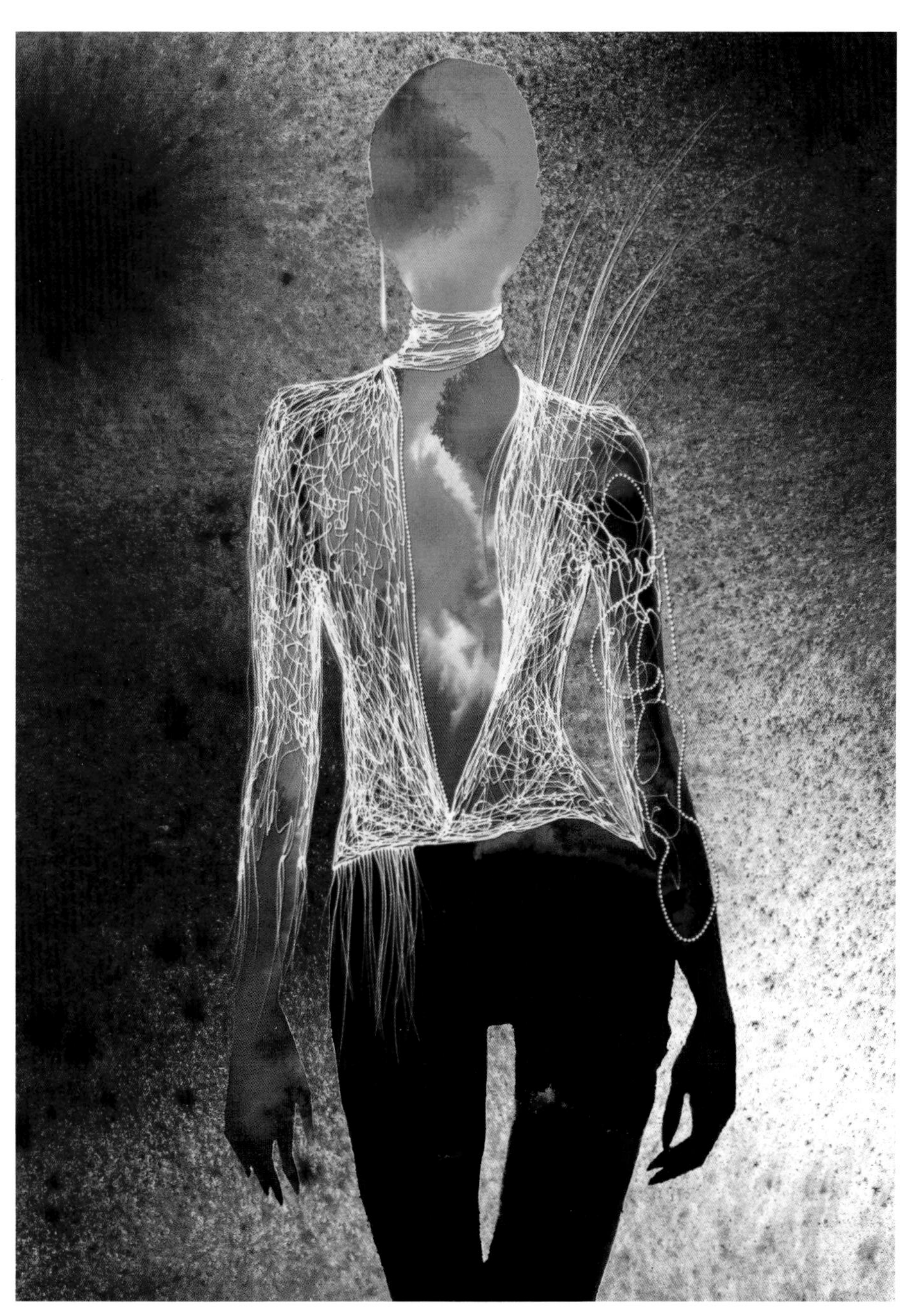

Bethan Morris

FASHION ILLUSTRATOR

Drawing and Presentation for the Fashion Designer

Abrams Studio
Abrams, New York

INTRODUCTION
Who is this book for? 6
What is in the book? 6

1
INSPIRATION
Discovering sources of inspiration 10
Researching themes 14
Working sketchbooks 18

2
THE FIGURE
Drawing from life 24
Templates 32
Body proportions: theory and practice 48

3
ARTISTIC TECHNIQUES
Art materials and equipment 48
Color 56
Fabric rendering and pattern reproduction 60

4
PRESENTATION FOR FASHION DESIGN
Mood boards 68
Design roughs and range building 70
Flats and specification drawings 76
Fashion-design presentation 78

5
HISTORICAL AND CONTEMPORARY FASHION ILLUSTRATION
The beginnings of fashion illustration 82
Contemporary fashion illustration showcase 93

6
TUTORIALS
Hand embroidery 160
Painting 162
Drawing with ink 164
Collage 166
Computerized machine embroidery 168
Adobe Illustrator 170
Adobe Photoshop 172

7
THE FUTURE: GUIDANCE
Portfolio presentation 176
The future: making choices 180
Interviews 185
- Stephanie Pesakoff—illustration agent 185
- David Downton—fashion illustrator 186
- Lysiane de Royère—trend forecaster 190
- Jeffrey Fulvimari—commercial fashion illustrator 192

• • •

Further reading 196
Trade publications and magazines 199
Useful addresses 199
Glossary 202
Index 204
Picture sources and credits 207
Acknowledgments 208

Book design: David Tanguy, Praliné
Abrams cover design: Eric J. Diloné

Library of Congress Cataloging-in-Publication Data

Morris, Bethan.
Fashion illustrator / Bethan Morris.
p. cm.
Includes index.
ISBN 0-8109-9171-3 (pbk.)
1. Fashion drawing. I. Title.
TT509.M67 2006
741.6'72--dc22

2006003181

First published in 2006 by Laurence King Publishing Ltd., London.

Published in 2006 by Abrams, an imprint of Harry N. Abrams, Inc.

Printed and bound in China
10 9 8 7 6 5 4 3 2 1

Front cover (main image): Kareem Iliya
Front cover (left to right): Annabelle Verhoye, Stephen Campbell, Edgardo Carosia, Matthias Frey, and Marion Lefebvre

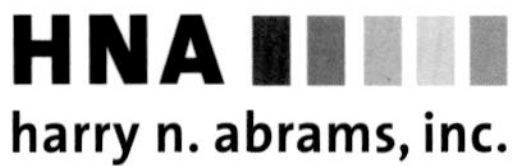

a subsidiary of La Martinière Groupe
115 West 18th Street
New York, NY 10011
www.hnabooks.com

INTRODUCTION

Fashion illustration titles line the shelves of bookshops, magazines often illustrate features rather than use photographs, and illustration is a popular medium for fashion advertising. The art of fashion illustration is once again in vogue, but will this trend continue? The answer must be yes. In an age of increasing standardization and automation, we yearn for the individuality expressed by the new trend-setting image-makers. Fashion illustrators who experiment skillfully with unusual media and innovative design are warmly welcomed. While fashion illustration continues to develop and offer fresh interpretations, its place in the future commercial world is assured.

WHO IS THIS BOOK FOR?

For the purpose of this book, the term "fashion illustration" is broad. It covers a wide range of artwork created by fashion designers and fashion illustrators. Under the umbrella of fashion illustration, this book focuses on the fundamentals of fashion drawing and presentation throughout the design process. As the fashion design student must present fashion ideas to gain employment on graduation, *Fashion Illustrator* explores the skills required to create an effective portfolio. Imaginative research directions are revealed, as well as how to illustrate fashion ideas, how to represent garments technically, and how to compile mood boards.

While *Fashion Illustrator* provides a valuable knowledge base for the fashion designer, many successful designers only design clothes. It is common for such designers to employ fashion illustrators to present their collections and promote their labels. The fashion illustration student's portfolio will therefore be geared toward advertising and promotion. A flexible approach is required for working to briefs from a variety of clients, so *Fashion Illustrator* reveals how to experiment effectively with color, how to use art materials and equipment, and how to select the appropriate artistic style, character, and media for a particular client.

Whether you want to be a fashion designer or a fashion illustrator, the most important skill to master is drawing the human figure. *Fashion Illustrator* dedicates a practical chapter to the figure, and this should be referred to regularly throughout your studies.

Covering the broad area of fashion illustration and presentation, this book will prove invaluable for both fashion design and fashion illustration students. Many books aim to teach the skills required to illustrate fashion, and these manuals are displayed alongside showcase books featuring edited collections of illustrators' promotional fashion artwork. These categories have traditionally been separate, but *Fashion Illustrator* combines a how-to approach with a visual overview of historical and contemporary fashion illustration. By explaining the fundamentals of fashion illustration and presentation, and bringing this rewarding creative process to life with rich detail, *Fashion Illustrator* serves as a valuable resource and teaching aid. It is useful for anyone with an interest in fashion, design, and illustration.

WHAT IS IN THE BOOK?

Enriched by case studies, example illustrations, practical exercises, and tips, *Fashion Illustrator* covers all aspects of fashion illustration and presentation. It explores how artists find inspiration in the world around them, and how they use this inspiration in the creation of their work. *Fashion Illustrator* encourages readers to challenge themselves by experimenting with varied media such as collage, different drawing tools, digital enhancement, and embroidery. Through this exploration, an understanding of the figure, and experimentation with different illustrative styles,

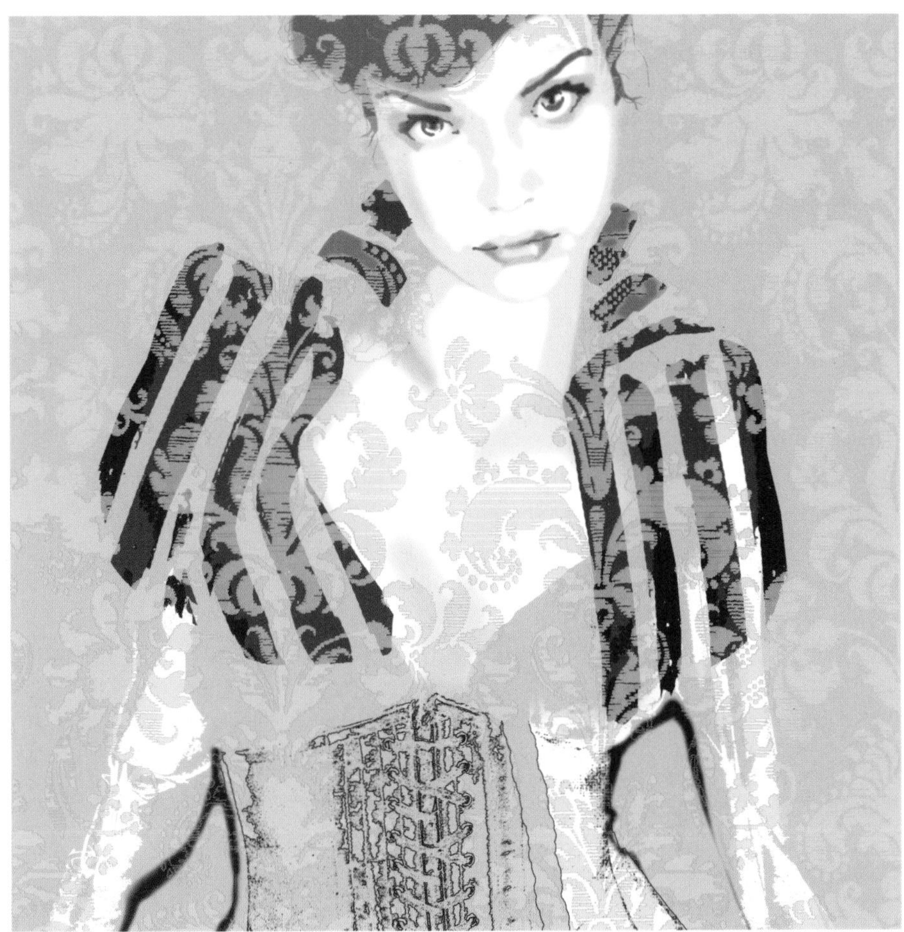

A digitally enhanced fashion illustration by Rebecca Antoniou.

the reader will learn how to present the clothed human form artistically. Examining the work of both past- and present-day fashion illustrators encourages students to gain the confidence and skills to push the boundaries of their own work. In-depth discussions with leading contemporary fashion illustrators provide insights that inspire students to think beyond graduation to a career in fashion illustration or design.

The content of *Fashion Illustrator* is presented in an easily accessible format, with each color-coded chapter broken down logically into subheadings. Each chapter can be read in isolation, and the book can be read in any order so that the reader can dip in and out to focus on current concerns.

Chapter One, "Inspiration," explores the things that inspire the creative mind, revealing how to find rewarding ideas, understand visual expression, and produce innovative fashion illustrations, sketchbooks, and artwork. The chapter begins by discussing the importance of looking for sources of inspiration from which to develop ideas. With this in mind, the reader is encouraged to look at the world with fresh interest. Inspiration for fashion illustration can be found through travel, music, television, film, museum and gallery visits—even product packaging. The varied processes for capturing ideas and investigating themes on paper are also explained to help the budding fashion illustrator tackle the daunting blank page.

Artists are invariably avid collectors of what, to the uninitiated eye, looks like junk. Chapter One emphasizes that accumulating anything and everything of interest is a fascinating way to build an idea bank for future design or artwork.

Compiling ideas in a sketchbook is also an essential part of both a designer's and an illustrator's development. Practical advice is given on completing useful sketchbooks that provide a source of rewarding inspiration.

Chapter Two, "The Figure," focuses on basic drawing skills, providing a solid understanding of anatomy and the physical structure of the human form. Through a series of observational exercises the reader learns to draw the nude and clothed figure from life and photographs, understand correct proportions, and draw features of the body accurately. The use of a template and the effective exaggeration of the proportions of a fashion figure are also explained clearly.

Chapter Three, "Artistic Techniques," gives a technical overview of how to use art equipment and materials, experiment with color, and render various fabrics. This guidance is visually enriched by a series of informative sketches and relevant fashion illustrations.

Chapter Four, "Presentation for Fashion Design," reveals how fashion illustration is used in the design industry. It explores the process of producing design roughs to build fashion ranges. It also explains the purpose of specification drawings, flats, and mood boards, and their significance in a fashion designer's portfolio.

Chapter Five, "Historical and Contemporary Fashion Illustration," describes the social journey of fashion illustration over the last 100 years. The illustrative styles of the twentieth century's most influential illustrators are discussed by decade. Illustrators of today inevitably look to the past for inspiration, and this section also features work that demonstrates this synthesis of past styles and modern techniques. The second part of the chapter showcases work by thirty-six leading international fashion illustrators from fourteen countries. Each illustrator defines his or her work and career by answering a series of interview-style questions. All offer interesting advice and inspiration to students who are thinking of following similar paths.

Chapter Six, "Tutorials," explains how the illustrative styles indentified in the previous chapter can be realized through a series of step-by-step tutorials. This chapter encourages the reader to build fashion illustrations in stages, experimenting with new techniques. The tutorials focus on collage, embroidery, traditional painting and drawing methods, and digital manipulation.

Finally Chapter Seven, "The Future: Guidance," takes the reader through the final part of the fashion illustration journey by outlining effective portfolio presentation techniques. There is also instruction on self-presentation, interview techniques, applying for further education, and embracing a career in fashion illustration. The role of the illustration agent is clearly described, and other industry specialists speak exclusively about their fashion illustration careers. David Downton offers advice on capturing the magic of couture shows with pen and ink. Lysiane de Royère of Promostyl describes the role of the fashion illustrator in publications forecasting future trends, and Jeffrey Fulvimari describes how his doe-eyed girls have wooed Madonna and are taking the fashion world by storm; we see examples of his highly successful commercial product packaging.

At the end of the book you will find a further reading guide, a list of trade publications and magazines, useful addresses, a glossary, an index, and the picture credits, which include contact details for the illustrated artists.

INSPIRATION

1

This book gives a solid grounding on all aspects of fashion illustration, but it is only a guide to help you on your journey. Sometimes embarking on that journey is the hardest part. Creating something new from scratch is a daunting prospect for any artist. This chapter will help you ensure that your portfolio stands out from the crowd. You will discover how to find inspiration and how to use it.

DISCOVERING SOURCES OF INSPIRATION

American painter George Bellows (1882–1925) once stated, "The artist is the person who makes life more interesting or beautiful, more understandable or mysterious, or probably, in the best sense, more wonderful." This is a tall order for the artist. With such expectations, you are not alone if you feel daunted by the prospect of creating artwork, and not the only one who finds it hard to know where to begin. To help you discover a starting point, this chapter reveals how to find inspiration, how to make visual use of the world around you, and how to apply your observations in creating innovative fashion illustrations, designs, and artwork.

Where exactly do you look for inspiration? As British designer Sir Paul Smith says: "You can find inspiration in everything … and if you can't, you're not looking properly—so look again." This is good advice. Inspiration for creative artwork is everywhere. Begin by wandering around your home, looking at it with fresh eyes. You will be surprised how mundane, everyday objects suddenly have new meaning and potential. The old wallpaper in the living room could be a good background for an illustration, or a photograph of your sister may supply the perfect fashion figure silhouette for a template. The illustration on the facing page has been drawn directly onto old-fashioned wallpaper.

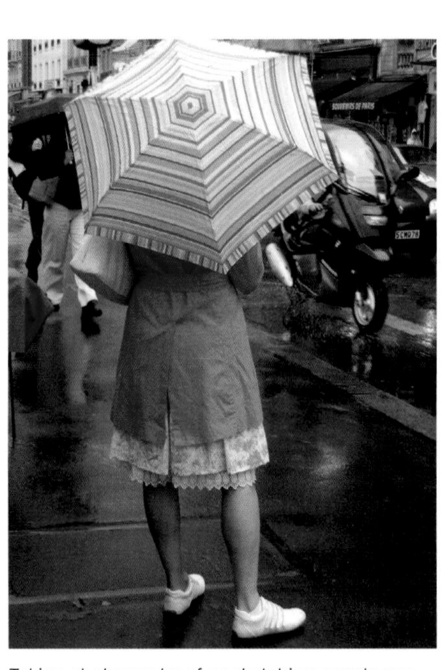

Taking photographs of or sketching people you see in the street gives you a rewarding variety of figures and stances for your illustrations. This girl on a busy Paris street stood out because of her brightly colored umbrella and coordinating outfit. The image provides an ideal starting point for a fashion illustration.

When you open your eyes to the world, you will discover that it is overflowing with potential to trigger your imagination. Don't be put off if you find that your ideas already exist somewhere else. The truth is that few ideas are entirely new; as Pablo Picasso said: "Everything you can imagine is real." However, when you bring to the idea your own personal response, you provide an original interpretation.

Like all artists, designers and illustrators look for sources of inspiration to develop their work and focus on absorbing new ideas all the time. Read a variety of books and magazines, familiarizing yourself with interiors trends, music and lifestyle editorials, as well as fashion. Theatrical costume and set design can also stimulate interesting ideas. Never be without a camera or sketchbook to capture and record inspirational scenes, objects, or people.

Experiencing other environments through travel stimulates creative imagination and need not involve the expense of going overseas. If you live in the city, visit the countryside, and vice versa. If you are lucky enough to travel abroad, visit local markets and communities, observe traditional costumes and everyday clothing, eat new foods and recognize cultural differences. By embracing the experience, you will come away from your trip with a wealth of inspiration.

Keep up to date with the news and world events, television, and film releases. Monitor changes and behavioral shifts in big cities around the world, watching for new trends in cities such as New York, London, Tokyo, Paris, and Copenhagen. For example, how might you apply the trend for knitting cafes in New York or permanent spray cosmetics (whereby colors are applied permanently like a tattoo) in Tokyo to your artwork? Additionally, never underestimate the importance of visiting galleries and museums. No matter how seemingly irrelevant to fashion contemporary-art exhibitions might sometimes seem, it is worth visiting them. Often the exhibition you least expect to enjoy delivers the most inspiring results.

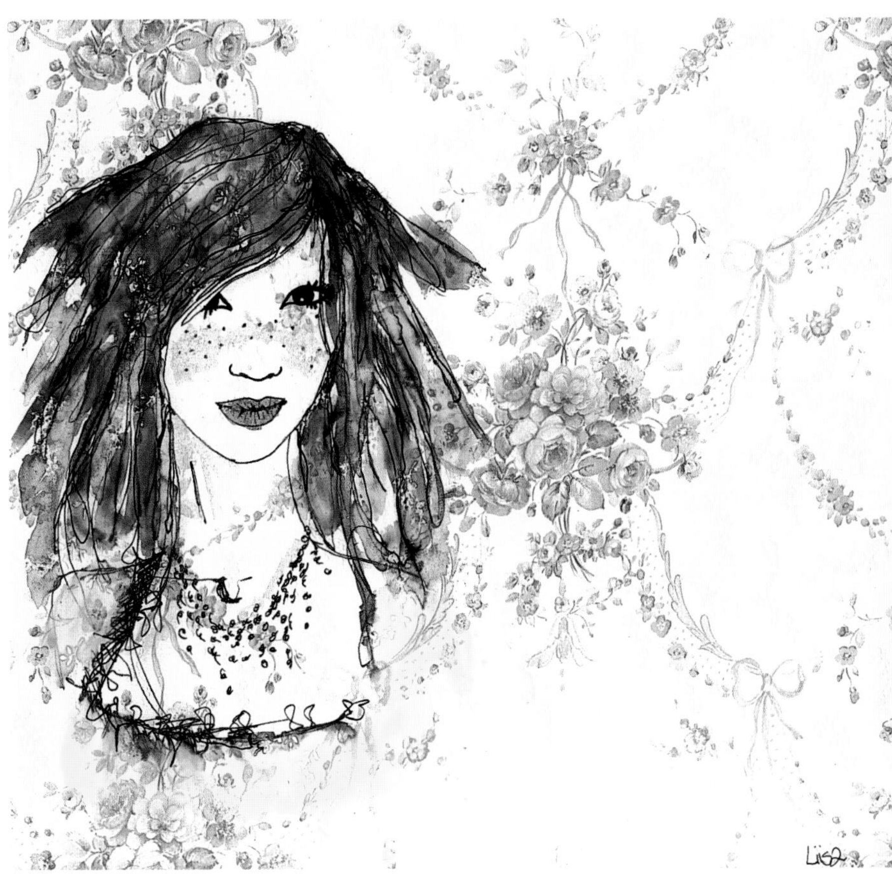

Here the illustrator has been inspired by a patterned wallpaper, drawing a fashion figure directly onto it. To complement the wallpaper background, this student artist has used a subtle color palette. An ingenious touch is to allow the pattern of the wallpaper to become the fabric of the garment. No artist can produce creative ideas without a knowledge base of ideas gained from magazines, books, advertisements, and a wide variety of other sources. Keep up to date with the latest trends and open your mind to new sources of inspiration.

In museums, too, a wealth of inspiring artifacts and memorabilia awaits your artistic interpretation. Nostalgia for the past will always captivate us. In fashion, for example, today's garments date quickly, yet bygone eras are always a source of inspiration. Every decade sees a revival of the style of a past decade. It seems that it is second nature for us to draw from the past to illustrate the future.

As an artist, designer, or illustrator, you are always open to visual stimulation in your normal day-to-day life. Even a trip to the supermarket can awaken new ideas as you look at the variety of vibrant packaging on the shelves. Your journey home might take you past architecture, a landscape, or gardens whose intriguing shapes and textures trigger your imagination. Your thoughts might be awakened by listening to compelling music, an image in a magazine might inspire a new idea, an absorbing television documentary might activate your creative energy, or a favorite poem conjure up engaging imagery. This type of inspiration is all around you waiting to be discovered.

COLLECTING INSPIRATIONAL ITEMS

Artists are invariably avid collectors of what to the uninitiated eye looks like junk. Accumulating anything and everything of interest is a fascinating way to build an idea bank for future designs or artwork. Keep everything that captures your imagination, as you never know when it might be useful in the future. Arguments about the amount of clutter you possess might occur with those who share your home, but stand your ground! This clutter could one day make you a famous artist—think of Tracy Emin's *Bed*. Art materials, unusual papers, wrapping, packaging, and scraps of fabric are worth storing as you may well be able to utilize them in

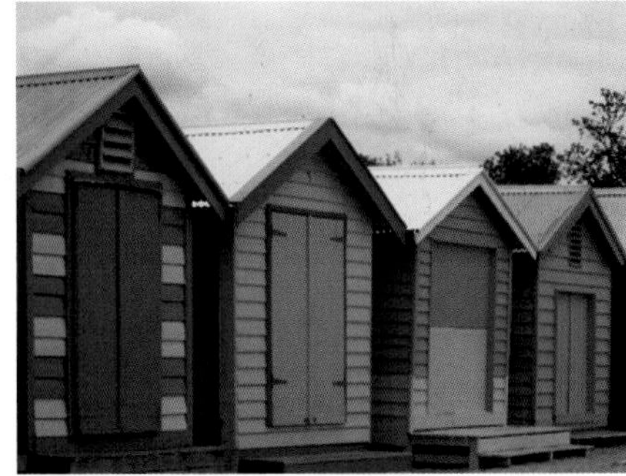

Beach huts seen on an Australian beach have added interesting accents of color to the dramatic shoreline. This scene could be used in a fashion illustration, or it could be that the colors inspire future artwork.

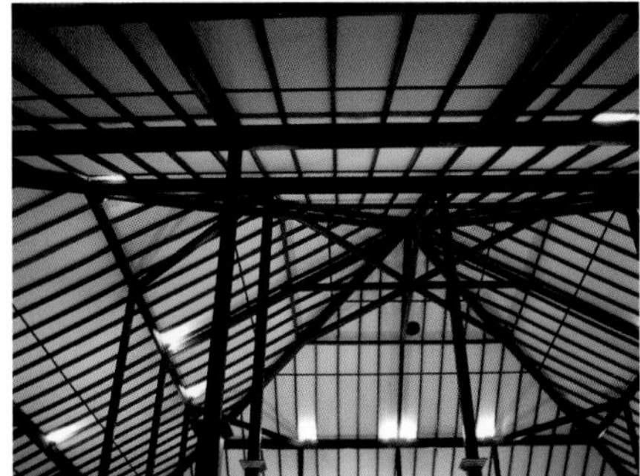

A building's interior structure can be as much a source of inspiration as that of the exterior. Interesting lines for fashion design or illustration can be seen in the timber structure of this wooden roof.

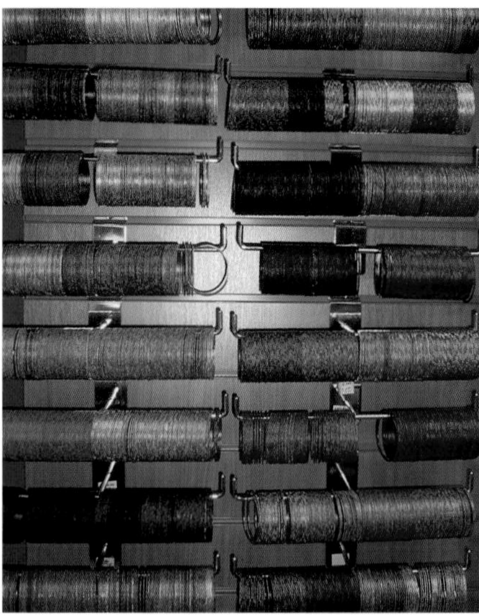

A trained eye can spot artistic potential in almost anything. Look closely at the colors, shapes, and details of these rows of brightly colored bangles, and see how they have inspired the background for this fashion illustration. The striped clothing also reflects the brightly colored rows.

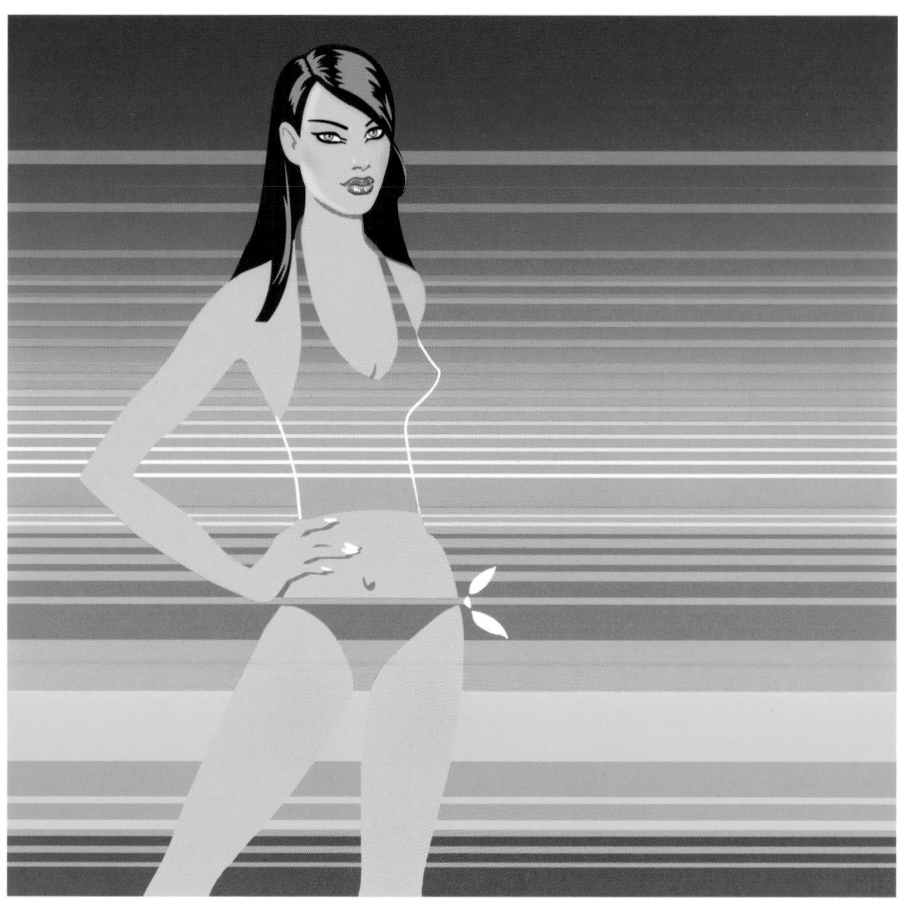

your artwork. In Chapter Five you will discover the work of Peter Clark, who uses found papers, such as maps and cigarette packs, to create delightful collaged fashion illustrations.

People collect all sorts of unusual items, either because they get pleasure from looking at them or because they can see creative potential in them. Many illustrators look for interesting stamps, cigarette cards, key rings, handbags, film memorabilia, calendars, buttons, and so forth in garage sales, flea markets, and thrift stores. They then put their own original slant on the ideas generated by their collections. The trained eye can spot artistic potential in almost anything. A collection of bangles above, for example, makes a marvelous starting point for a fashion illustration. Look closely at the colors, shapes, and details, and think how they could be incorporated into a piece of work.

Books form a particularly useful collection, providing a constant and varied source of inspiration. The Further Reading guide on pages 196–98 provides a list of fashion and fashion illustration titles worth finding. Additionally, remember that books on all sorts of other subjects might spark ideas, too. Look in secondhand bookstores for older, out-of-print titles as well as keeping up to date with new titles, broadening your collection so that it offers an ever expanding variety of ideas. Collecting books is costly, so it is worth becoming familiar with your local library. Just browsing through the shelves in a peaceful environment can be a stimulating process. If you take a sketchbook along, you could even practice making some observational figure drawings while you are choosing which book to borrow.

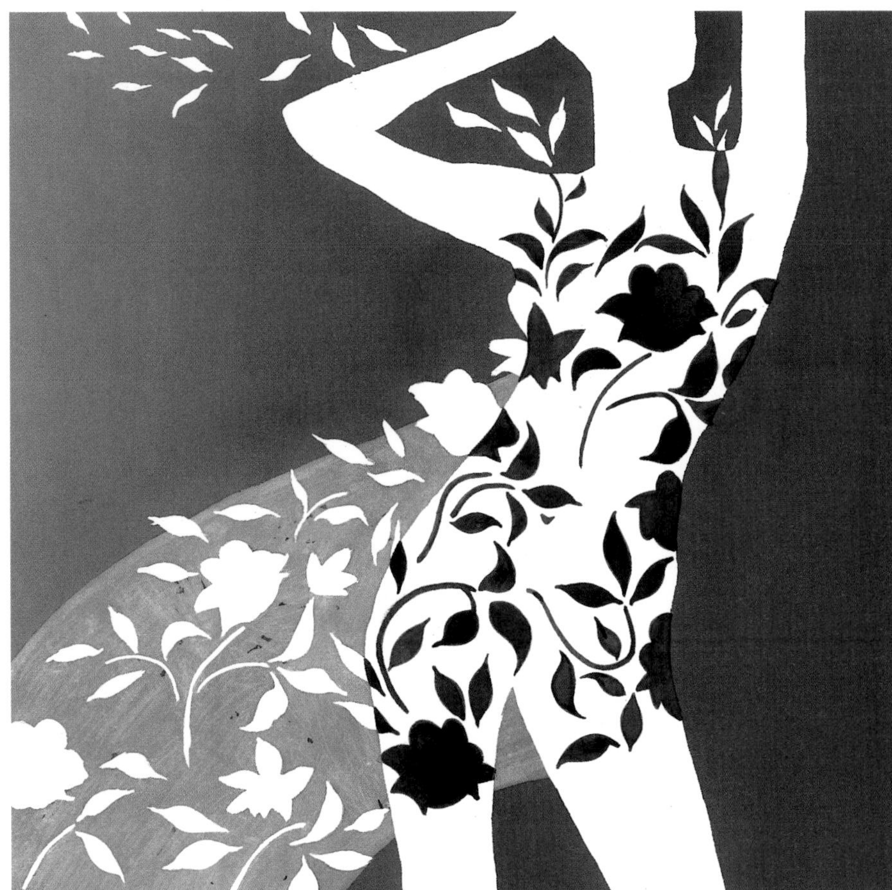

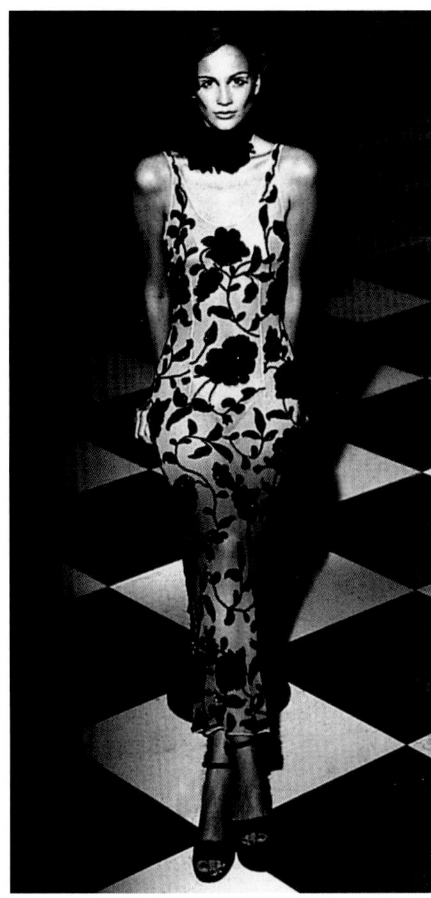

Invest in other forms of printed media, too, such as magazines, journals, and postcards. As magazines are printed more regularly than books, their content is usually "of the moment." Such up-to-date images can inform and inspire your artwork. Postcards from galleries can also be an economical way of taking home a little piece of inspiration, particularly if you can't afford an exhibition catalog. Many artists have boxes of postcards, saved from a lifetime of visiting exhibitions, that they use repeatedly as inspirational references for fashion illustration.

Maintaining a lively interest in the world is vital for the fashion illustrator, who must combine keen observational skills with creative interpretation.

Above
Visit as many exhibitions as possible because you never know which one might provide valuable inspiration. If the exhibition catalog is too costly for you, buy postcards of your favorite images. This postcard was bought at the Royal Academy of Arts, in London, during the exhibition *Giorgio Armani: A Retrospective.*

Left
This fashion illustration has been created in a monotone palette to reflect the black-and-white photograph of a Giorgio Armani dress. The floral design of the fabric is instrumental to the artwork.

RESEARCHING THEMES

There is no doubt that one of the most daunting aspects of creativity for the artist is being faced with a blank page. The prospect of plucking new ideas out of thin air and arriving at an original artistic solution can be unnerving. This is why it is important to develop a knowledge base from which creative ideas can grow.

Albert Einstein said that "imagination is more important than knowledge." However, before most artists can begin to produce artwork from their imagination they need to establish the knowledge base from which they will work. The simplest starting point for this is to select a theme to investigate and develop. This can be anything that interests you, from an antique Japanese silk fan to graffiti art on train station walls—the range of inspirational resources in the world is endless. With so much to stimulate your imagination, it is easy to become indecisive. The key is to be selective, only choosing themes that truly inspire you. Your chosen theme must continue to hold your attention while you explore its creative elements.

A good starting point in the investigative process is to form a list of words that are associated with the theme. This is known as "mind mapping" or "brainstorming." A butterfly theme is explored (facing page) by listing the words that spring to mind while concentrating on the image, or idea, of a butterfly. The words create a number of research avenues to follow, the initial subject of a butterfly having a wealth of associations, with almost every word capable of inspiring a new investigation.

The images below show how a theme can also be investigated artistically. Notice how the butterflies have been used to create repeat patterns. The textures of their wings and the symmetrical patterns across them have been represented through painting and drawing. Color studies have been made of many butterfly varieties. The popularity of the butterfly as decoration in fashion has also been emphasized. This exploration shows how a butterfly theme can be used to inspire fashion designers as well as the fashion illustrators who illustrate their garments.

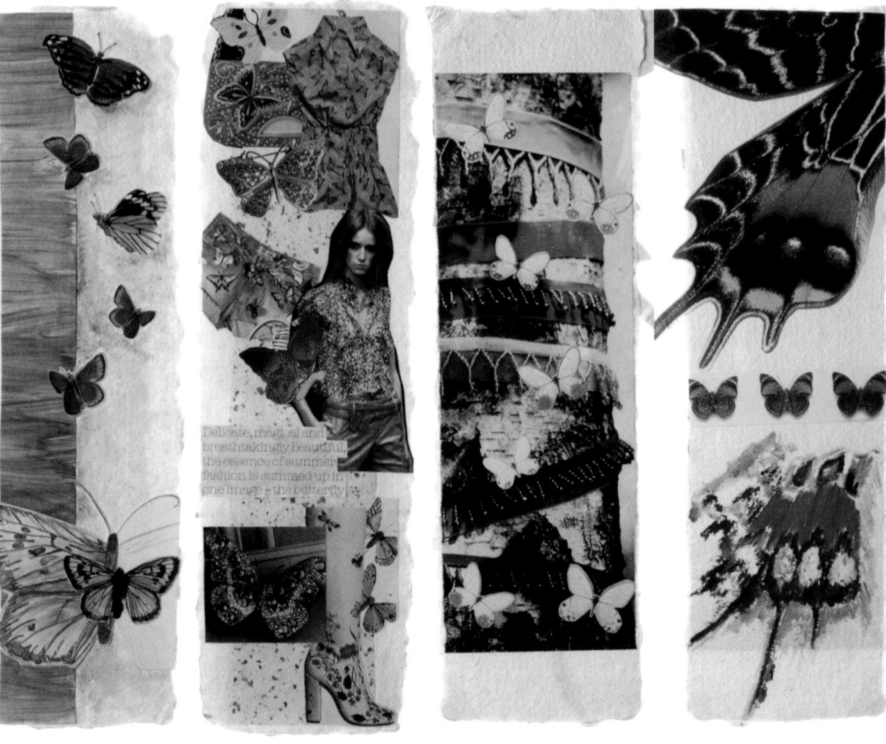

Four studies investigating the butterfly as a theme show different media, including collage, painting, drawing, and cutouts from magazines, mounted onto handmade paper. The images demonstrate a visual exploration of the butterfly theme, revealing its diversity as a research direction.

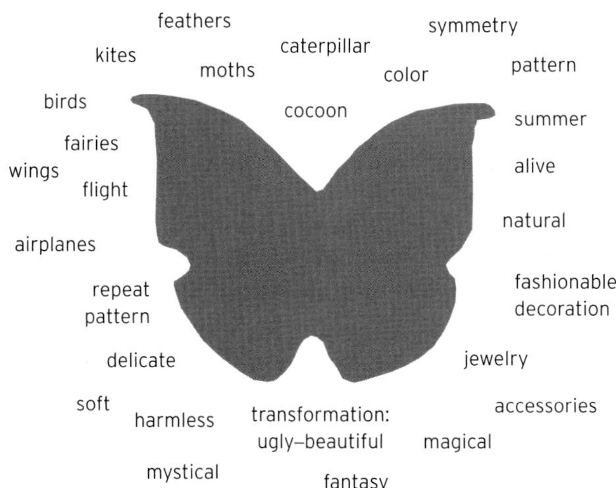

Left
This mind map shows a selection of words linked to a butterfly theme. A pattern of words produced in this way can inspire many ideas for fashion illustrations.

Below
The role of the imagination is as significant as that of knowledge. Once inspiration is found, research material collected, and a theme established, the illustrator conceives a wealth of imaginative ideas. This illustration has been created using a mix of traditional drawing techniques for the figure and Photoshop collage to add the butterflies.

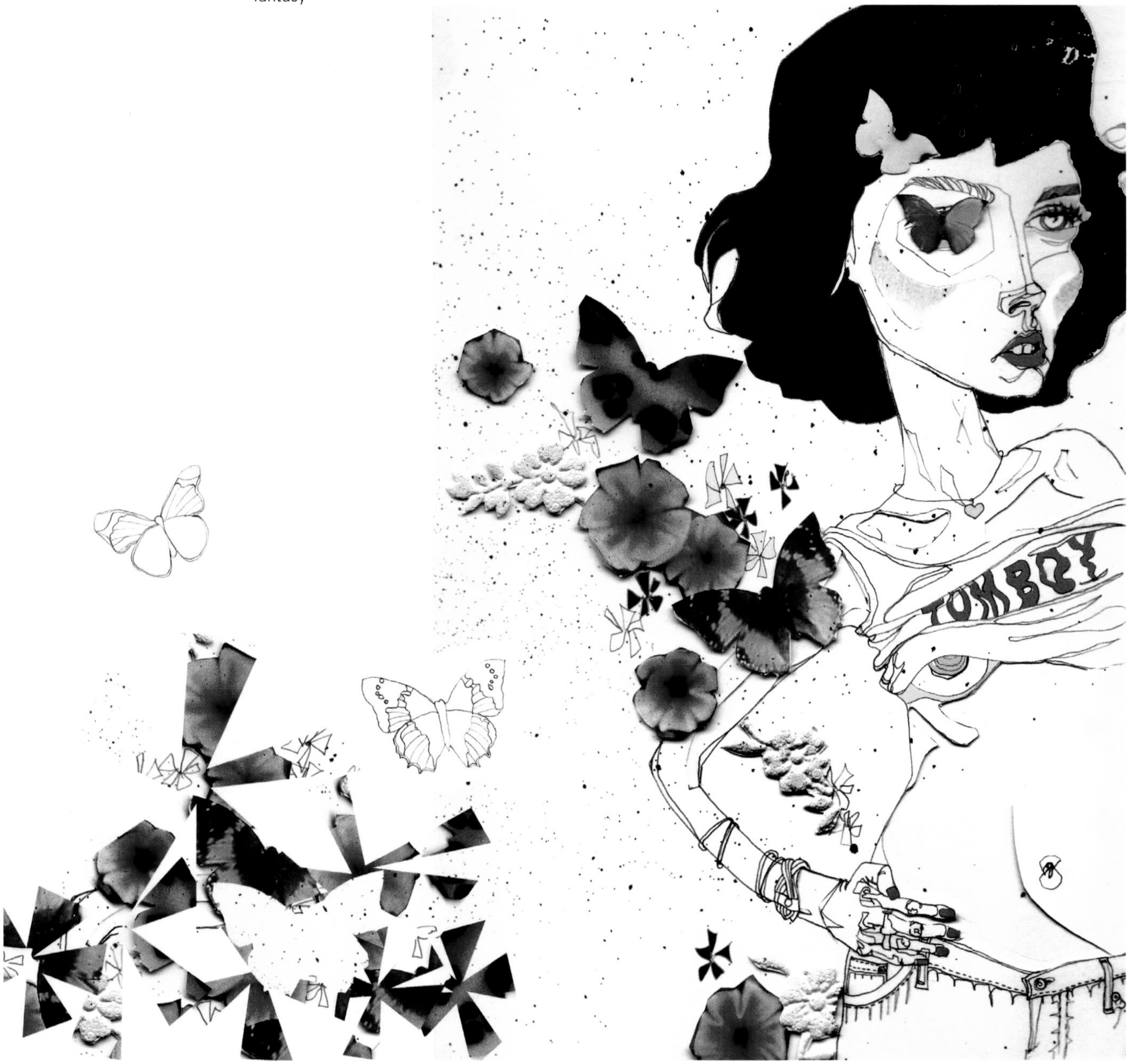

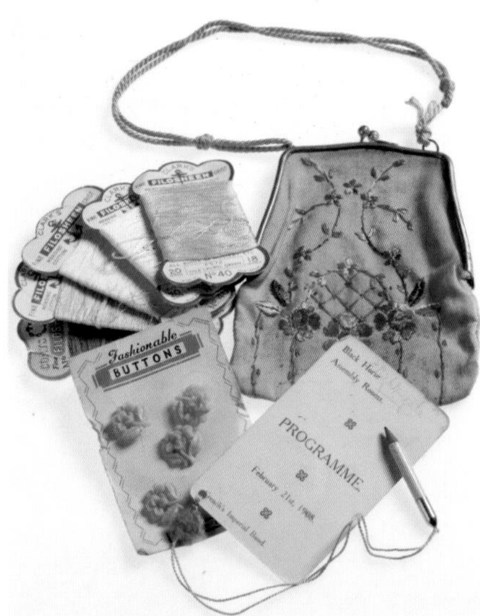

INVENTIVE INSPIRATION

An interesting way to find inspiration for a fashion illustration is to invent a story around found objects. Try carrying out the exercise demonstrated on this page, and see how your ideas differ from the illustrator's finished artwork.

Start by looking carefully at the objects. Certain aspects will appeal to you more than others. You may find that a particular detail sparks off a train of ideas for a fashion illustration. The objects were chosen because they are commonly linked by age and color—all have an antique, aged feel and date back as far as 1908. Focus your attention on the objects to absorb as much information as possible before you begin your illustration.

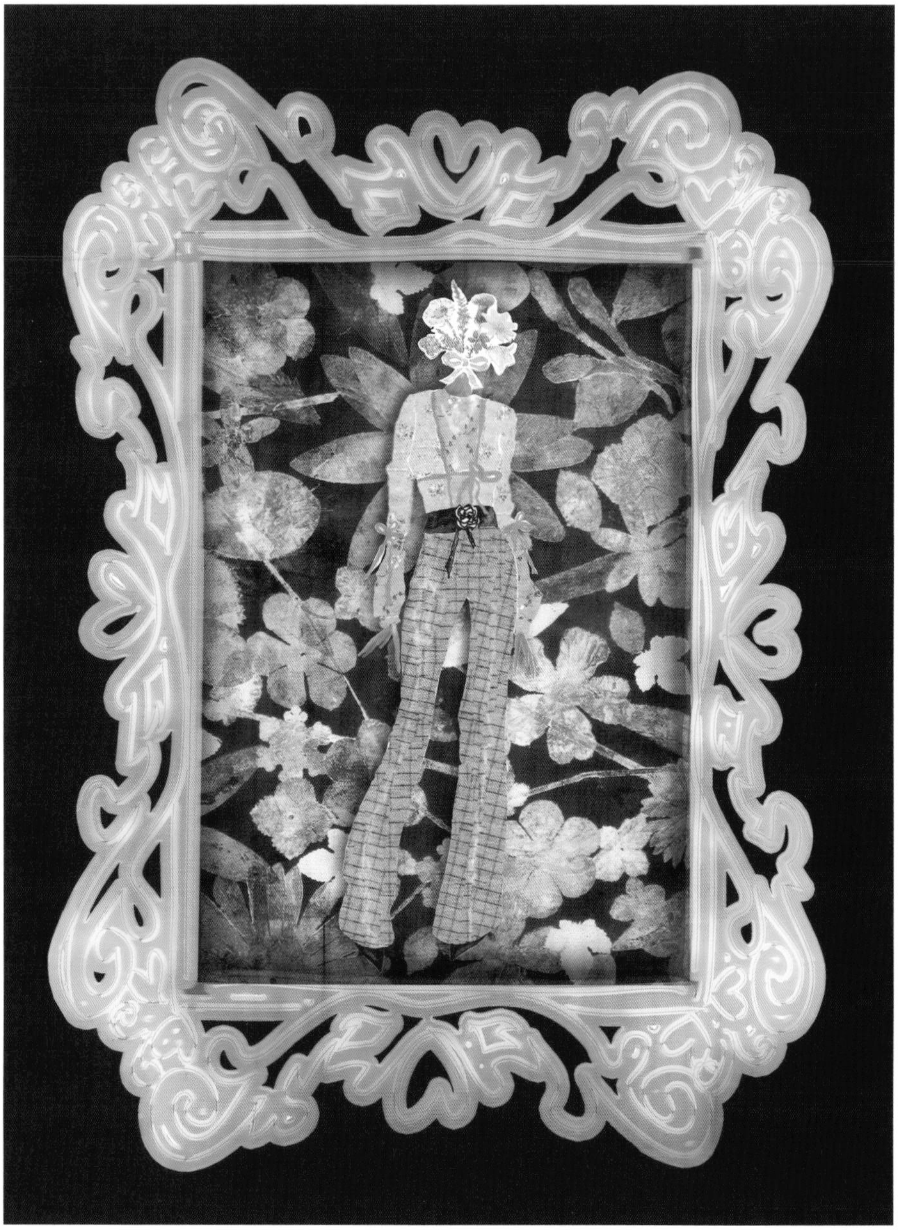

Above
The dance card is an interesting object. In years gone by, women used it to record the names of the men who asked them to dance. This innocent means of flirting and dating could inspire an illustration based on nostalgic romance. Almost 100 years old, this handbag is decorated with the sort of hand embroidery that has enjoyed a revival during the recent resurgence in traditional craft techniques for fashion and interiors. Such embroidery could inspire decorative clothing in a fashion illustration or be used as a medium for the artwork itself. The floral buttons could be drawn onto fashion garments or the flowers utilized somehow in the illustration. Retro graphics on the packaging could also stimulate creative thinking. The cottons provide a tonal color palette that links the objects and provides a starting point for color choices in the illustration. It is often difficult to make color choices when illustrating, and many images are spoiled by using too many colors. Consider that most people dress in a limited palette, and bear in mind that it is therefore often advisable to limit your fashion illustration to a few complementary shades.

Right
Although nothing dates more quickly than fashion, objects of the more remote past are endowed with nostalgic imagery that can inspire contemporary artwork. This illustration has been created using hand-drawing methods and enhanced using a computer. Fabrics of a similar color palette to the inspirational objects above have been scanned and combined with the hand-drawn garments. The background and antique frame were also added using a computer.

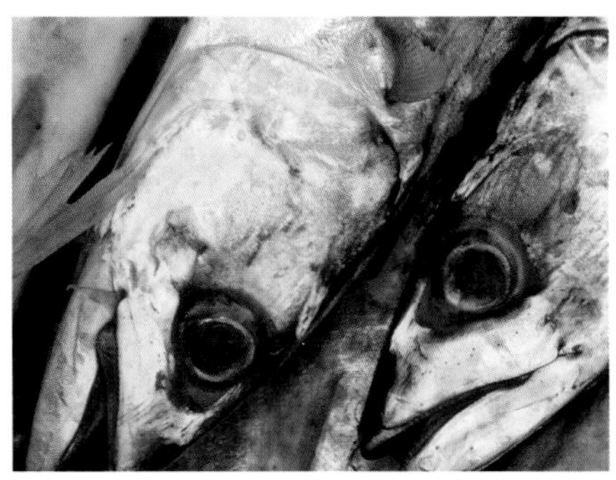

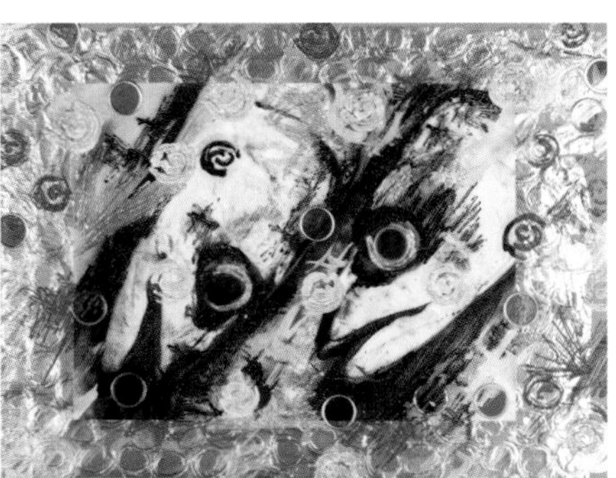

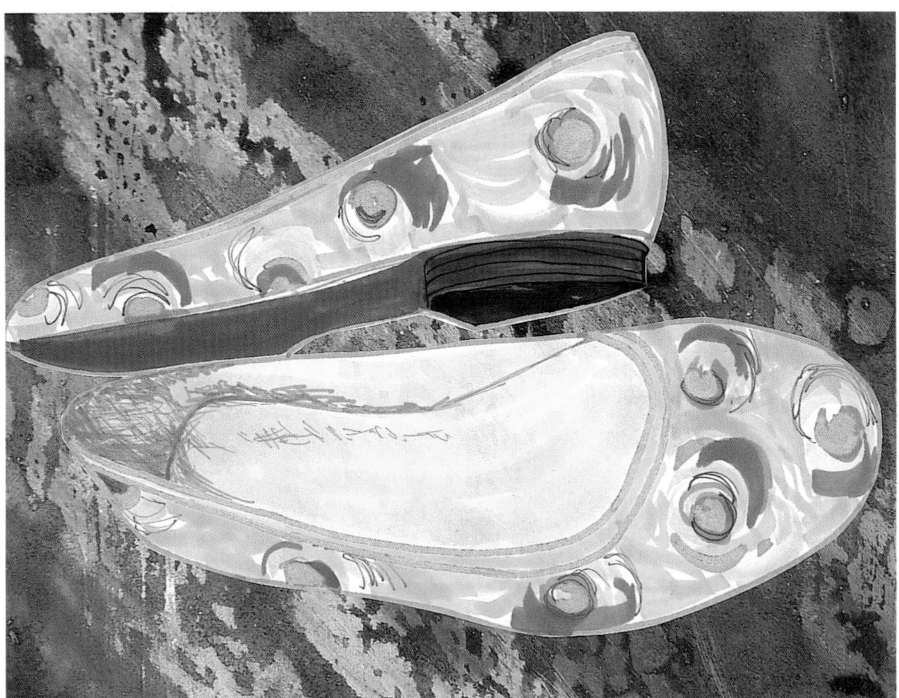

Top left
A close-up photograph of freshly caught mackerel from Aberporth beach in west Wales provides an inspiring starting point for stimulating creative ideas. Notice, for example, the light-reflective textures and interesting patterns.

Top right
In a mixed-media collage, silver foil represents the shiny texture of the reflective fish scales, and the shape of the eyes is re-created with transparent colored disks and metallic paints.

Left
These shoes have been designed with the fish-eye patterns in mind, using marker pens. To create the effect of water, the background of the illustration is achieved using wax resist and ink.

IMAGE INSPIRATION

When you have found a theme that interests you, explore it further to discover your own personal artistic response. For example, look closely at the patterns, textures, shapes, and colors in an image that you find appealing, then experiment by reproducing and interpreting them using a variety of media and techniques.

The three images above show how simple it is to work using a theme. The starting point is a close-up photograph of freshly caught mackerel. It was selected as a source of inspiration because of the many elements it offers for creative development. For example, the shapes created by the fish eyes were the designer's inspiration for the patterns on the shoe, while the reflective colors and textures depicted in the study helped the illustrator decide on the shoe's tonal contrasts.

WORKING SKETCHBOOK

A sketchbook is a visual notebook or diary. It is a personal response to the world and can assume many different guises, varying from being a portable scrapbook in which to collect interesting pieces of fabric or pictorial references, to a book of observational drawings and ideas. All may, one day, provide that essential spark of inspiration. A sketchbook provides you with the opportunity to practice design, drawing, and illustration skills at any time and in any place. You can develop figure studies by sketching the people you see at a local park, or on a train, or even by sitting on a bench on a main street and drawing the shoppers. Sketching scenery, such as interesting architecture, also helps to create ideas for illustration backgrounds.

Most artists keep sketchbooks in which they experiment with ideas and collect insightful imagery. Picasso is said to have produced 178 sketchbooks in his lifetime. He often used his sketchbooks to explore themes and make compositional studies until he found the subject and concept for a larger painting on canvas. Like Picasso, you will have numerous sketchbooks throughout your education and career. Some you will use for researching specific themes while others become constant companions for recording ideas that will provide future inspiration.

Producing useful working sketchbooks is an essential part of an art student's development. Academic design and illustration briefs often request a sketchbook containing appropriate research to be submitted for assessment. Ideally, the sketchbook presents an explorative journey around a chosen subject area.

A working sketchbook should be impulsive, experimental, and in constant use, becoming an accumulation of ideas and research from which to draw inspiration for design and illustration. Sadly, this advice is frequently ignored, and sketchbooks are produced whose clean pages are decorated with neat cuttings, ordered sketches, and unused material from presentation boards. Generally this method of working results in tedious sketchbooks of carefully planned pages, often with Post-it notes acting as a reminder to fill blank pages. By organizing a sketchbook into a precious album in which the artist arranges experimental work at the end of a project, creative spontaneity is often lost. The sketchbook then becomes a useless tool rather than a rich resource for imaginative artwork.

The "Hot Metal" sketchbook research (facing page) gave the designer plenty of scope to create a collection of womenswear. The design roughs show how the colors explored in the research and the woven, metallic fabric experiments, were interpreted in the garments. Much of the research imagery of rusting metals and soldered cars is also reflected in the garment shapes.

Inspiration from the research also carries through into the fashion illustration. Instead of the obvious white paper, sheet aluminum was used as a background for the artwork. The figures were sketched in permanent marker and paint, with the clothing added separately. Heated copper was used to create a bodice and skirt, while other outfits are made up of appliquéd leather and denim. Topstitching and garment details were drawn using a silver pen. All of these techniques, first explored in the research, demonstrate the value of researching and exploring a theme in your sketchbook.

Opposite, top
Research for the theme "Hot Metal" was collated and mounted into a sketchbook for easy reference and to provide inspiration for future designs and illustrations. The black pages act as a strong background for magazine cutouts, textile sampling, fabric manipulations, sketches, photographs, rough designs, and personal reflections.

Opposite, below left
A womenswear fashion collection based on the "Hot Metal" theme has been drawn to produce what is known in the industry as a "lineup," in which a designer views the collection on one page to see if the garments work together as a whole. The original designs were photocopied onto gold paper.

Opposite, below right
To continue the theme, "Hot Metal" fashion illustrations have been presented on sheet aluminum. The figures have been painted and their clothes added with fabric collage. The fashion illustrator or designer is always open to experimenting with new materials.

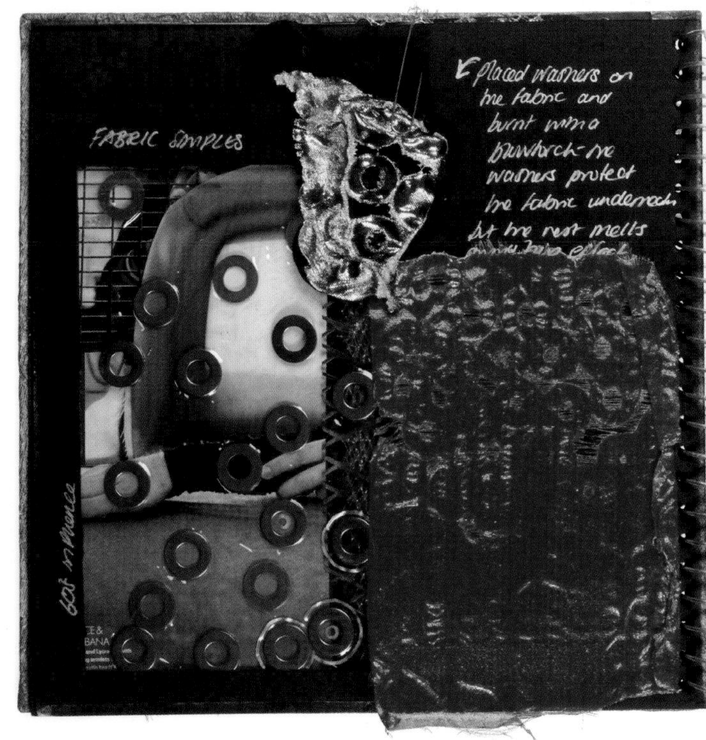
FABRIC SAMPLES
placed washers on the fabric and burnt with a blowtorch - the washers protect the fabric underneath but the rest melts

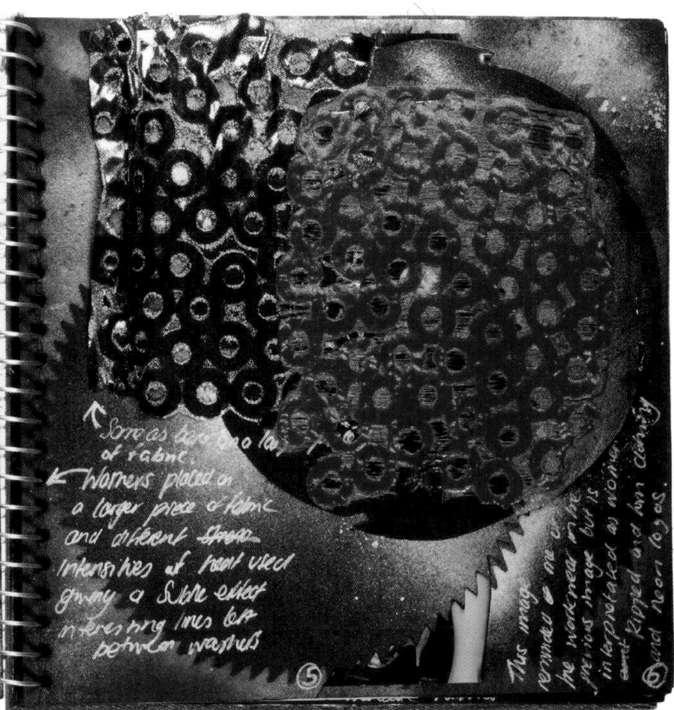
Washers placed on a larger piece of fabric and different intensities of heat used giving a subtle effect interesting lines left between washers

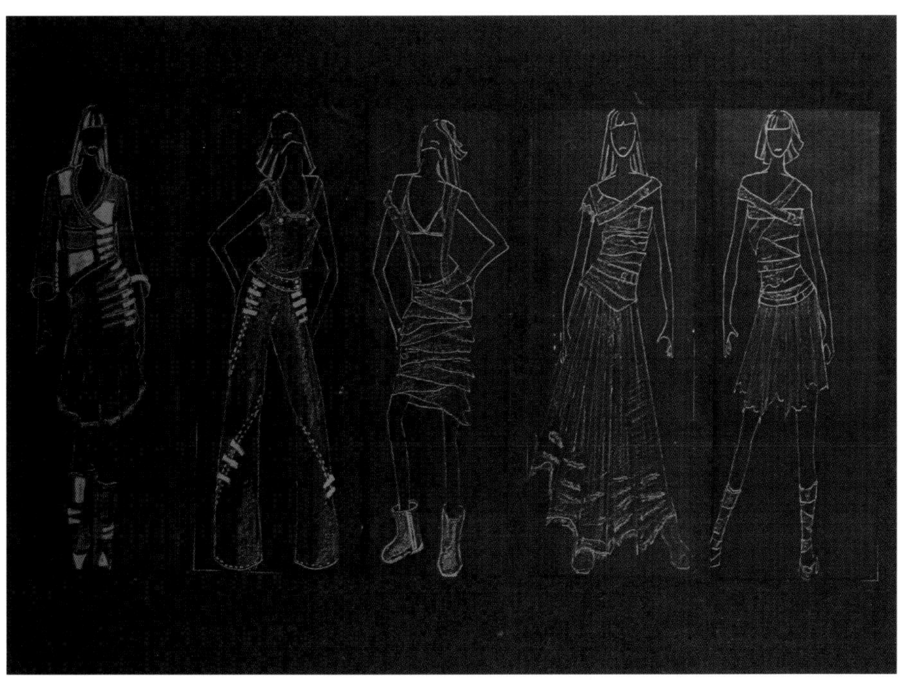

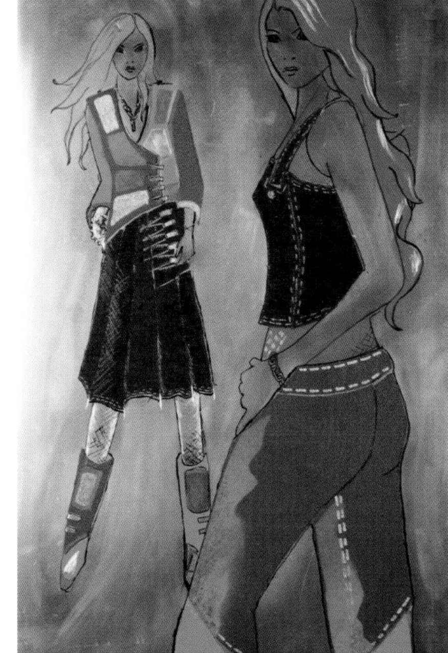

The best way to begin creating a useful sketchbook is to gather research material from a variety of sources. This can include any or all of the following:

- observational drawing
- painted visual studies
- color studies
- photographs
- collage
- relevant imagery, for example from magazine cutouts
- fabric swatches
- found objects
- Internet research
- exhibition information
- artist/designer references
- postcards
- historical references (text or visual)
- personal recollections

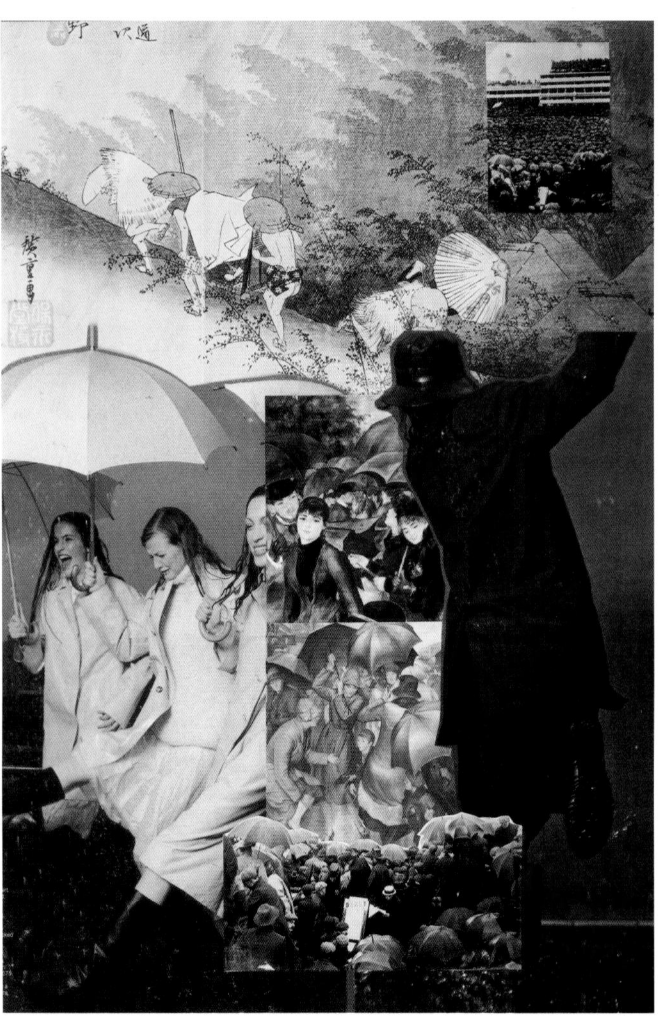

Below left
Find a theme to explore and research it, using your sketchbook for experimental work and to collect inspirational material. This sketchbook page is like a mini mood board (see p. 68), showing how the theme of bad weather was investigated through a series of magazine cutouts and references to original artwork.

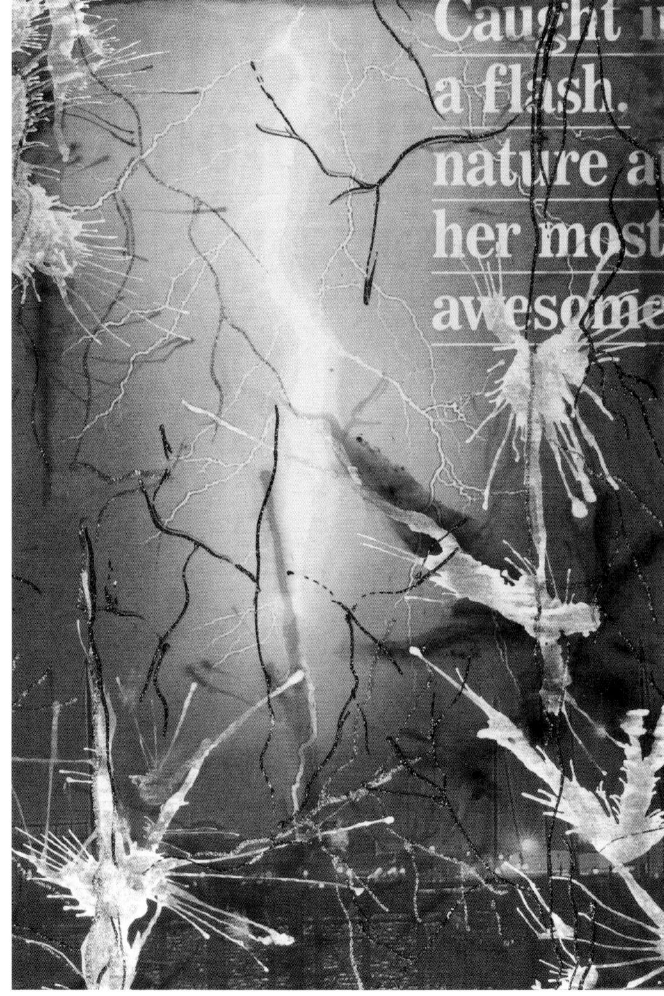

Below right
Experiment with various media in your sketchbook. Here, lightning has been reproduced onto a newspaper background with colored inks and metallic glitter pens.

Sketchbooks are available in a variety of sizes. Some are small enough to fit into your pocket for convenient location drawing, while the bigger ones can be used for larger-scale artwork. The paper used in most sketchbooks is a good-quality white cartridge paper, but you can also choose brown or black paper, or paper for a specific medium such as watercolor or pastels.

Buy a durable sketchbook with a hard back and strong binding. Investing in sketchbooks that will last a lifetime is worth it—in years to come, your visual studies might inspire you to produce new work. Keeping sketchbooks also gives you the pleasure of looking back through them to see how your skills have progressed.

These pages (facing page and below) show how an artist has investigated the theme of weather, in particular rain and thunderstorms. This research has not yet been used for any form of finished art, but the potential for future work is evident, and the artist can refer to the sketchbook at any time for inspiration. Ask yourself what artwork you might produce using the diverse and experimental work from the sketchbook pages as your starting point.

Below left
Preparing your sketchbook pages so that you can work on them at a later date reduces the fear factor of the blank white page. Keep in mind the themes you are exploring—for example, this page has been prepared using a watercolor wash to produce a rain effect.

Below right
Practice drawing from magazines with a range of media to improve your skills. Here, pastels and silver ink are used to illustrate a woman in wet-weather clothes splashing in a puddle.

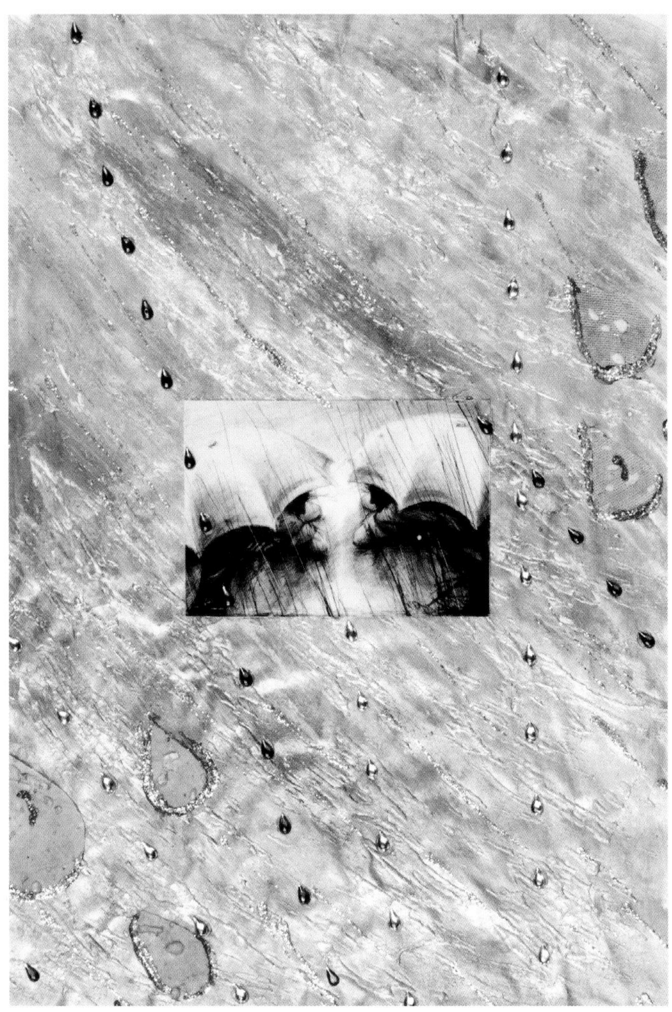

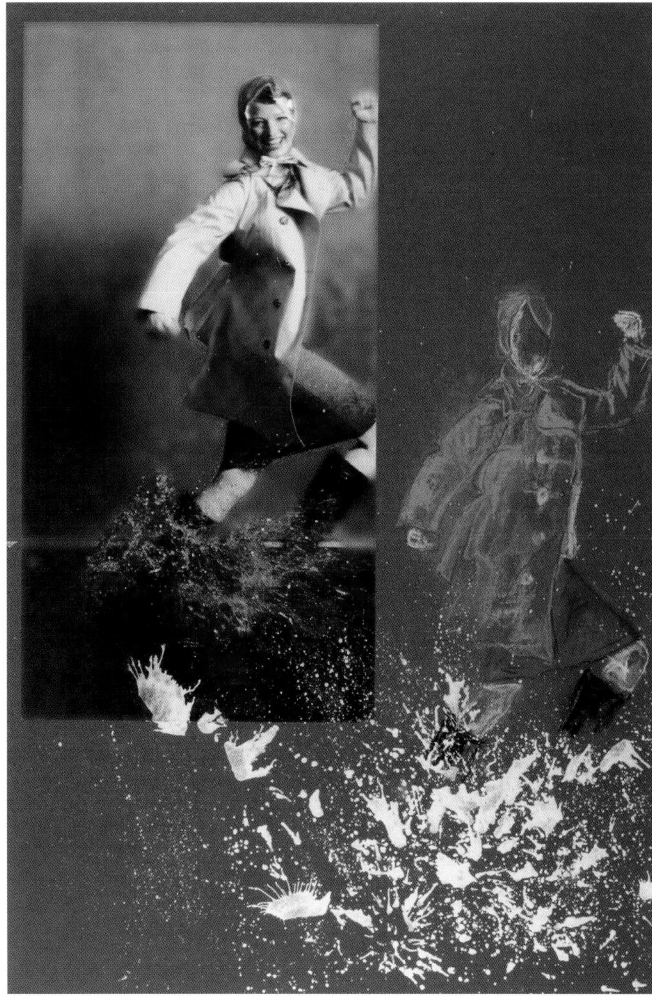

Make your sketchbooks working tools that you add to and update continually. The pages below, from a fashion design student's sketchbook, clearly map the stages from completing initial research to garment design. As garments are finished, the designer has placed photographs next to the original drawings to compare the two-dimensional and three-dimensional versions. The pages also show how the designer planned each outfit for the catwalk show, listing details of the garments and the models. Creating a photomontage of the outfits in the collection, the designer links this to the other pages in the sketchbook with color. The figures are placed on the page to provide a unique layout. Snapshots from behind the scenes of the fashion show complement the two-dimensional designs and finish the story.

This series of sketchbook pages shows how a designer has planned a collection to progress from two-dimensional sketches to three-dimensional garments. Working on graph paper throughout, the designer sticks to the same color palette. On the first page (*Top left*), the design is highlighted by a line drawing that reveals the outfit's silhouette.

Top right
Marker pens are used to illustrate this garment, although its back view is shown on a mannequin in a photograph. The designer links the images cleverly with a broken line drawn around the outfits.

Below left
A planning page on which the designer has listed the items that make up the outfit. This is for the model and dresser at the catwalk show.

Below center
A photomontage of the collection shows photographs placed at the top and bottom of the page, which is an unusual arrangement. Most people use the center of a page as a starting point, but the originality of this display is far more interesting for the viewer.

Below right
Behind-the-scenes snapshots from the fashion show display finished garments next to the initial designs in the sketchbook.

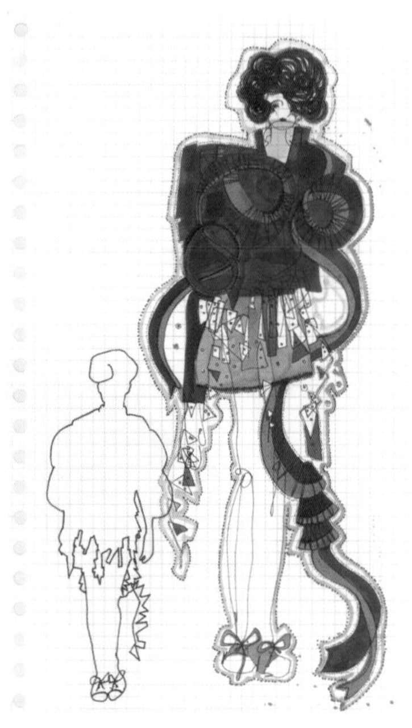

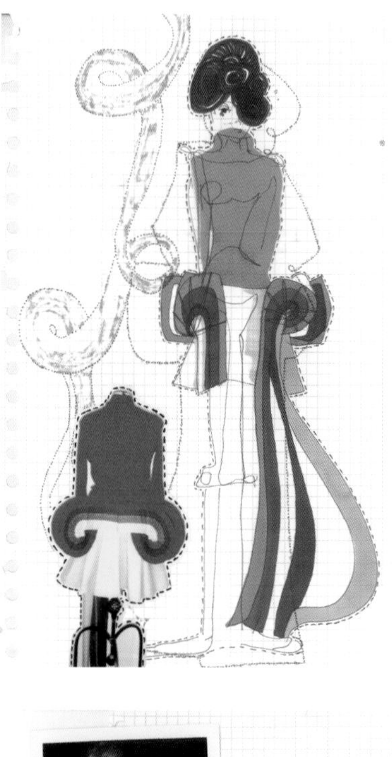

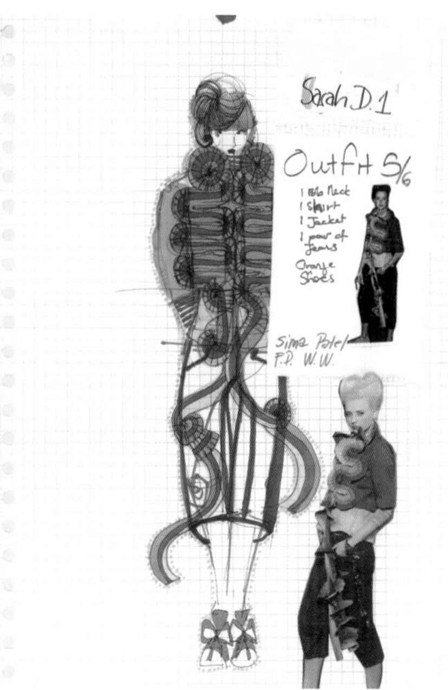

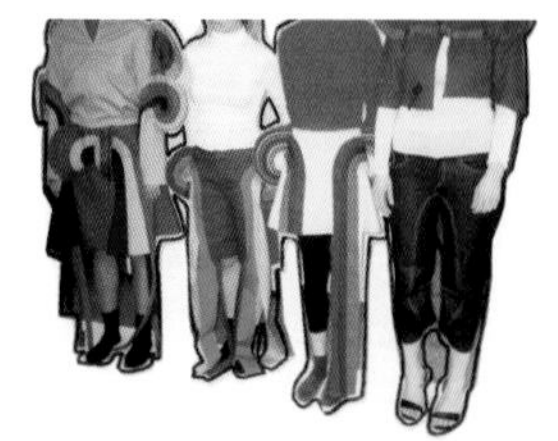

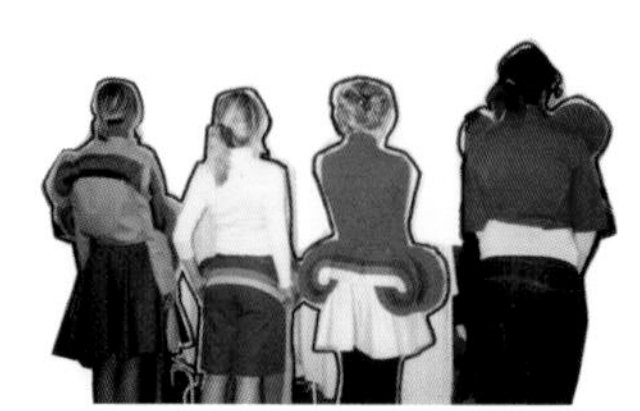

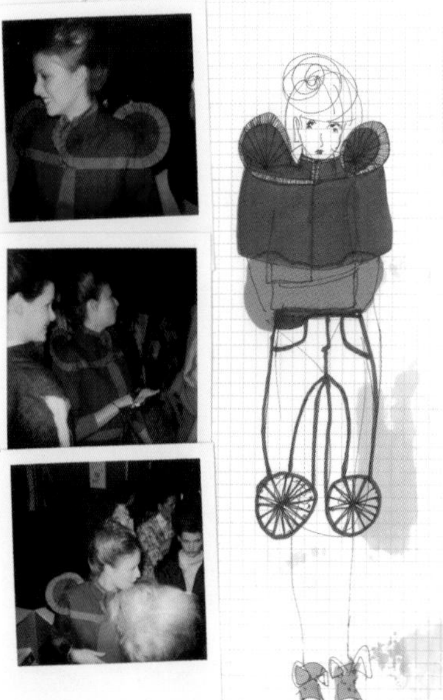

THE FIGURE

2

Central to fashion illustration and fashion design is the figure. An understanding of the accurate proportions of the human body and how it is constructed is vital for producing convincing fashion illustrations and garment designs. This chapter provides essential information and advice, and easy-to-remember tips, that you will find useful throughout your artistic career. To understand the figure beneath the clothes, practice the exercises described on the following pages regularly.

DRAWING FROM LIFE

The figure has occurred throughout art history as a central theme for exploration—drawing the nude figure from life has been practiced in art academies for centuries. Clothing brings further challenge and diversity to drawing the figure and, from this, the art of fashion illustration has developed.

If you are relatively new to figure drawing, you may feel daunted by the apparent complexity of the subject. It is a common belief that drawing the figure is the hardest artistic talent to develop. How many times have you heard phrases such as "I can't draw faces" or "I can't draw hands"? In fact, good drawings of figures are not so much the most difficult to achieve as the easiest to judge. We know the layout and proportions of our bodies so well that we notice inaccuracies instantly. The result is that, unless a drawing is remarkably accurate, it is deemed poor and the artist loses confidence.

At its most basic, a drawing is nothing more than a series of marks made on a surface by one person that another can understand. In fashion illustration, drawing the figure is more about developing your own style, and creating individual studies that convey personality and meaning, than about accuracy. However, this is not an excuse to draw a figure with, say, a disproportionately large head because you are

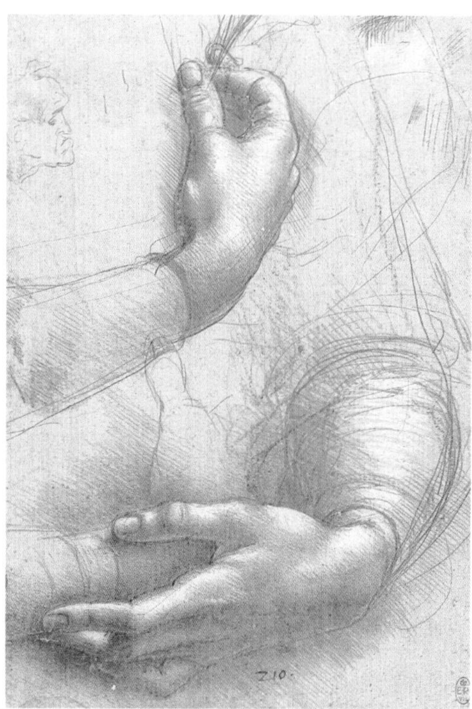

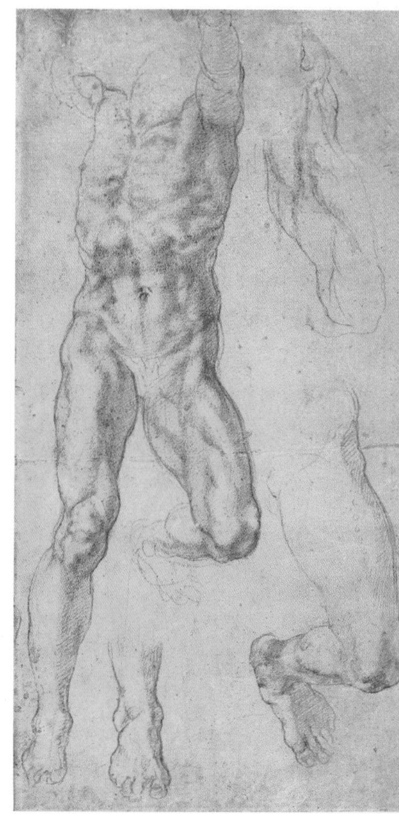

Left
Leonardo da Vinci, *Study of a Woman's Hands*, c. 1490. Charcoal on paper.

Right
Michelangelo, *Study of a Male Nude Stretching Upwards*, sixteenth century. Chalk on paper.

To create a fashion illustration, you need to be aware of the body shapes that lie beneath the clothes. The Italian Renaissance artists Leonardo da Vinci and Michelangelo made many rigorous studies of the nude figure in which they acutely observed anatomy before painting clothed figures.

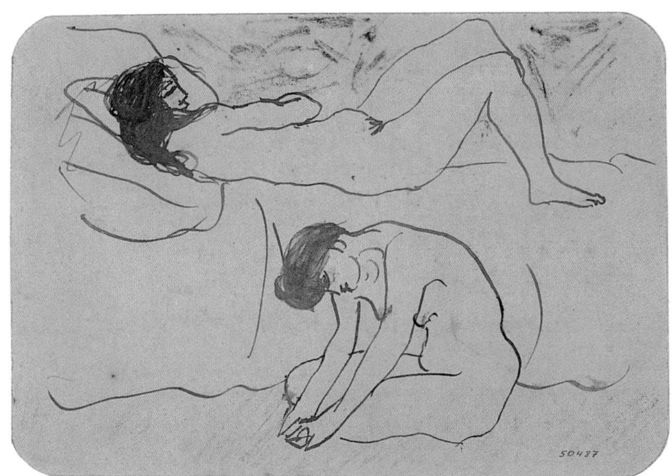

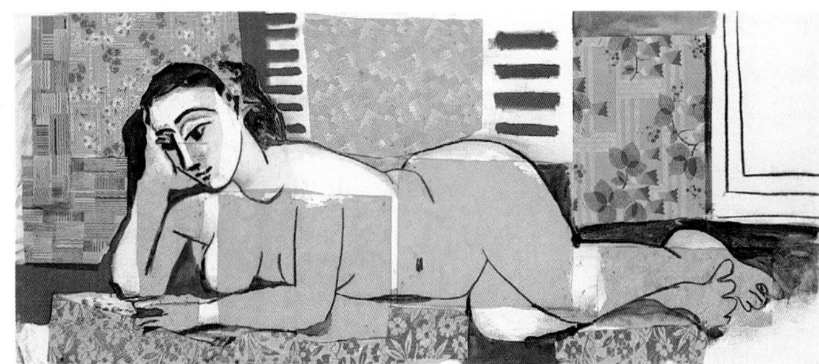

unable to assess proportions correctly. An illustrator must understand accurate body proportions before it is possible to create a unique style.

Through drawing we learn to see. We may think we know the human figure until asked to describe it accurately. By recording a figure on paper, we cannot help but understand it better. Our drawings vary because we all see things differently. Look with fresh eyes to achieve an honest drawing, and never rely on memory or what experience tells you is correct. Free yourself from what your mind already "knows" and draw only what your eyes see.

THE NUDE FIGURE

The nude human figure must serve as the basis for all figure study and fashion illustration. It is impossible to draw the clothed figure without knowledge of the structure and form of the body underneath. In the twenty-first century, artists and illustrators no longer tend to study anatomy as part of their formal training. However, a sound knowledge of how the body is constructed can only increase your perception. When thinking about the figure you may use in a fashion illustration, consider the body shapes that lie beneath the clothes. It is inspirational to look at the work of Michelangelo and Leonardo da Vinci (facing page), whose observations of anatomy in pen and ink capture the reality and the beauty of the human body.

To broaden your knowledge of anatomy, visit a natural history museum or refer to books to make studies of the skeleton and the joints and muscles that operate to move the bones. By gaining an understanding of how joints move and which bones fit together, you can create more realistic figure drawings.

A clear understanding of anatomy allowed Pablo Picasso to base a significant amount of his work around the nude human form. The works selected here (this page) outline important lessons for the art student. *Two Nude Women* demonstrates Picasso's economic use of line. Both women are lost in thought, and Picasso captures their mood with decisive pen-and-ink strokes. The nudes are drawn on a colored background, using only a limited palette, enhancing the purity of line and form.

In *Femme nue allongée* Picasso uses mixed media to create blocks of color and pattern, his experimental approach enriching the artwork. It is doubtful that Picasso knew what result he would achieve when he started this piece, once saying: "If you know exactly what you are going to do, what is the point of doing it?"

Left
Pablo Picasso, *Two Nude Women*, 1902-03. Ink and pencil on card.

With economical line and a limited color palette, Picasso captures the main lines and forms of two reclining nudes in this uncomplicated image. His technique is bold and decisive.

Right
Pablo Picasso, *Femme nue allongée*, 1955. Paper collage and oil on canvas.

Experimenting with mixed media without a fixed idea of the outcome is a way of achieving unpredictable and exciting results, as Picasso demonstrates in this image. He uses haphazard blocks of patterned paper and color to express his ideas, the finished effect most likely unplanned.

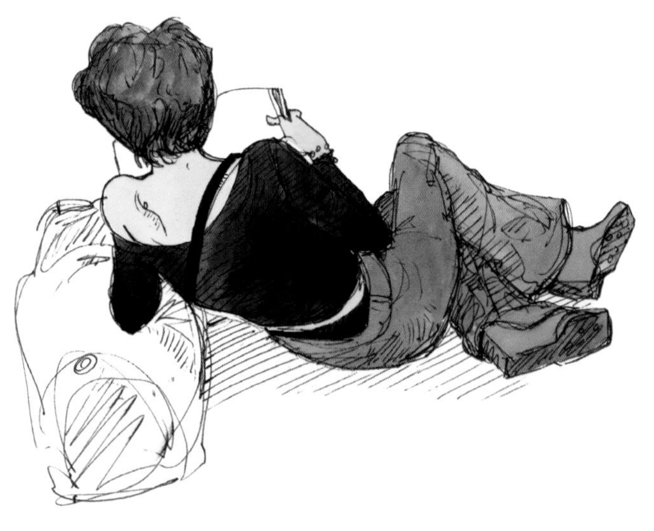

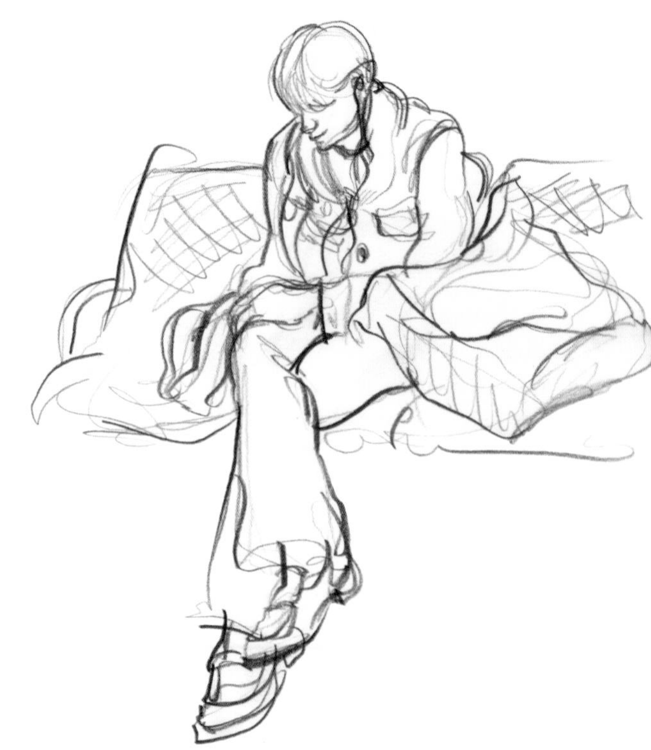

Observing the human figure is vital for the fashion illustrator. Keep a small sketchbook in your bag and draw from life whenever you have the opportunity, using portable media such as pen and wash, or pencil and watercolor. The train station is an excellent place to begin. In these sketches we see a woman reading while leaning on her bag and a man in the waiting room.

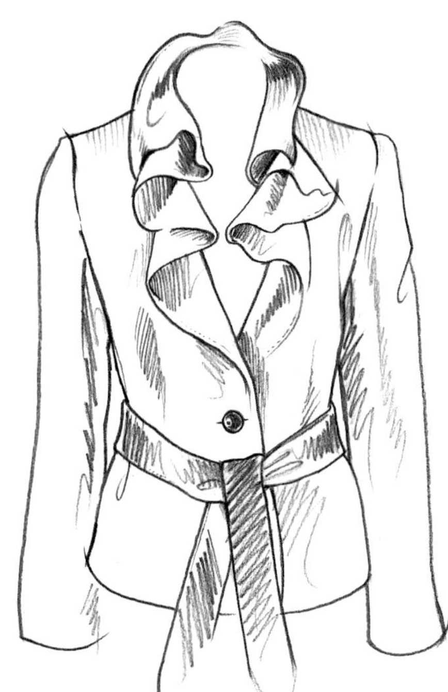

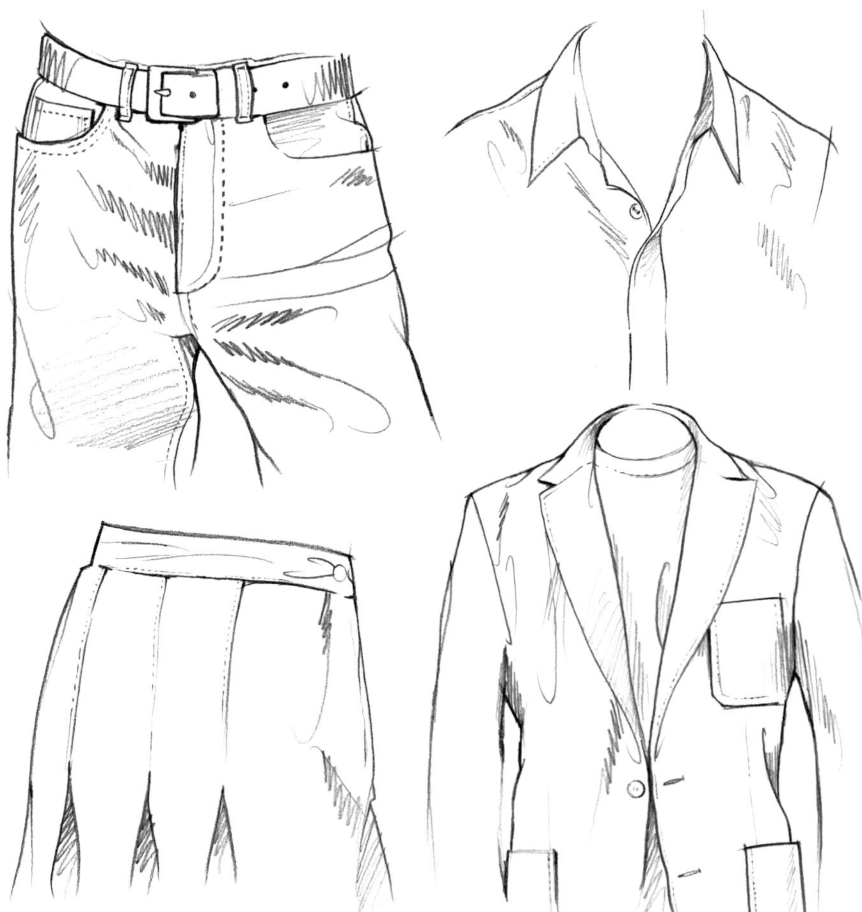

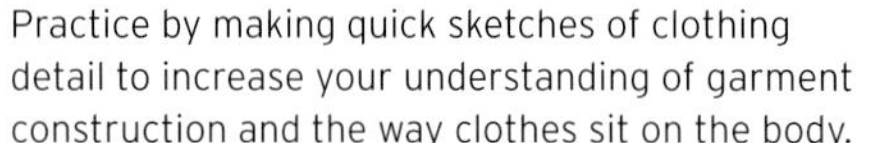

Practice by making quick sketches of clothing detail to increase your understanding of garment construction and the way clothes sit on the body.

THE CLOTHED FIGURE

An understanding of how fabric drapes around the body is vital for drawing the clothed figure convincingly, as is a knowledge of how seams, gathers, pleats, and darts affect the fit of garments on the figure. You do not need to know how to sew to illustrate, but it helps to be aware of the construction of clothing, just as it does to understand the structure of the body. Make detailed studies of sections of clothed figures to build your awareness of the ways in which clothes fit and drape on the body, before you begin to illustrate.

An important aspect of drawing the figure is awareness of its scale in relation to its setting. Consider how figures fit into their surroundings, and how much their appearance is dictated by the scene in which they are set. Focusing on scale, composition, and clothing, practice drawing figures in various locations: children playing on a beach, customers shopping, teenagers playing football, a couple dining in a cafe, a person curled up in an armchair or asleep on a sofa, employees at a meeting, friends watching television, passengers on a bus, or old ladies chatting on a park bench. This type of sketching increases your ability to create a sense of perspective, and to draw figures to scale in their environments. By sketching on location, you will also gain ideas for backgrounds and settings for your fashion illustrations.

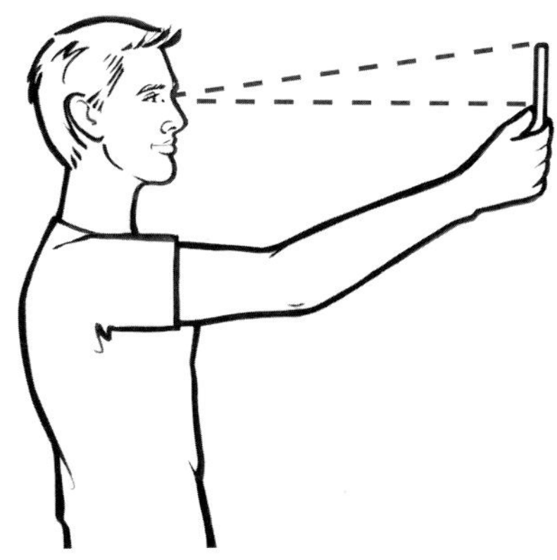

By holding a pencil at arm's length and focusing on your subject, you can measure the figure in front of you. Close one eye, and use the pencil point and your thumb as markers to measure, say, a leg in relation to another part of the body.

MEASURING THE FIGURE AND USING A VIEWFINDER

When drawing the nude or clothed figure from life, the most difficult skill to master is that of correct body proportions. To enhance their skills, many artists use a pencil to measure the figure and a viewfinder to frame a model and give proportionate width to height.

By holding a pencil at arm's length and focusing on your subject, you can measure the figure in front of you. Close one eye, then use the pencil point and your thumb as markers to measure each part of the figure in relation to another. You can also hold your pencil at the same angle as the figure's arm, then transfer this angle to your drawing. This method allows you to assess approximately relative angles of parts of the body that would otherwise be difficult to draw correctly.

A viewfinder is a piece of card with a window cut into it of the same proportions as your drawing paper. Hold the viewfinder in front of one eye to frame the figure. A viewfinder helps you to disregard the figure's wider surroundings and draw only what is inside the window. It allows you to try out different framing options for your picture, including more or less of the setting around the figure.

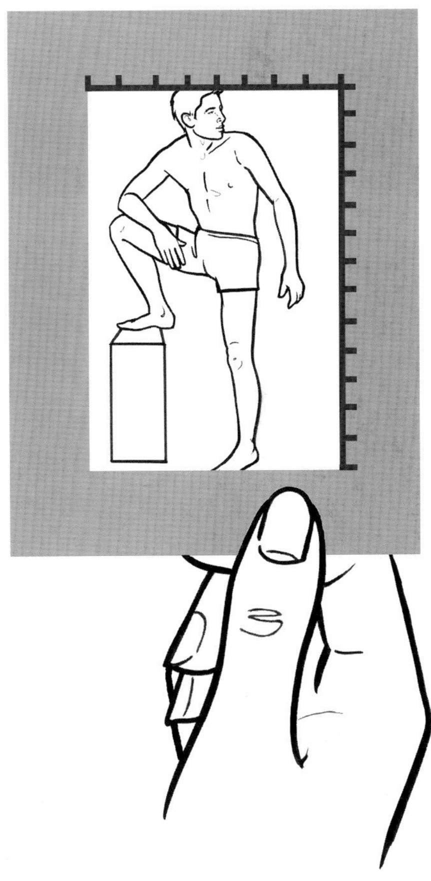

A viewfinder is a simple-to-make device that helps you to select how much of a figure's surroundings you want to include within the confines of your picture. By moving the viewfinder, you can select the view that works best.

Below left
Life drawing on a large scale can be bold and dramatic. This artist brings drama and atmosphere to the work by using intense color, and strong lines, shapes, and patterns using charcoal and pencils.

Below center
Experiment with varied media when drawing from life. While charcoal is a popular choice for many artists because it encourages bold, expressive lines, this study has been created with oil pastels on brown paper. Oil pastels are richly colored and have a dense, waxy texture that can be exploited to provide additional interest in a figure drawing.

Below right
Here, a single page has been used for a series of quick studies. Working with pencil, the artist concentrates on several poses in order to build an understanding of the figure and the way it moves.

LIFE DRAWING

The best way to represent figures confidently is to draw from life as often as you can. Many local art centers or art schools offer life-drawing classes. Attending your first life-drawing session can be a frightening prospect. Where will you sit? What materials should you use? Will you feel embarrassed? Where do you start? Many artists advise that in life-drawing classes the best way to proceed is to view the nude figure as a series of lines and shapes and forget that there is a person in front of you. Drawing the nude figure is the ultimate test in observation and understanding, and demands your full concentration, so you will find it easier than anticipated to dismiss other thoughts.

To practice drawing the clothed figure, make the most of opportunities such as family or friends watching television. Most people stay fairly still for about fifteen minutes when relaxing. Public transport also offers an excellent opportunity for capturing interesting poses. Always carry a small sketchbook when traveling on a train or bus, or attending an event where there are lots of people to draw.

The sketchbook page opposite shows how Francis Marshall, although famous for couture-show sketches of Balenciaga, Jacques Fath, and Dior, has always found time to practice figure drawing.

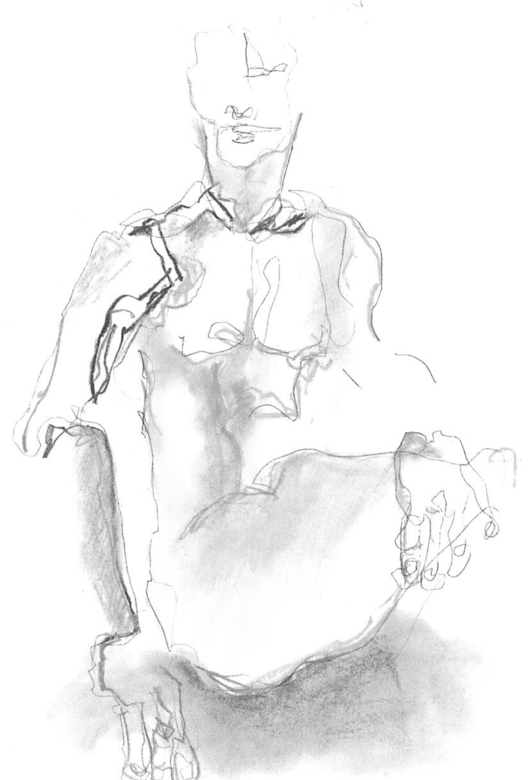

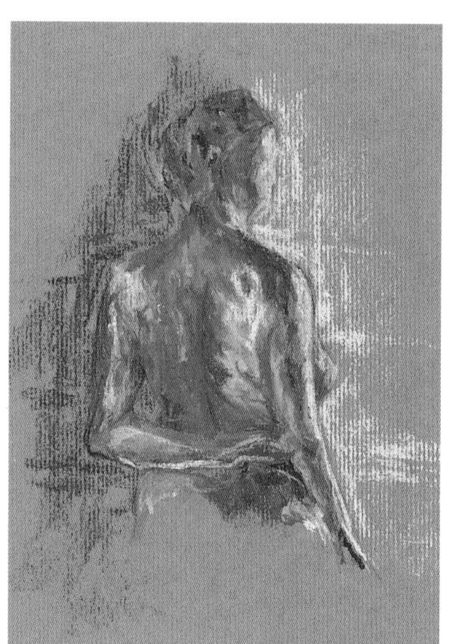

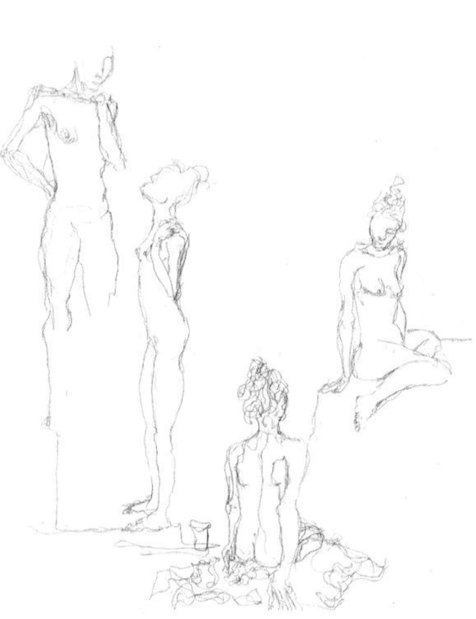

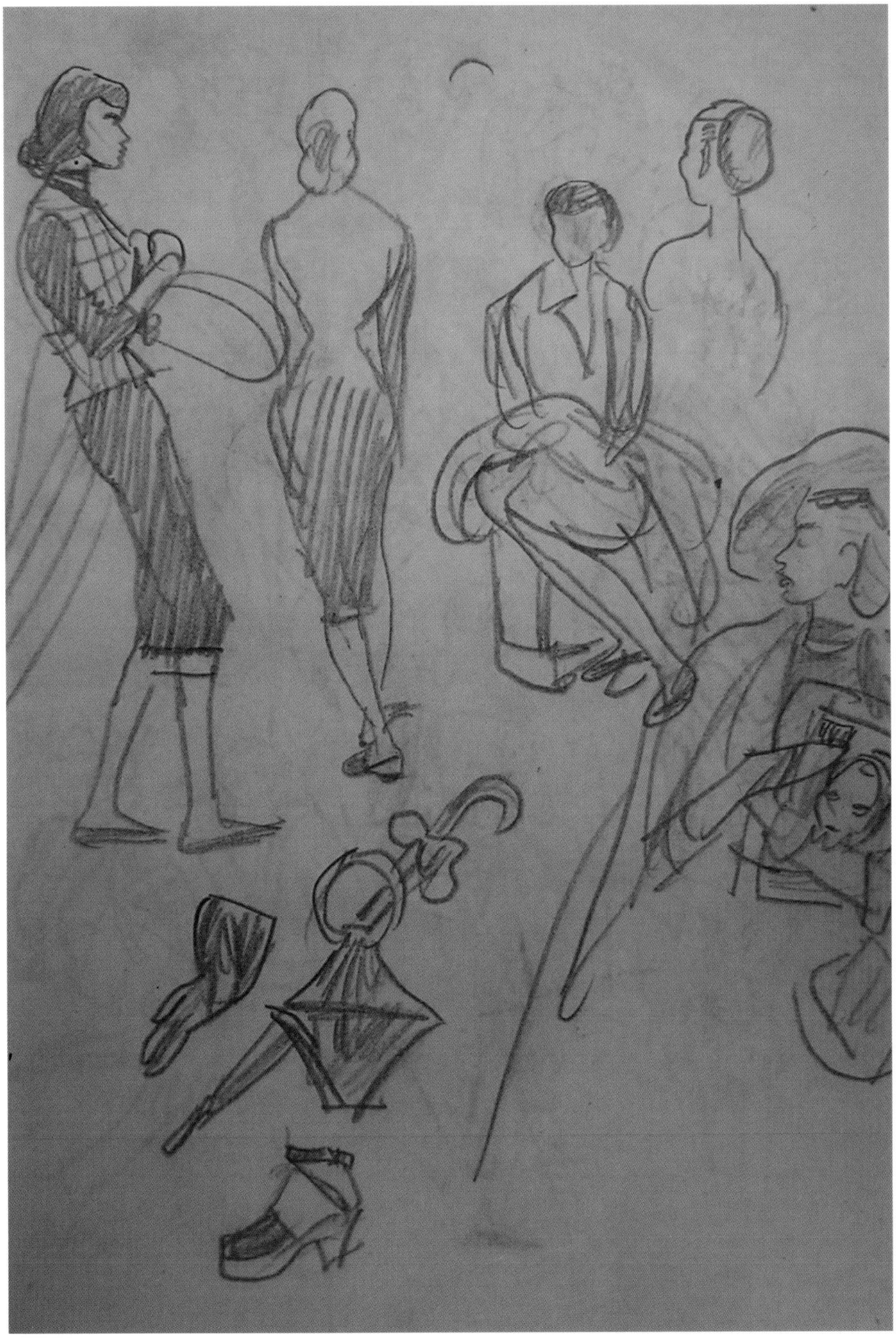

To improve his talent for capturing catwalk styles, Francis Marshall draws frequently from observation. His sketchbook pages show women walking, detailed pencil drawings of facial features, and clothing accessories.

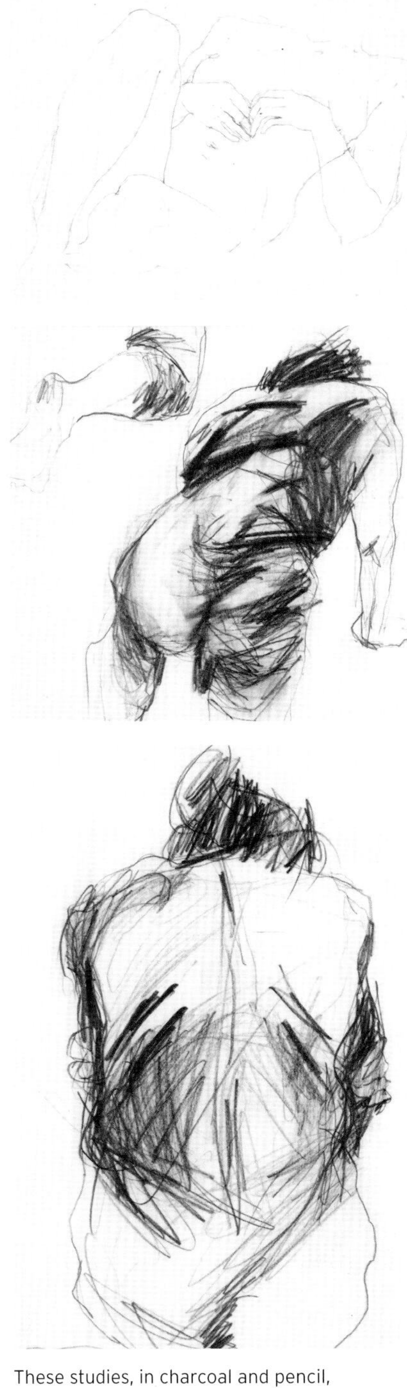

These studies, in charcoal and pencil, demonstrate how drawing from life can help you gain valuable knowledge of the figure beneath the clothes. Perfect finished artwork is not attempted; instead the artist has focused on understanding particular parts of the body.

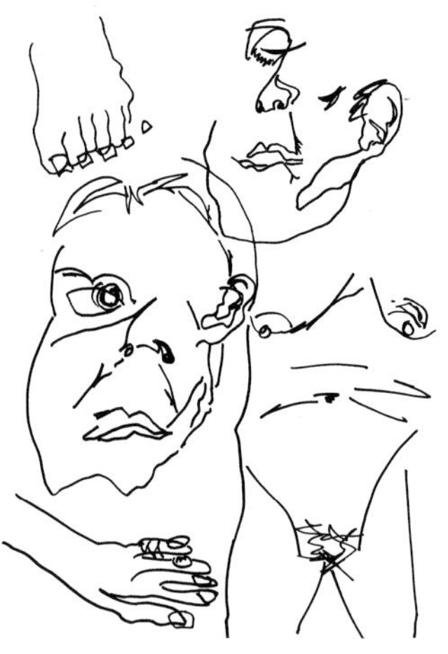

The "don't-look-back" exercise encourages you to focus your thoughts entirely on the figure you are drawing. The aim is to draw without looking at your page. The result is not supposed to be a perfect artwork, but a valuable lesson in concentration and confident expression.

OBSERVATIONAL DRAWING AND INTUITIVE EXERCISES

Drawing from life is also known as "objective" or "observational" drawing, meaning an image that is created to represent what is seen during direct observation. The aim is to show the figure (or object) truthfully, exactly as it appears. Drawing in this way is about believing and trusting your visual judgment as you record what you see. Before embarking on more elaborate studies of the figure, try some simple exercises using intuitive observation. The purpose of these exercises is to train your mind to accept what your eyes—rather than your preconceptions or your mind's interpretations—deem to be true.

The "don't-look-back" exercise

Focus all your attention on the figure in front of you and draw exactly what you see. Do not examine the drawing once you have started—just look at the figure and recreate its shapes on paper. Try not to use your critical judgment. Concentrate on the contours of the figure and the shapes contained within. This type of drawing is about forgetting what you think you know, and believing in what you see. When you look at a figure, your brain interprets for you what you should see. The result is that you may draw the figure as you *believe* it to be, rather than how it *actually* looks. By checking your drawing constantly, it is tempting to correct what you think are mistakes. Trust your eyes, and you will produce a truthful drawing.

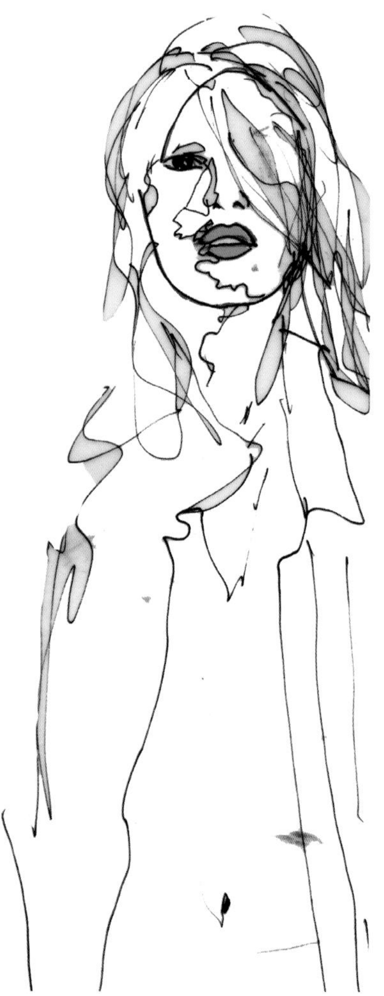

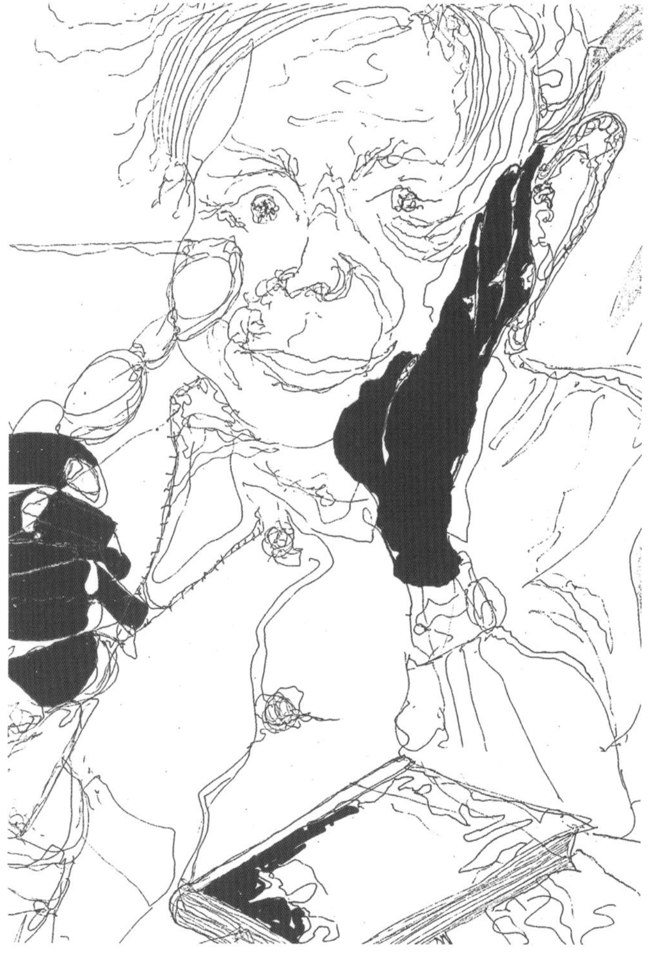

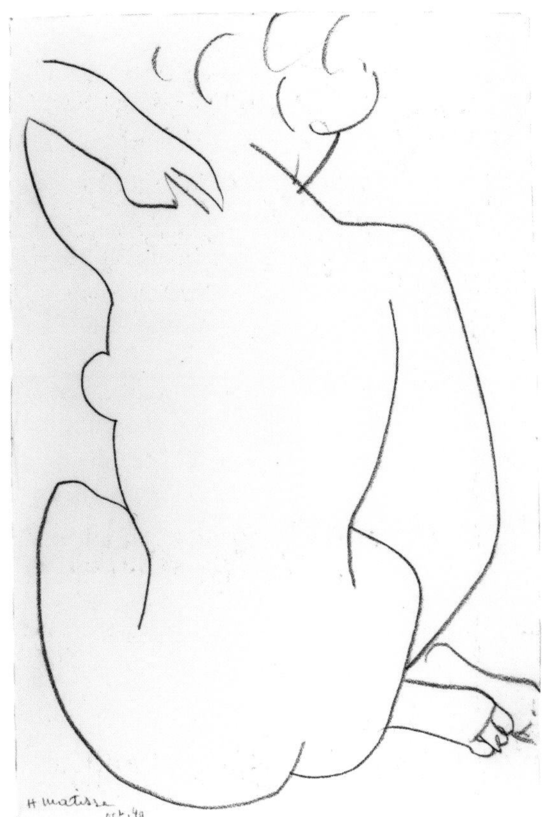

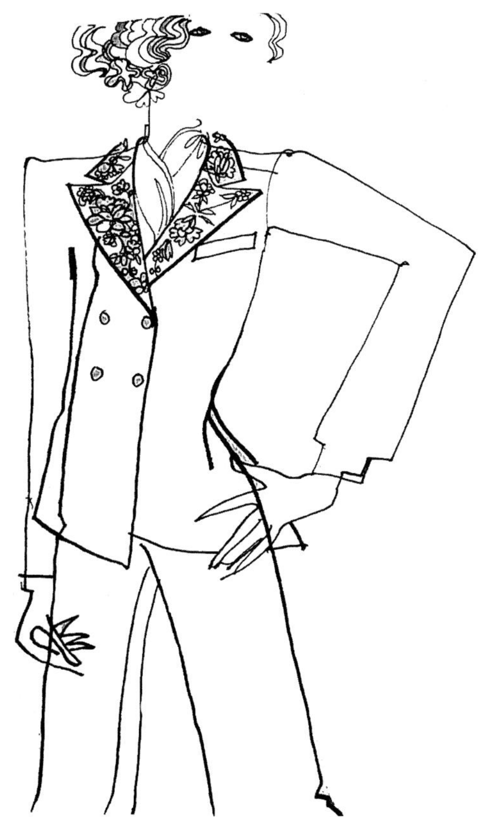

The continuous-line exercise

Working from observation, make a continuous line drawing of the figure. As you look at your subject, keep your hand moving constantly so that the line remains unbroken. You can complete this exercise using any medium—charcoal, pencil, or pen. Avoid the temptation to create accurate details, such as those of the face, with lots of small lines. The purpose of this exercise is to record all information with one single, flowing line. The illustrations opposite (below left and right) have been created using continuous lines. They are extremely free images, only refined by a hint of color added digitally. It is a good idea to experiment with freehand drawing and the computer to create unique effects.

The outline exercise

A useful skill to acquire when learning to draw the figure from life is to look past the detail to concentrate on the shape as a whole. Simplify what you see, flattening the figure in your mind's eye so that you focus on its outline. Learn to pay close attention to "negative spaces"—the areas of background enclosed by parts of the figure. If you concentrate on drawing these shapes, the figure should emerge with some accuracy into the foreground of your illustration. Look at the back view of the figure drawn by Matisse (above left). The lines are simply the outline of the shape he sees. Likewise, Ossie Clark shows off his designs with strong outlines (above right). The space around the figure is vital to the outline.

Above left
A master of the outline technique, Matisse captures this figure (1949) with only a few simple lines, so that the viewer comprehends it entirely.

Above right
This line drawing, by British designer Ossie Clark, from a sketchbook of c. 1970, provides just enough detail to appreciate the design of the clothes.

Opposite, below left
Line drawing has been a major influence in this fashion illustration even though there is no obvious outline to the figure. Instead, it is made up from many interconnecting lines. A small amount of color has been added digitally at the end of the process to finish the illustration.

Opposite, below right
The continuous-line exercise involves creating a figure drawing with one, flowing line. This one has been scanned and color blocked in digitally to emphasize the hands.

TEMPLATES

TRACING FROM A PHOTOGRAPH

Tracing is not always cheating. Sometimes making a simple copy of a figure from a photograph is the most helpful way to start a fashion illustration. You are already working with a two-dimensional image, which is easier than working directly from a three-dimensional figure. Moreover, if you do not have access to a life model at the appropriate time, drawing a figure accurately from memory is not a common skill. Most people need a source of inspiration to begin a drawing. Trace the outline

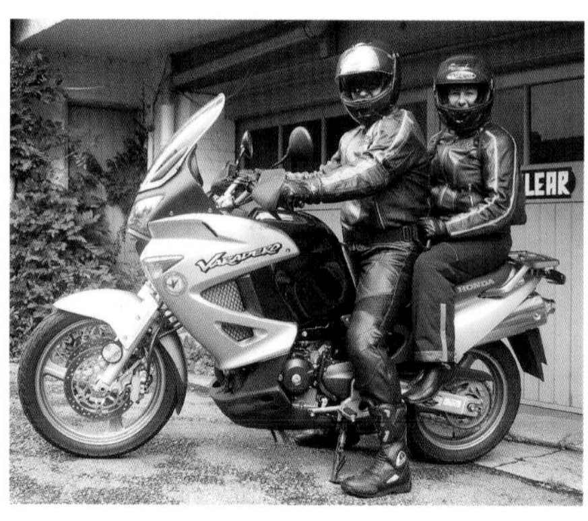

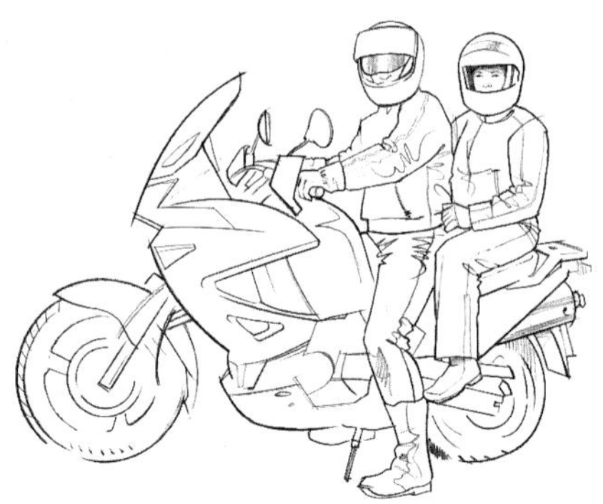

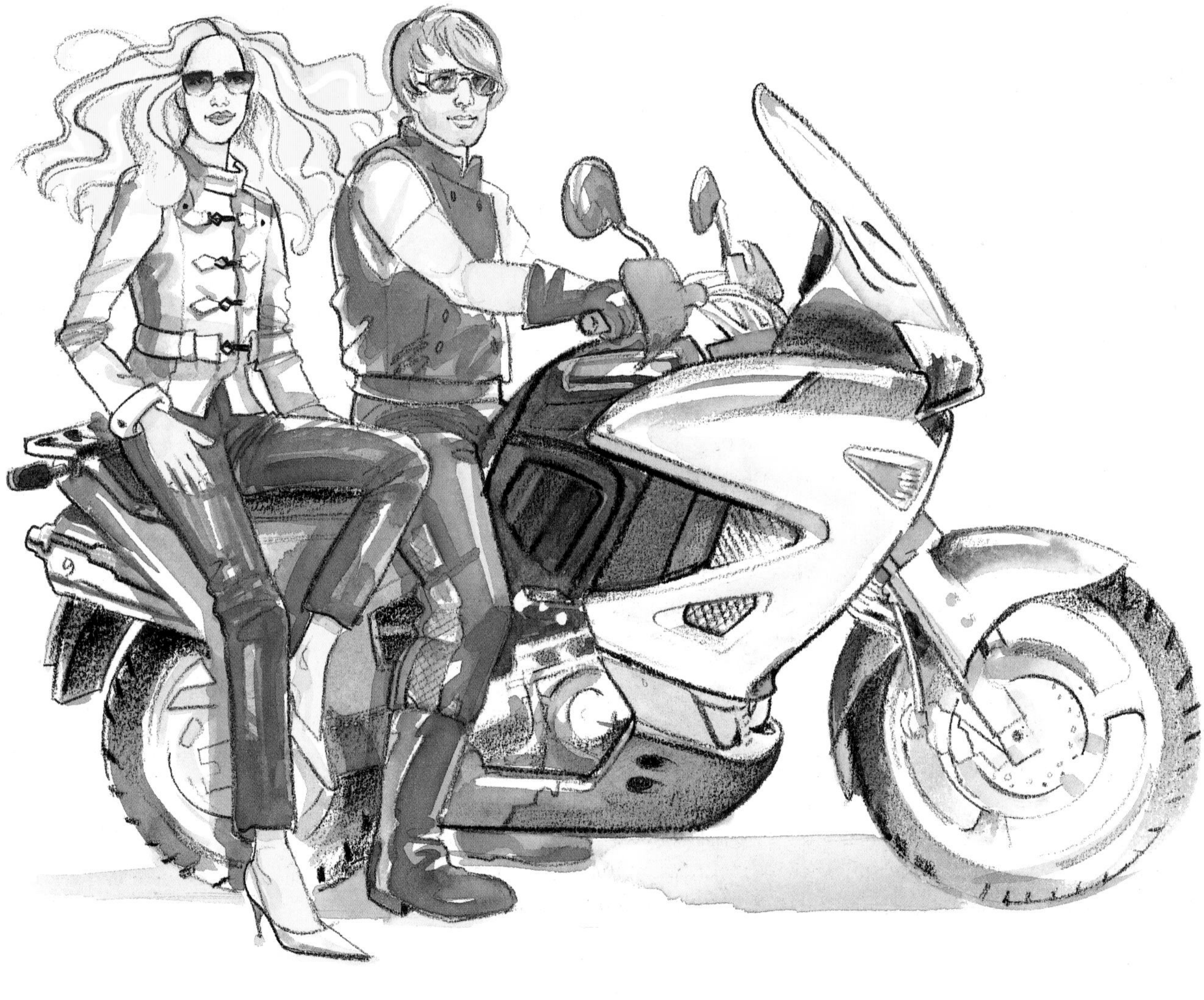

Right
Copying a figure, or figures, from a photograph or magazine can form the foundation of a fashion illustration. Even an ordinary photograph of a couple on a motorbike wearing full leathers can be used as a starting point.

Far right
Trace the main lines of each figure by placing your paper over the photograph on a light box.

Below
Inspired by the photograph, this is the final fashion illustration. Although life drawing is necessary to understand the human body, it is still valid to use a two-dimensional image as the basis for your figure.

of a figure from a photograph or magazine to give yourself a starting point, then apply your own illustrative style as you develop the artwork.

Place the photograph on a light box, or light tracer, or against a window so that you can see the most important features of the figure clearly. Decide on the main lines that define the figure's shape, then trace them carefully. Use a sharp pencil to avoid lines becoming fuzzy and confusing.

HOW TO USE A TEMPLATE

If you select photographs from a magazine that give a clear indication of body shapes and proportions, your tracings can be used as the basis for a fashion-figure template. A figure template is a tool used by fashion designers to help them speed up the design process. It is placed under semitransparent layout paper upon which the designer draws the garments, moving the template along the page to repeat the process. The template is used as a guide only. When the clothes are sketched in, the template is removed and the artwork completed. Depending too heavily on templates can inhibit a fashion designer's creativity, a common mistake being to design only clothes that fit the templates. Likewise, the illustrator must bear in mind that the template is a useful tool but not a means of creating a unique piece of artwork. The constant use of a template to initiate an illustration tends to lead to stilted results.

Copying a template from a fashion illustration book as your starting point for an artwork is not recommended. Often, those who view your work will recognize the pose. It is far better to create your own figure using the techniques suggested below.

CREATING A TEMPLATE

Select one of your own figure drawings or a suitable magazine photograph, place layout paper over it, and trace the image. Now simplify the drawing to create a clear outline, ensuring the proportions of different parts of the body are correct in relation to one another. Suggest the face and hairstyle, but do not draw every hair and eyelash. Unless you are adding accessories, the hands and feet also need only be implied.

You may adapt the pose to your own requirements. A simple front and back view of a front-facing figure will enable you to design quickly and precisely, but vary your templates so your work does not become predictable. The easiest method is to develop your first template, repositioning the legs and arms to create a variety of poses. Think about the stance of the templates, too. The way a figure is standing can often reflect the mood of a collection. Study models in magazines, and try to re-create similar poses and gestures in your templates. Drawing a line down the center of the template, front and back, creates a marker against which design details, such as button plackets, pockets, and seams, can be positioned correctly. If a template is too large, it can be scaled down by hand or by using a photocopier or scanner. When you have a selection of templates, you could reduce their size to repeat a series of poses across a page.

When creating your templates, consider the market for your illustrations or designs. For example, an expensive eveningwear collection will not look right if templates developed from street figures are used as a starting point. Collect a number of templates with varied looks and character.

Templates are used as an aid to freehand design, but they can also be adapted for the computer. Scan a template and use it as a foundation for your artwork, adding to it with a program that allows you to make decisions on color and pattern.

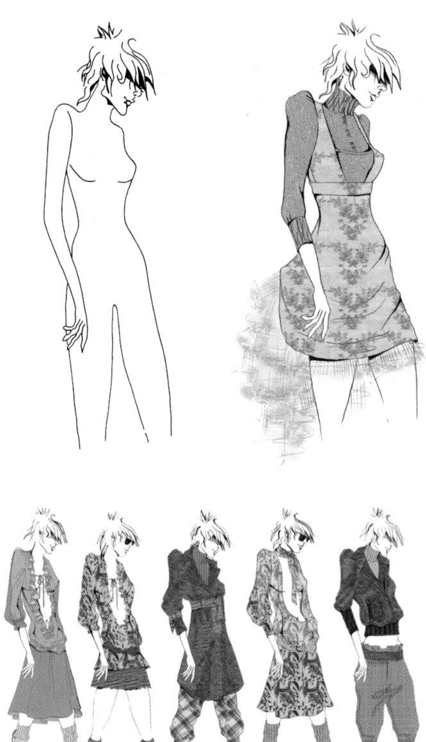

Above, top left
This female-figure template can be used traditionally on paper, or scanned for use on the computer.

Above, top right
The template has been scanned and clothing added using the computer. Fabric was scanned, then copied onto the garments.

Above
A full collection lineup, which uses the same template and illustration process for each figure.

Overleaf
Templates are created by reducing the body to a clear, simple outline. They enable the designer to work faster, using the template as a guide. To show garments from the front, back, and sides, the designer creates a range of templates. Templates for design are usually realistic and body proportions are not exaggerated.

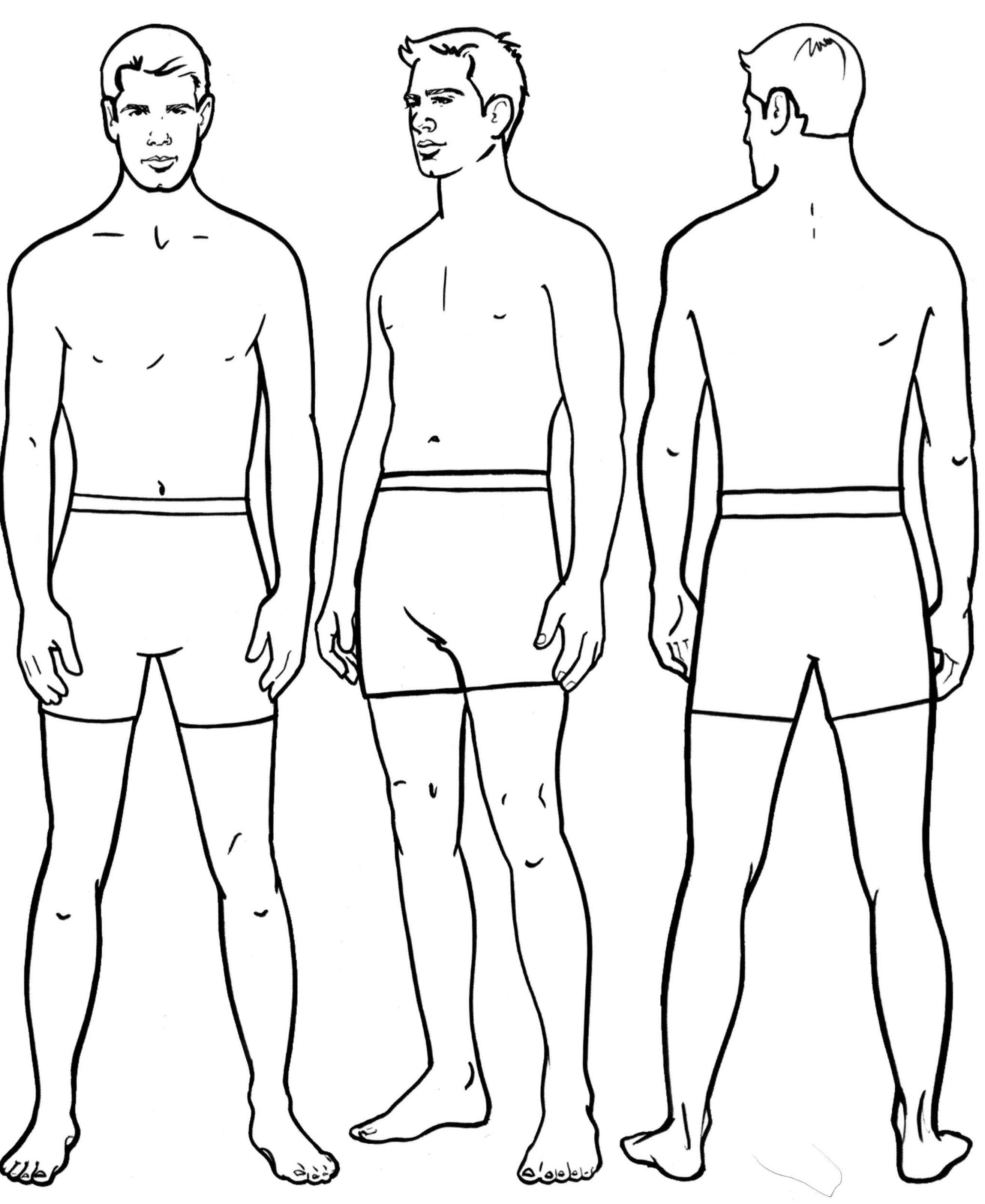

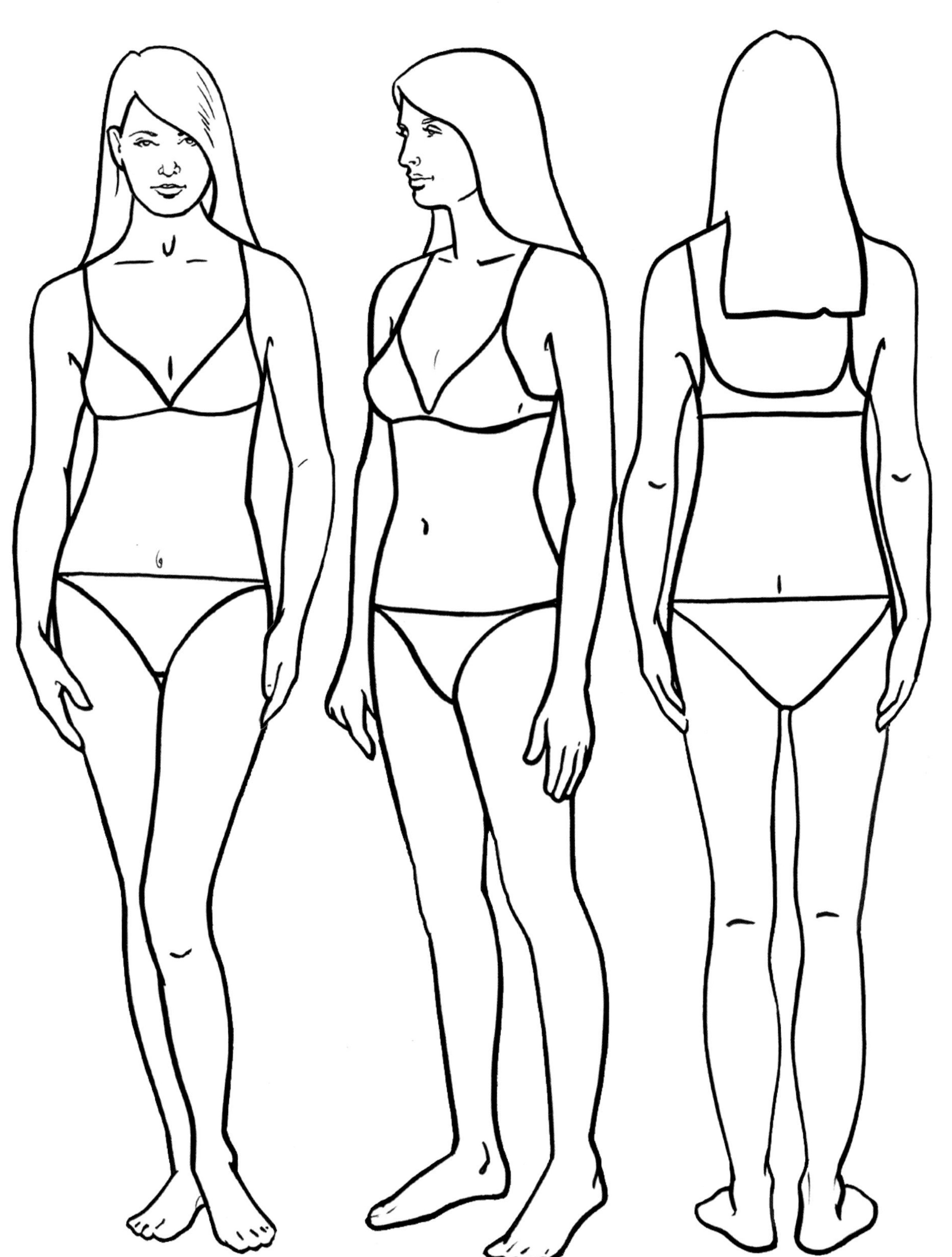

BODY PROPORTIONS: THEORY AND PRACTICE

THE HUMAN FORM

When drawing the fashion figure, it is important to know the standard proportions of the human form, as well as bearing in mind that people vary greatly in shape and size. Clothing the body is a means of self-expression and an opportunity for creativity, so the impression created by a fashion illustration must be based on careful observations. Fashions change from culture to culture, and from decade to decade. For example, a curvaceous figure and short, wavy hair were desirable in the 1950s, while a decade later a thin figure and poker-straight hair were most admired. The fashion illustrator often aims to express the features that society currently perceives as beautiful, and may choose to highlight these features through exaggerated illustration.

So, while body shapes and proportions may vary from person to person, and the fashionable ideal may change, the artist must keep in mind the essential components outlined in the following diagrams. The easiest way to begin your study of the human body is to see it as a series of shapes. For simplicity, imagine that it is made up of eleven basic parts (see below):

The human figure can be divided into eleven basic parts, which assists in seeing the body as a series of shapes.

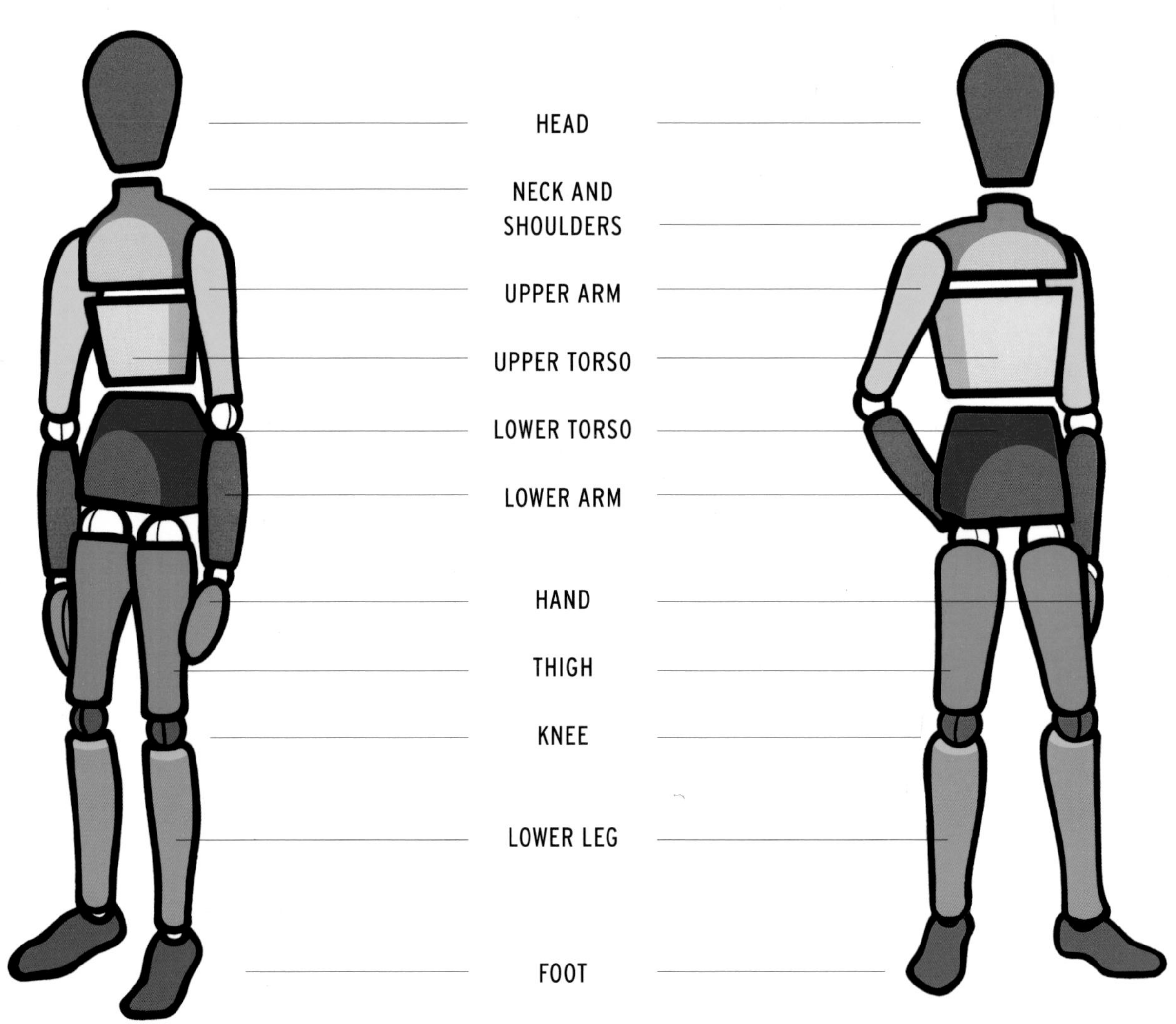

These basic parts can be manipulated to create different poses. Practice this by adjusting the parts of a wooden mannequin and drawing it at different angles (below). Your objective is to notice the way the eleven body shapes move in relation to each other. Then, once you understand how all the body parts fit together, focus on remembering their proportionate sizes.

This exercise is an important preparation for fashion illustration, as it will allow you to experiment with poses before you begin to concentrate on the details of the clothing.

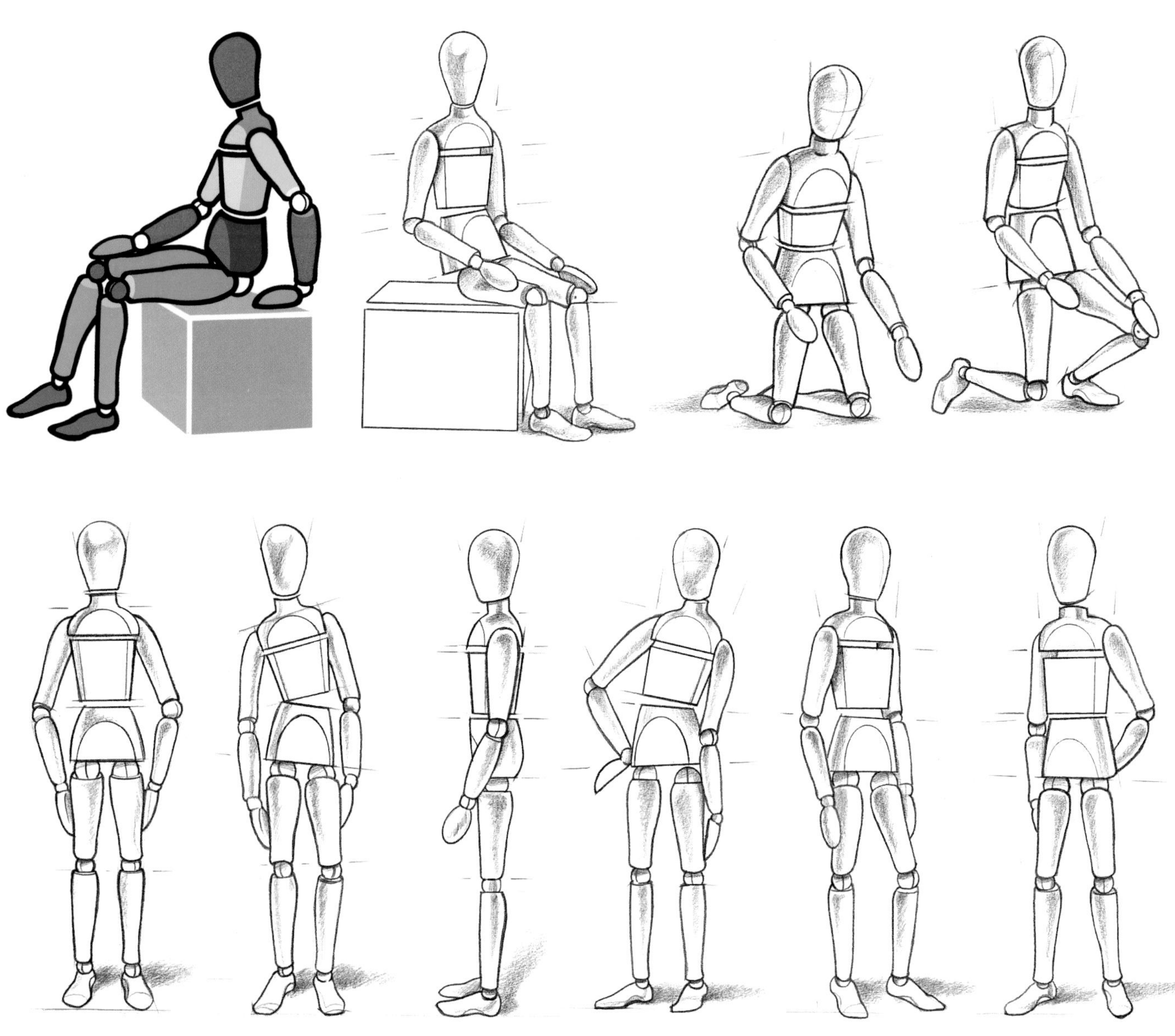

Practice drawing poses from a mannequin, observing how the 11 body parts move in relation to each other.

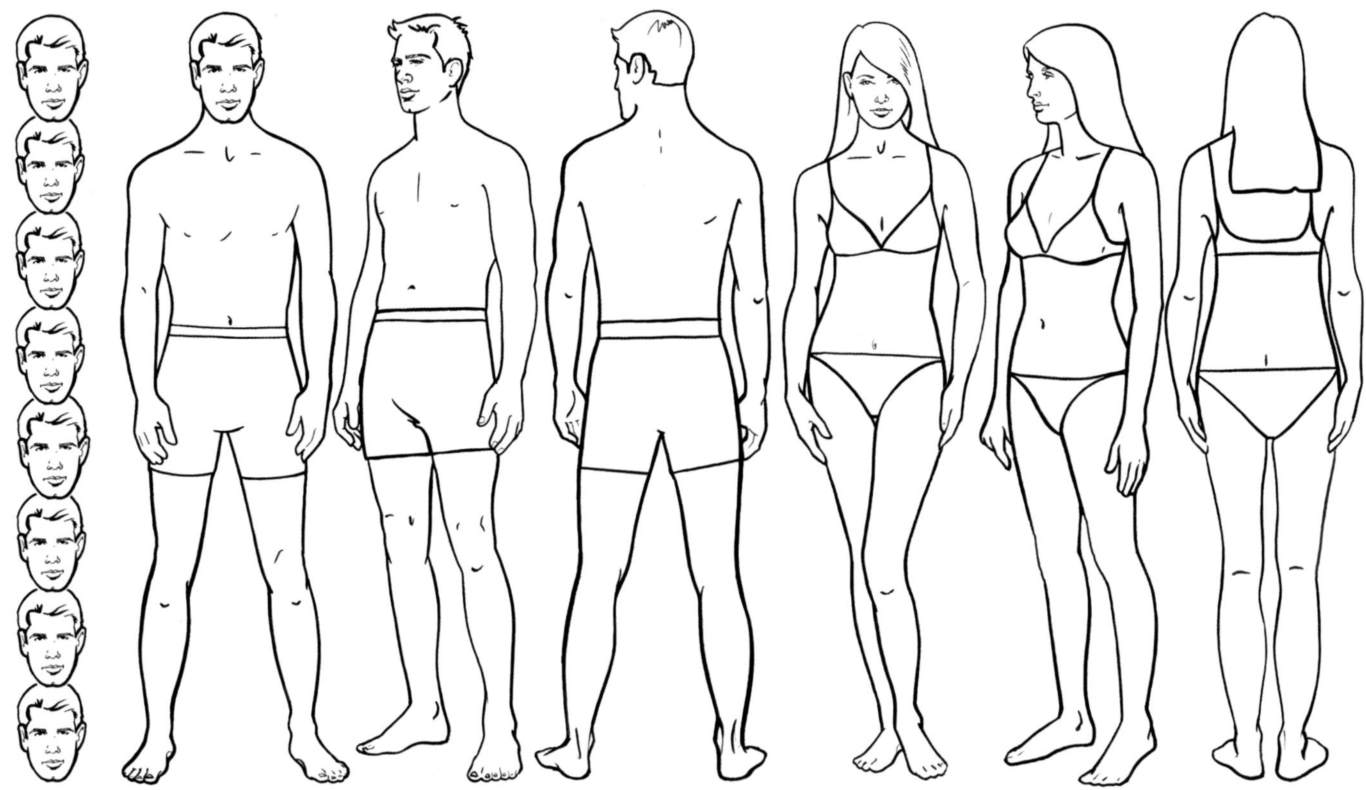

These diagrams show how the height of the body can be divided into eight equal parts, each equivalent to the height of the head. This fairly accurate system, invented by the ancient Greeks, is still used by artists today.

TRADITIONAL MEASURING METHODS

The ancient Greeks invented an ingenious method of measuring the height of the human body. They used the length of the head as a unit of measure, then counted the number of times it fitted into the body's total height. During classical Greek and Renaissance times, the ideal number was eight, which was the standard for perfect proportions. This simple way of measuring is still used today. Try it yourself by using a tape measure to find out how many times your head length fits approximately into your body height, from crown to toe.

DIFFERENCES BETWEEN MEN AND WOMEN

Men's and women's body proportions differ greatly, and men are generally taller. Women's shoulders are narrower and slope downward, whereas men's are broad and fairly straight. Women have proportionately wider hips than men, who have wider necks. The most common exaggerations in fashion illustration are for the female figure to be drawn with longer legs and a smaller waist, and for the male to have broad shoulders and muscular, toned arms. The following diagram demonstrates useful facts for the illustrator to keep in mind when drawing the figure.

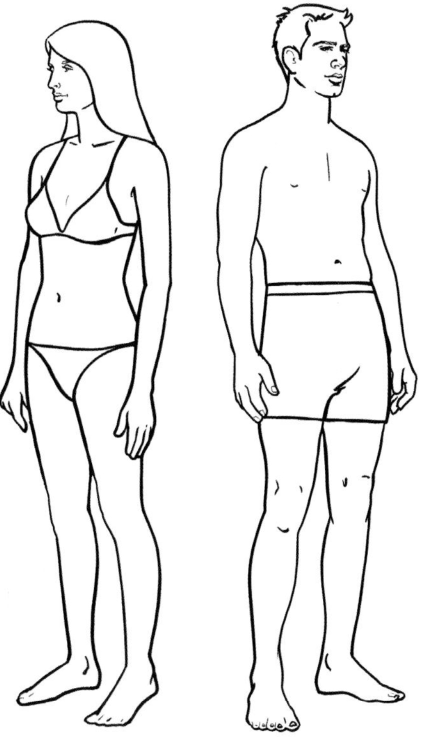

Left
A few useful body-proportion facts that a fashion illustrator should always keep in mind are shown in this diagram.

Below
Although accuracy is important when understanding the human form, fashion illustration sometimes exaggerates particular features. Here, the neck and hairstyle have been exaggerated to create an appropriate character for the fashion collection.

EXAGGERATION FOR FASHION

Although it is important to gain a thorough understanding of how the body is constructed, a fashion illustration is not always an accurate representation of reality. Exaggerating some aspect of the figure can add interest and character to the work. Fashion designers and illustrators often elongate the figure to give it more elegance and grace. To elongate a fashion figure, use the traditional measuring technique but increase the amount of heads used in the body length. For example, a figure could be stretched to ten or more heads in height. When stylizing a drawing by increasing the height of the figure, fashion illustrators usually emphasize the length of the legs. To keep proportions relatively sensible, calculate the legs as making up two thirds, rather than half, of the total height. The step-by-step exercise on the following page teaches you how to exaggerate leg length and fit the tall figure on a page. Use a figure from one of your life drawings, or from a magazine, for the exercise rather than attempting to draw from imagination.

Today, leg elongation is not as common as it once was in fashion illustration, which is employing a greater variety of figure shapes and body proportions. Contemporary illustrators are not afraid to portray reality and challenge fantasy. Illustration is not only about elegance and beauty, but creating a character that complements the clothes. However, given that exaggeration has dominated fashion illustration decade after decade, it may be worth exploring the very technique that has served illustrators for so long.

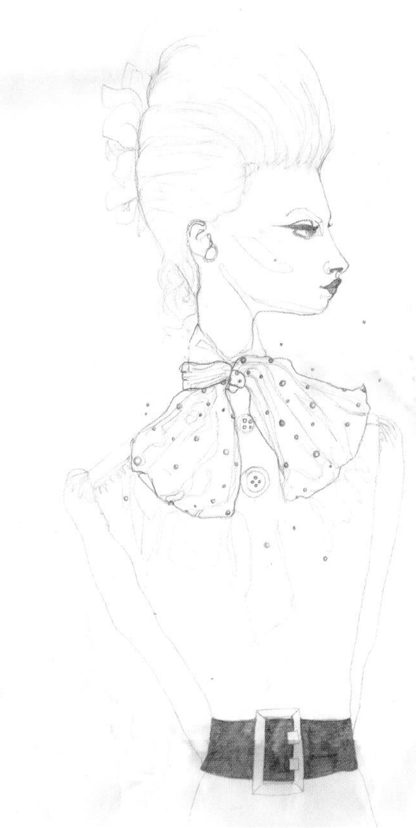

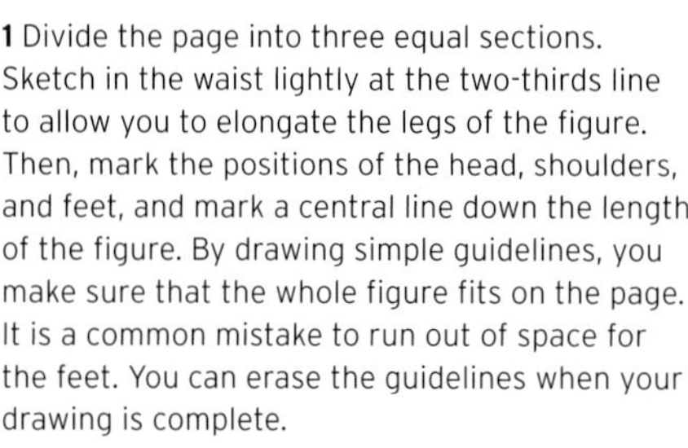

1 Divide the page into three equal sections. Sketch in the waist lightly at the two-thirds line to allow you to elongate the legs of the figure. Then, mark the positions of the head, shoulders, and feet, and mark a central line down the length of the figure. By drawing simple guidelines, you make sure that the whole figure fits on the page. It is a common mistake to run out of space for the feet. You can erase the guidelines when your drawing is complete.

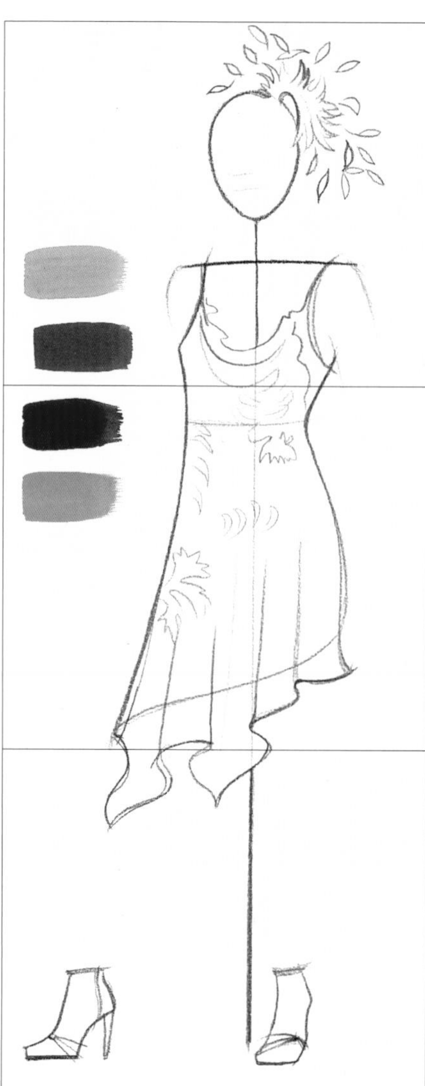

2 Sketch in outlines for the clothes and any decorative details, and decide which colors to use.

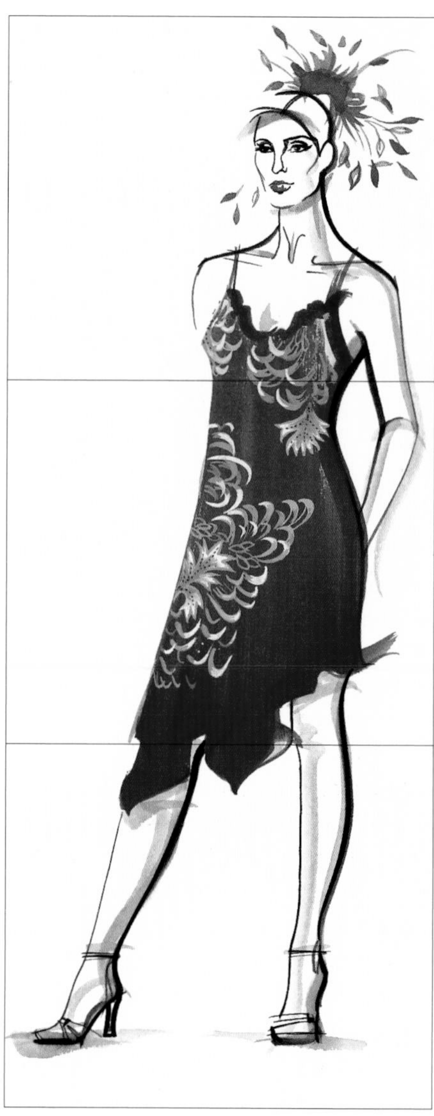

3 Complete the fashion illustration using appropriate media for the clothes and other important features.

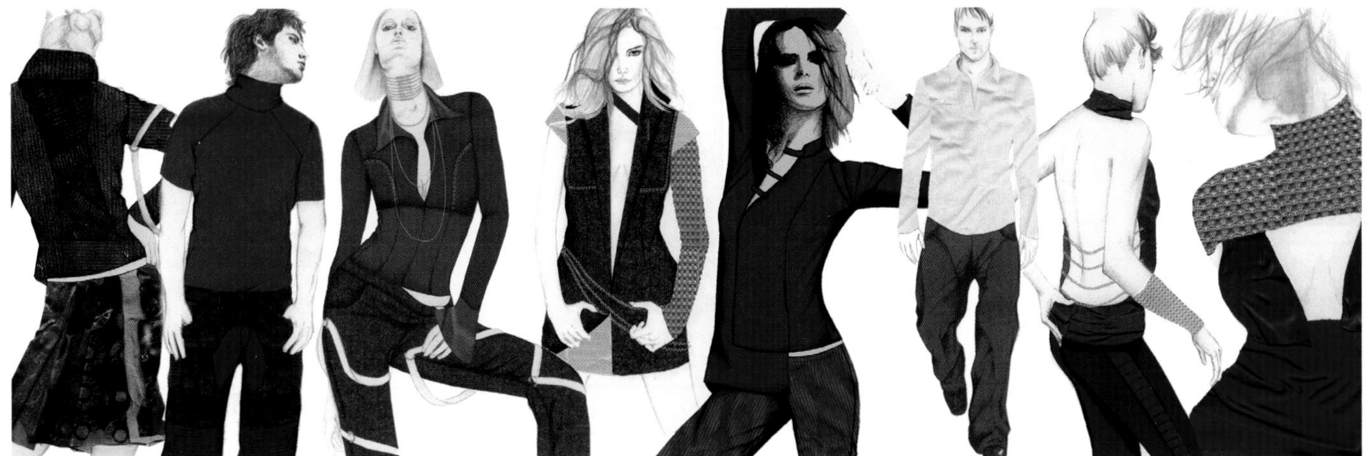

This fashion illustration combines realistic faces and figures with digital manipulation to show the garments to best advantage. The figures have been drawn in pencil and the clothing added by computer. They are arranged in a montage that contains a range of poses. Front and back views, close-ups and full figures have been placed in a lineup that illustrates the collection from all angles.

DECIDING ON A POSE

To best promote the garments in a fashion illustration, consider the stance of your figure. The way a person stands expresses much about their mood or emotions. For example, a figure with head tilted and hands behind the back may be thought coy or demure, while a figure with hands on hips and feet apart may be seen as strong or bold. Think carefully about the type of fashion you are promoting. For example, is it your own collection, or are you illustrating for a name-brand clothing company, or a designer with a particular client base? This will help you decide on the most appropriate pose for your figure.

Build a collection of poses from magazines that you can refer to for your work. Collect images from a range of magazines, including fashion, photography, and sports magazines—you may be required to draw action poses for a sportswear range. Look back, too, at your own life drawings and photographs for inspiration.

HOT SPOTS—FACE, HANDS, AND FEET

Do you leave out the face in an illustration because you are scared of ruining the image by drawing it in? Do you tuck hands into pockets so that you need not illustrate them? Perhaps you draw the figure off the page to avoid tackling the feet? It is true that one small line in the wrong place can spoil an otherwise perfect fashion illustration, but the best illustrators avoid the temptation to hide these difficult features. By practicing until you can approach these elements with conviction, your illustrations will gain in diversity and sophistication.

Indicating these hot spots authentically can be a daunting prospect for the novice, but it need not be. It is increasingly acceptable to suggest features imaginatively, rather than always to represent them correctly. On the following pages are tips on combining an accurate rendering with an imaginative approach to create an illustration that you are happy with.

Advice for drawing the head and face

- A ball, egg, or square shape can be used to construct the head
- The head divides into three masses: the cranium, the facial bones, and the jaw
- Draw in guidelines to define the position of the eyes, nose, and mouth
- The guidelines can be positioned to represent the planes of the face looking in different directions
- A male figure has thicker eyebrows, a larger mouth, and squarer jaw line than the female
- The face provides a focal point for an illustration, but must harmonize with the rest of the body rather than standing out from it
- When drawing profiles, symmetry does not need to be considered
- A badly drawn face can ruin an otherwise good illustration

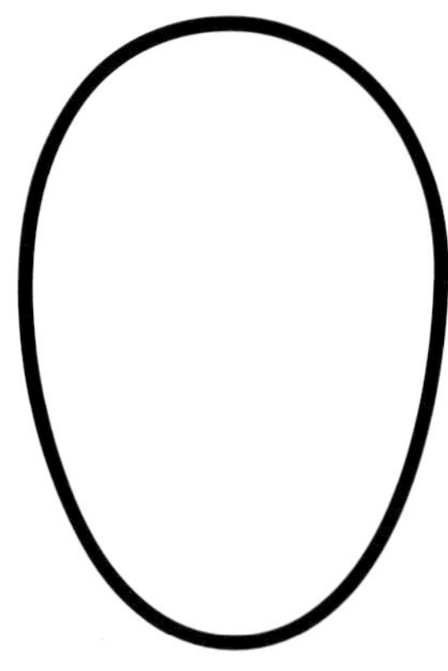

1 First, outline the head. This will probably be close to an oval or egg in shape.

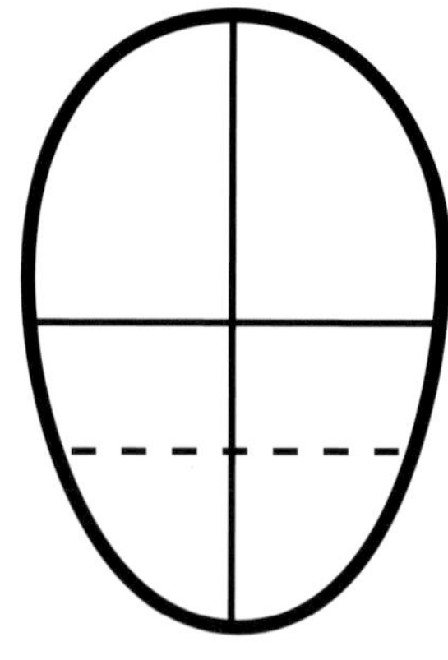

2 Divide the head in half vertically and horizontally. Then divide the bottom half in half again in a horizontal direction. These guidelines can be erased later.

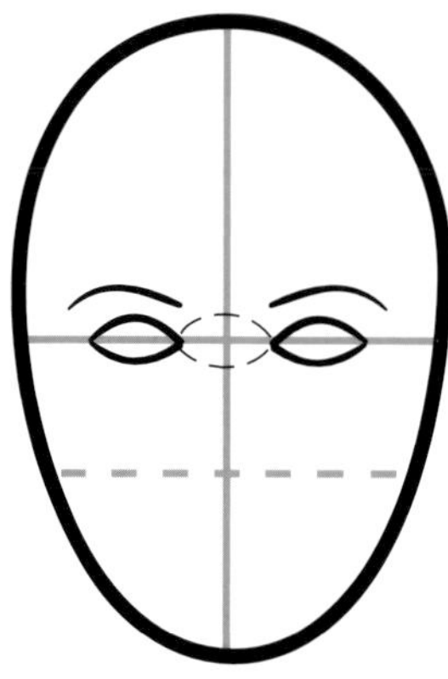

3 Map out the eyes on the top horizontal line. Leave a space of one eye width in between the eyes. Draw in the eyebrows.

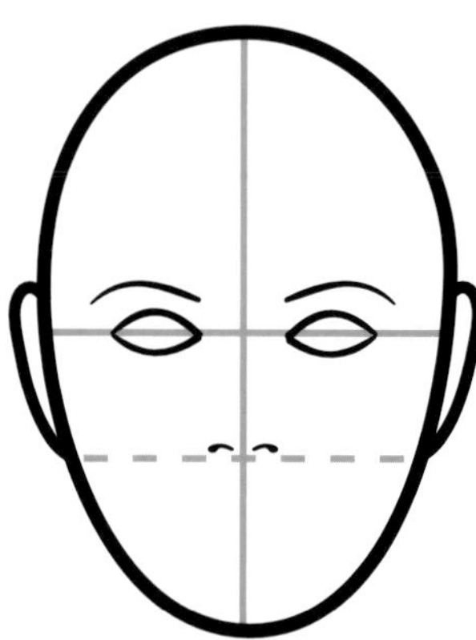

4 The base of the nose should fit on the next horizontal line. Draw in the ears; their size is usually the distance between the eyebrow and the bottom of the nose.

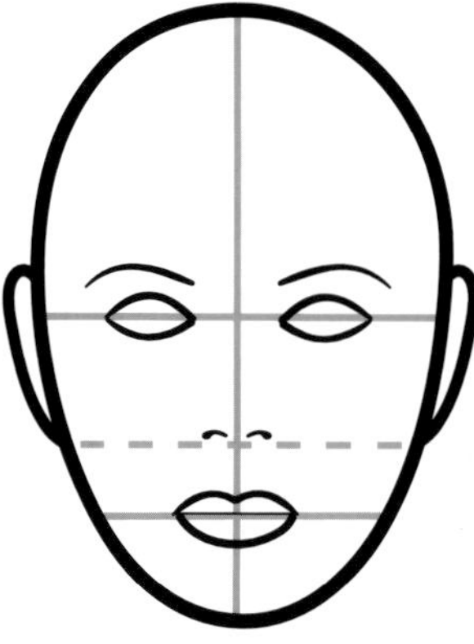

5 Divide the bottom half of the face again, and use the lowest horizontal line as a guide for the mouth. The top lip usually sits above the line and the bottom lip below.

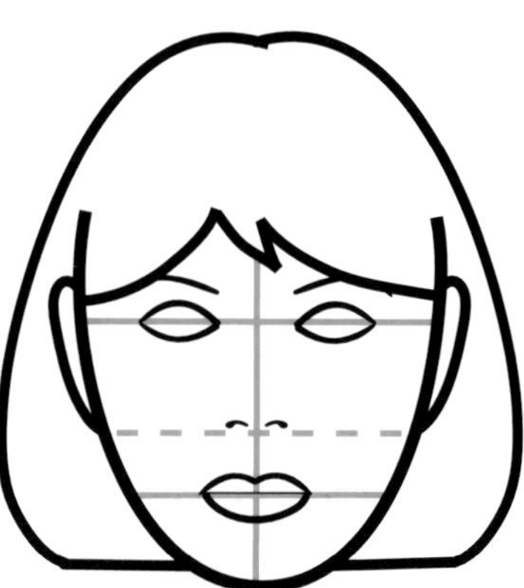

6 Finally, draw in the hair. In fashion illustration it is usually best to attempt to draw the overall shape the hair creates, rather than each individual hair.

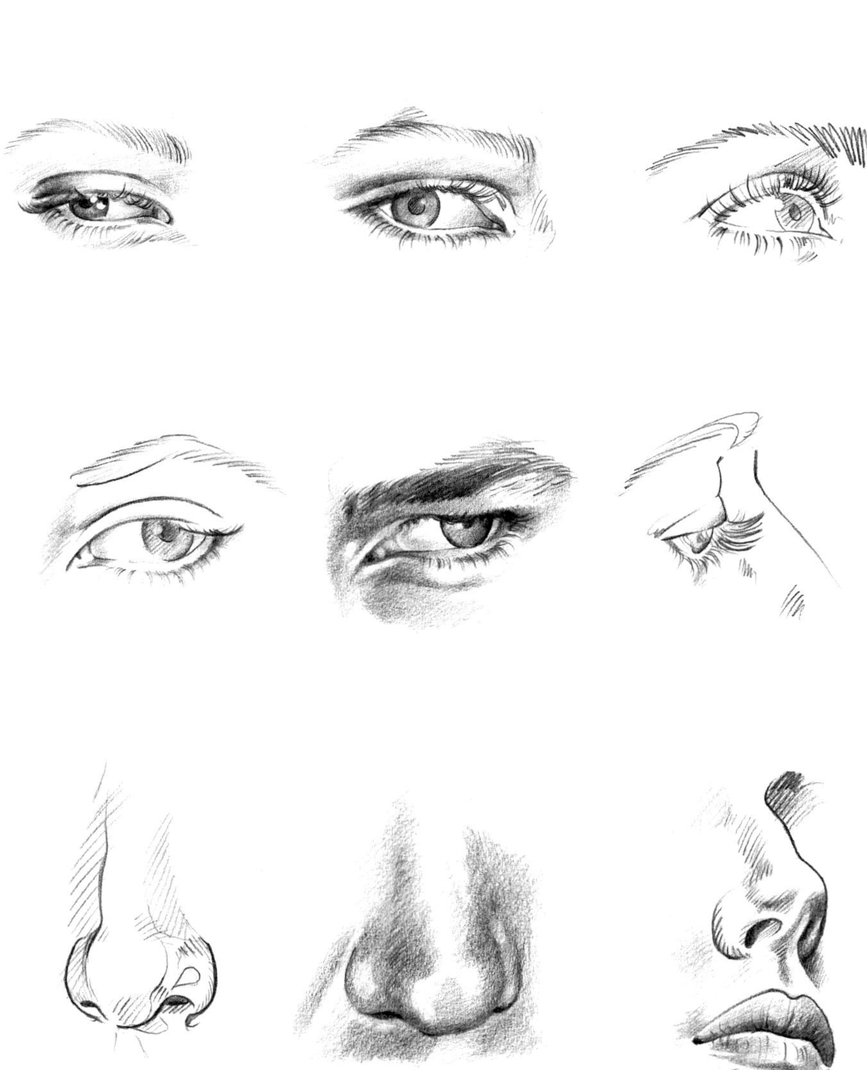

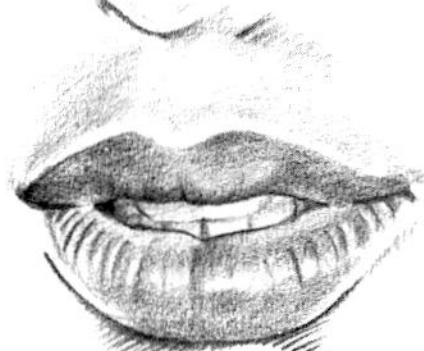

Advice for drawing features

- Suggest the features and, if in doubt, don't draw them in
- Features are usually smaller than you expect. For example, a hand can cover the face easily
- Ears and eyes are in line with each other between the eyebrows and the nose
- Eyes are at the halfway point of the head length—it is a common mistake to draw them higher up
- Most commonly in the center of the face, eyes are set one eye-width apart
- The iris of the eye is always partly covered by the upper eyelid, creating a shadow on the eyeball
- Eyelashes on both lids become progressively thicker toward the outer corners of the eyes, although the bottom lashes are shorter
- The upper lip often appears in shade as it curves in toward the teeth
- The bottom lip is usually fuller than the top one
- Lips stretch horizontally around the curving face, so do not draw them in a straight line
- Rather than draw each individual tooth, suggest teeth by drawing a shadow between them
- The nose starts at the forehead and has an indentation where the bone ends and the cartilage begins
- Made up of planes that form the sides, top, and the base, the nose has a ball at the bottom and wings on either side where the nostrils flare

Advice for drawing hair

- Lines for the hair should flow away from the scalp and continue in the directions set by the chosen style
- Try not to make the hair too uniform or like a hat
- Rather than attempting to draw every individual hair, outline large tufts
- The female hairline is usually higher than the male, emphasizing the roundness of the forehead
- A female's hair is drawn with longer, more flowing lines than the shorter strokes of a male's hair
- Hair should vary in tone, having highlights and definition, rather than be treated as a single mass
- Hair can be styled in all sorts of ways: tied back, neat, wild, trendy, bobbed, wavy, long, curly, fringed, short, spiky, cropped, straight, braided, and so on

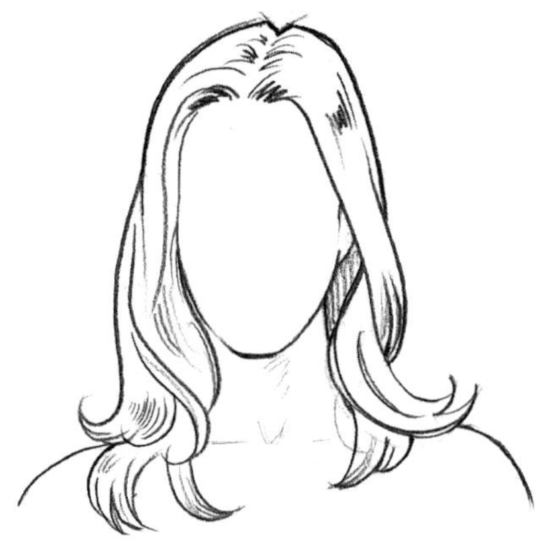

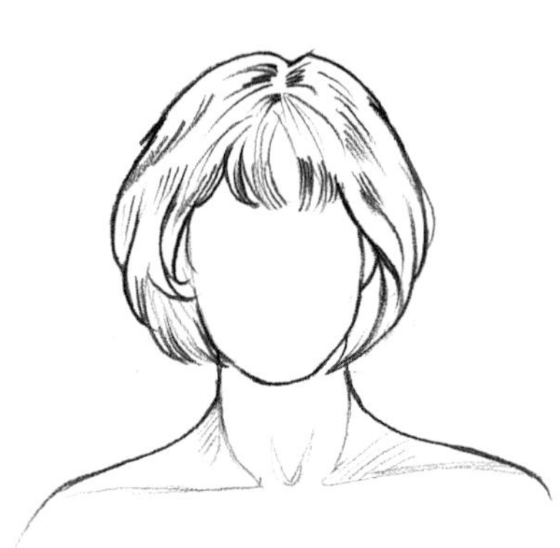

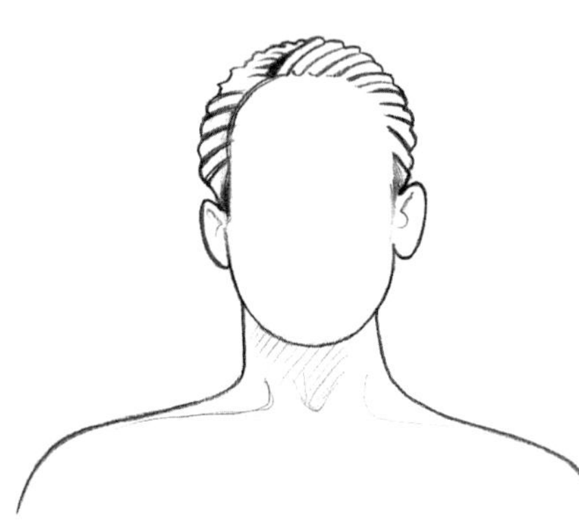

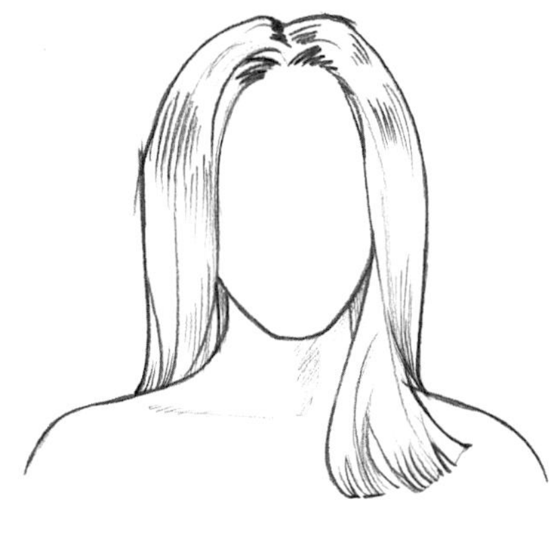

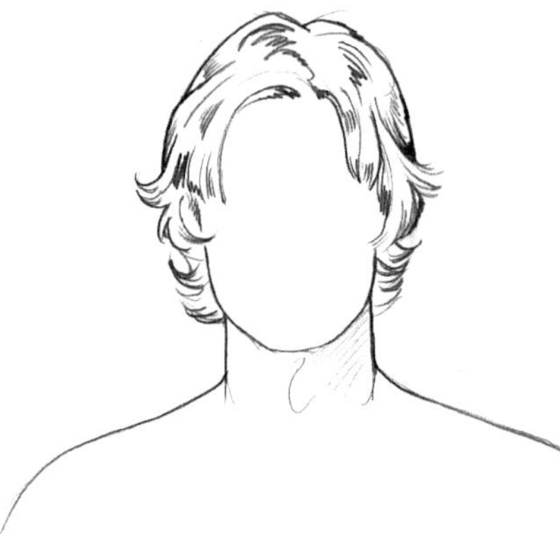

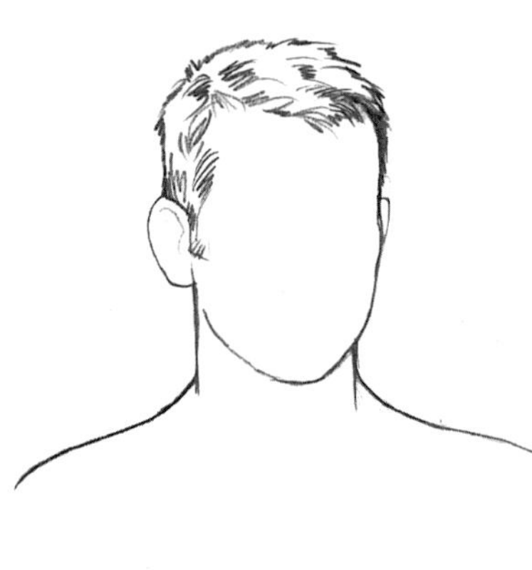

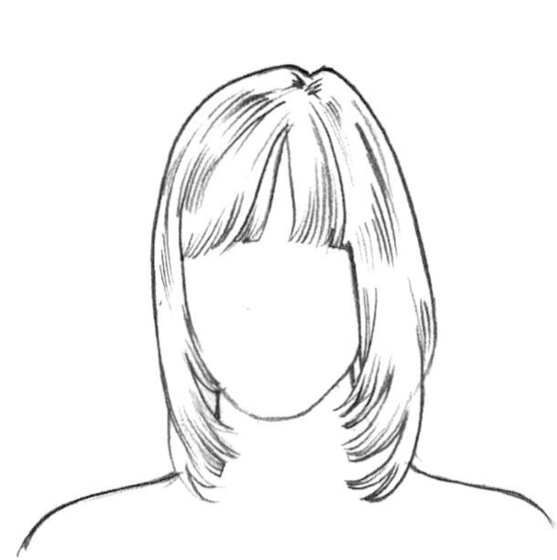

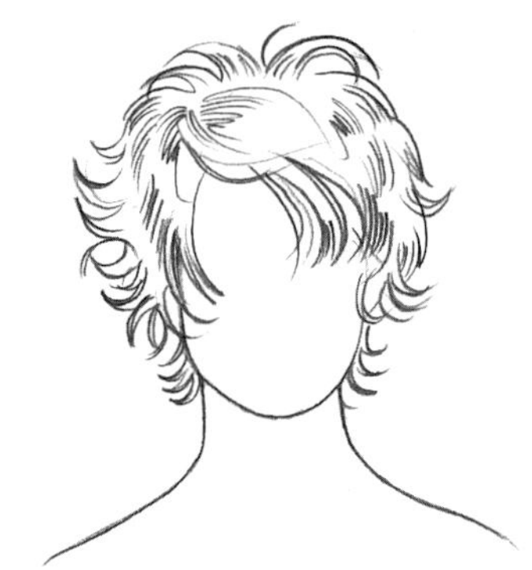

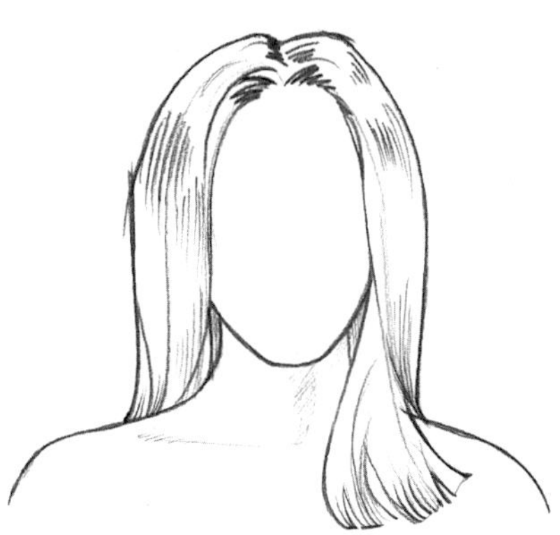

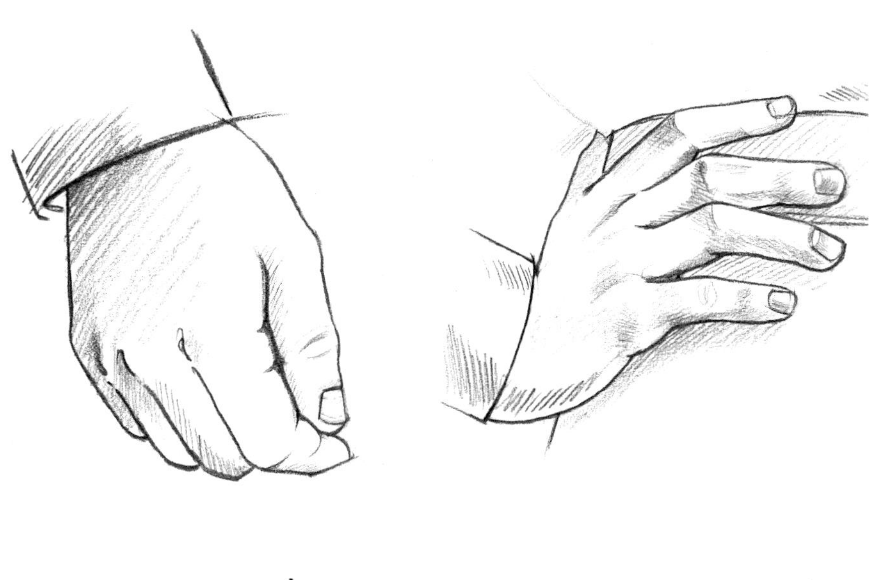

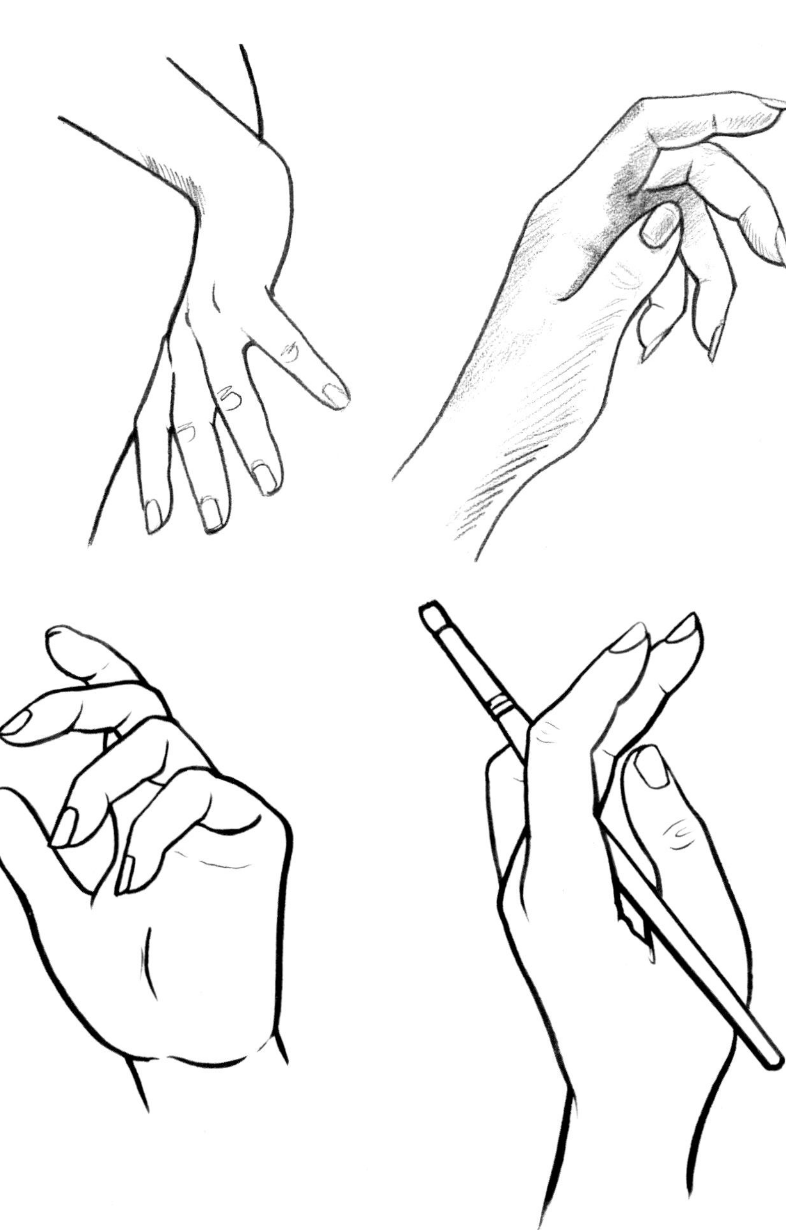

Advice for drawing hands

- The surface of the hands reveals the skeleton beneath
- It is a common mistake to draw the hands too small
- The hand should cover the face when outstretched—its length is about equal to the face from hairline to the base of the chin
- The palm is concave, the back of the hand convex
- Simplify the drawing of hands in a fashion illustration—you do not need to indicate every knuckle and fingernail

Advice for drawing feet and shoes

- The body's weight rests mainly on the heel and the outside edge of the foot
- Not including the toes, the sole of the foot is equal to the length of the head
- The big toe is approximately one quarter of the whole foot
- Shoes and boots must be in proportion to the rest of the body—a figure with tiny feet looks as though it might fall over
- When drawing footwear with a heel, ensure that the heel and sole are on the same plane or surface
- The fashion foot is usually drawn long and slender—the higher the heel, the longer the foot appears
- The higher the shoe, the greater the angle in the arch of the foot

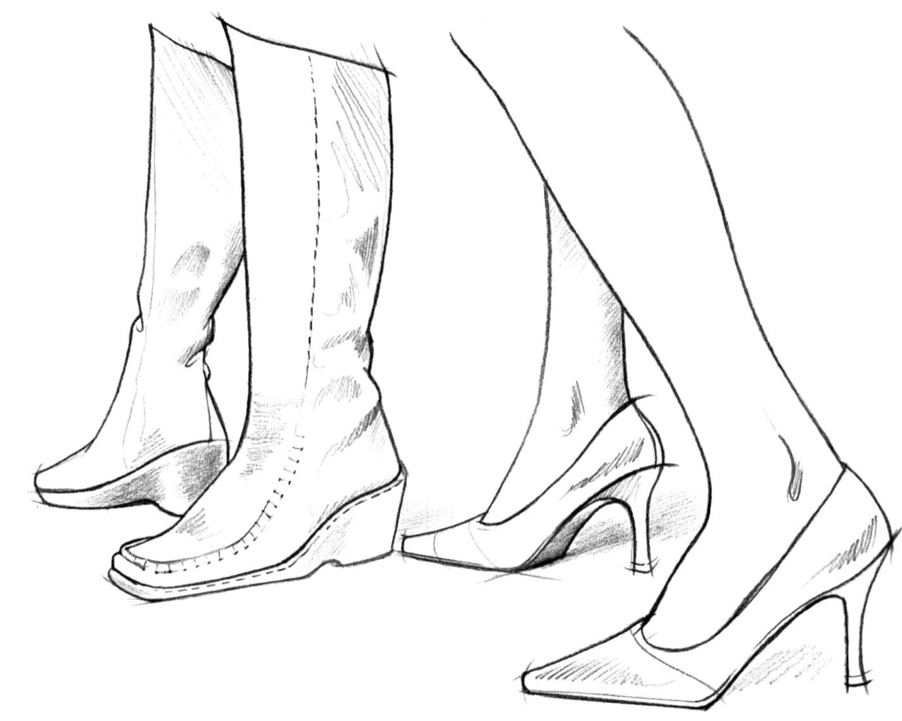

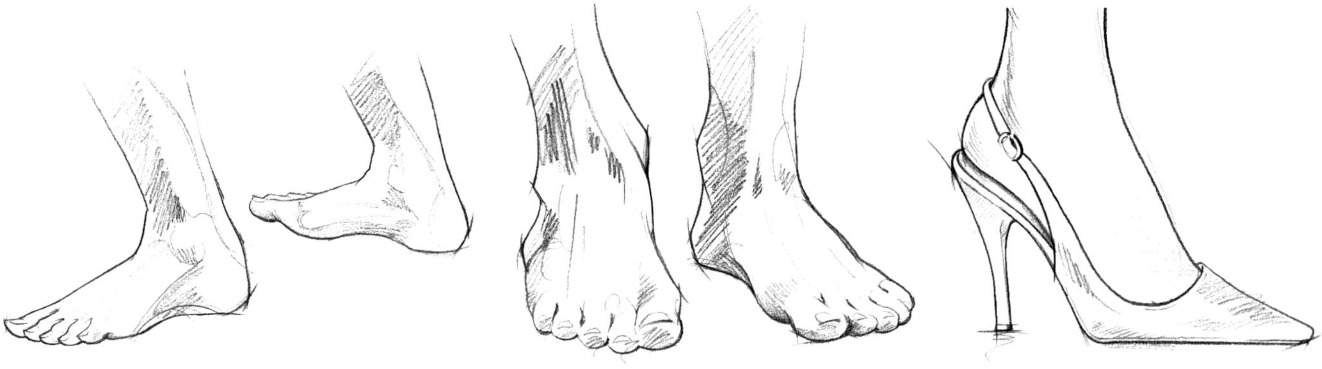

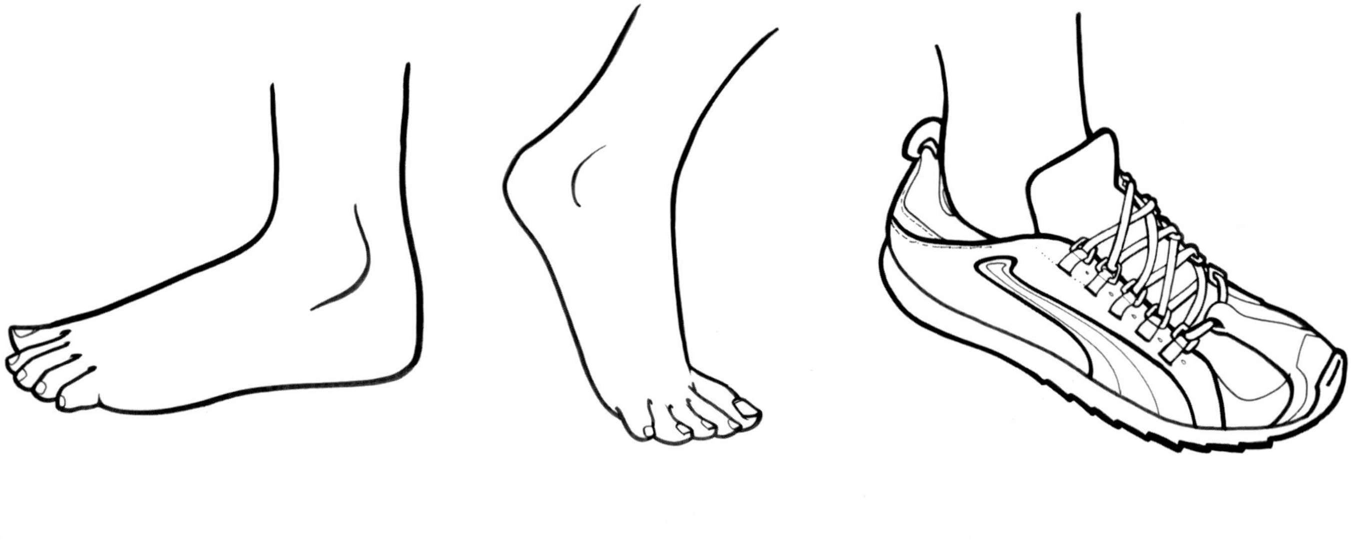

ARTISTIC TECHNIQUES

3

Once you have started finding inspiration, researching themes, using a sketchbook, and practicing figure drawing, you will be keen to experiment with different art materials. In this chapter you will find out which art materials to use to achieve particular effects, how to convey fabric realistically, and how to select a color palette. Even professional artists can find these aspects of illustration challenging. To provide a useful reference source, the chapter divides into sections that you can dip in and out of easily to find the information you need.

ART MATERIALS AND EQUIPMENT

The range of materials and equipment available to illustrators and artists today is vast and can be a little overwhelming at times. Searching for appropriate materials in an art supplier's can feel like being surrounded by irresistible confectionery in a candy store. To the creative eye, everything looks tempting, and the correct choice of medium is difficult to make.

Finding a medium that suits your own particular method of working and your style is the best way to proceed. You should feel comfortable enough with it to produce work confidently. Consider your personality when selecting your artistic tools. If you are a careful, meticulous perfectionist you may be most at ease with precise art materials such as a pencil or pen. If you have a more energetic, fast-and-furious approach to illustration, you may enjoy the freedom of oil pastels, charcoal, or paints. Experimenting frequently with new materials will encourage you to be more innovative in your work. Brand-new pots of ink, sharp, colorful pencils, and acrylic tubes just waiting to be squeezed may look inviting but, to a beginner, they also hold an element of anxiety. The next section covers how to use art materials and equipment in fashion illustration, so that you can make your selection with confidence.

The quirky figures in this illustration were created using mixed media, combining hand drawing with photocopied paper cutouts in a collage.

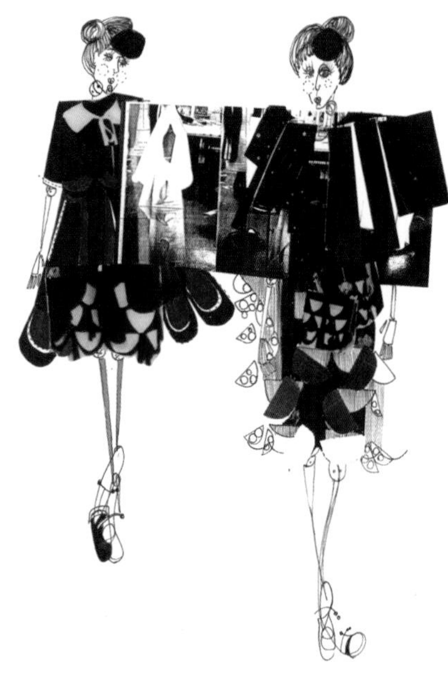

PAPER

Paper is the first element to consider when beginning a fashion illustration. There are many types to choose from, available in various colors and thicknesses. All can be used as a surface on which to work or as a material from which to create a collage.

Cartridge paper is one of the most basic, commonly used papers, and is suitable for drawing and dry artwork. It is not generally recommended for painting or heavily rendered work, as it is made of wood pulp, so that moisture causes it to buckle. It can be made suitable for painting by soaking it with a wet sponge and stretching it over a drawing board. Secure the edges with brown gum tape, then allow the paper to dry thoroughly before beginning your painting.

Layout paper is a fine, semiopaque paper that allows you to see an image faintly beneath it. Suitable for roughs, marker drawings, and color tests, it is often bleed-resistant so that colors do not run. The translucency of layout paper enables you to trace over it to produce one rough from another. It is also suitable for mounting onto background papers and cards for fashion-presentation purposes.

Unlike smooth cartridge paper, *pastel paper* has a grain running through it. Soft art materials such as pastels and charcoal pick up the grain, and the artist can exploit this effect in the illustration. This paper is often tinted in tonal ranges upon which black-charcoal illustrations look particularly effective, the background color adding increased intensity.

Tracing paper and *acetate* are clear sheets that are also excellent for use on presentation boards. You can photocopy images onto them, then overlay the images—the transparency of the sheets means that the image beneath is not

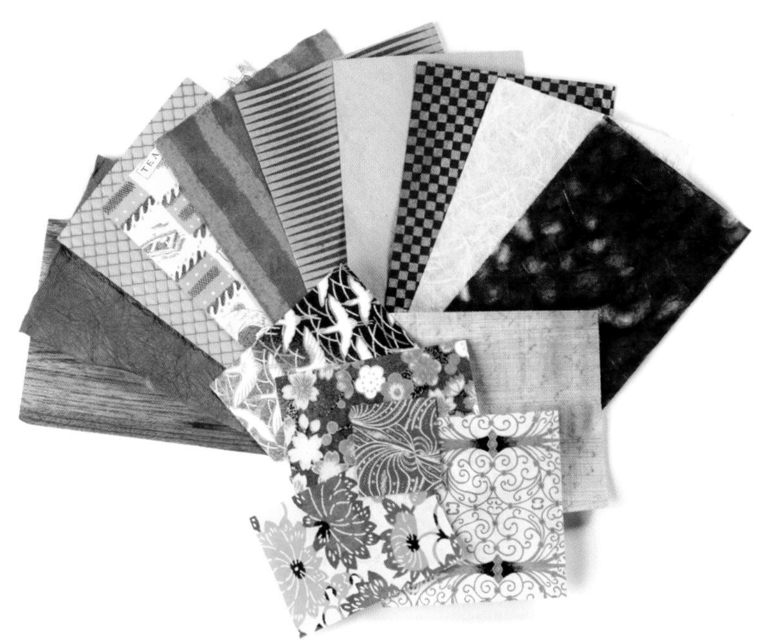

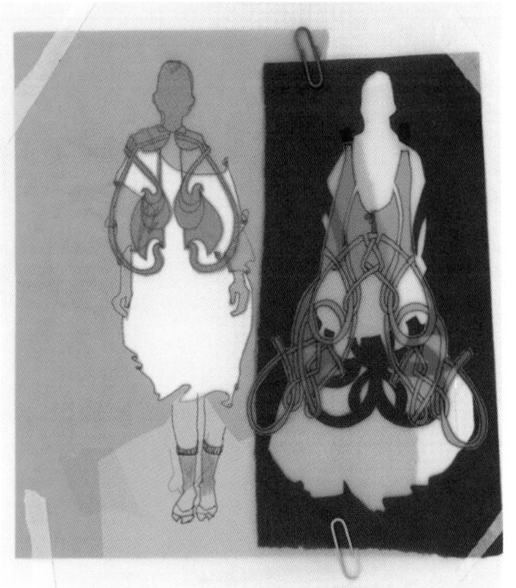

Left
A selection of papers. Some are printed, while others have unusual textures.

Right
Colored, transparent papers have been cut intricately and overlaid to create the outfits in this illustration. Using such a technique means that your designs change every time you overlay the cutout in a different position.

obscured completely. Drawing and painting directly on acetate creates a unique effect, with light shining through the image.

Watercolor papers are available in many weights and textures. Good-quality watercolor paper is a must, as cheap, thin paper makes colors look flat and lifeless. With its ability to absorb liquid, watercolor paper can be used with many wet media, such as ink, paints, or water-soluble crayons.

Tissue paper, card stock, colored backing papers, wrapping paper, wallpaper, candy wrappers, and other packaging can all be used in fashion illustrations. Use your imagination as to how to incorporate them into your work.

PENCILS

Every artist—even painters, sculptors, and printmakers—benefit from being skilled at drawing with a pencil. The pencil is a convenient and expressive means of evolving a composition and of recording visual information quickly for translation into another medium later on. Most works of art begin with a pencil drawing.

Lead pencils are available either in the form of traditional wood-cased pencils or in a mechanical pop-up style. The advantage of a mechanical pencil is that it is always sharp. You can also select a variety of lead thicknesses for this type of pencil, ranging from 0.3 to 0.9. Pencil leads are graphite, and they are made in several grades ranging from hard (H) to soft (B—the "B" stands for black). The hardest make fine, pale-gray lines, and the softest produce thicker, black lines. The grades are usually designated as follows: 9H, 8H, 7H, 6H, 5H, 4H, 3H, 2H, H, HB, F, B, 2B, 3B, 4B, 5B, 6B, 7B, 8B, 9B. HB and F (which stands for fine point) are midway between hard and soft.

Soft pencils are ideal for rapid sketches and expressive line-and-tone drawings. They work especially well on textured paper, but take care when using them, because they smudge easily. Hard pencils best suit artists with a confident, clean, and accurate style of drawing. Try experimenting with several grades of pencil to create a rich interaction of line and tonal contrasts in your fashion illustrations. Many illustrators add texture and detail to finished paintings, especially watercolors, using pencil. *Graphite sticks* are made of compressed and bonded graphite. They glide across the page to produce the boldest and most expressive drawings. You can change the marks they make by using the point, side, or flattened edge of the stick.

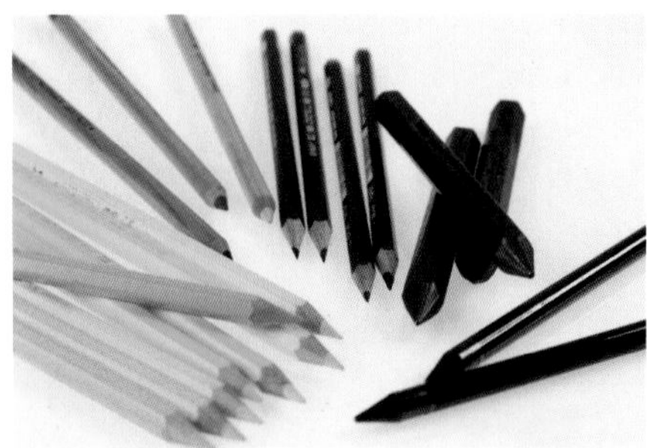

Left
A selection of pencils, ranging from chunky graphites to colored pencils.

Right
To create the effect of smudged makeup, a combination of lead pencil drawing with soft-pastel coloring is ideal.

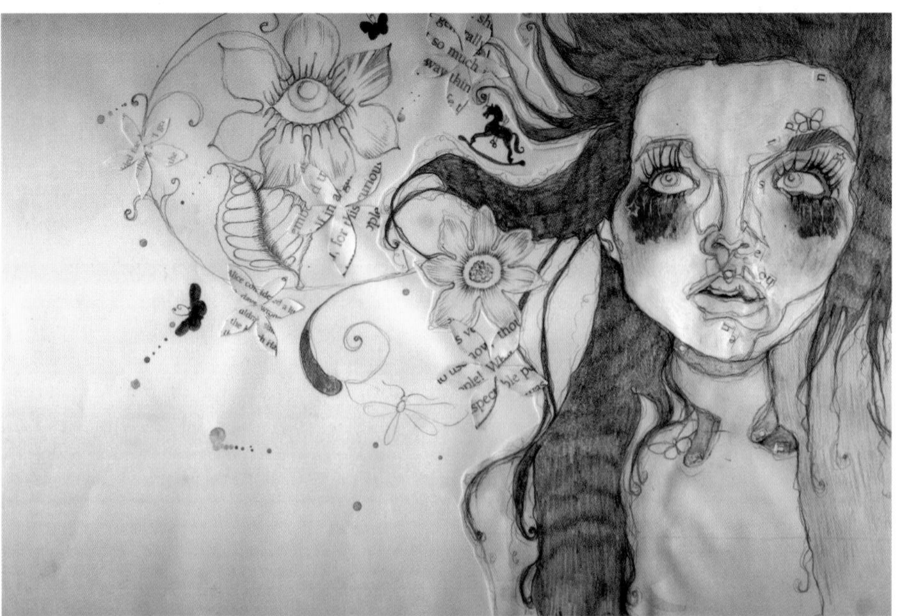

The water-soluble versions produce beautiful, silvery gray washes. Graphite sticks are especially popular for life drawing and clothed-figure drawing because they allow a fluid technique.

Colored pencils are made from a mixture of pigment, clay, and filler bound together and soaked in wax before being encased in wood. Colored pencils are not just a safe drawing medium for children. The fashion illustrator can use them to make a varied range of marks, while controlling the finished effect. You can use them like a graphite pencil to shade areas, only in color. You can also blend shades together carefully with a paper stump (a tightly rolled, tipped paper), eraser, or your fingers. As with all pencil drawing, tonal areas can be built up with hatching (short parallel lines drawn closely together) or crosshatching (a fine mesh of crisscrossing lines that builds depth of shade). Colored pencils are particularly useful in the early stages of developing your abilities, because they allow you to build confidence with a controllable medium.

WATER-SOLUBLE ART MATERIALS

Water-soluble pencils offer the advantages of colored pencils, but they have a water-soluble ingredient in the lead. This means that you can apply the color dry but create a subtle watercolor effect by loosening the pigment with brushstrokes of water. A controllable medium, water-soluble pencils are useful for bridging the gap between drawing and painting, when developing illustration skills. *Water-soluble crayons* work in the same way as the pencils, but are softer and more malleable. They create bolder marks and denser hatching, making them more of a painter's tool.

The advantage of both water-soluble pencils and crayons is that they are easy to carry with you, allowing you to sketch figures quickly on the street or catwalk. You can develop a picture further with paint when you return to your home or studio, if you so wish.

WAX CRAYONS

Experimenting with the wax-resist technique might seem like revisiting your childhood, but it produces some interesting effects. Drawing with a wax crayon, then overpainting with watercolor is an effective means of creating a textured finish on clothing in a fashion illustration. The wash of color is repelled by the wax but soaks into the unwaxed paper to leave a unique pattern. Try also the time-honored technique of coloring a sheet of paper with wax crayons, shading over the top with a black crayon, then scratching out your figure, which will appear in a rainbow of colors.

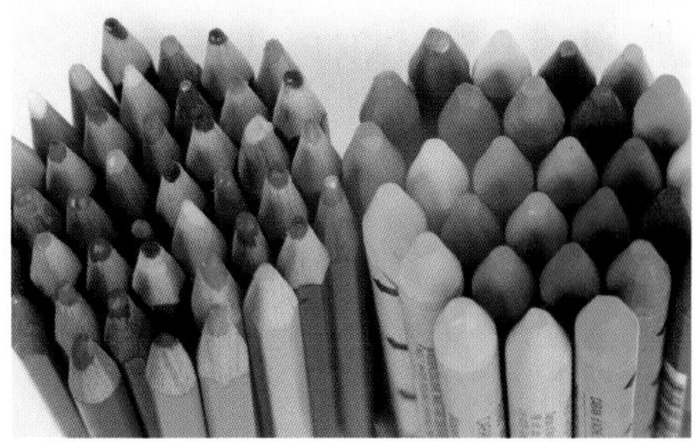

Water-soluble colored pencils and a mixture of wax crayons.

CHARCOAL

Made from twigs charred at high temperatures in airtight kilns, charcoal usually comes in the form of *sticks* of various thicknesses about four to six inches long. It is fragile, tends to snap easily, and can be messy to work with. However, this soft medium is ideally suited to blending and smudging, and creating strong dramatic lines.

Charcoal sticks are most commonly used for life drawing, but could just as easily lend themselves to drawing monotone fashion illustrations. A charcoal drawing is full of atmosphere and life, and therefore ideal for fashion illustration. Drawing with charcoal encourages a freedom of creative expression that you do not get with a pencil. It is excellent for adding shadows, depth, movement, and texture to your fashion illustration, too.

There are also *charcoal pencils* made from compressed charcoal encased in wood, which are slightly easier to handle, and cleaner to work with, than sticks. The pencils have a harder texture, and the tips can be sharpened for more precise line work.

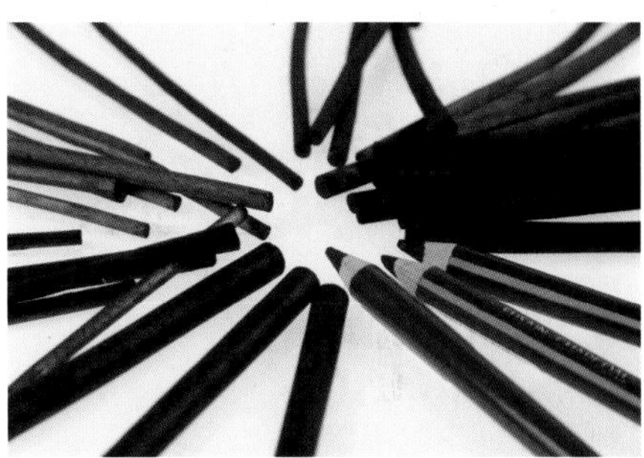

Charcoal sticks are available in a variety of thicknesses. It is also possible to buy charcoal in pencil form.

PASTELS

Considered both a drawing and a painting medium, pastels are made from finely ground pigments mixed with chalk and bound together with gum to form a hard stick. They are available in a wide range of colors because, although they can be blended, pastels cannot be mixed to make new colors. An opaque medium, pastels work best on colored backgrounds that unify the artwork, or on textured surfaces such as a heavy watercolor paper.

Soft pastels are creamy and popular for their vibrant colors. *Hard pastels* are easier to handle as their consistency makes them less fragile. *Pastel pencils* provide a greater degree of control as they do not break and crumble as easily as the crayons. They are good for outlining and crisp, detailed work, and can be used in combination with other types of media. For an illustrator, the dusty, delicate surface of the picture is the disadvantage of using pastels. When you complete the illustration, remove excess dust with a tissue, and correct the edges of your work with an eraser. Apply fixative cautiously—if your application is too heavy, it will change the colors of the illustration.

Oil pastels are waxy, creating a waterproof resist when applied to paper. Rich in color, they can be used to create wonderfully evocative illustrations. Applied thickly, they leave a pastelike residue on the surface that adds a unique texture to a fashion illustration. Scratching through a layer of oil pastel is an effective means of creating patterns to represent fabrics.

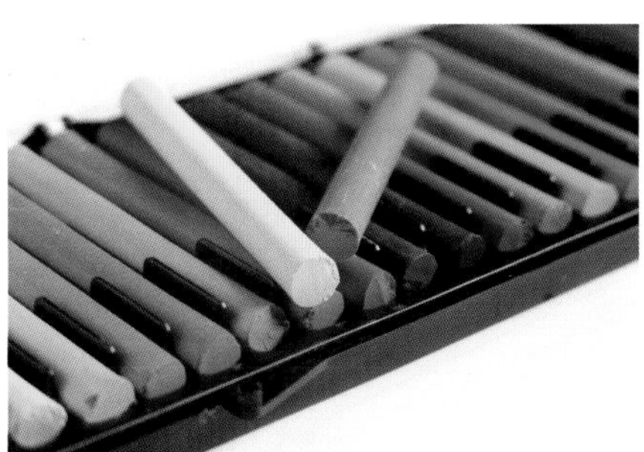

A selection of pastels.

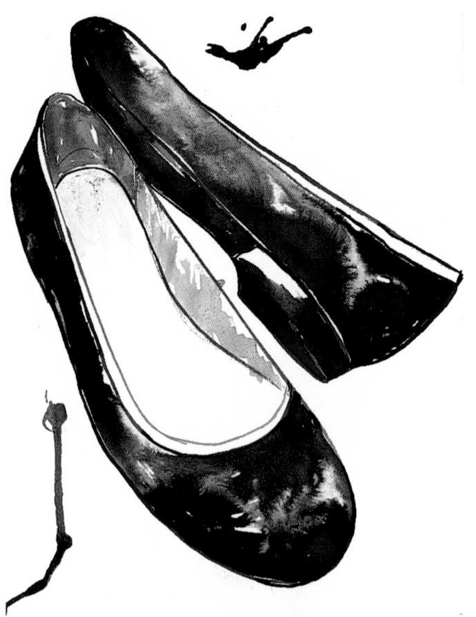

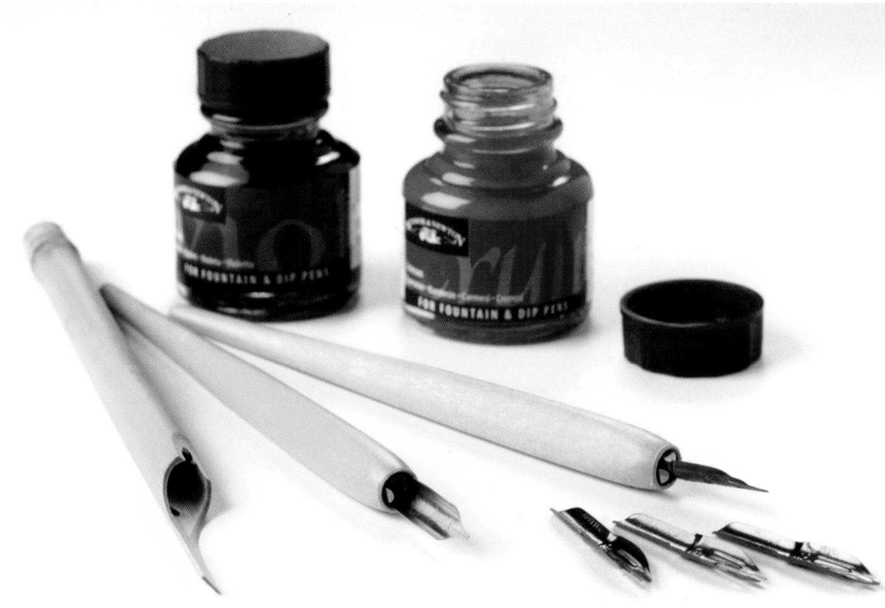

Left
Black India ink has been used here on watercolor paper, and the ink diluted with water to provide different monochromatic shades. Using ink, you can vary your drawing tool for a range of interesting effects.

Right
Ink can be applied in a variety of ways. We see here a selection of dip pens with different nib sizes and a bamboo stick. Inks are available in a wide range of colors and can be waterproof.

INK

When drawing with ink, the first aspect to consider is whether or not it is *waterproof*. Black waterproof India ink is the first choice of most illustrators as washes can be applied over a shiny line drawing. A monochrome illustration is then created using a dip pen, brush, or bamboo stick. By varying your drawing tool, you can achieve a range of wonderful effects.

Non-waterproof ink sinks into the paper and dries with a matt finish. Diluting it produces a wide range of lighter tones. You can enjoy experimenting with non-waterproof inks by dropping them onto paper soaked in water. The ink disperses in the water, creating beautiful patterns and textures on the paper surface. Painted lines will be fuzzy, rather than sharp, as the ink spreads.

Inks are available in a wide range of colors, not just black, so the more you experiment, the more diverse the effects you can create for your illustrations.

PAINT

Many illustrators favor a particular paint, but it is sometimes difficult to decide which type will most suit the style of your work. Qualities of the different paints available are described below to help you make a selection.

Watercolor is often the most popular choice as it is so convenient. You only need a paint box, brush, paper, and water to get started, while being so portable makes it ideal for location work. Watercolor paint is sold in tubes or pans. Tubes are available in many sizes and are recommended because you can mix stronger colors in larger quantities. Pans are small slabs of solid paint that fit into easy-to-carry boxes, the box lid usually acting as a palette for mixing colors. However, applying watercolor to your illustrations is not as easy as it looks. Using the correct watercolor paper and quality brushes is important, but you must also know when an illustration is finished. Overworking can lead to mistakes that are difficult to correct.

Watercolor is the perfect medium for adding subtle color to pencil fashion illustrations. It is also excellent for applying washes to pen-and-ink drawings and for adding colored details to sketches. You can exploit its natural properties by allowing a

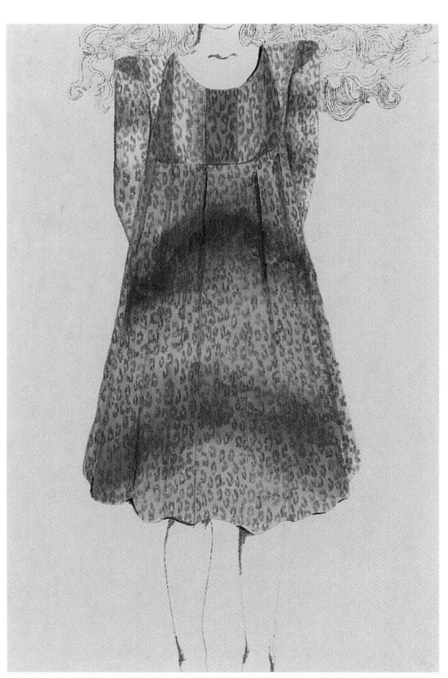

thin wash to run and drip over your fashion figure, adding a sense of movement to the illustration.

Acrylics are incredibly versatile as they can be applied straight from the tube or diluted, using a brush or knife—the latter creating a dense texture. Producing strong colors, acrylics dry with a tough, plastic waterproof skin. Try painting fashion figures onto fabric in acrylics. Once dry, use a sewing machine to add decorative stitching.

Oils are historically the professional painter's medium. The buttery consistency of the paint arises from a high concentration of pigment mixed with the finest-quality oil. Although rarely used in fashion illustration today, oil paint is not as difficult to handle as you may think. You can buy water-mixable oil paint that can be thinned with water rather than turpentine. Alternatively, oil sticks give you the same control as pastels and charcoal but also the rich, vibrant colors of oil paint. The advantage of oil paint is that you can model it on the canvas, molding the textures you want in your fashion illustration, and even creating a three-dimensional effect by applying the paint with a knife.

Gouache is a type of watercolor that has been mixed with white to make it opaque. It is excellent for laying flat, solid color as it dries without streaks, and is popular for illustration because its strong, matt colors are suited to reproduction. To use the paint creatively, apply the colors boldly in undiluted form. Imagine your illustrations as poster art, making them powerful and eye-catching.

Spray paint gives unexpected results, and is therefore the medium to have fun with. You can buy fairly cheap cans of spray paint for artistic use in a wide range of colors. It is excellent for stenciling and adding finishing touches to your fashion illustrations.

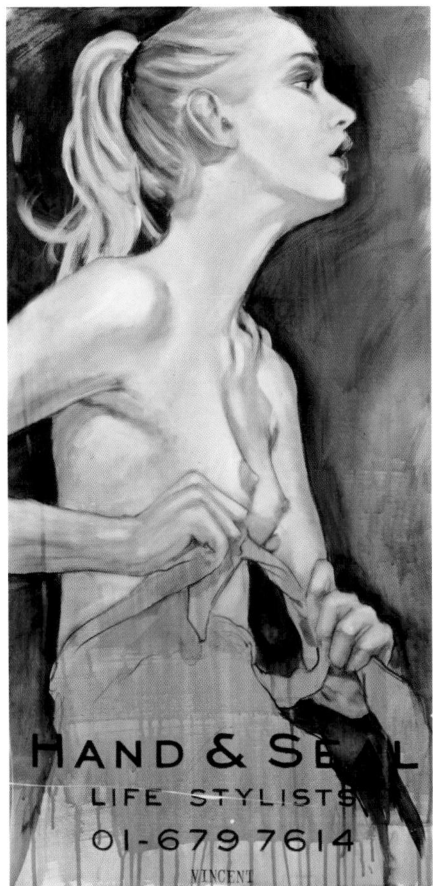

Above
Traditional painting skills are combined with accurate observation to render this figure in acrylics on canvas.

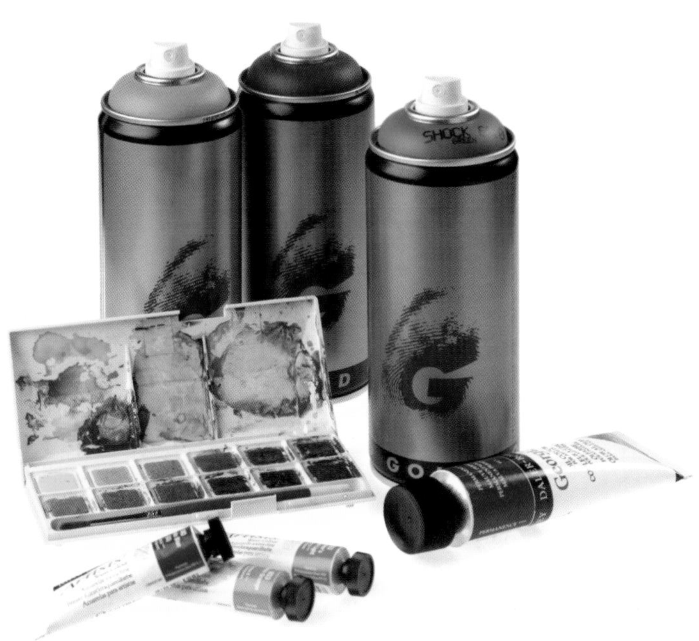

Left
Paints are available in many forms.
Here are tubes of oil and gouache, a palette of watercolors, and cans of spray paint.

Opposite, below
Watercolor and fineliner are used on a colored paper to create this vivid, printed dress. The bright translucency of watercolor paint is perfect for conveying the patterned fabric, with detail added using the fineliner. The face is unimportant in this fashion illustration and so has been left out to place emphasis on the dress.

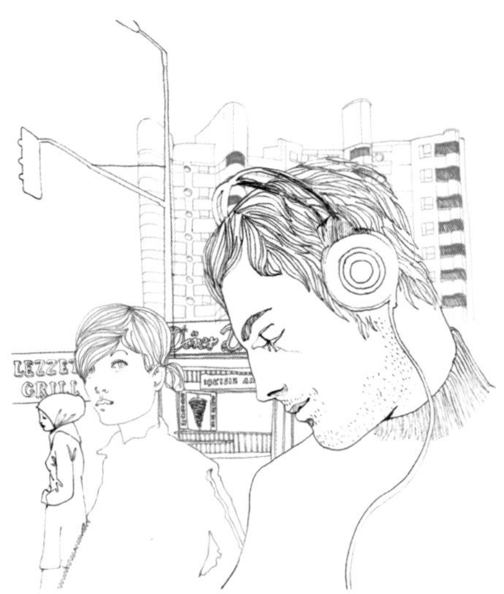

PENS

There are all sorts of *markers,* including a variety of felt- and fiber-tip pens. High-quality markers can be costly but give good, non-blotchy results. They are usually supplied in packs of toning colors or sold singly. The best types have a variety of nibs—wide, medium, and fine. Wider nibs are useful for blocking in areas of color evenly. Skin-tone markers are invaluable for fashion illustration, giving a realistic flesh color. However, while using markers is a quick, convenient way of adding color, it takes a confident illustrator to apply them with conviction.

Ballpoints, although not always considered an art material, are worth experimenting with. Working in a single color with a line quality that does not alter can produce interesting results. A ballpoint is often at hand, and doodling in a relaxed atmosphere provides a perfect creative environment.

Fineliner pens are wonderful for emphasizing fine details, such as intricate embroidery or knitted textures, in fashion illustrations. A nonpermanent type can also be watered down to create a flowing line.

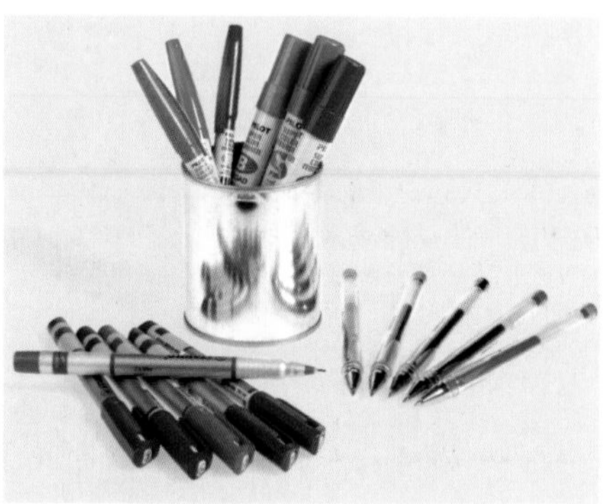

EMBROIDERY THREADS

Hand embroidery threads offer a vast choice of color. Stranded cotton is the most popular type, and the strands can be separated to give you the thickness you want. Silk, wool, linen, synthetic, and metallic threads are also available, giving you a variety of options ranging from smooth, shiny stitches to textural, matt ones.

Machine embroidery threads are presented on spools and also vary in color, thickness, and finish. Usually made of rayon or cotton, they come in a wide range of single colors or variegated shades in matt, shiny, and metallic.

To embroider, use the needle as a drawing tool on the fabric. There is a great variety of different embroidery stitches you can use to create patterns on the fabric, demonstrating creative flair in your fashion illustration.

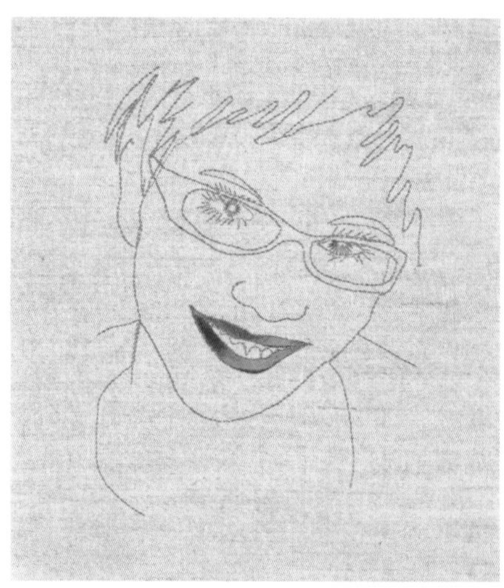

EQUIPMENT

The *sewing machine* is an important piece of equipment for many fashion illustrators. If possible, yours should offer a number of embroidery stitches. Many now have computer-software programs that link the sewing machine to your computer, allowing you to stitch a design created on screen.

To cut out mount boards and papers, the *steel ruler* is useful as both a measuring and a cutting tool. It is preferable to a wooden or plastic ruler, as it is more difficult to slice into steel and create unwanted irregularities along the cut edge. A *cutting mat* provides a safe, steady surface for cutting with a sharp *scalpel* or *knife*. The most useful blades are those with an angled top over a straight cutting edge.

A *light box* is a handy tool for the illustrator. It is simply a screen lit from below that allows you to see through paper placed over photographs and magazine cuttings, so that you can trace figures or other elements. As light boxes are fairly expensive, you might prefer to use a window for the same purpose. However, if you can afford a light box, you will own it forever. They are also useful for looking at details in photographs or transparencies.

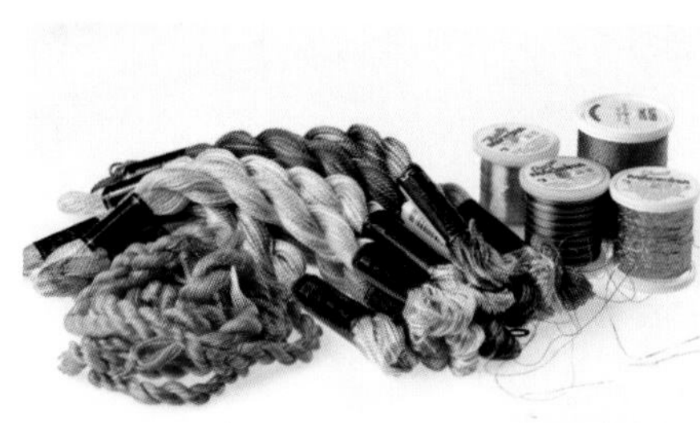

Spray adhesive is an essential for the illustrator. It should be applied evenly to one surface in a well-ventilated room. Be careful to protect areas you want to remain free from glue, as spray adhesive can be messy. It does, however, provide the most professional results when producing presentation boards, collages, and illustrations.

Masking tape is essential for fixing paper to a drawing board, and it peels easily off the board and your artwork when you have finished.

A *photocopier* can save you time by enlarging and reducing images or by providing you with repeated copies for collage. You can experiment with color in your illustrations by altering the tones on the copier to, say, make a red garment green. You can also set the copier to "reverse" so that it copies all dark lines and areas light and vice versa, allowing you to create, for example, a white line drawing on a black background. Some copiers are more sophisticated than others, but be creative with what is available to you, and experiment with the results.

A *computer* is becoming increasingly popular for fashion illustration. Many creative software programs are on the market to help you draw, manipulate images, and alter photographs, the best-known being Adobe Photoshop and Adobe Illustrator. There are tutorials in Chapter Six that will inspire you to create fashion illustrations using these programs.

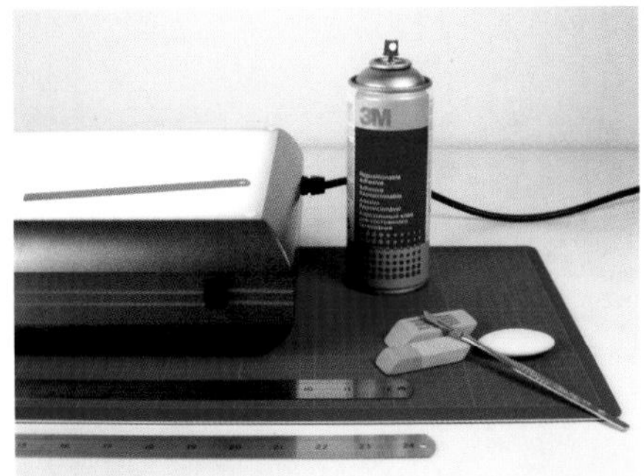

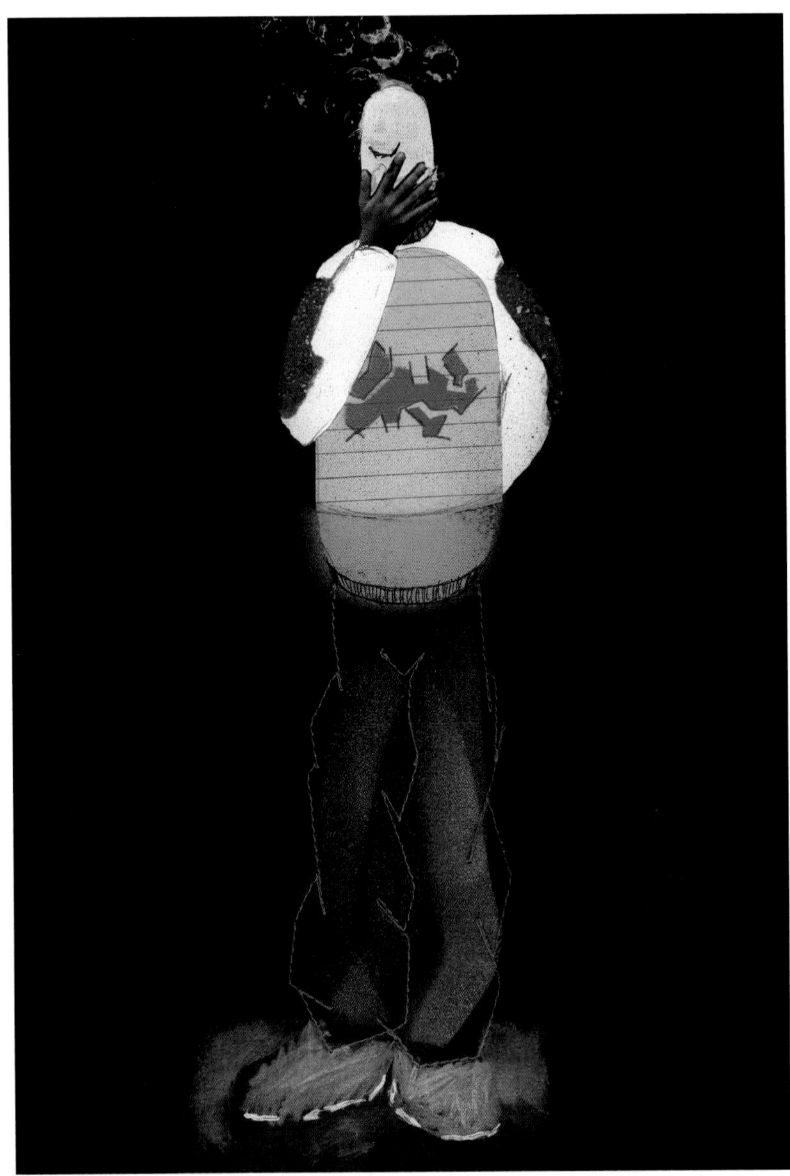

Opposite, from top
This line drawing has been completed in black and pink ballpoint pens. Although not always seen as an art material, ballpoint pens are easily available and allow you to sketch freely.

A selection of pens, ranging from markers and ballpoints to fineliners.

A computerized sewing machine with different embroidery options is a useful tool for the illustrator. This illustration was first drawn and scanned. The scanned image was then embroidered in red thread onto a linen fabric, using a sewing machine.

Embroidery threads are bought on a spool for use on a sewing machine or as individual skeins for hand embroidery.

Above
A light box, cutting equipment, and adhesive—valuable tools for any artist.

Left
Using a black background gives dramatic effect to this mixed-media illustration. Photocopied images and colored-pencil drawing are combined with some digital manipulation.

COLOR

In our daily lives we are surrounded by color and make choices about it regularly in the way we dress, decorate our homes, and even when we buy a car. Having an eye for which colors work well together is essential for the fashion designer or illustrator, whether you are choosing a scheme for a portfolio project, planning a color-themed collection, or selecting colors for a dramatic fashion illustration.

THE COLOR WHEEL

Understanding the basic principles of color theory and knowing how to apply colors will help boost your confidence as a fashion illustrator. The simplest way to learn about the theory is to study the color wheel. When the sun shines on a rainy day, a rainbow often forms. The basic colors in a rainbow are red, orange, yellow, green, blue, indigo, and violet. The color wheel is a simplified version of this spectrum (excluding indigo) and arranges six colors into a circle. The wheel is then made up of colors that fit into the following categories: primary, secondary, tertiary, warm, cool, and complementary.

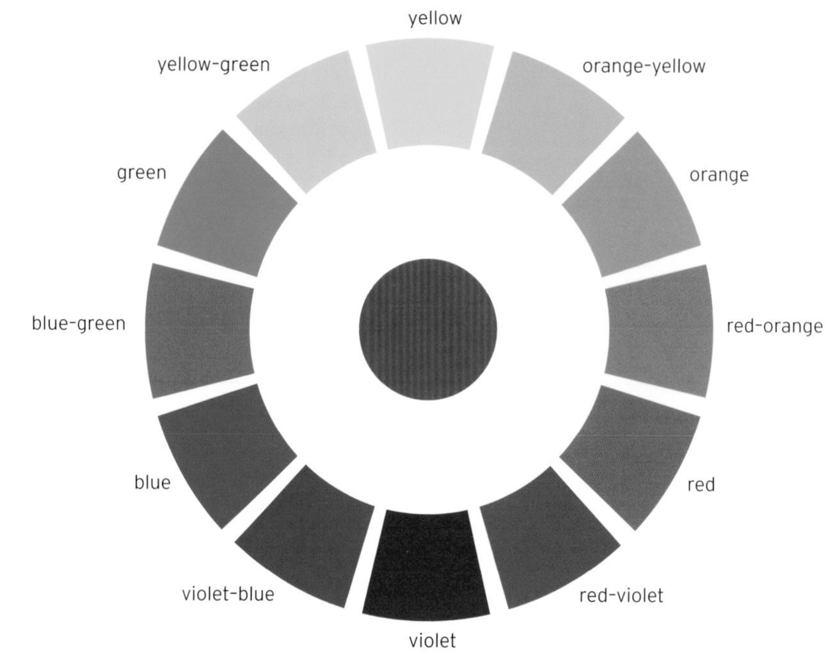

PRIMARY COLORS

Primary colors are ones that cannot be made by mixing other colors. The three primary colors are red, yellow, and blue. They are equidistant on the color wheel.

red

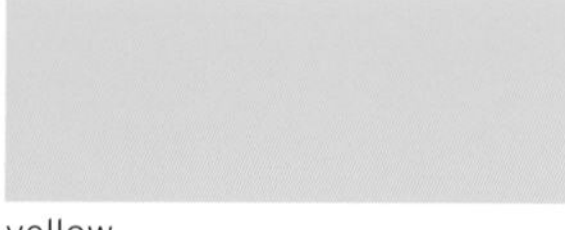
yellow

blue

SECONDARY COLORS

The secondary colors are orange, green, and violet. They are produced by mixing two primary colors. When mixed, red and yellow make orange, blue and yellow make green, and red and blue make violet. The secondary colors are also equidistant on the color wheel, in between the primary colors.

orange

green

violet

TERTIARY COLORS

Mixing a primary color with its adjacent secondary color on the wheel produces a tertiary color. For example, mixing red with orange creates red-orange and red with violet creates red-violet. Again, these are equidistant on the wheel.

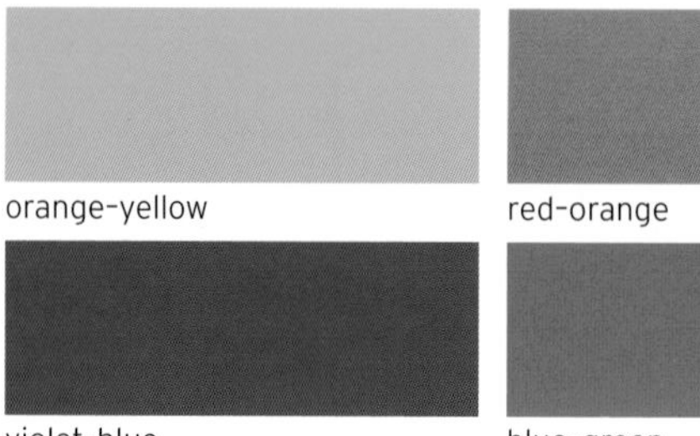
orange-yellow

violet-blue

red-orange

blue-green

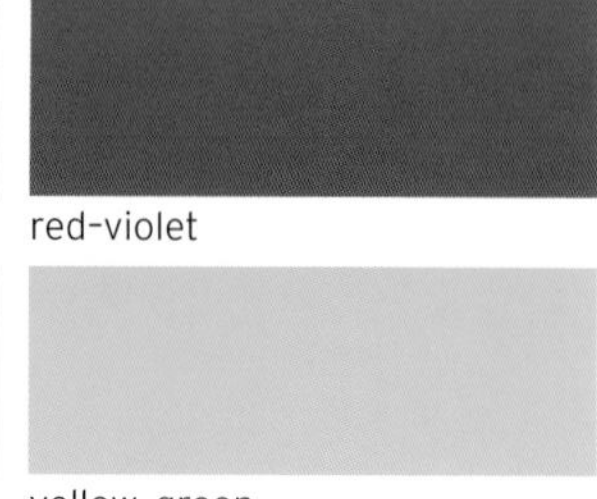
red-violet

yellow-green

WARM AND COOL COLORS

All colors have associations. Warm colors such as reds, oranges, and yellows are associated with sunlight and fire. They tend to stand out in an illustration and seem closer than cool colors, which recede into the background. Cool colors include the blues of the sky and water, and the greens of rolling hills and the landscape. Bearing in mind how warm and cool colors affect the viewer enables you to enhance the atmosphere of your artwork.

COMPLEMENTARY COLORS

The opposite colors on the color wheel are contrasting partners called complementary colors. The partners consist of one primary and one secondary color. The pairings are red and green, blue and orange, and yellow and violet. They appear brightest when placed next to each other. When mixed together, complementary colors produce a gray, neutral tone. To make a color darker, add its complementary partner, rather than shading with black. For example, if you would like a darker yellow, add a hint of violet.

USING COLOR-WHEEL THEORIES

Mixing colors yourself in your chosen medium is the best way to discover how the color-wheel theories work. Start with three primary colors—red, yellow, and blue. When the primaries are mixed together, they produce a muddy black. Experiment by mixing the secondary colors, then the tertiary colors. The amount of any one color added to the mix affects the shade produced. Make notes on how you mix the colors, so that you can re-create them in the future.

Three distinct characteristics account for the appearance of colors: hue, value, and saturation. Each of these can be manipulated by color mixing or, more subtly, by altering the context in which a color appears. *Hue* is the name of a color—for example, red, green, or blue—that identifies it in the color spectrum. *Value* is the relative quality of lightness or darkness in a color. This varies on a scale of black to white. *Saturation*, also known as intensity, is the relative purity of hue present in a color. A highly saturated color will give a strong sense of hue, and a low saturation will have a weaker presence.

The result of mixing a color with white is known as a *tint*.
Mixing gray with a color is known as a *tone*.
Mixing a color with black creates a *shade*.

Below left
Remember that the white of the page can be used as part of the illustration. Here, the white page has been allowed to show through for the snow, hair, and fur coat. The strong background shade of the sky is also picked up in the face, providing a good balance of color. Visual impact is achieved with a simple color palette. The pink is used as an accent color on the lips and gloves. This illustration was created using paint and Adobe Photoshop.

Below right
The artist has limited the color palette to a few complementary shades to create a particular, desired effect. By mixing lead-pencil sketching with watercolor paint, subtle colors are created and contribute to a calming atmosphere in what seems to be a fantasy land.

COLOR FORECASTING

Have you ever wondered how the colors for fashion, interiors, cosmetics, and even cars seem to complement each other every season? How do fashion designers all decide that, say, green is this summer's color? Or that our homes will be decorated in brown? The answer is that there are teams of professionals—known as "color forecasters"—analyzing data to provide color predictions for up to two years ahead. Chapter Seven contains an interview with Promostyl, a fashion- and color-prediction house. The company has a group of agents who travel the world to research upcoming trends. Promostyl then produces seasonal books recording their predictions, which are sold as reference sources to designers and businesses worldwide.

USING COLOR IN FASHION ILLUSTRATION

In the fashion industry color palettes for clothing change from season to season. When designers produce new collections, they are aware of the season's predicted colors through attending trade shows and seeking advice from fashion- and color-prediction agencies. However, the illustrator is free to select a personal palette for fashion artwork. Although it is important to describe the garments, using color confidently is preferable to paying too much attention to the seasonal color trend. Be bold with color, keeping in mind the way that children splash color onto a page and experiment with bold brush strokes and strong shades. Not adding color for fear of ruining a perfectly drawn figure is self-limiting for an illustrator.

Think about the viewer and what you want the eye to be drawn to in your illustration. Limiting your color palette, then using an accent color cleverly is one

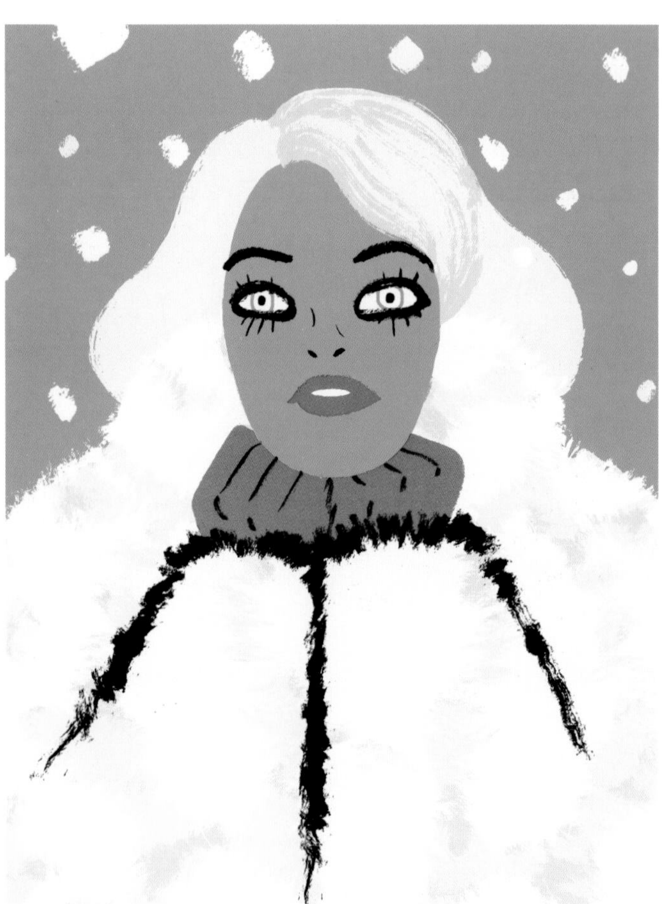

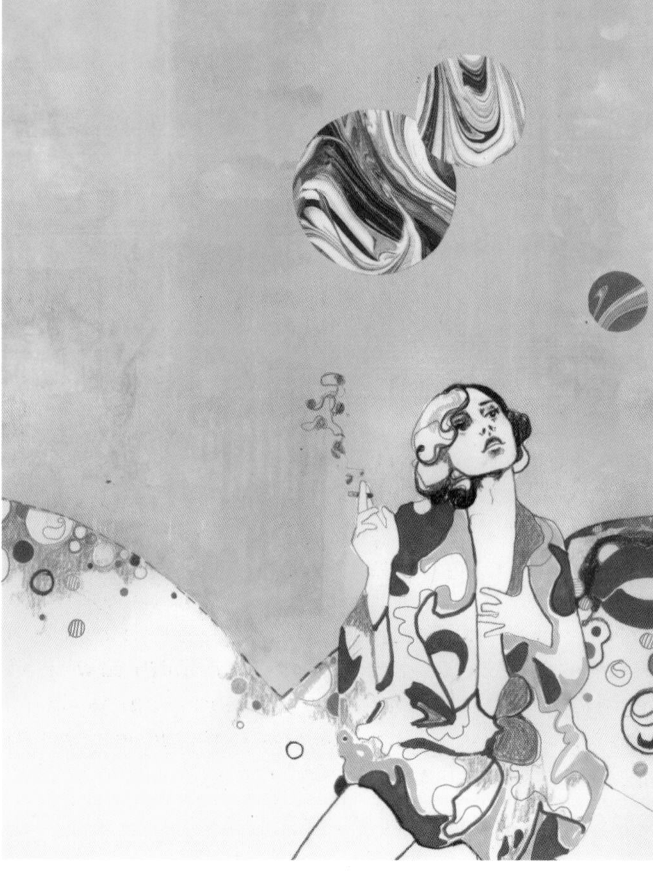

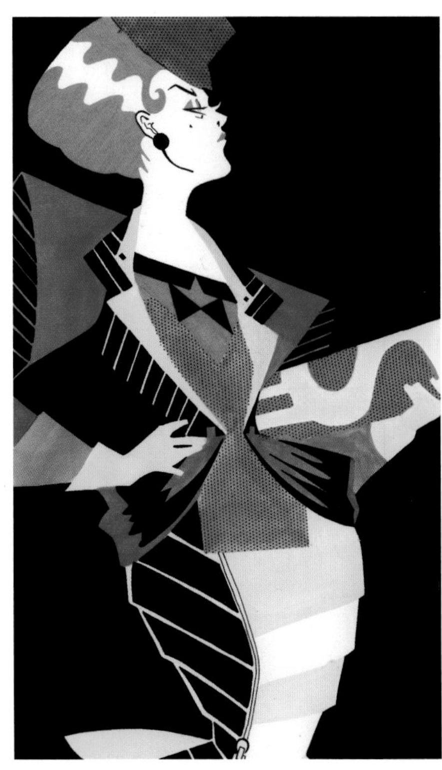

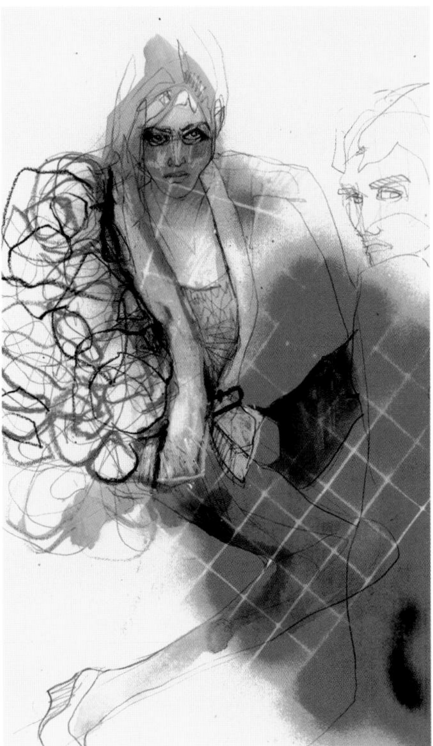

Left
In this illustration, created on the computer, color underlines the power and attitude of the strong woman portrayed. The black background is interjected with bold, bright colors that create a striking impression.

Right
Figures have been drawn directly onto a pale-lemon background paper, with colors stronger in the places where the illustrator wanted to focus attention. The hair, for example, is a brighter orange, and the same technique is used for the clothes to draw the viewer's eye through the illustration. Mixed media have been used, including pastels, pencils, paint, and charcoal.

way of controlling what the viewer notices. By adding a few, carefully placed accessories in the accent color, you can create a flow across the page from top to bottom, left to right. In this way the accent color guides the viewer's eyes over the illustration. For example, think of an illustration of a man in a black suit wearing a red belt, a red hat, and red shoes. The red would draw the viewer's eyes to follow it over the ensemble but without detracting from the predominant black suit.

For further inspiration, look at how other artists and illustrators use color in their work, for example in the contemporary illustrations on these pages. Try similar techniques yourself, adding your own fresh, individual response.

The subtle colors used in the fashion illustration (facing page, right) produce a calm atmosphere for the viewer. The image is dominated by patterns of color. The balls in the sky are created with a marbling technique, and their colors are reflected in the patterns on the garment. This serene image of a woman smoking a cigarette is in stark contrast to the next illustration (above left), in which the dramatic pose of the woman creates a powerful atmosphere. Here, the bright colors stand out from the black background, and her outfit fills the whole page. The remaining illustration (above right) uses the same technique to create a strong image that puts the clothes on center stage. This illustrator has chosen to work on a lemon-colored background paper rather than white. The images, therefore, are bonded by subtle shades and tones, the colors stronger in areas the illustrator wanted to draw attention to. The brighter orange of the hair is repeated in the clothes to move the viewer's eye through the illustration, and the figure's cheeks are highlighted with red as are her painted lips. A large area of dominant color distinguishes this illustration. Demonstrating a powerful way of using color in illustration, this image shows the benefit of experimenting with it in your work.

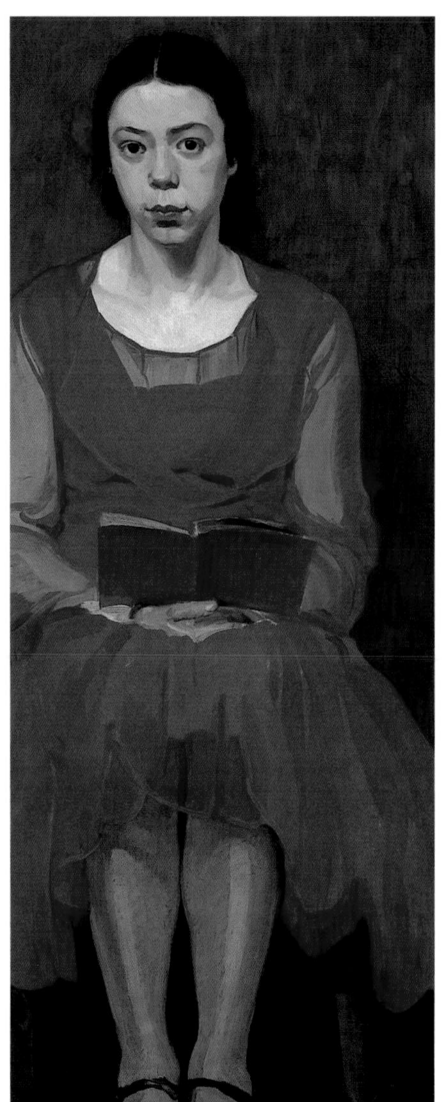

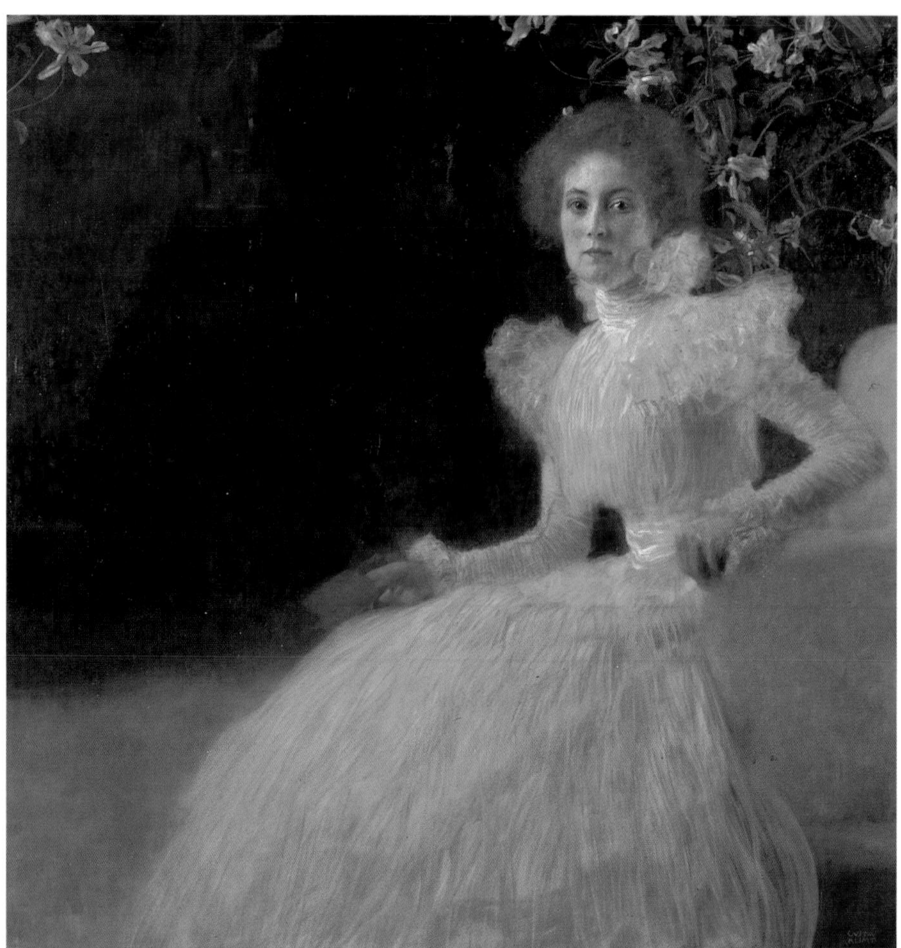

Left
Ferdinand Andri, *Girl in a Red Dress*, 1917.
Oil on canvas.

Right
Gustav Klimt, *Portrait of Sonja Knips*, 1898.
Oil on canvas.

Studying how artists convey the qualities of particular fabrics is a fascinating way to learn about rendering skills. These oil paintings by Andri and Klimt show differing methods of conveying the characteristics of sheer fabric when worn by a female figure.

FABRIC RENDERING AND PATTERN REPRODUCTION

Depicting the qualities of fabric accurately brings authenticity to a fashion illustration. To achieve a professional standard of fabric representation, develop an understanding of different fabrics, and observe the way in which they drape and fall on the body. The best way to gain this knowledge is to sketch clothed figures. Notice the shapes the fabric makes around the body, rarely lying flat but molding itself around the contours of the figure. Observe the way that looser garments hang while tighter fabrics stretch on the body, and practice drawing the effects. It would be useful to collect a range of fabric samples and practice drawing them, observing the way they fold and fall. It is also worthwhile visiting a museum or gallery and sketching from figurative sculptures to discover how fine fabrics are cleverly rendered in heavy stone. Visit the old-master paintings, too, to observe how these artists skillfully represented fabric.

The oil paintings above show two very different chiffon dresses that each artist has portrayed in a contrasting style. In Andri's *Girl in a Red Dress*, the transparency of the chiffon is rendered by allowing the sheer sleeves and neckline to reveal the flesh beneath the fabric with such realism that it is almost like looking at a photograph. The area where the undergarment is apparent is a denser, darker shade of red, and this contrast itself serves to emphasize the sheer quality of the sleeves. Every fold and crease in this dress has been observed and accurately rendered, and even the girl's silk stockings shine with reflected light. In Klimt's *Portrait of Sonja*

Knips, the pink dress is made from ruched, pleated chiffon, the many layers of the dress evident in the opaque paintwork. The delicate, sheer quality of the fabric is revealed on the shoulders, cuffs, and at the hem of the dress.

Always keep in mind that, although your fashion illustrations may be highly creative and individual, the intention of the artwork is to convey a garment or outfit. The representation of the fabric from which the clothing is constructed must play a significant role in your artwork.

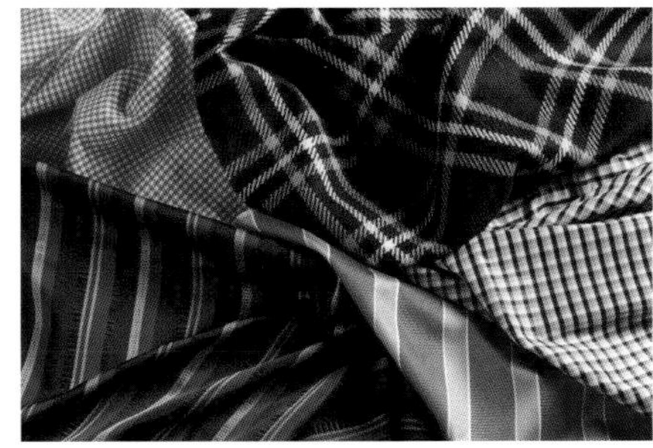

Striped and checked fabrics

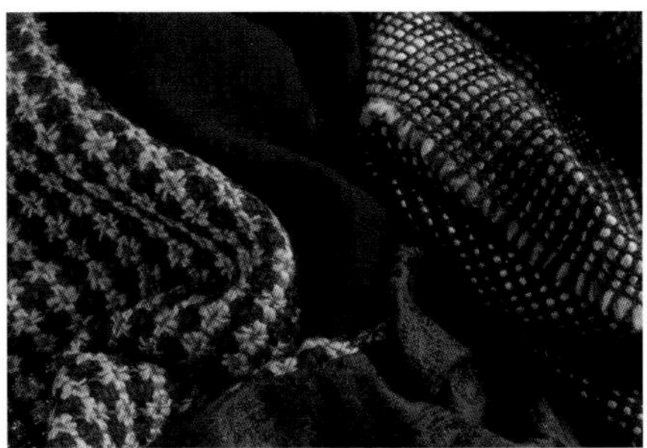

Woolen fabrics

Stripes and checks

When drawing stripes, keep in mind that they move with the body. Stripes run across, down, or around the body, regardless of their width or the direction of the print. A common mistake in fashion illustration is to render stripes using straight, parallel lines. If you look at a horizontal-striped jumper off the body, then the lines of the stripes are, indeed, straight. However, imagine a person wearing that jumper. The stripes will wrap around the torso and arms and so must be drawn with curved lines.

The correct way to draw stripes is to begin at the center of a garment, then follow the lines of the stripes over the curves of the body, up to the shoulder, and down over the hips to the hem. It is a mistake to start from the top or bottom, as the direction of the stripes will become confused with the shift in hip and shoulder positions of the figure. When you plot your stripes from the center of the garment, ensure they are of equal proportion if that is true of the fabric. Some striped fabrics have uneven stripes that are not symmetrical. Stripes may run in a vertical, horizontal, or diagonal direction.

Checks, or plaids, are stripes running in two directions. Like stripes, they can be drawn straight or on the bias (diagonally) to form either repeated "+" or "x" shapes. Again, checks are made up of straight lines that will curve with the body. These lines usually run down the center front of a garment and are equidistant from each other.

Plan your drawings with faint pencil lines before you begin to render striped and checked fabrics. Accuracy at this stage is vital if the finished artwork is to look professional.

Wool

Woolen fabrics are generally woven in a variety of weights, and include flannel, gabardine, fleece, and mohair. They can also be patterned—for example, tweeds, pinstripes, and herringbone. Wools are best rendered in a soft medium that will produce one base color and a darker shadow because, unless it is textured, a drawn woolen surface often appears flat. Markers are excellent for drawing flat fabrics, and you can soften the edges with a nonpermanent fineliner, sweeping a wet brush over the outline. Other art materials that work well for rendering wool are pencils, inks, watercolor, and gouache. Try applying the base colors with paint and the highlights or shadows in pencil.

Textures and weaves can be rendered with a dry-brush technique, in which a fairly limited amount of almost-dry paint is applied, leaving part of the page white. You could also try scratching directional lines into the surface of wet paint. Tweeds and herringbones can be represented with inks and markers, which convey the fluidity of the pattern. To create the intricacies of the weave, crosshatch with two or more colors.

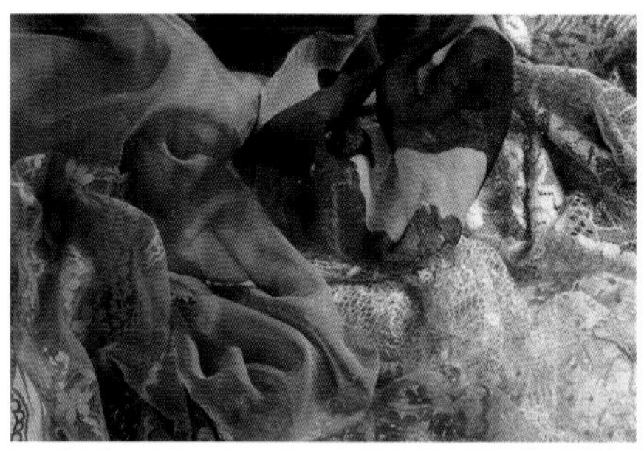

Sheer fabrics

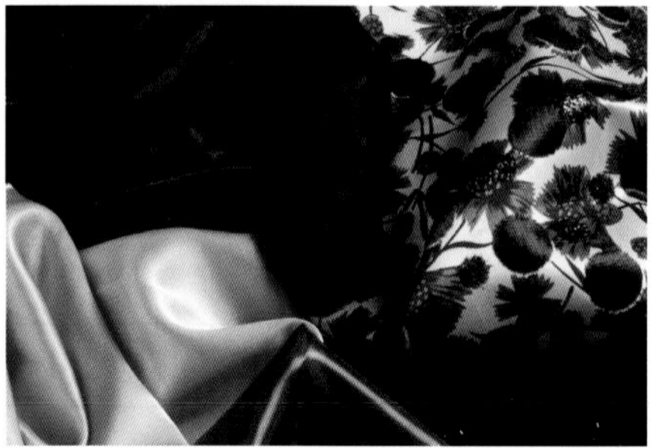

Shiny fabrics

Sheers

Sheer fabrics are so fine that a single layer is transparent, and you can see skin tone through it. With the exception of lingerie, most garments in sheer fabrics are made up of many layers, or include undergarments.

Sheers can be categorized into two groups: the softer sheers, such as chiffon, voile, georgette, and some laces, and the stiffer types, including organza, tulle, net, and organdie. To render transparent fabrics, begin by applying skin tones to your fashion illustration. Add the color of the fabric over the top of the skin with a light touch in either pencil or marker, avoiding heavy outlines. The skin must be visible under the fabric, so be careful not to choose too dark a color.

Where sheer fabric touches the body, shading should be darker. Where it floats freely, use lighter tones. This technique also applies if you are rendering many layers of chiffon—the more layers, the denser the shading. For lace or net, the appearance of the fabric as it lies over the skin must, likewise, be rendered sensitively. These meshlike fabrics can be represented with fine crosshatching that becomes darker where the fabric folds. For lace, you can build up the floral patterns and embroidery by using a fineliner to indicate the details. Your drawing lines for such a delicate fabric should be fluid and without sharp corners. The edges of lace may be scalloped and heavily patterned, but it will be impossible to draw every intricate detail. Simply *suggesting* the style is perfectly acceptable in fashion illustration.

Organza and organdie have a stiffer consistency than the sheers discussed above. Garments made from these fabrics stand out from the body and create a sense of drama. They can be rendered with the same techniques used for other sheers, but there is a difference in the way that they fall and catch the light. When sketching them, try overlapping blocks of color to show where one fold of fabric lies on top of another. The deeper shading conveys the double thickness of the fabric.

Shiny fabrics

To illustrate shiny fabrics, observe where the light source falls on the garment. Clever rendering will create the illusion of reflected light. To add a highlight to the garment, draw on a white shimmer line or leave the white of the page to shine through. Shiny fabrics divide into three categories. First, there are the light-reflective types, including firm fabrics such as taffeta, satin, and leather, and softer velvet and velour. Second, there are the decorative fabrics with a sheen, which are usually beaded, and sequinned lamés. The third category includes heavily patterned reptile skins and brocades.

Shiny fabrics are usually rendered in three shades. The darkest shade is for the folds and shadows, a medium shade is for the general garment color, and the lightest for the highlights. The lightest shade, usually white, often surrounds the dark shadows, and touches of it should be added to the edges of the garment. Add highlights where the body juts out from the fabric, at the chest, arms, or legs, for example. Choose any art material for these three shades, but focus on imitating shine.

Softer sheens such as that on velvet should be approached in the same way, only without areas of solid color or solid outlines. Instead, create feathery edges. A soft, dry medium such as pastel is ideal for creating a velvety smooth surface to your fashion illustration. Treat the shimmer of lamé, sequins, and beads as a pattern, stippling with a hard brush, using fairly dry paint and creating sharp white highlights. Alternatively, tap all over the drawing with a medium-nibbed marker. To give your illustration extra sparkle, use metallic pens.

Feathers and fur

Both natural and imitation feathers and fur are difficult to render realistically. It is a common error to overwork these parts of an illustration by sketching in too many lines. The best method is to use watercolor paper, dampening the page, then adding ink or paint in light touches. This creates fuzzy, soft lines that represent the delicacy of feathers and fur well. For white feathers or fur, paint a dark background, then use bleach to add fine lines.

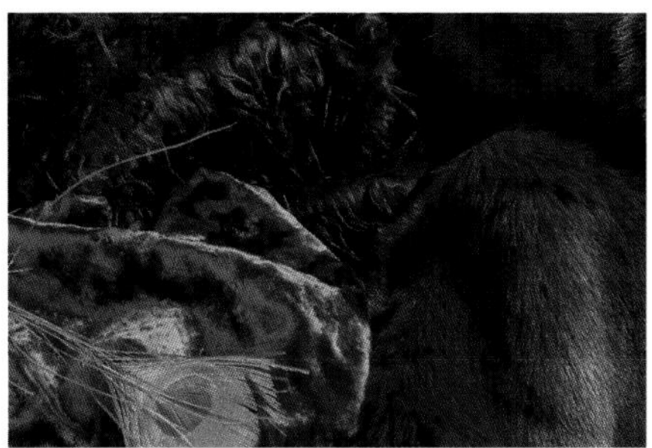

Feathers and fur

Knit

This fabric has a texture created by its looping and twining threads. Knit differs from woven fabric in its stretch as well as its texture. Knitted garments are either constructed by hand or machine, and produced in various wools and yarns, such as angora, cashmere, mohair, chenille, bouclé, and metallic. Gain awareness of knitwear variations because they demand very different rendering techniques.

To render knitwear differently from a woven fabric, you need to draw in the rib. Rib, or ribbing, is the term used to describe a series of raised rows in knitted fabric. Ribbing is often found around the neck, cuffs, and edges of a garment and can be indicated with repetitive line. You will also need to master authentic representation of the stitches used in knit. For example, cable and braiding can be indicated with a combination of curved and straight lines in a rope pattern, while purl and garter can be rendered with a series of loops and ellipses. Knit patterns often include geometric shapes, raised textures, and flowers. These are usually known as Fair Isle or Argyle and are best shown by blocking in the patterns before adding texture and color.

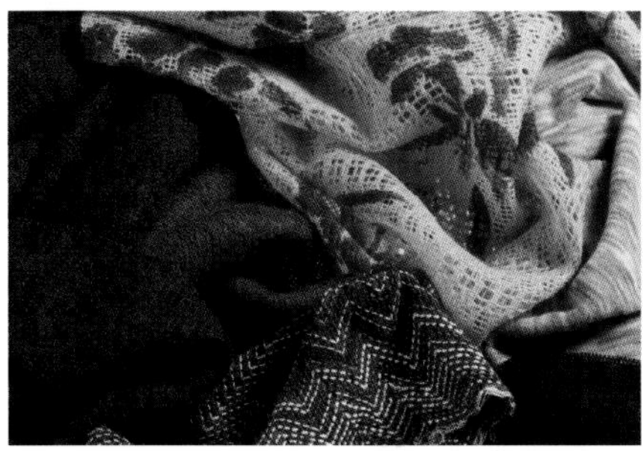

Knitted fabrics

Pattern and print

Fashion fabrics can be printed with almost any design or motif, including floral, abstract, animal, and polka dot. A design that is duplicated or copied is called a repeat pattern. In addition to the repeat, you need to bear in mind scale. For example, a life-size floral fabric must be reduced to fit into the proportions of a drawn figure. The simplest way to calculate this is to hold the fabric up to the center of your body and count the repeat in the directions of the side seam and along the waist. To achieve the scale, fit the same count into your drawn figure.

When you reduce a fussy print, remove some of the detail, as it can look overworked on a smaller scale. Render some of the pattern, and disguise areas with soft shadows, using a limited color palette.

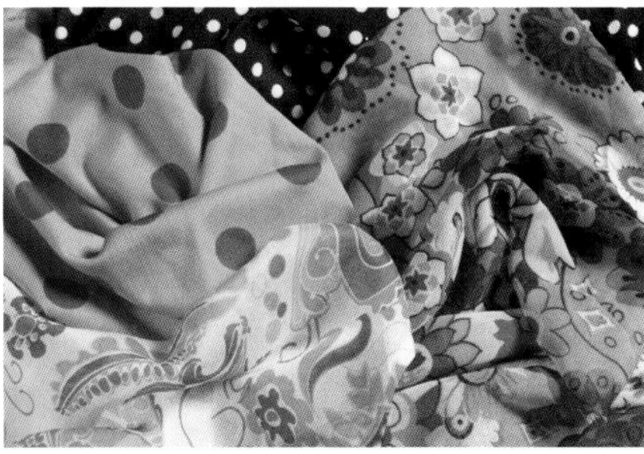

Patterned and printed fabrics

Embellished and embroidered fabrics

Not all fabrics are the same through their length; some vary in texture. Handmade fabrics are often embroidered or otherwise embellished, and you will need to change your rendering style accordingly. Embellished fabrics are often manipulated through stitching. For example, some are raised with padding or wadding, then decorated with hand- or machine-stitched patterns. To capture such techniques on paper, the fabric must look raised from its background. Embellishments will appear closer to the viewer if worked in light colors on a darker background. Embroidery thread also catches the light, so again this should be rendered with highlights. It is impossible to record every detail, but draw in elements every now and again to indicate the presence of decorative stitching.

Denim, a heavy, woven fabric, is often adorned with topstitching, rivets, and prominent seams, all of which can be rendered by the illustrator. If you look carefully

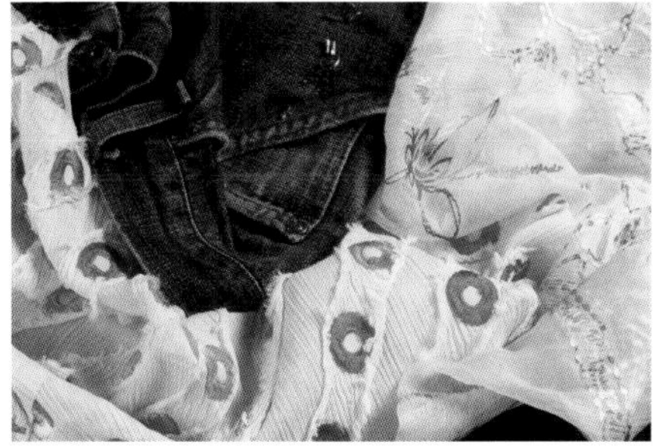

Embellished and embroidered fabrics

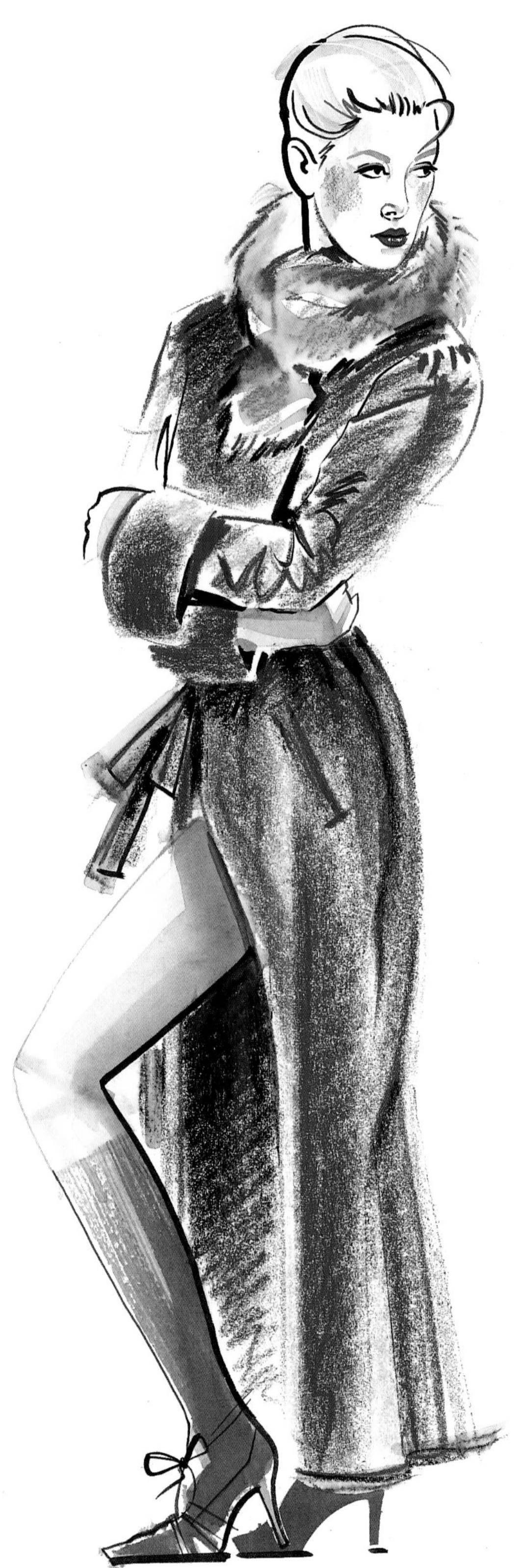

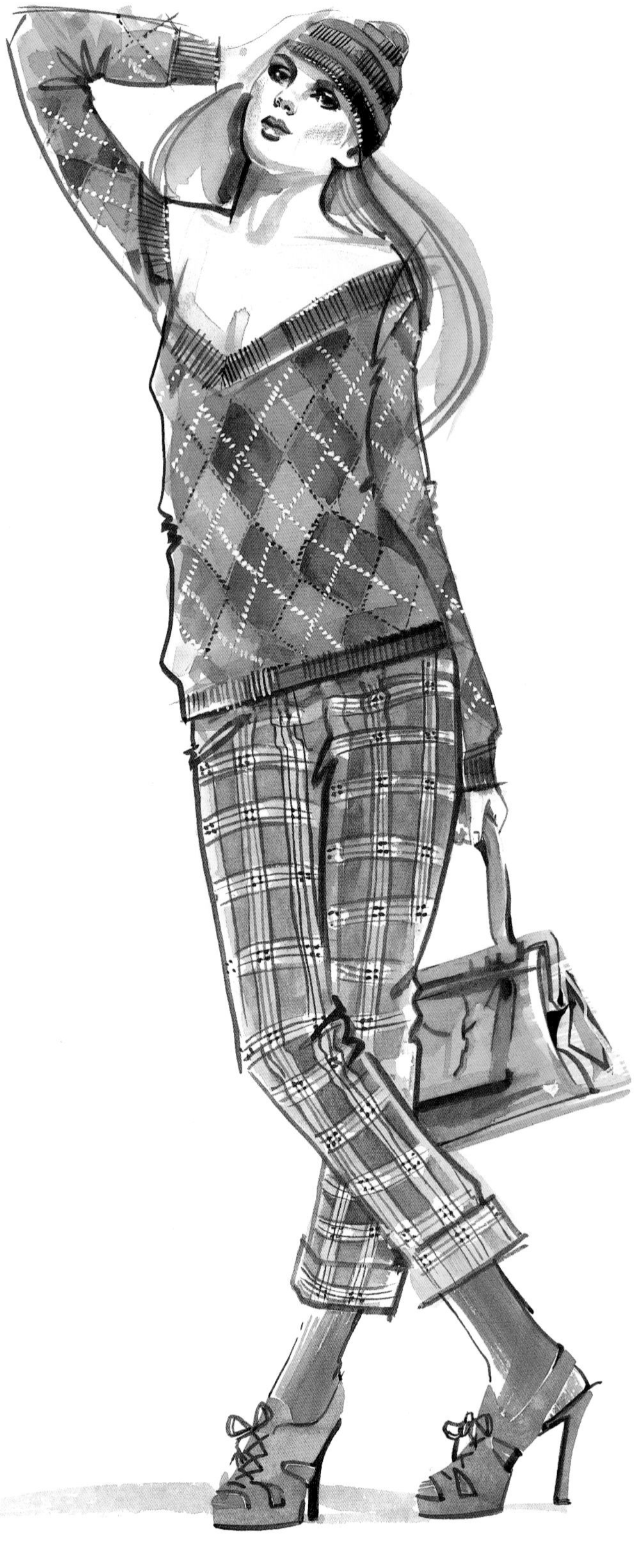

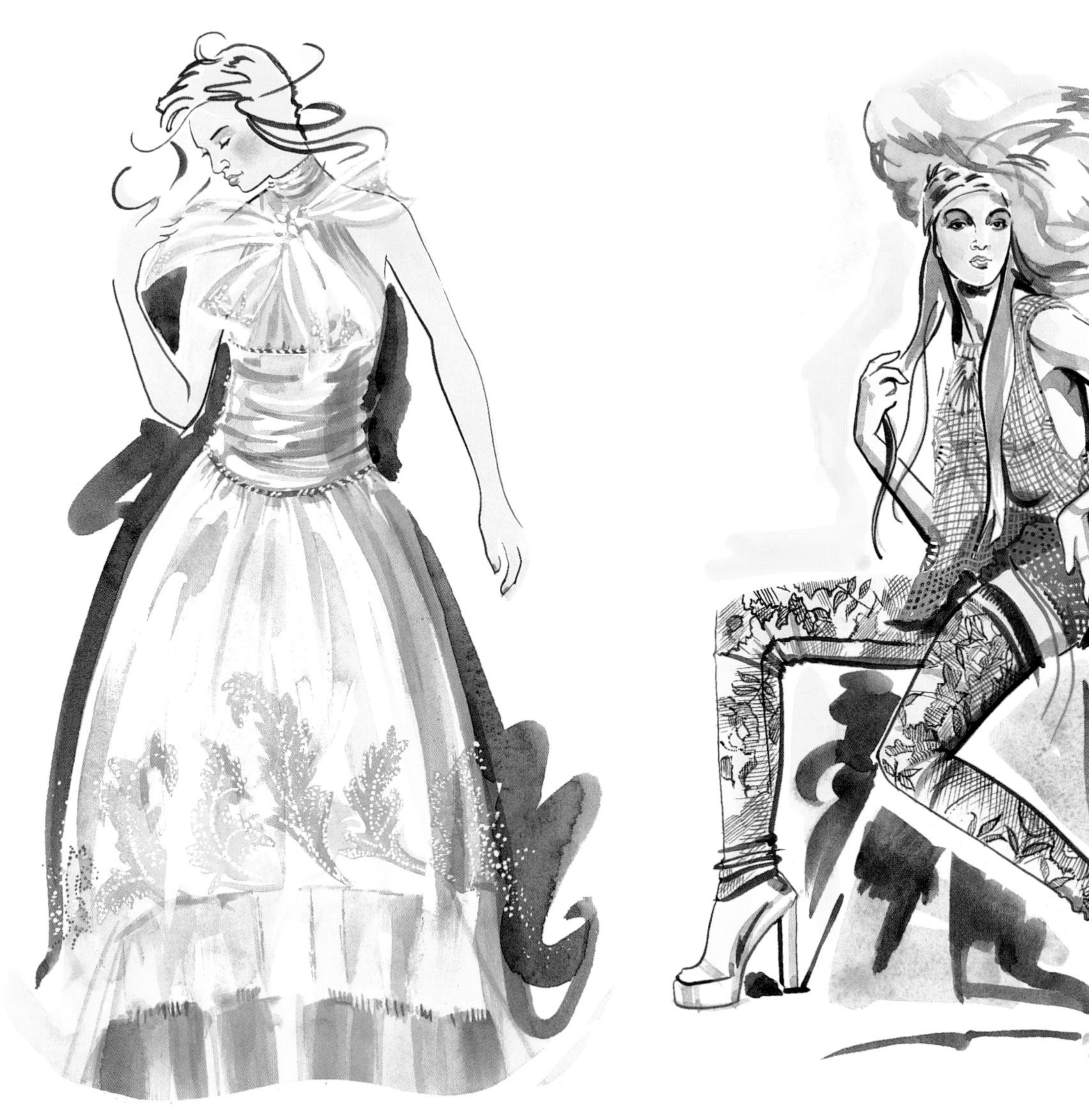

These illustrations have been created using the rendering techniques described in the preceding section.

at a piece of denim, you will see that it is made up of a series of diagonal lines broken up by the weave. Copy this effect using sharp, water-soluble pencils of varying shades of blue. Use darker shades for the diagonal lines and paler ones for the weave. For areas where the denim is worn, dilute the pencil marks with water to create the effect. Denim rivets are often metallic and can be rendered effectively with a metallic pen or paint. Highlight the topstitching in areas where it is prominent, using a simple, broken line. Today, denim is often customized to include embroidery, rips, print, and jeweled accessories, all of which the fashion illustrator must draw attention to.

Fabric reference exercise

To make the most of the information discussed in this section, experiment by rendering fabrics yourself to create a set of reference illustrations. Divide a sheet of plain paper into a grid of blank squares. Place a viewfinder with a square view over various fabric samples. Try to create the same effects that you can see through the viewfinder in your squares. Experiment with a range of media until you find the best way to represent each of the fabrics. Make notes next to your accurate renderings to remind you how to create similar effects again. Building up a library of authentic rendering techniques is certain to be a useful aid when creating fashion illustrations in the future.

PRESENTATION FOR FASHION DESIGN

4

Throughout your education and career as a fashion designer, you will need to present your design ideas, technical drawings, mood boards, and promotional fashion illustrations in an effective way. This chapter looks at how to use your initial inspiration and sketchbook ideas to create original designs and build ranges. It will show you how to present your ideas to a professional standard without limiting your creative flair, and how to gear your presentation style to suit a particular client or market.

MOOD BOARDS

Creating a mood board is an excellent way to organize your research and ideas at the beginning of a project. A mood board captures the style and theme for a set of designs by displaying images, fabrics, and colors that are to be influential in the creative process. An effective mood board will make a clear, cohesive statement to the viewer, who gains an understanding of your design direction. A mood board is also sometimes known in the industry as a story, or concept, board.

Below is a useful checklist of items to gather when compiling a mood board:

- Mount board
- Defining image(s)
- Backing papers
- Foam board
- Spray adhesive
- Cutting equipment
- Color samples
- Fabric swatches
- Textile samples
- Text (to include title and season)

First, lay out all your research material and decide which image, or images, best define the mood or theme for your design ideas. These images can be photocopies

Mood boards based on a theme of traditional blue-and-white china display images that define a classic, timeless style, with color palettes and fabrics also represented.

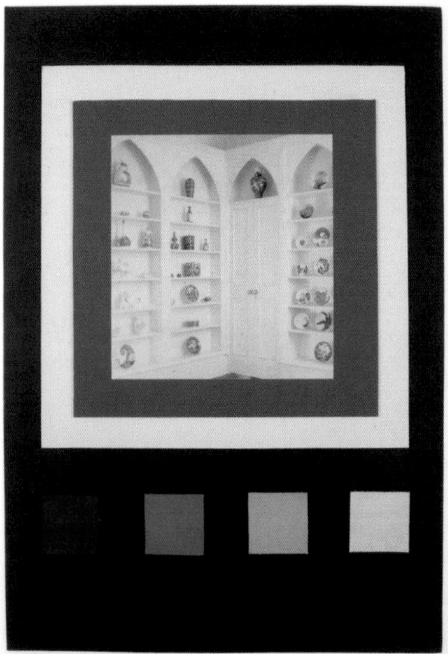

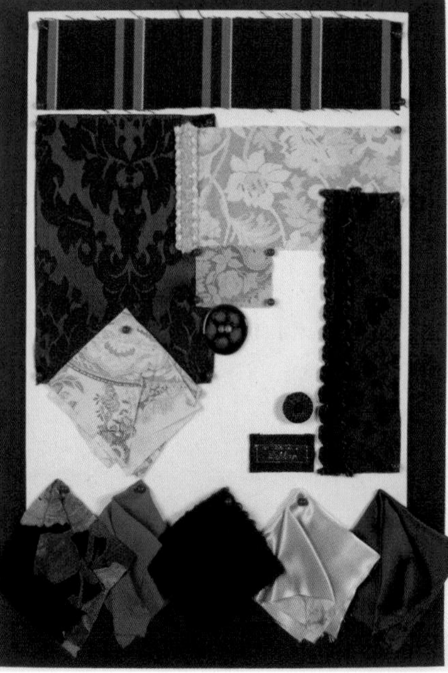

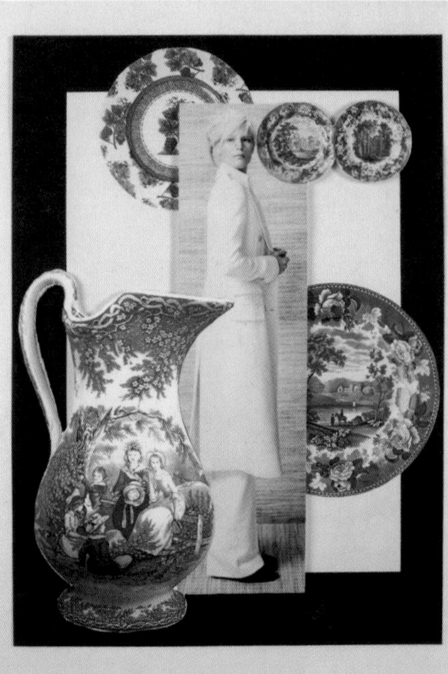

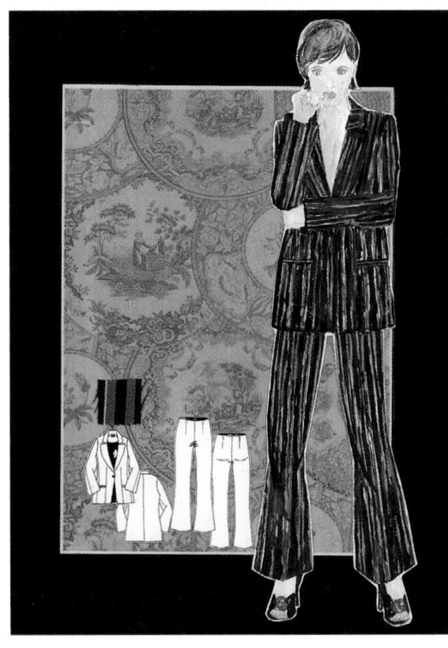

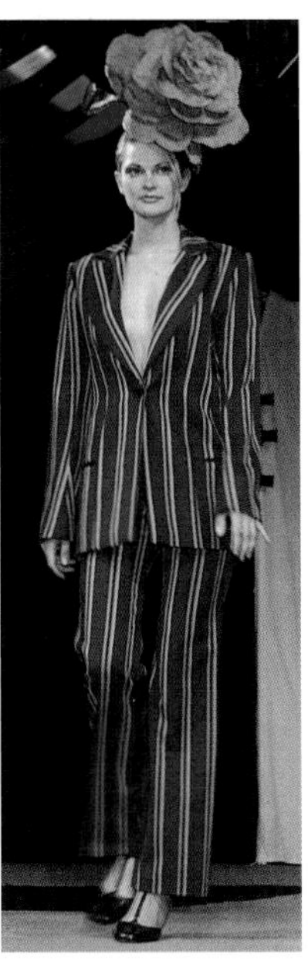

Left
The design of this striped trouser suit was inspired by the colors of the china in the previous mood board. The fashion illustration has been displayed on complementary mounting board. Printed fabric has been color photocopied onto acetate to provide a background. Flat drawings of the garments have also been mounted with fabric samples.

Right
This photograph shows the completed suit being modeled on the catwalk in a fashion show. The headdress was inspired by the floral designs on the blue-and-white china. It is important to display photographs of your creations in your portfolio.

from a sketchbook, magazine cuttings, or photographs. If you use more than one image, there should be a common link between the colors, patterns, or themes. The images all need to tell a similar story.

Pay attention to prevailing colors as you select images. Color choices must be coherent throughout the project, so think about them as you compile your mood board. When you have selected your color palette, decide how to display it creatively. Various means include cutting out paint-swatch cards, wrapping threads around card stock or painting your own samples. Limit the amount of colors you display, otherwise the board will become confusing and difficult to read.

Fabric samples should complement the images in color and theme. Think about how to display these samples, too. Untidy, jagged, and frayed edges will spoil your mood board. Frame your fabrics, stretching them over card stock or neatly sewing the edges. Treat any textile sampling, such as embroidery or fabric manipulation, in the same way. If you want to apply text to your mood board, avoid doing so by hand. Unless handwriting is paticularly beautiful, it can make a mood board look amateur. Use a computer to print text, or use Letratone. The next step is to plan the layout of the mood board for maximum impact. Make some rough sketches to see how best to arrange your items, and decide on the color of the mounting board and backing papers you will use.

The mood board (facing page) shows ideas for a refined collection based on blue-and-white Spode china. The presentation colors have been limited to shades of blue and cream, with images mounted onto foam board to give a three-dimensional effect. The selected fabrics have also been pinned on. It is easy for the viewer to appreciate the theme of this mood board.

A promotional fashion illustration (above left) for the collection demonstrates how decisions made in the mood-board process can be applied when illustrating. The artist has continued the theme by linking the colors, and by using the same mounting board to frame the illustrations. The mood board and illustration show how vital it is to think ahead and plan carefully when presenting your artwork. The final outfit (above right) seen on the catwalk demonstrates how the theme moves through the whole process.

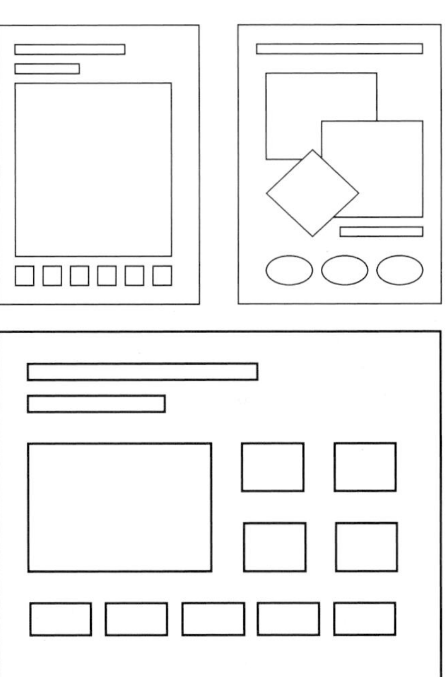

Example diagrams of possible layouts for mood boards show that it is essential to plan your ideas before fastening elements in place. Use the shapes in these diagrams to represent the things you will place on your mood board. For example, the boxes represent the color palettes and the larger rectangles the defining images that illustrate your mood or theme.

DESIGN ROUGHS AND RANGE BUILDING

Fashion designers produce a series of connected ideas that are later realized in their clothing range. While garments work as part of individual outfits, they share linking elements such as color, fabric, shape, and styling so that, when viewed together, they create a cohesive collection. When a collection is shown on the catwalk, it is easy to wonder how fashion designers produce so many new garments. How do their ideas get from paper to the bright lights of the fashion show, and how many designs do they complete to present a full range? Also, how do they create the story of their collection? The simple answer to all these questions is "careful planning."

The first stages of planning should include a thorough breakdown of the design brief. Gain an understanding of who you are designing for, identifying your target market and customer profile. Ask questions such as who will be wearing the clothes you design—how old are they, and are they male or female? Pinpoint the budgets and price points you are aiming for. Is it a couture clothing range or a collection for a retail outlet? Are you producing a casual range or occasionwear? What season is the collection destined for? It is only when you are clear on all these points that you can begin to design.

Remember the lessons from previous chapters when planning your fashion range. From discovery of sources of inspiration, and the exploration of ideas in your sketchbooks, will often spring the theme for your collection. This foundation work provides a starting point for experimental fashion sketches, known in the industry as "design roughs." When representing your thought processes on paper, forget about perfection, and let your ideas flow freely. Have the confidence at this stage to draw rough sketches without worrying about mistakes and bad designs, but be sure to maintain correct body proportions. In this way you are most likely to commit unique ideas to paper.

Some designers draw ideas onto the figure using a template (below), while others prefer to design flat (facing page), drawing garments directly onto the page. Find the method that best suits your personal design style, again always using correct body proportions.

Opposite
These fashion designs have been drawn directly onto layout paper. They have been designed flat without the aid of a figure template and by drawing only the garment. Occasionally the designer includes part of the figure, but this is drawn freehand to show what the garment might look like on the body. You can almost see the designer's brain working faster than the pencil to record these design roughs!

Below
To produce these fashion designs, the designer drew directly onto a figure template, then moved it along under the layout paper for each new figure, creating a new design on top of it. Serving only as a rough guide, the template does not influence the shape and design of the clothes.

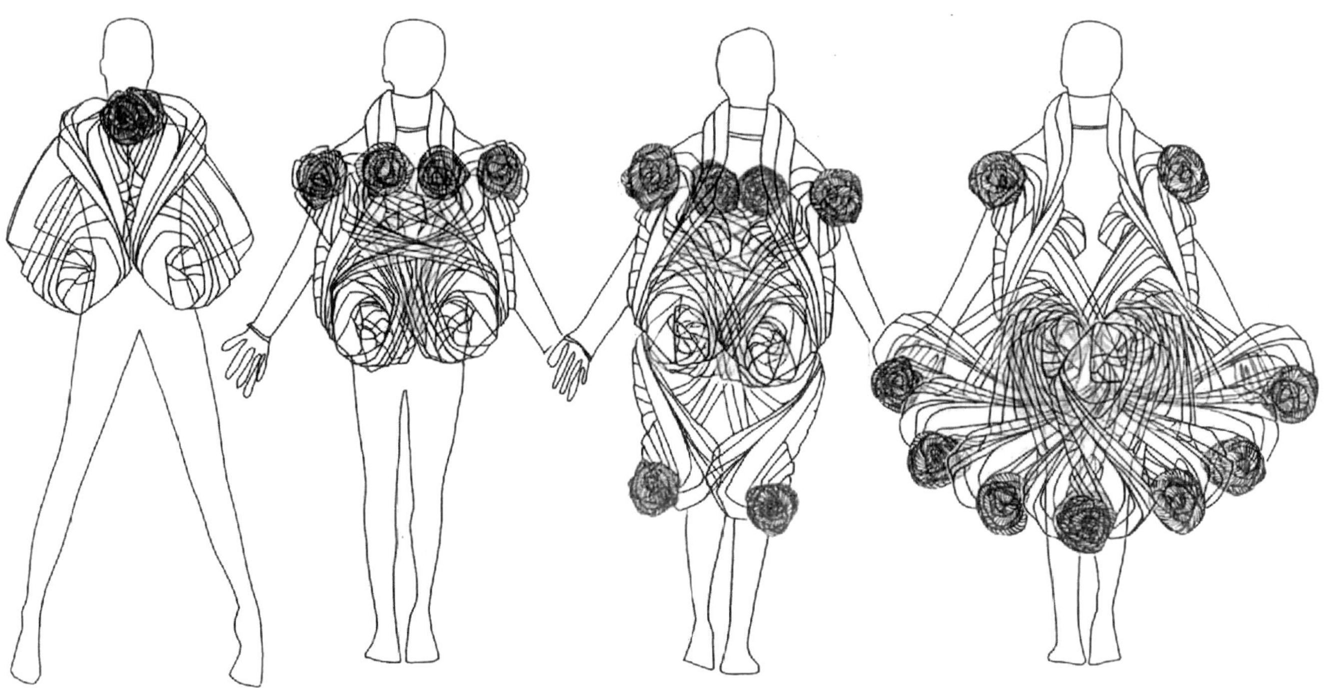

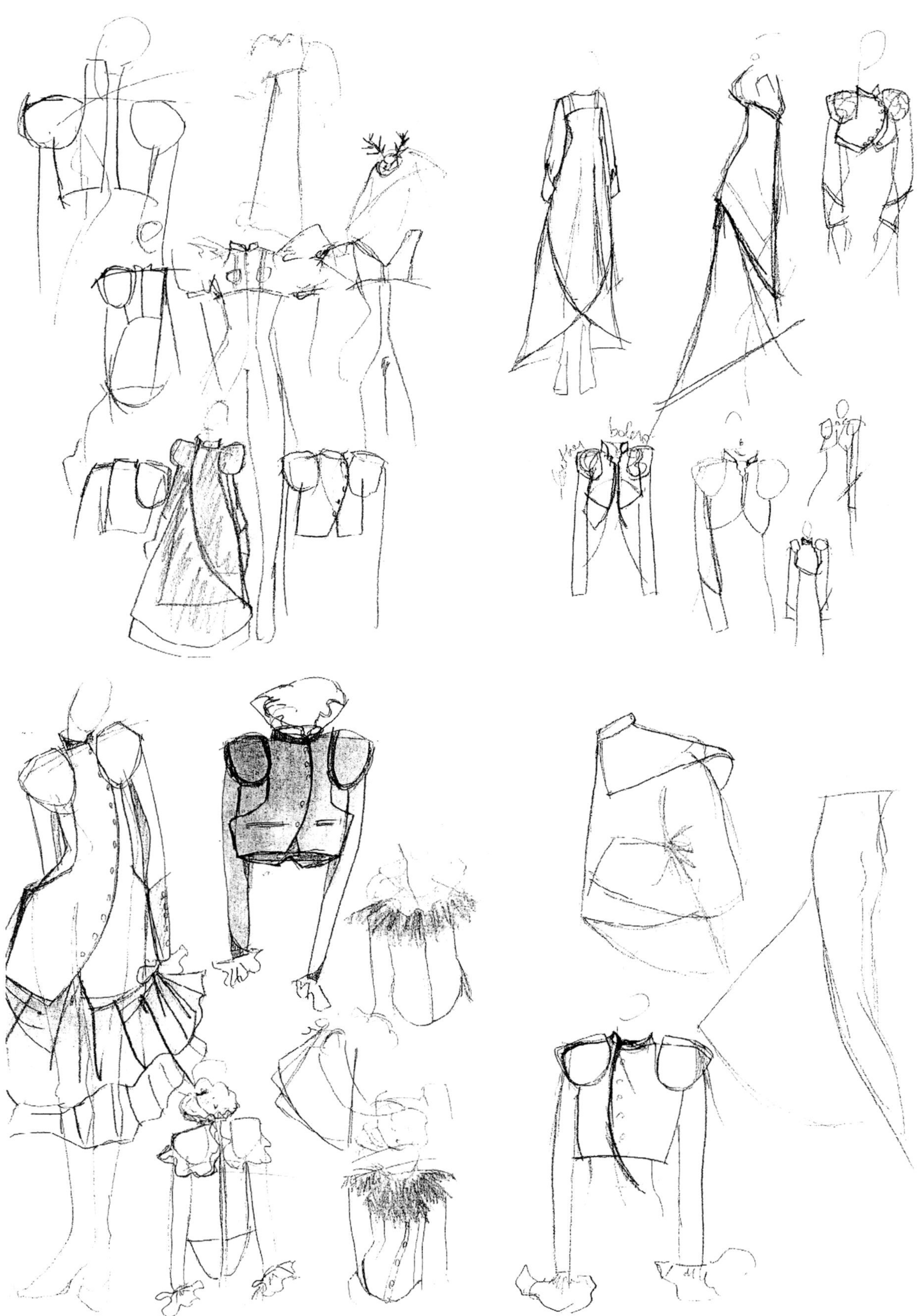
bolero

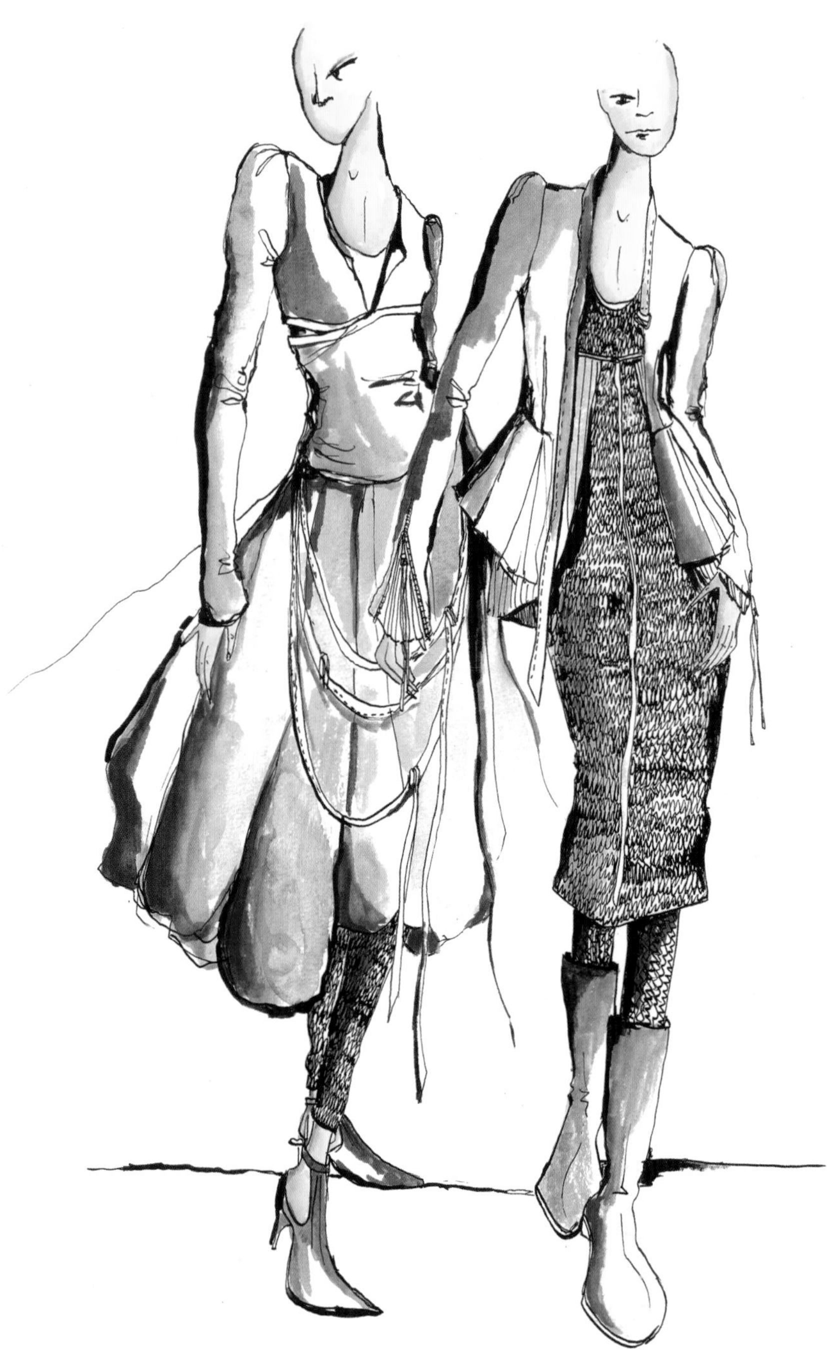

To produce your own design roughs, plan the fabrics and trims from which your garments will be made. This design rough clearly shows the differences between the fabrics in both outfits.

A design rough does not have to be well executed or a perfect piece of art. Faces and figure details are not important when designing at this stage. Do not worry about creating beautifully finished sheets—the purpose of design roughs is to assist you on your design journey. As your skills continue to improve, your presentation style will develop.

When producing design roughs, decide which fabrics and trims your garments will be made from. Source fabrics by visiting shops and contacting factories that supply via mail order. For specific fabrics, look on the Internet. Always ask to see a sample and check that you like the way the fabric handles before buying. Attach small pieces of your chosen fabrics to your designs as you draw, to enable you to see which fabrics and designs complement each other. When designing, avoid portraying flat, lifeless fabric. Instead, see it as three-dimensional, considering how it will drape and hang on the body. Take into account any embellishments you might add. For example, if you intend to embroider or manipulate the fabrics, add experimental samples to your design roughs.

The design rough (facing page) shows the differences between the fabrics in both outfits clearly. This student has drawn the texture of the knit using many close, wavy lines in direct contrast to the smooth fabric of the other garments, which only have paint applied in the areas of shadow.

To develop your designs, use a layout pad. This is a pad of thin paper that allows you to trace ideas easily. Place a template underneath a page, and design over the top, adapting the original design but keeping the related template outlines. This method of working not only saves you time, but allows you to see the range developing. Repeating this process of designing over a template encourages a cohesive collection of designs.

At the rough-design stage, start making decisions about color. Designers often use a limited palette when building a range so that colors harmonize and outfits can be coordinated. The design roughs (below) have been painted using subtle watercolor shades of cream and brown, with green and pink acting as highlights. As you produce design roughs, your ideas will flow like these, and your designs should be linked by color and shape. Importance should be placed on the clothes themselves, rather than on the figure. At this stage, you should not aim to produce a polished fashion illustration, rather an image that focuses all attention on your designs.

The next step is to build your designs into a range. As you select outfits, you will notice common design themes running through your choices. Repetition is an important tool in creating a cohesive collection. The designs overleaf show how variations of a similar garment have been tried. Sleeve lengths vary, and the necklines change with each design. To encourage your ideas to flow like this, try

These designs are all drawn onto fairly unrealistic figures. However, the small proportions of the heads help to emphasize the exaggerated size of the padded garments in the collection. Watercolor has been used to add detail to the designs and to suggest a color palette for the range. The paint runs and splashes, but it doesn't seem to matter. This student did not spend hours meticulously perfecting the figures or a painting style, yet in the design roughs captures the character of the collection.

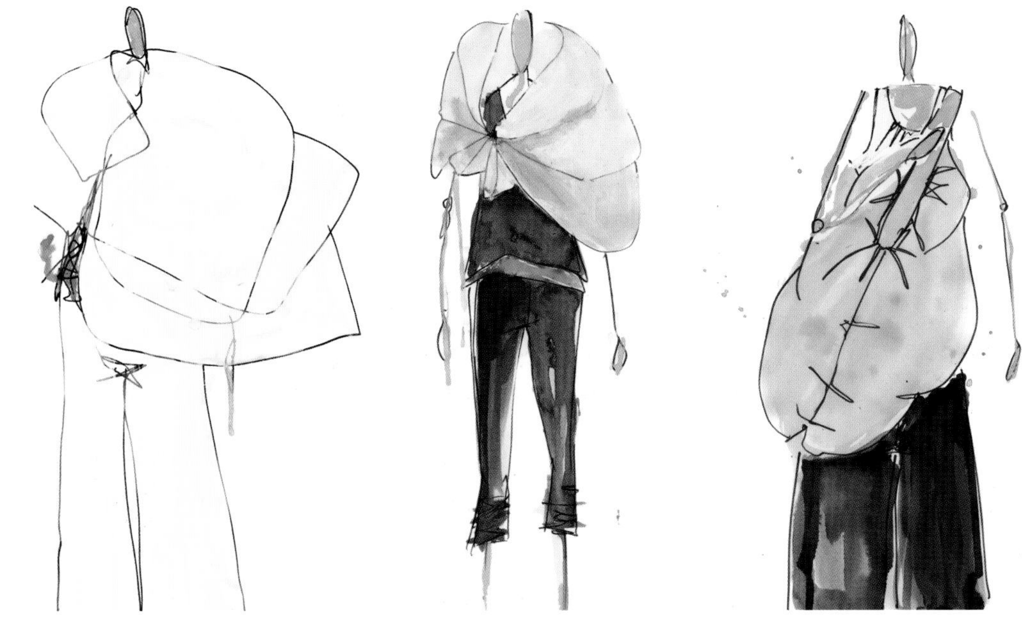

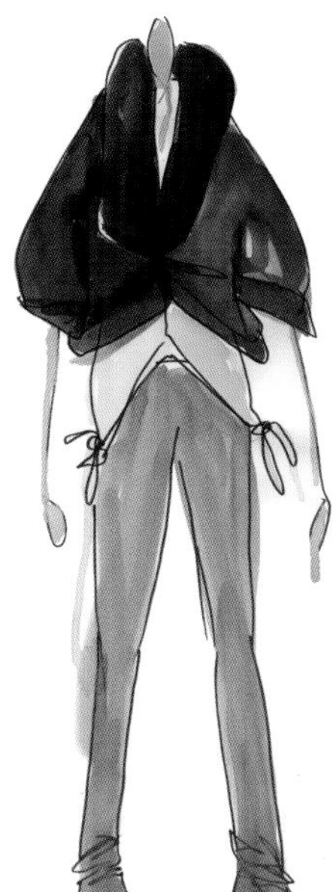

sketching about six garments on one theme. For example, incorporate frills into a series of garments, changing one feature with each new design. Repeat this process of design experimentation until you have a store of fashion designs from which you can build your range. The easiest way to make a selection for your range is to lay out all your design roughs and choose the outfits that look good in their own right, but which also sit well with others when mixed and matched. You may need to include a selection of balanced separates such as skirts, tops, trousers, dresses, and outerwear. A complete, interchangeable wardrobe such as that shown below, in which garments work in harmony with each other, is often the ideal.

When you have built your range, draw it onto one page so that it can be easily viewed as a complete collection. Depending on the size of your range, you may need to reduce your designs on a photocopier or scanner to fit them onto a single page. Think creatively about how to present your collection at this stage, because it is the first time you are telling its story. The images on the facing page show various

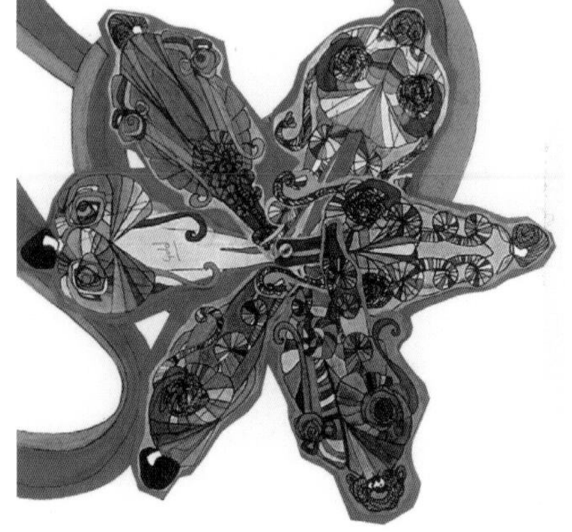

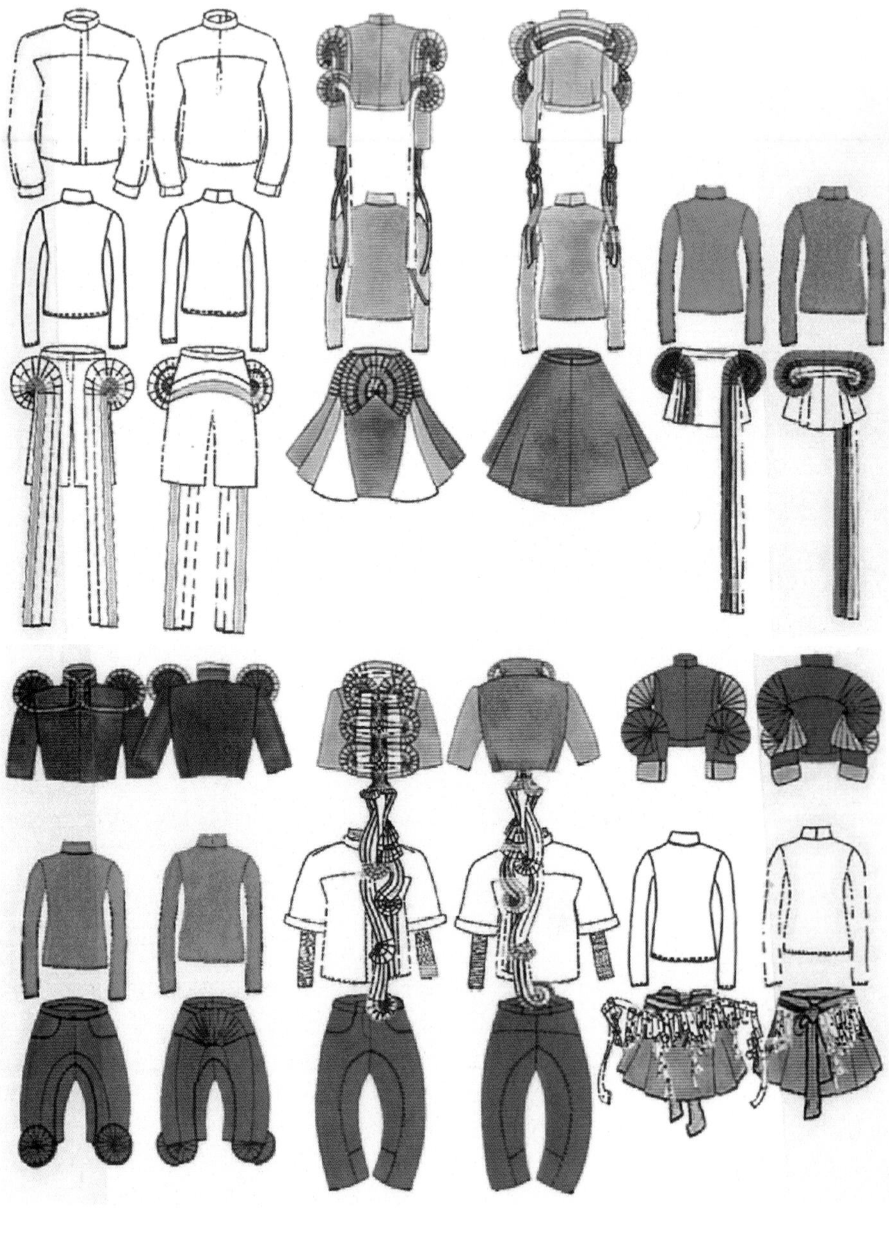

Above
These design developments have been presented in an unusual style: joined in the center by a split pin, the outfits can be fanned out and rearranged to discover which look good together.

Right
These design roughs show the benefit of repetitive design in exploring different detail options. Note how the basic shape of the top is the same throughout, yet small elements such as the neckline or sleeves change with each new design.

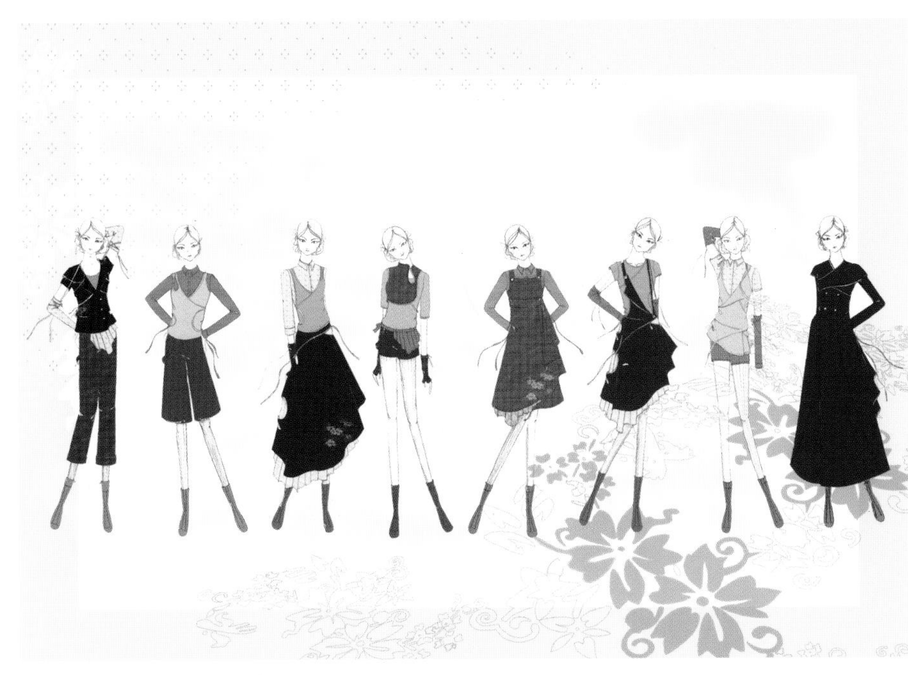

Top
This collection lineup is shown in a clean, uncomplicated style with subtle colors and background patterns enhancing the designs.

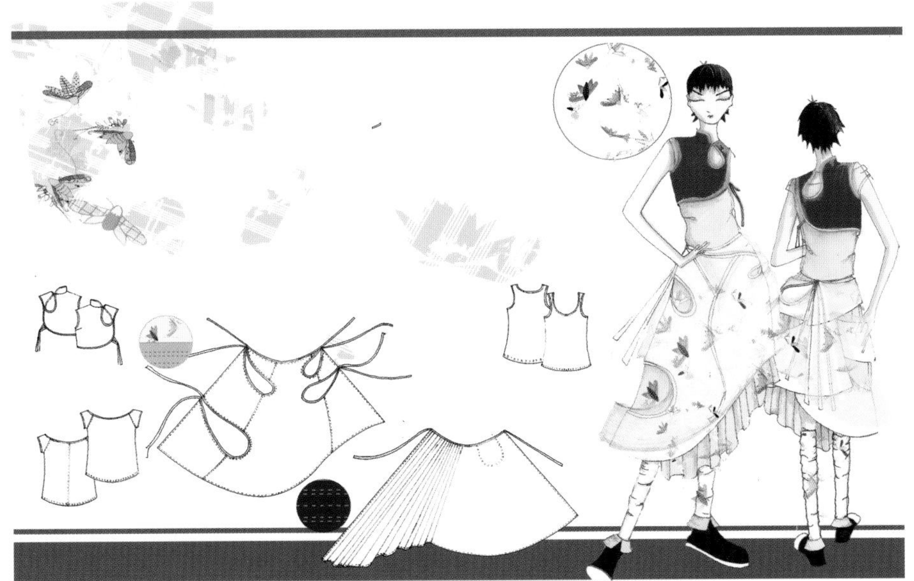

Below
For clarity of understanding, this fashion illustration is accompanied by flat designs of the garments. The precision of the flats (see next page) enhances understanding of the designs and allows the illustration to be freer in style.

methods of displaying a collection. The first image (top) presents the range in a simple but effective outfit lineup. Background patterns and color choices are subtle but clearly emphasize a cohesive collection. The whole collection has been presented on one page, and the viewer can clearly see how the outfits fit together. The poses are simple, with various stances showing off the front of the garments, and the back views could be treated in the same way on another page of your portfolio. The second image shows both the front and back views of the garment, and focuses on the clothes in greater detail. The figure is accompanied by flat designs, which allow the viewer a better understanding of the shape of the garments. Even the pattern detail of the fabric has been emphasized in the circles. The block of color at the bottom of the page gives it grounding, ensuring that the figures look as if they are standing on the floor rather than floating in midair.

FLATS AND SPECIFICATION DRAWINGS

A variety of terms are used to describe the drawing of a detailed garment specification. Flats, working (or technical) drawings, specs (or schematics) all describe the diagrammatic styles of representing an item of clothing. They are two-dimensional drawings of garment construction, showing front, back, and side views with technical descriptions. They also show design details such as topstitching, trims, and pockets. This style of drawing is most often used to accompany a fashion illustration, giving the viewer more information about how the garment is made, to back up its visual description. We saw (on p. 75) how the flats interpreted the illustration. Without them, it would be difficult to imagine the shapes that make up the outfit. Some designers actually work out their design roughs in this way if they find it easier to design ranges flat, rather than on a figure, in order to consider technical aspects as they work. The image (facing page, top left) shows a series of flat designs, created on a computer, accompanying an illustration.

Drawings for flats should be clean, sharp, and precise. This style of accurate drawing is difficult for those who like to draw freely using sketchy lines. Practice drawing clothes from your wardrobe and, to enhance your understanding of your own designs, from your design roughs, too. You will learn about the construction of garment details by drawing them. In particular, practice drawing more complicated details such as trouser seats, collar revers, pleats, pockets, and unusual sleeves.

The simplest way to produce a flat is to sketch a garment in pencil, then draw over the top in black ink. For this purpose, buy a set of fineliners made up of three different nib thicknesses. Use the heaviest to outline the garment, the medium one for the garment structure, and the finest to emphasize the details. The working drawings (facing page, top right) for a coat have been created in this way, with its seams and topstitching clearly identified on both the front and back views. A detailed sketch shows a close-up of the collar construction and the button positioning hidden beneath the lapel. Notice that the proportions are of a realistic body size—scale and accuracy are important for the purpose of this type of drawing, and exaggeration is not appropriate.

In industry and the commercial world, the details indicated in the flat are also shown in a more precise version, known as a spec (specification), or schematic, drawing. For this, a garment's correct specifications are mapped out to the last millimeter. Accurate measurements are added to the drawing, along with details about lining, trims, threads, fusing, and fastenings. A sample specification sheet used in factories (such as the one on the facing page, below) will even have meticulous details about darts, pleats, pocket placement, pattern matching, hems, buttonholes, and pressing. Compiling this information on a sheet, with a detailed spec, means a sample machinist is able to make a garment simply from the information provided. Creating the design from an illustration would be virtually impossible, with the machinist having to make crucial decisions about the garment construction that could differ from the designer's ideas. Specs provide a safety net for all and eliminate the possibility of error. They are also vital in the costing process. From a spec, it is possible to work out all the materials required to make a garment, and cost its production accordingly. Much of this information is compiled using a computer system known as CAD/CAM (computer-aided design/computer-aided manufacture). CAD/CAM systems speed up many of the manual-design procedures and operate specialist-manufacturing machinery efficiently. Specific training is required to be a CAD/CAM operator, but with every detail of the garment logged, it should be simple enough for the garment to be produced anywhere in the world.

Opposite, top left
Flat designs can also be done on the computer, serving the same purpose as hand-drawn flats in allowing the designer to explain technical aspects of the garments.

Opposite, top right
An accurate specification of a coat drawn to scale has been worked using fineliners of varying thickness. More complex parts of the garment, such as the collar, are clearly explained.

Opposite, below
A mock example of an industry-style specification sheet produced using CAD/CAM software, based on the scale drawing above it.

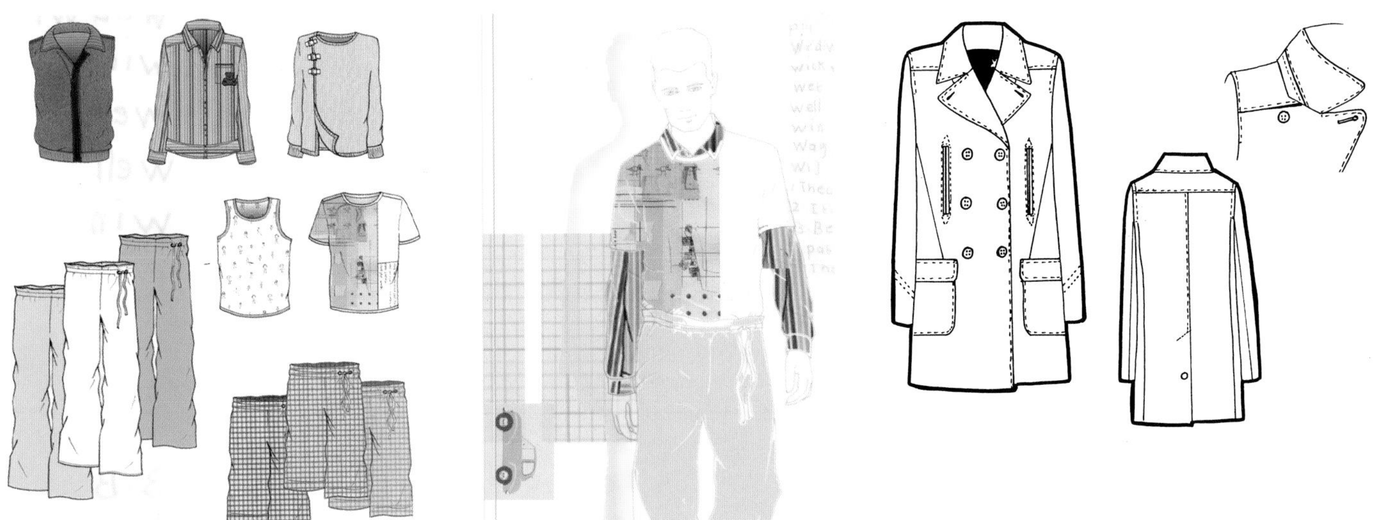

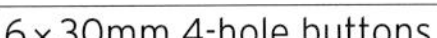

6 x 30mm 4-hole buttons

Top-button placements:
Drill 130mm and 30mm from front edge
540mm from lower hem edge
80mm spacing

Buttonholes:
35mm length
Placement 15mm from collar edge

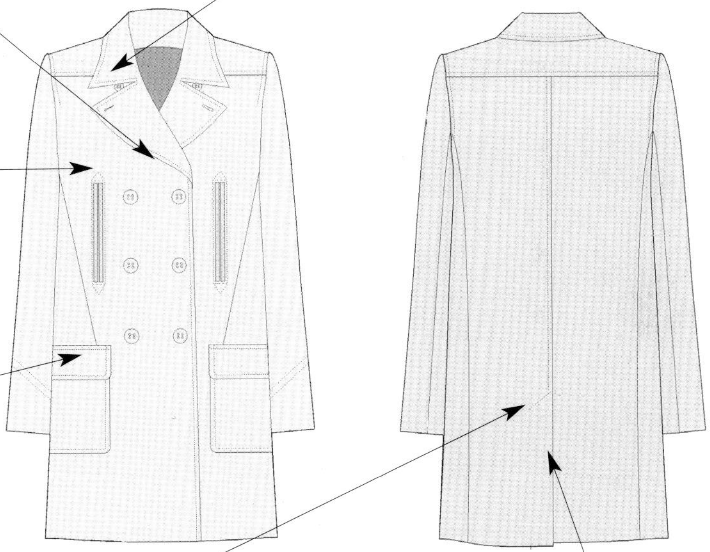

Vertical welt pockets:
120mm length
5mm topstitching and reinforced

Top of welt placement:
560mm from lower hem edge
150mm from front edge

Pockets:
Bag 160mm x 160mm
Flap 65mm x 65mm

Lower pocket edge placement:
110mm from hem
Distance 130mm from front edge

Fabric	Supplier Fabric Code	B 400/T24
Lining	Supplier Code	J 5574N
Fusible Interlining	Supplier Code	J 4671
Thread	Supplier Code	J 70000/F744 120 gauge poly
Topstiching	Supplier Code	J 7741 / F74B 100 gauge poly

Topstiched bar tack reinforcement 50mm

Flap depth 220mm

Classic rever collar with concealed stand

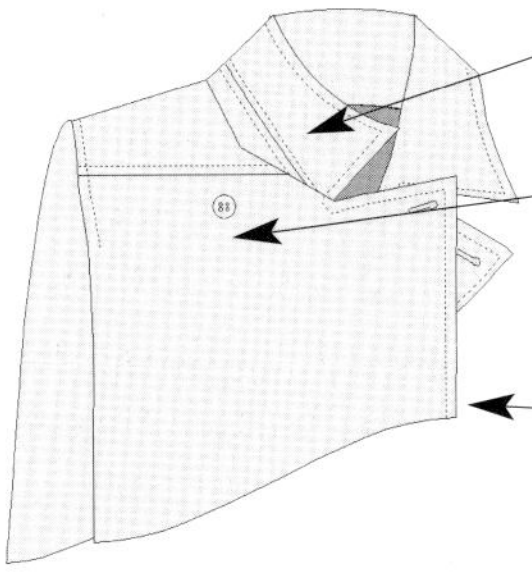

Button placement:
Drill 25mm from saddle seam
150mm from shoulder seam

All topstiching:
5mm from edge/seam
Lockstich 3.5cm per centimetre

Below
These figures are ideal for showing certain fashion garments, such as street- or sportswear, but would be inappropriate for more formal designs, such as tailoring or workwear.

Opposite, top left
On this mood board are displayed some of the defining images that determined the collection designs shown in the following pictures. Notice the links between elements on the mood board and the finished garments.

Opposite, top center
The front and back views of the garments are drawn to specification, with a small thumbnail image showing what the garment will look like on the figure.

Opposite, top right
This illustration, describing the personality of the customer who will wear the clothes, accompanies the accurate specifications for each outfit in the collection.

Opposite, below
The fashion collection has been presented as a clear lineup, featuring six outfits that are stylistically linked by the use of a similar figure template. Altering the pose provides slight variations.

FASHION DESIGN PRESENTATION

As a fashion design student, you are expected, on completion of a project brief, to present not only a fashion illustration but all the design work leading up to it, in a portfolio. If you have planned carefully, then the same color palette, characters, media, and so on will have been used to work through the project, building a cohesive theme for the final artwork.

The four images (facing page) show a selection of pieces from a design student's project brief. Immediately, it is possible to establish some common features that link the work together. The mood board displays some defining images that have influenced the collection designs. The same character runs throughout all four pieces. A similar color palette links the artwork, and a computer has been used throughout. The promotional fashion illustration does not require front and back views of the garments, as the designer has produced accurate specifications of each outfit in the collection. Creating an atmosphere and describing the personality of the customer who will wear the clothes is what this illustration is primarily about. The overall presentation is crisp, original, and, most importantly, professional.

When you work in the industry as a designer, you will have to make presentations to buyers from all types of companies. It doesn't take long to realize that, if you have one specific style of presenting your fashion designs and always stick to it, you will soon be unemployed! Be adaptable in your approach to your work. For example, the fun figures below are highly appropriate for a street-, surf-, or skatewear company, but not for a tailoring firm. Your design presentation should always be driven by a client's market.

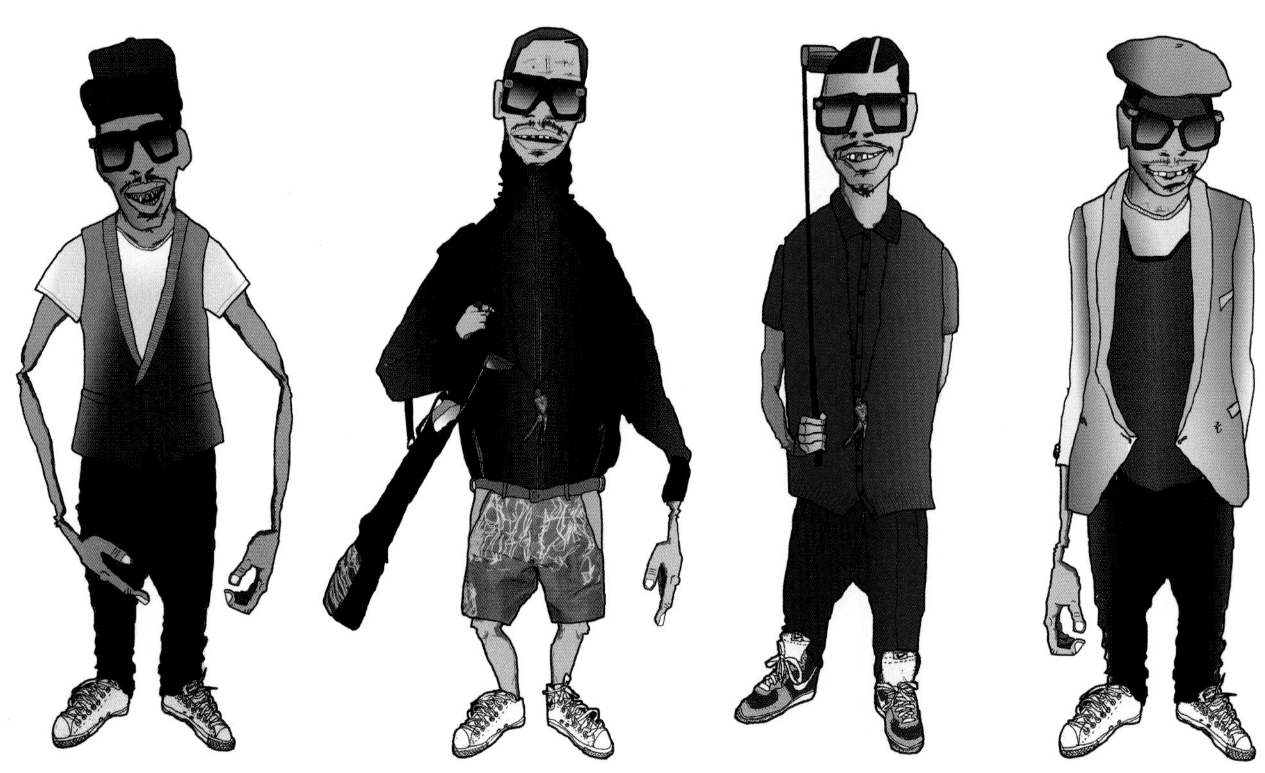

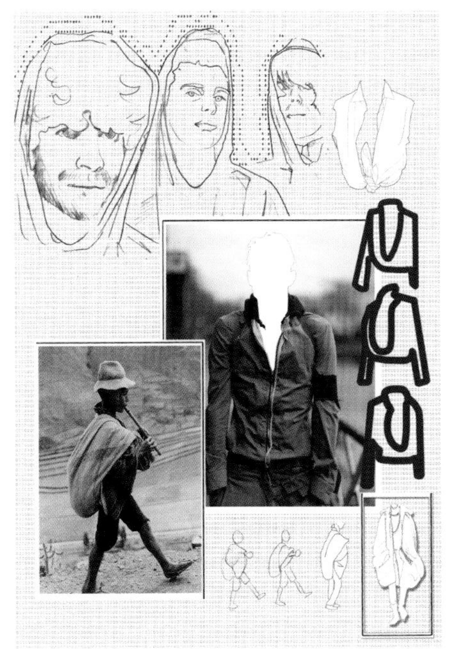

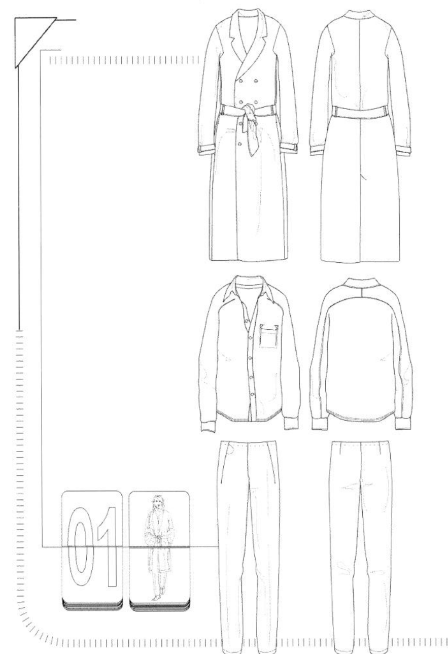
01

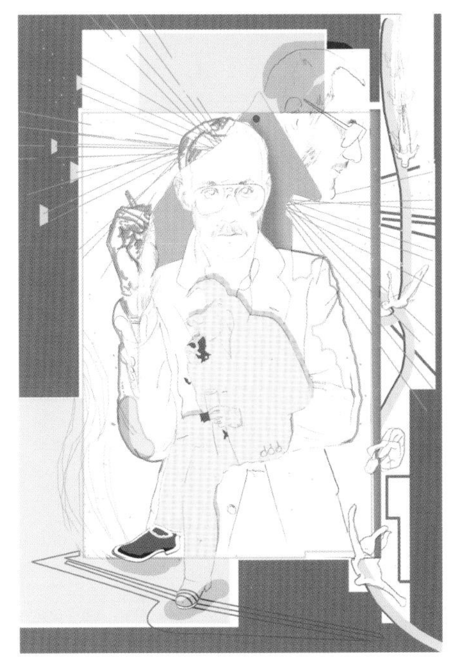

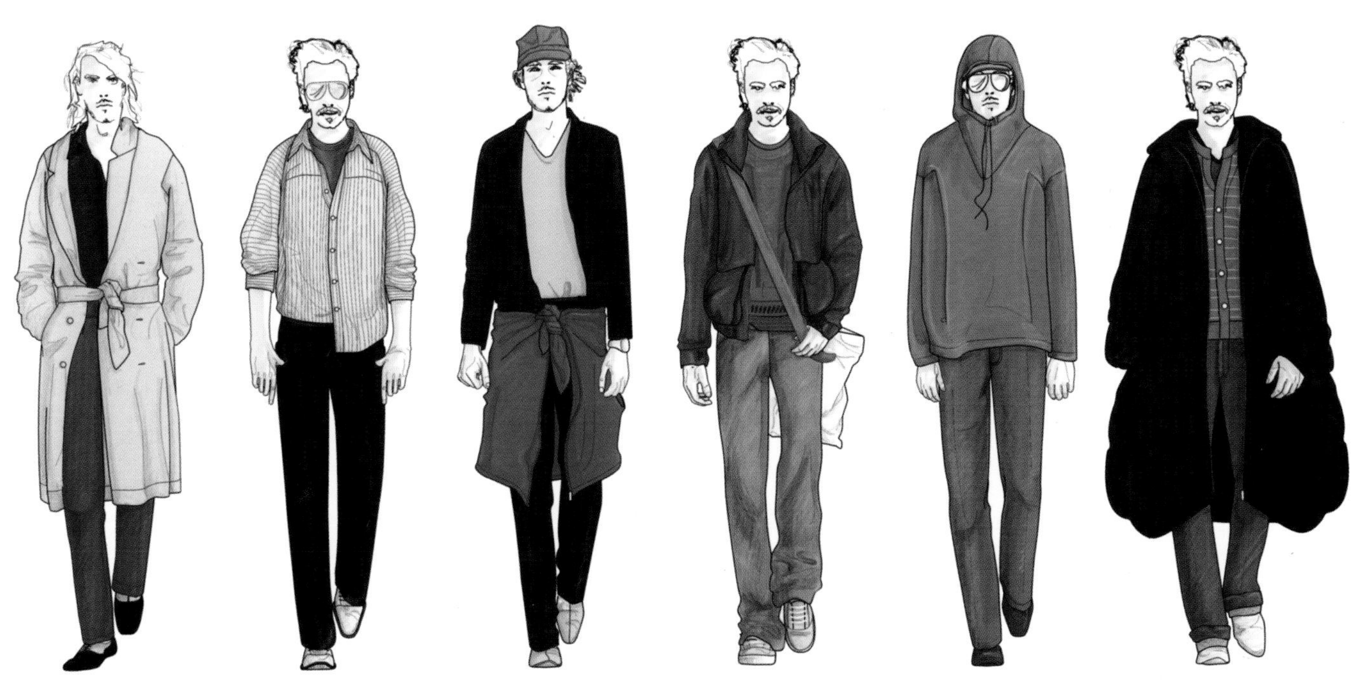

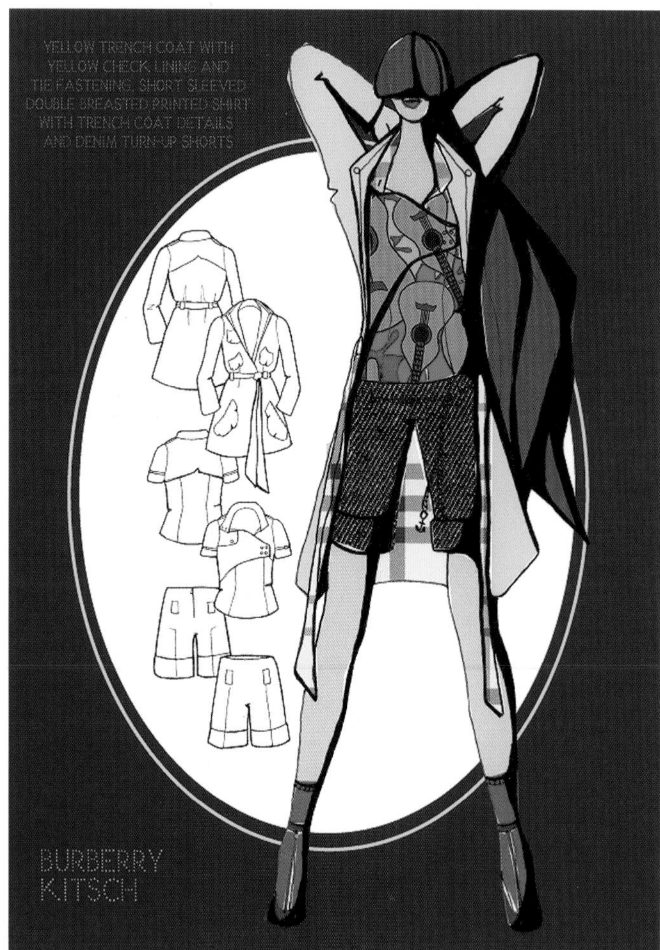

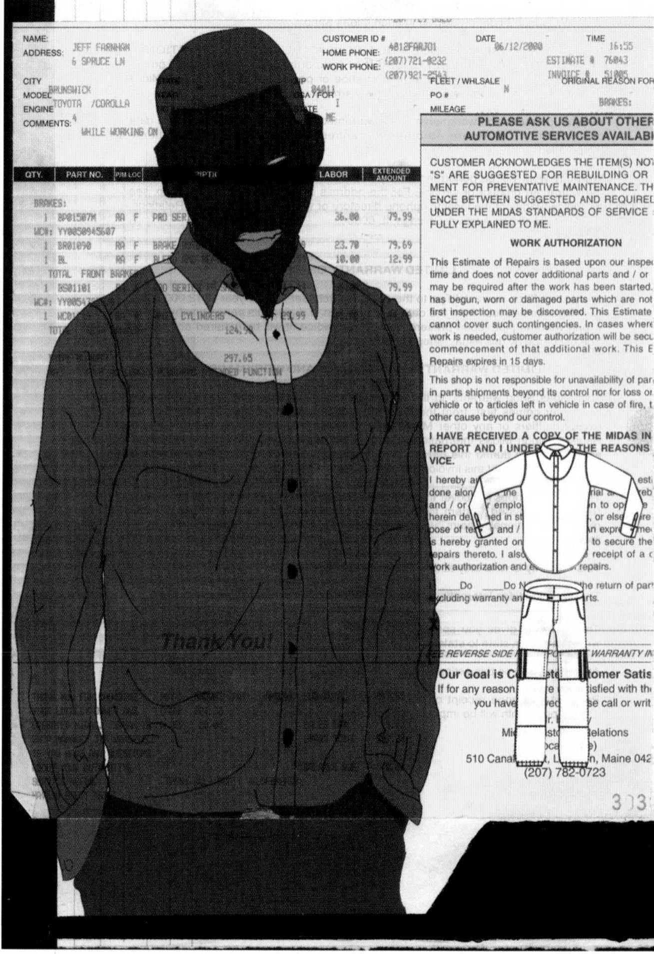

Left
An illustration aimed at selling an outfit should give the buyer comprehensive information in a clear layout—this one answers its purpose perfectly.

Right
Be imaginative in your presentation, and remember that there are many alternatives to the blank white page. This final design is presented on top of a collection of old receipts and bills.

The layout of the design board (above left) is easy for a buyer to understand. It shows the outfit clearly on a figure, but also the front and back details on small flats. The fabrics for the garments have been scanned on a computer and could be presented to the buyer on separate fabric cards. An oval background frames the designs, allowing the viewer to focus on each outfit.

This final design (above right) is enlivened by the humorous approach of using old receipts and bills from the automotive world instead of a blank page for the background. The stance of the figure conjures a relaxed mood for the collection. Detailed specs describe the front views of the garments. Don't forget to include back views too, because a buyer requires every garment construction detail. Always provide the viewer with as much information about your designs as possible. The presentation of your fashion designs could mean the difference between securing a job or not. It is vital that you adopt a professional approach to your work at all times.

HISTORICAL AND CONTEMPORARY FASHION ILLUSTRATION 5

The story of fashion illustration is one of change. Through the last century alone, distinct changes in illustrative styles, and the popularity of the illustrated figure, have taken place. Different drawing styles have emerged, encouraged by the development of new media. Fashions have evolved constantly, and the representation of the fashion figure has altered dramatically. This chapter will examine why these changes occurred and, more significantly, how styles from the past still influence illustrators' work today.

THE BEGINNINGS OF FASHION ILLUSTRATION

Throughout the centuries, artists have been inspired by costume and fabric. Fashion illustrators have depicted the latest fashions, publicizing not only the garments but their creators. As early as the mid-seventeenth century, the detailed and descriptive etchings by Wenceslaus Hollar represented the beginnings of fashion illustration. By the eighteenth century fashion ideas began to circulate via newspapers and magazines in Europe, Russia, and North America. The first engraved fashion plates were published in the *Lady's Magazine* in 1759 and, by the nineteenth century, technical improvements in print meant fashion, and the outward expression of wealth it conveyed, was never out of the press. At the turn of the twentieth century, fashion illustrators were strongly influenced by art movements such as Art Nouveau, Art Deco, and Surrealism. These were instrumental in determining new styles of illustration. During the same period, artists such as Matisse, Degas, Dalí and Toulouse-Lautrec demonstrated a keen interest in what their subjects wore. Their work also had a vast impact on the way that fashions were illustrated.

PRE-1900s

Before the turn of the twentieth century, Alphonse Mucha and Charles Dana Gibson had both begun to make their names by painting beautiful women, and would go on to become famous illustrators of fashion in the new century. Their drawings had a profound effect on the fashions of the time.

Alphonse Mucha created posters in the style of Art Nouveau, with swirling, floating, and twisting lines, and detailed patterns. Mucha's women were languid, with flowing hair and dramatic elegance, and many society women tried to imitate the beauties he portrayed in their styling and dress. In the same way, others

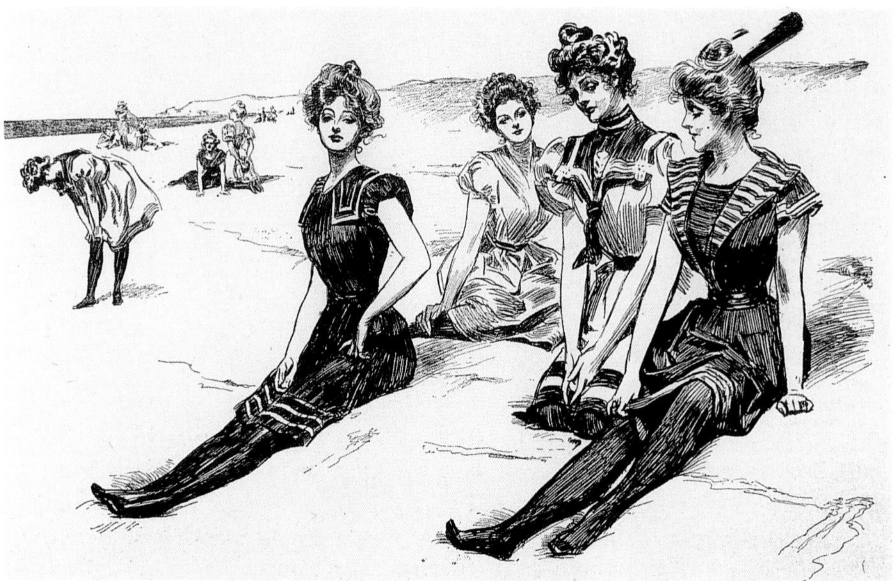

Charles Dana Gibson illustrated for magazines such as *Time*, *Life*, and *Harper's Bazaar*, but it was the creation of the "Gibson Girl" that made him most famous. This character was tall and slender, and said to be based on his thoroughly modern wife. She was realized on stage, endorsed products for manufacturers, and even inspired songs. Women everywhere tried to emulate the "Gibson Girl" by copying her clothes, hairstyles, and mannerisms. This truly shows the influential power of fashion illustration at the time.

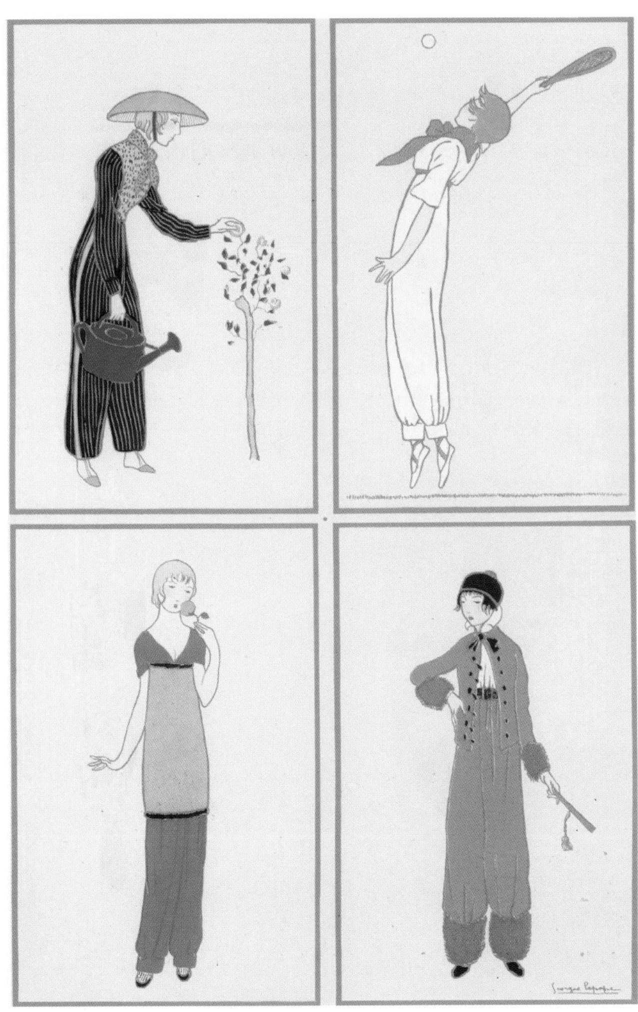

Pochoir images from the book *Les Choses de Paul Poiret* by Georges Lepape. This technique of simple stenciling originated in Japan.

emulated the clothes, hairstyles, and mannerisms of the tall, slender "Gibson Girl" created by Charles Dana Gibson. Gibson first worked with paper cutouts and silhouettes before becoming famous for his pen-and-ink drawings. He illustrated for magazines such as *Time, Life,* and *Harper's Bazaar.*

THE EARLY 1900s

The first 30 years or so of the twentieth century were the golden years of fashion illustration. These were the decades before the photographer and camera took over the task of showing fashion to the world. In the early 1900s, illustrators such as Leon Bakst and Paul Iribe captured the true spirit of the new fashion trends and portrayed them in an individual manner, conveying the mood and hopes of the time.

The elaborate Ballets Russes and its costume designer, Leon Bakst, introduced brightly colored Oriental fashions to the world, challenging the subtle shades of Art Nouveau. The vivid colours of his drawings influenced fashion for years to come. Through Bakst, an enthusiasm for Orientalism, was introduced to fashion, influencing the couturier Paul Poiret to produce his innovative designs. These feature in the colorful fashion illustrations of Georges Lepape, many of which were line drawings, highlighted with watercolor through finely cut stencils. This technique, known as *pochoir,* originated in Japan. Stenciling is a simple form of printing that is still a popular means of adding color to an illustration today.

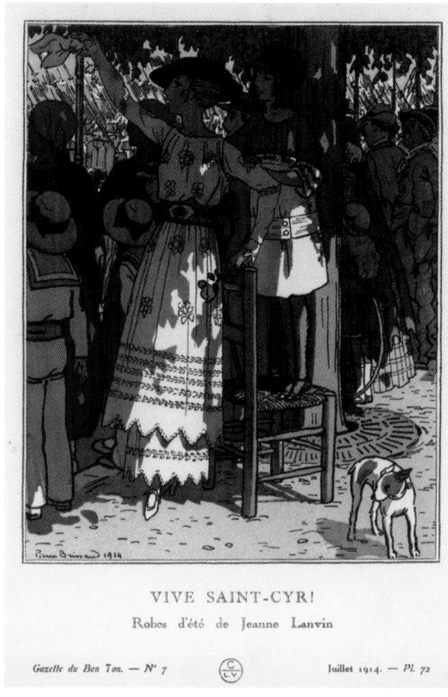

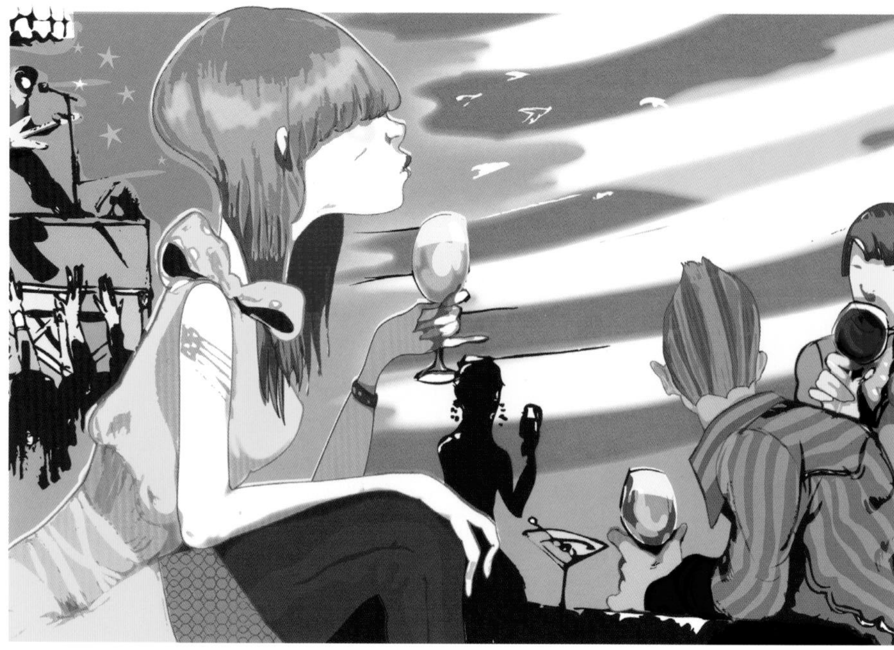

Left
Jeanne Lanvin walking dress (1914) for *La Gazette du bon ton* by Pierre Brissaud, the cousin of Georges Barbier and another advocate of the *pochoir* style. His illustrations often contained more than one figure and depicted social scenes.

Right
Today's illustrators are also fond of showing their fashion figures in a busy environment. Marcus Chin's illustration shows a well-dressed woman at a music gig, sipping a glass of wine, surrounded by other revelers.

THE TEENS

Contemporaries of the illustrators discussed above, Georges Barbier and Pierre Brissaud were French illustrators working for an early fashion magazine called *La Gazette du bon ton*, eventually acquired by Condé Nast. Many of the illustrators later went on to work for the company's prestigious fashion magazine, *Vogue*. Georges Barbier was the chief illustrator. His style owes much to Oriental ballet, theater, and the sinuous lines of Art Nouveau. He also greatly admired the work of Aubrey Beardsley, whose influence can be seen in Barbier's strong outlines and bold figures.

The illustrative styles of the decade from 1900 to 1910 were landmarks in the development of twentieth-century illustration. Many illustrations showed fashions in busy social scenes, a trend followed by some of today's fashion illustrators, including Marcus Chin. Art Deco design also began to feature heavily in illustration, and Cubist geometry influenced the work of illustrators such as Charles Martin. Similar Cubist shapes were revisited in the 1980s by fashion illustrators such as Mats Gustafson and Lorenzo Mattatotti.

The four years of World War I had a significant impact on fashion illustration. Printed journals and magazines declined as a vehicle for fashion illustration, but the film industry grew dramatically. During this decade many fashion and costume designers for stage and film hit the headlines, the most famous being a Russian-born painter known as Erté. Perhaps best known for his elaborate costumes at the Folies Bergère in Paris, Erté also designed many lavish costumes for American movies. His life's ambition to become a fashion illustrator was fulfilled when he signed up with *Harper's Bazaar*, where he continued to contribute fashion drawings for the next twenty years.

THE TWENTIES

World War I was a period of great social upheaval, which had a dramatic influence on culture and the arts. The emancipation of women resulted in a new female image that rejected unnecessary flounces of fabric and impractical ornate frills. Two of the most influential women in the fashion world at this time were Gabrielle "Coco" Chanel and Madame Madeleine Vionnet. Chanel's simple styles, teamed with compulsory costume jewelry, and Vionnet's bias-cut dresses defined a new era. Both designers opened shops in this decade and went on to clothe women for many more.

Until the twenties, the illustrated fashion figure had been drawn with fairly realistic proportions. However, as artwork and fashions became simplified, angular, and linear in the twenties, so too did the fashion silhouette. Illustrations now featured longer and leaner figures. Exaggerated fashion figures appeared in the works of Eduardo Garcia Benito, Guillermo Bolin, George Plank, Douglas Pollard, Helen Dryden, and John Held Jr. In his many memorable covers for *Vogue* in the twenties, Benito captured the essence of the strong, emancipated women who epitomized the decade. His figures were elongated and somewhat abstract in style, appearing in graphic designs enhanced by subtle color contrasts.

The "flapper" became an iconic figure of the "roaring twenties." The cartoons of John Held Jr during the "jazz age" adorned the covers of the *New Yorker* and *Life* magazine. His style, featuring funny dancing cartoon characters with bright backgrounds and humorous scenes, is still mimicked today, and contemporary illustrators such as Stephen Campbell use character and humor in their fashion illustrations too.

Below left
The cartoons of John Held Jr became iconic in the "roaring twenties" and adorned the covers of society magazines.

Below right
Modern illustrators such as Stephen Campbell use personality and character to show off fashionable clothes. Campbell's preferred tool is the computer, to create his popular cartoons.

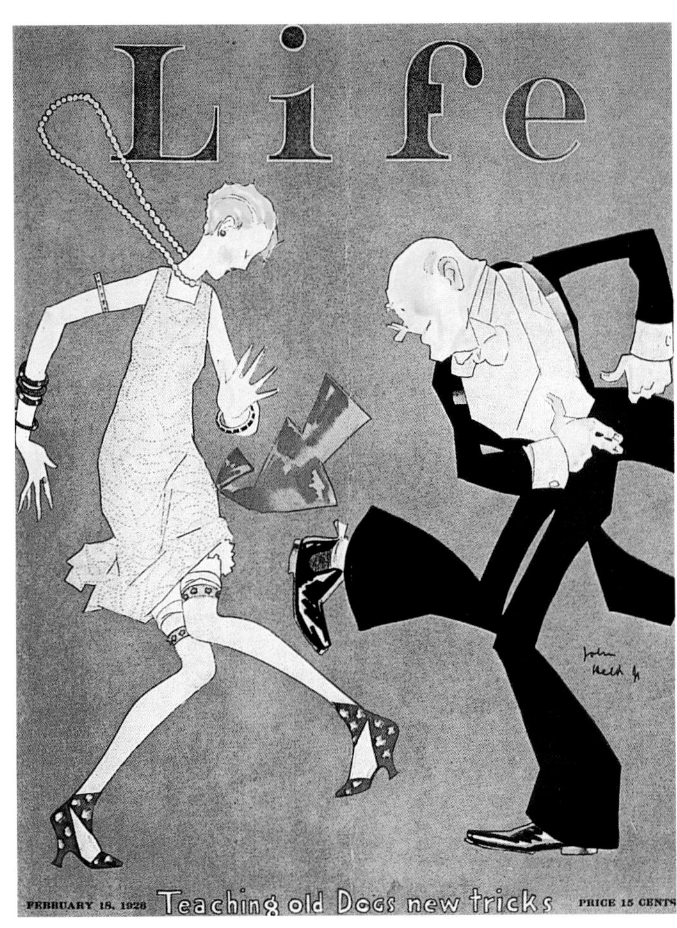

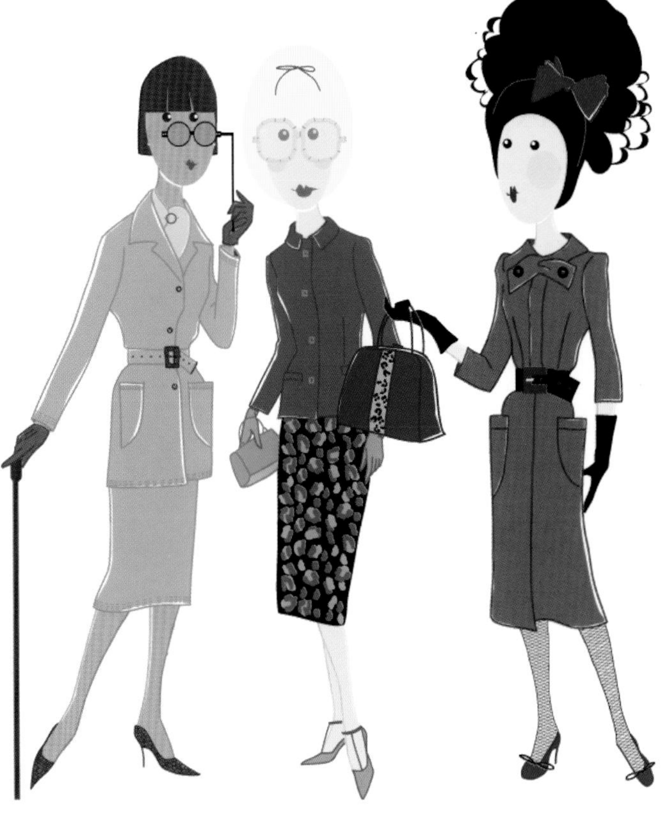

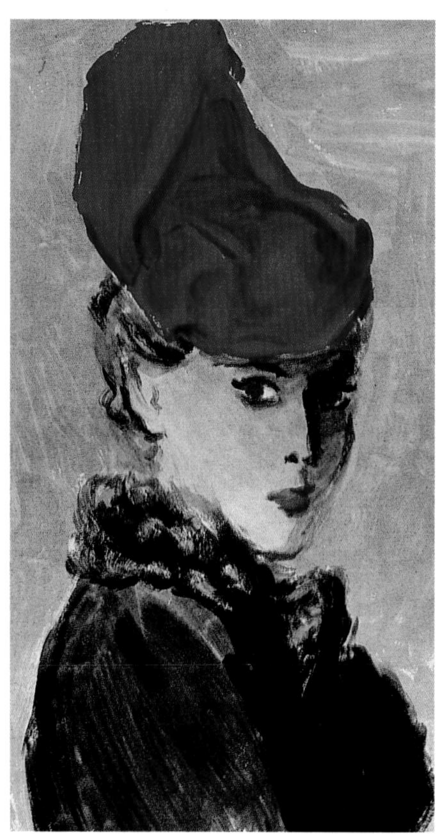

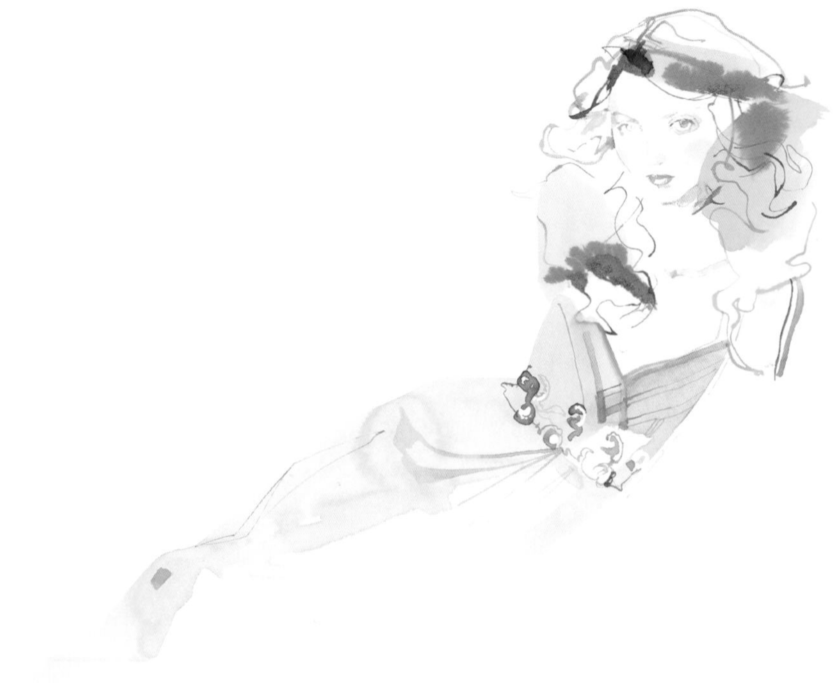

THE THIRTIES

The beginning of the thirties saw fashion magazines truly utilize fashion illustration in both editorial and advertising formats. The fashion silhouette returned to a more realistic feminine form, and drawing lines were softer, textural, and curved. A new romanticism was reflected in the illustrations of Carl Erikson, Marcel Vertes, Francis Marshall, Ruth Grafstrom, René Bouët-Willaumez, and Cecil Beaton.

Carl Erikson, known as Eric, emerged in the thirties as a remarkable draftsman who would become an influential fashion illustrator for the next three decades. Eric represented every detail of garments with the lightest of brushstrokes. An advocate of observing the human figure and capturing the beauty of real life, Eric drew only from life, never memory.

Vertes worked for *Harper's Bazaar* and *Vanity Fair,* his illustrations characterized by an economical use of line and color. He also illustrated the advertising campaign for Schiaparelli perfumes. Today, freelance fashion illustrators still work for advertising companies: the image above right)is an advertisement for the UK women's clothing retailer Topshop by David Downton. Cecil Beaton contributed amusing fashion sketches and cover designs to *Vogue* throughout the thirties but became most famous for Oscar-winning costume designs for stage and screen, and his photographs of Hollywood actresses. Towards the end of the thirties, the fashion photographer began to overtake the illustrator as the camera replaced the paintbrush as the favored means of advertising fashions.

THE FORTIES

During World War II, many European fashion illustrators went to the United States, where there were more work opportunities, and some never returned. The early part of the decade saw illustration styles continuing in the same romantic vein they had embraced in the thirties. Dominating forties fashion illustration, along with Christian Bérard and Tom Keogh, were three illustrators who coincidentally shared

Above left
Eric, cover of British *Vogue*, September 2, 1936. Schiaparelli's flaming red velvet hat and karakul (lamb's wool) scarf streaked with blue-green owe their wit and inspiration to the Surrealists, with whom she was closely involved. Eric's association with *Vogue* lasted for many years, on both sides of the Atlantic.

Above right
Fashion illustrators still contribute to advertising today. This image shows an illustrative advertising campaign for Topshop, UK, by David Downton. Promotional postcards featuring his work were available in the store for customers to take away as a keepsake.

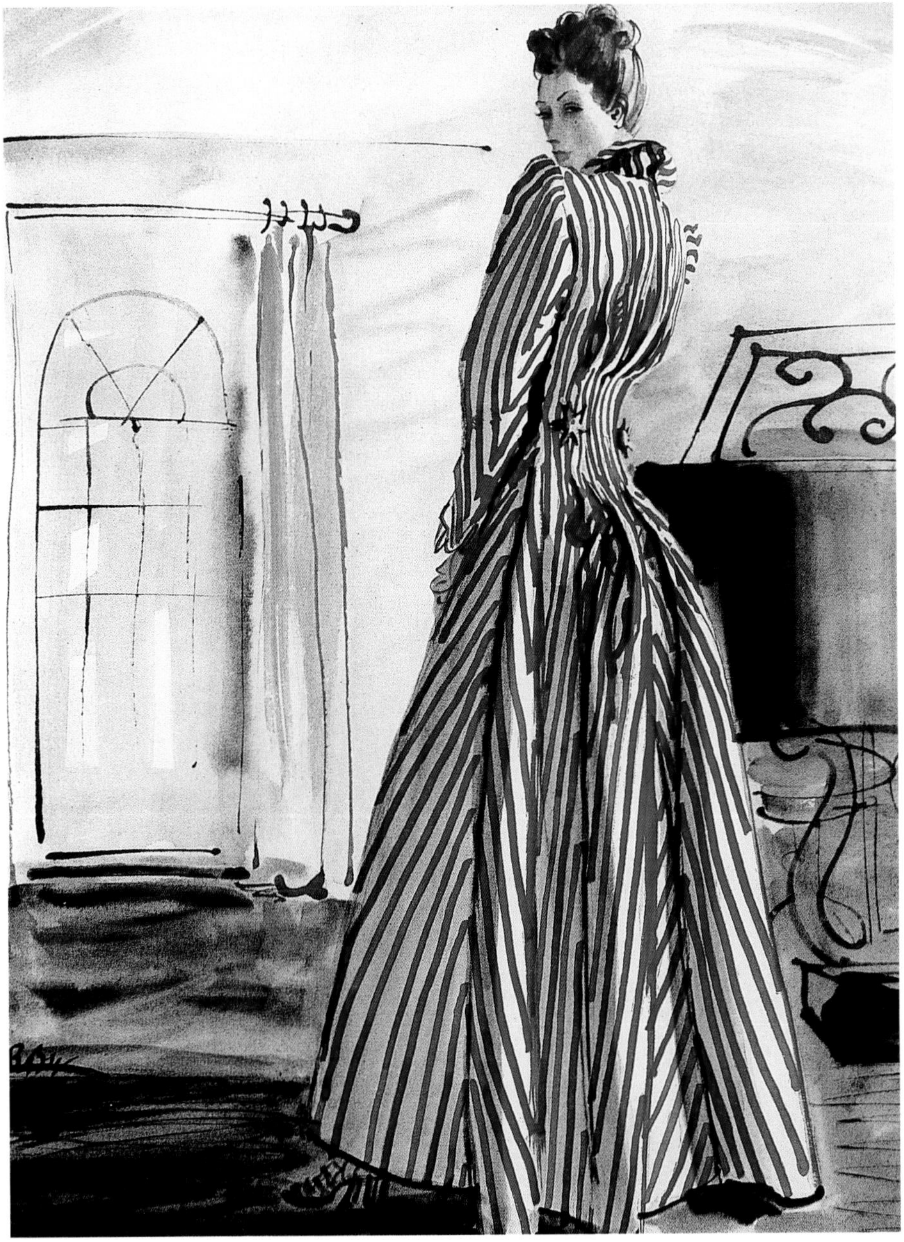

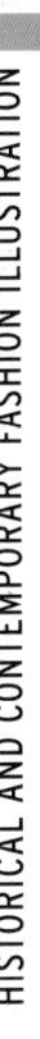

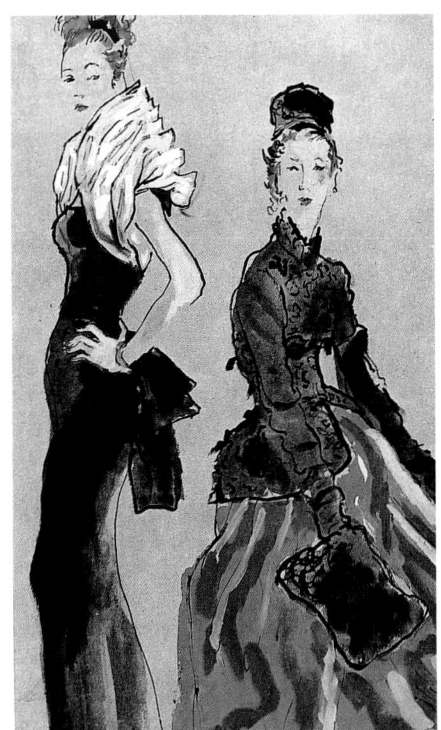

the name René. René Bouët-Willaumez worked for *Vogue* in the thirties but continued throughout the forties using an Expressionist style influenced by Eric. René Bouché began illustrating exclusively in black and white, though in his later illustrations he developed a strong sense of color. His decisive and accurate drawing style was derived from strict observation, and his images often appeared spread across double-page *Vogue* editorials.

René Gruau is perhaps best known for creating the advertisements for Christian Dior's "New Look," establishing a professional relationship with the Dior design house that lasted more than fifty years. He painted in a bold style, influenced by Picasso and Matisse, using black brushstrokes to outline the form, minimal detail but a generous amount of movement and shape. Gruau's style gives the illusion of speed and hastiness. However, he admitted that he completed at least thirty preparatory sketches before creating an illustration. A lesson to us all.

Left
René Bouët-Willaumez was influenced by Eric but refined his own style through adventurous use of color, swift, sharp hatching, and vigorous shading. His illustrations had a dramatic sense of style and commanded space on the pages of *Vogue* for many years.

Above
René Bouché had a firm and accurate drawing style that derived from strict observation. He used pen and ink or crayon, and cleverly merged the character of the garments with that of the wearer, as in this example from 1945. Bouché had a strong sense of color, and he passed on his knowledge to fashion illustration students at Parsons School of Design in New York, where he taught during the forties.

THE FIFTIES

Following the war, the fifties were a time of development and increased affluence. Technological advances introduced plastic, Velcro, and Lycra, creating for illustrators the challenge of representing new synthetic fabrics. The glamorous life depicted in the movies and on television showed up-to-date images of beauty, and the use of illustration began to decline. However, many illustrators from previous decades continued to work in the fifties, while new artists such as Kiraz and Dagmar arrived on the scene.

A self-trained artist, Kiraz, who emerged in the fifties, still illustrates fashion today. From Cairo, he moved to Paris, where he drew sexy, sophisticated Parisians as cartoon-style characters. His method of illustrating personality as well as fashion has influenced many contemporary illustrators such as Jason Brooks, who draws gorgeous comic-book girls with character. Dagmar had a simple, clear-cut, and direct approach to representing fashion. She worked at *Vogue* for twenty years, her modest graphic approach distinguishing her from some of her predecessors.

THE SIXTIES

In the "swinging sixties," youth culture was predominant, and being young, carefree, and abandoned was the fashionable ideal. The emergence of the teenager in the late fifties meant that fashion acquired a younger, modern look. Illustration poses altered from demure to witty and dynamic. However, the fashion illustrator had become less important than the photographer for magazines, so much so that photographers and models became celebrities in their own right.

Just one illustrator shone like the stars of illustration from previous decades—Antonio Lopez. His versatility meant that he went on to illustrate for the next three decades, but it was in the hedonistic sixties that he truly made his mark. Through his illustrations he portrayed the rebellious attitude of the young generation and reflected fashion as it took center stage in this colorful, visual decade. His wide imagination led him to experiment in every possible style, using a wealth of media and techniques. Each season, he tried a new illustrative technique, discarding styles as they became popular and were taken up by others. He was, and still is, a great influence on fashion illustrators.

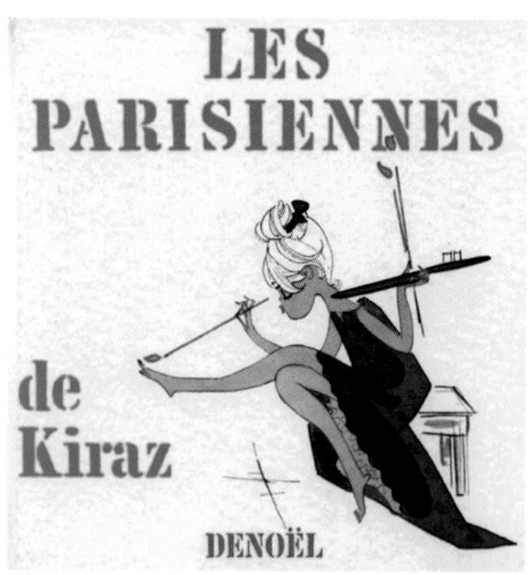

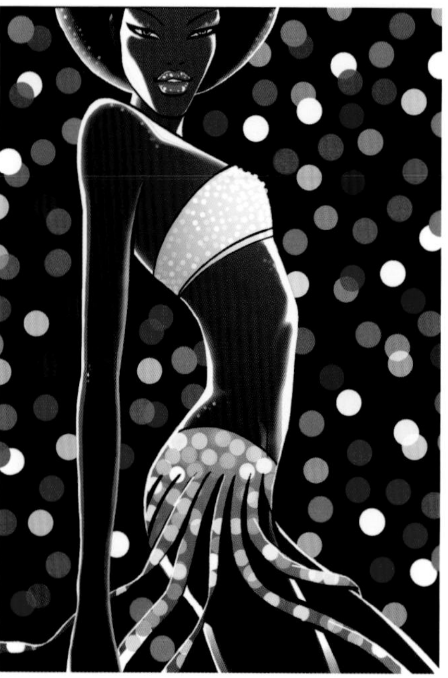

From top
Kiraz is a self-trained artist who emerged in the fifties. The sexy, sophisticated *Les Parisiennes* cartoon characters from his books became his trademark, as seen in this cover of 1953, and he still illustrates fashion today.

Jason Brooks works digitally, yet draws from historical influences such as Kiraz, to capture his infamous comic-book girls. This is a computer-generated flier for the London nightclub Pushca.

Opposite
In the hedonistic sixties, Antonio Lopez's fashion illustrations showed the rebellious attitudes of the generation. His huge imagination meant that he drew in every style possible, using a wealth of media and techniques. Here, we see how the background and furniture play just as important a part in his 1964 artwork as the figure.

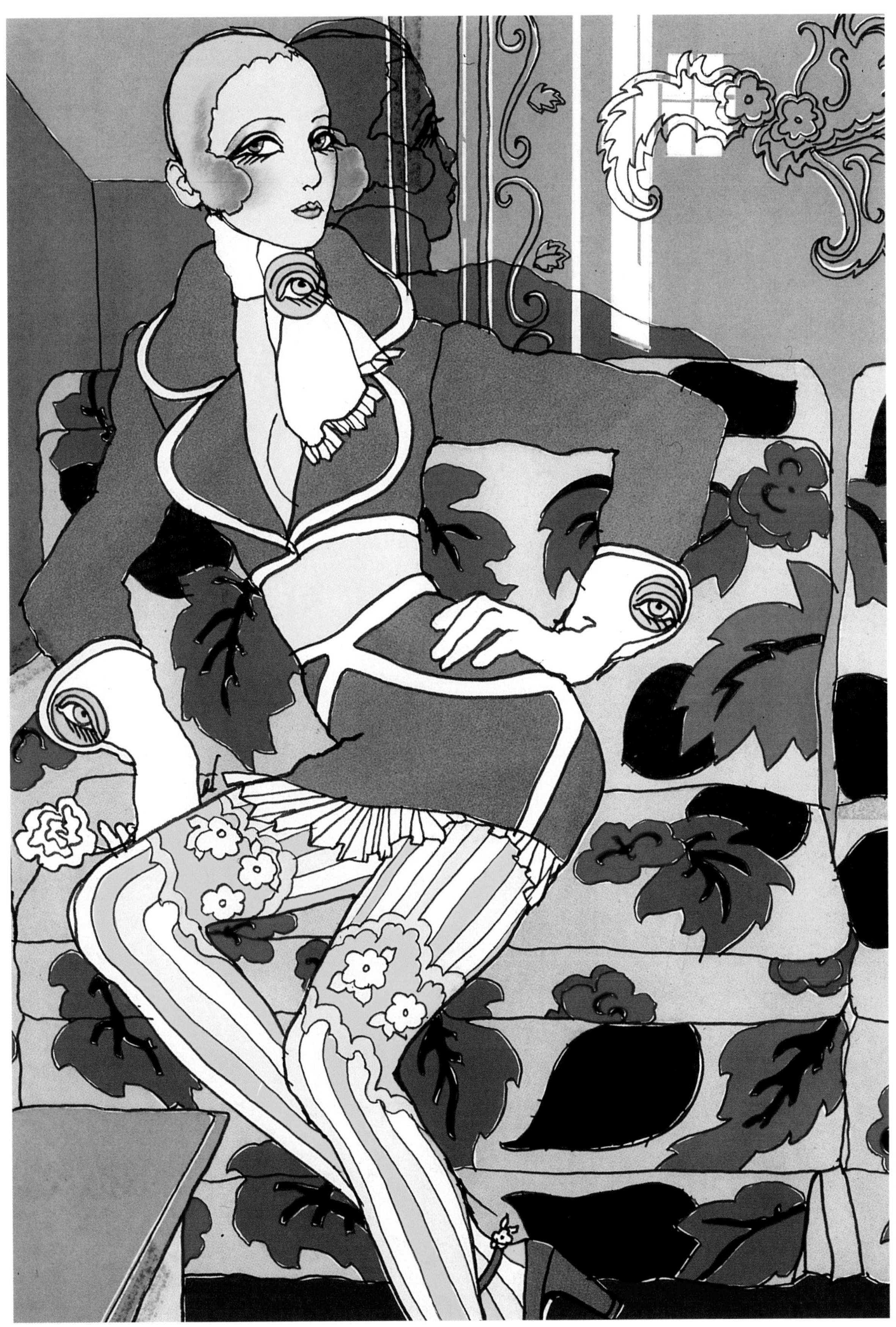

An illustration in watercolor by Tony Viramontes for an advertising campaign for Valentino couture.

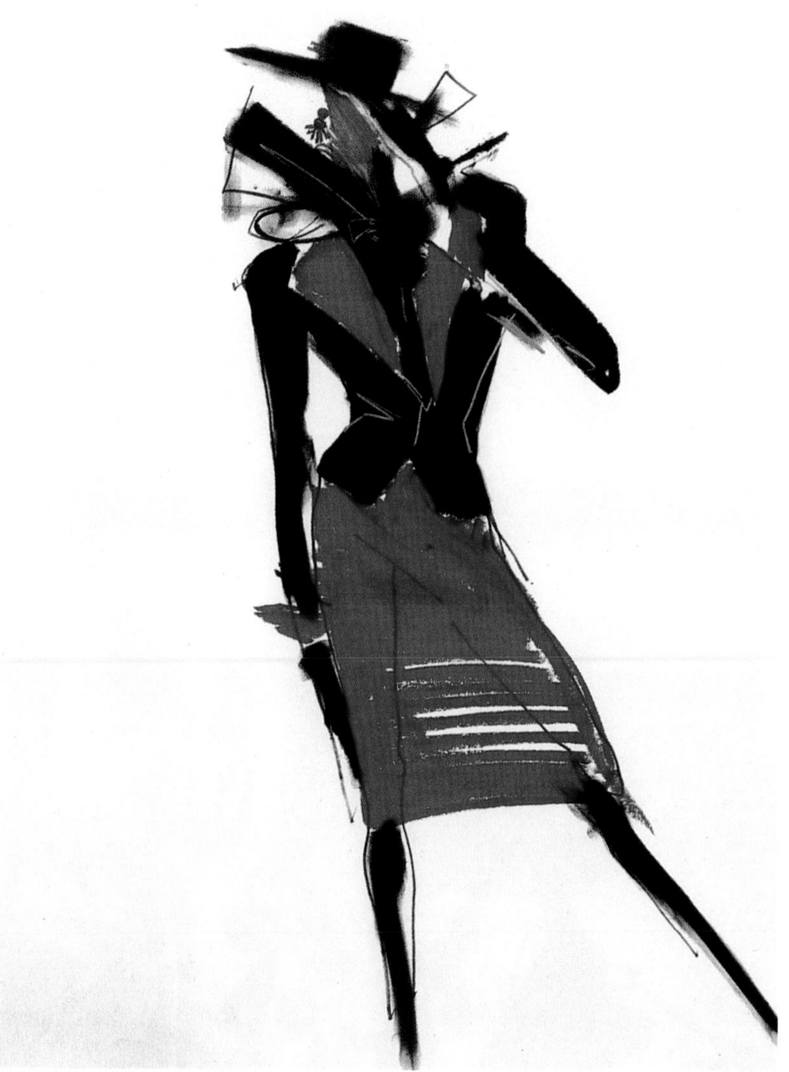

THE SEVENTIES

In the seventies, photography still dominated fashion editorials and advertising. Antonio Lopez continued to work, however, and was joined by a variety of new illustrators influenced by Pop Art and Psychedelia. In the early part of the decade, illustrations featured dramatic colors and bold patterns. New ideas were developed by illustrators such as Lorenzo Mattatotti, Mats Gustafson, and Tony Viramontes, whose striking images began to make their mark in the fashion world.

By the latter part of the seventies a highly finished realism emerged in illustration. This is evident in the work of David Remfrey, whose pen-and-ink drawings colored with a faint watercolor wash show realistically rendered women. The artist's straightforward technique captures the sexy, bold women of the era. Remfrey most recently illustrated the successful Stella McCartney advertising campaign with nostalgic, seventies-inspired drawings.

THE EIGHTIES

Th eighties saw the emergence of a style so distinctive it seemed impossible that fashion illustration would not return with a vengeance. The large shoulders and harsh angles of the fashionably dressed were crying out to be drawn by the great illustrators of the decade. Makeup was expressive, and poses were theatrical—a perfect excuse for fashion illustration to creep back into magazines.

Antonio Lopez once again answered his calling to epitomize the men and women of the time. He did so alongside illustrators such as Zoltan, Gladys Perint Palmer, and Fernando Botero, who were all producing innovative and experimental work.

Zoltan was one of the first illustrators to produce a series of fashion images ranging from three-dimensional photo-drawing montages to collage with found objects. He used fabrics, flowers, gemstones, and inorganic or organic materials to re-create fashion in the same way that illustrators had previously become more liberal in their choice of artistic materials. Palmer illustrated for magazines and various advertising campaigns for Vivienne Westwood, Oscar de la Renta, Missoni, and Estée Lauder. A well-known artist in the eighties, when asked to capture the French fashion collections, Fernando Botero did not alter his artistic style. The result was a series of fashion illustrations featuring large, rounded, voluptuous women. He confronted the view that "fat" can never be "beautiful" by illustrating high fashion with delightful results.

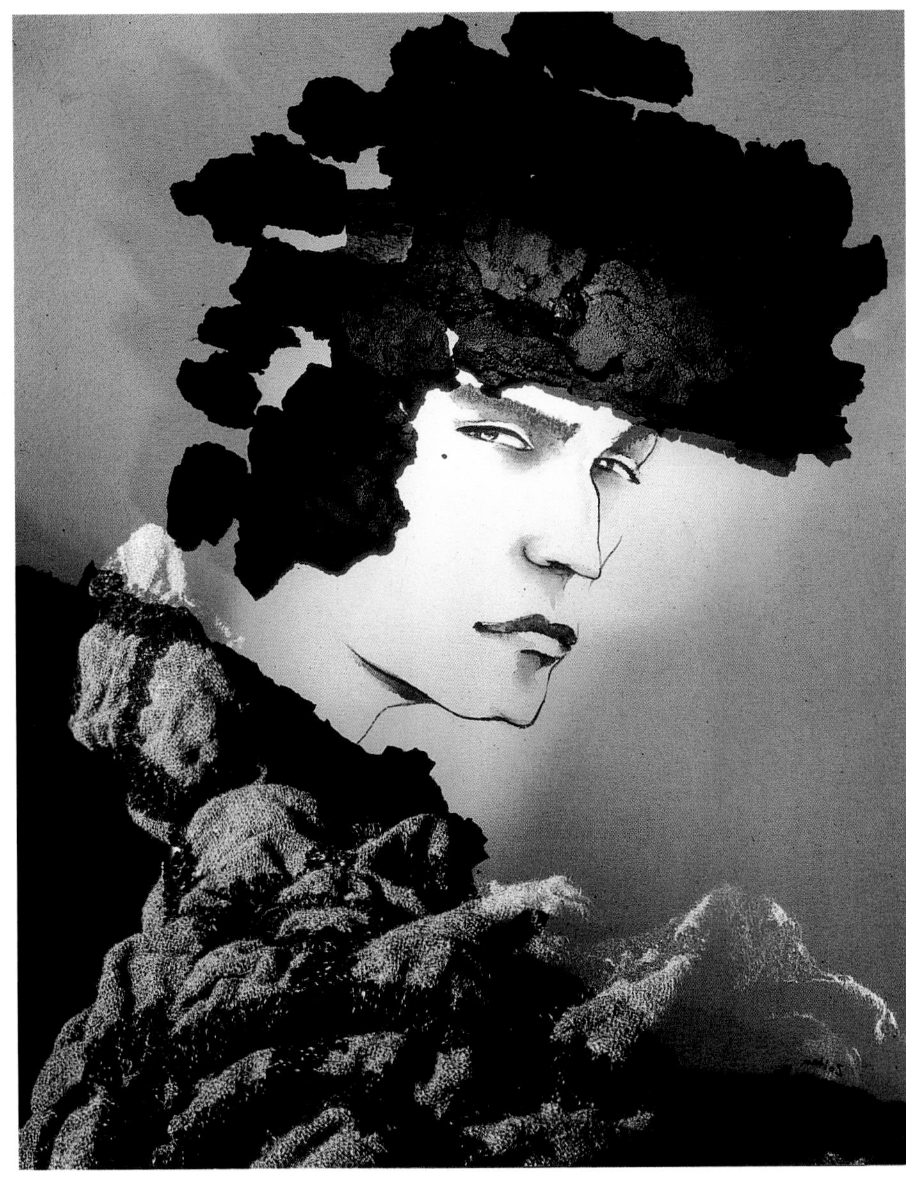

Zoltan became famous for his three-dimensional photo-drawing montages and collages of found objects. He represented fashion with a creative choice of artistic materials.

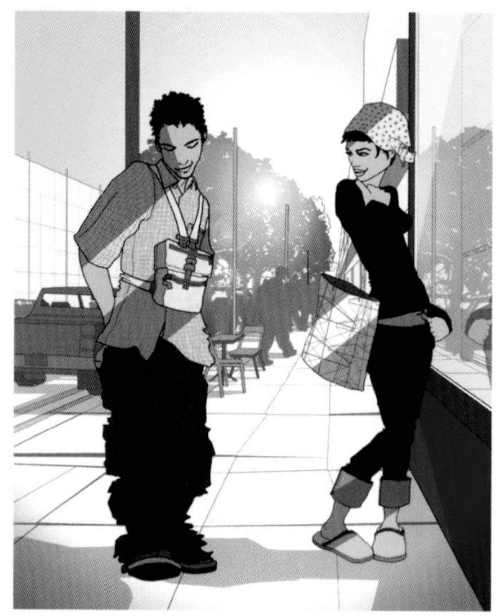

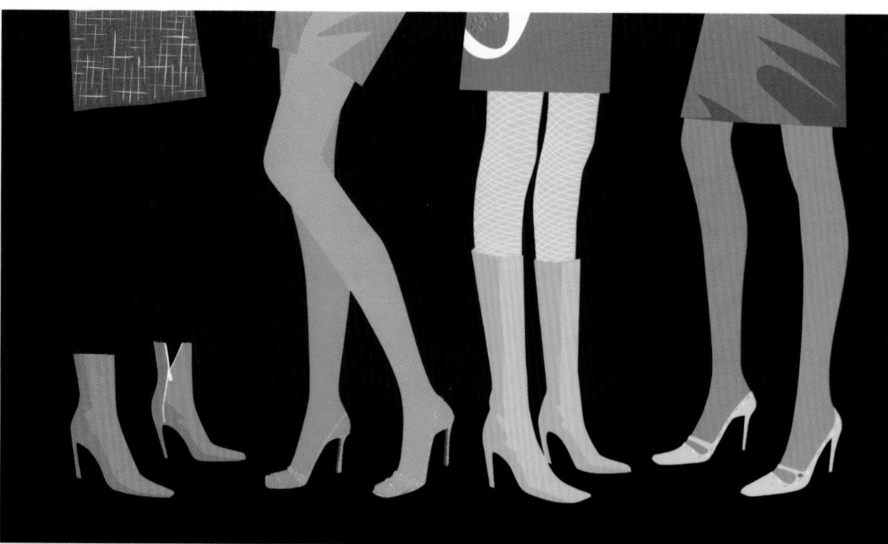

Above
Graham Rounthwaite's street kids show how, by the late nineties, fashion illustration began to depict real people rather than focusing solely on the perfection of fashion models.

Right
The digital age could not be more clearly outlined than by the work of Jason Brooks. His Pushca fliers became collectibles, and his illustrative style is instantly recognizable even when you only see legs and feet!

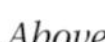

THE NINETIES

By the end of the twentieth century fashion illustration was no longer considered the poor relation of photography but instead a credible rival to it. Illustrators such as Jason Brooks, François Berthold, Graham Rounthwaite, Jean-Philippe Delhomme, and Mats Gustafson spearheaded illustration's comeback.

Berthold created a series of fashion illustrations that challenged previous styles. He presented cropped illustrations so that the head, shoulders, calves, and feet were missing. The viewer's full attention was thus given to the garments illustrated.

Computer-generated images and digital technology in the nineties signified a boomtime for illustration. There were illustrators who created small subcultures with intense fashionable followings: Brooks produced his computer-generated fliers for the nightclub Pushca, and Rounthwaite created a set of New York street kids generated on a Mac. His ads for Levi's were projected onto huge billboards on the sides of buildings—a true sign that illustration was back in town. Moreover, illustrations of the emerging, couture-clad supermodels by the likes of David Downton were splashed across every newspaper and magazine.

CONTEMPORARY FASHION ILLUSTRATION SHOWCASE

The turn of this century has brought about a new world that reflects on the old. Traumatic terrorist events and natural disasters have encouraged society to crave the comfort and safety of the past. There is an increasing desire to look back to old-fashioned values and explore bygone days.

Advances in technology will always improve and develop the artistic performance of fashion illustrators, but the return to safe traditional methods has brought about a new way to work. Today's illustrators use established handcrafted techniques such as drawing, embroidery, or collage and mix them with their digital counterparts to create a modern medium.

The next section provides an in-depth look at a selection of contemporary fashion illustrators from the twenty-first century. It focuses on their varied use of media and examines the way they clothe the body in art. Through a series of questions and answers, the illustrators explain what inspires them, how they create their work, and what it means to them to be a fashion illustrator.

RICHARD GRAY

What inspires you?
My inspirations change constantly according to whatever is appropriate to the commission I am currently working on. However, I would say that music is very inspirational when it comes to creating a mood for work: P.J. Harvey, Lamb, and Patti Smith are always good to work to. The artworks of Aubrey Beardsley, Leonora Carrington, and Dupas, or the beautiful illustrations of Benoit, Erté, and Antonio Lopez are very inspirational. I am lucky enough to have very creative friends who are kind enough to model for me. To work with them on projects is always completely inspiring and a real pleasure.

Are you interested in fashion?
I am very interested in fashion design. I studied fashion at Middlesex University and, although it was always quite obvious that fashion illustration was my main interest, I would have been perfectly happy to have followed a career in fashion design. Fashion is still the main focus of my illustration work, although it is not confined to fashion by any means. Great fashion designers with real intuition and true creativity are incredible to work with. They are such a catalyst for ambitious creative work.

Describe your work.
My work is very narrative, whether the logic of it is always apparent or not. My portfolio has a broad range of styles in it. I have never felt it necessary to confine myself to a single style, when I enjoy working in so many different ways.

Which media and techniques do you use?
I use gouache, pencil, airbrush, collage, and ink. I resolutely do not use the computer to do my work. Although there is some incredible computer-based work around, I really need to physically draw a pencil line or paint a brushstroke to make those dynamics. I much prefer to see the physical creation of artwork, even if it means there are mistakes, rather than something that may appear perfect but is homogeneous. I like to be able to work with spontaneity.

What, for you, makes a successful fashion illustration?
Something truly reflective of the illustrator's personality, inspired by the creativity of a designer's work, without losing the essence of either.

What artistic training have you undertaken?
BTEC National Diploma in General Art and Design at Great Yarmouth College of Art and Design (UK), and BA Hons in Fashion at Middlesex University (UK).

If you could give one piece of advice to a student, what would it be?
A good career is made from luck and opportunity, as much as it is from talent. Make your illustrations accessible to those who can appreciate, support, and use your work.

Describe yourself and your greatest achievement.
I am fortunate enough to have made a successful career from something I greatly enjoy doing.

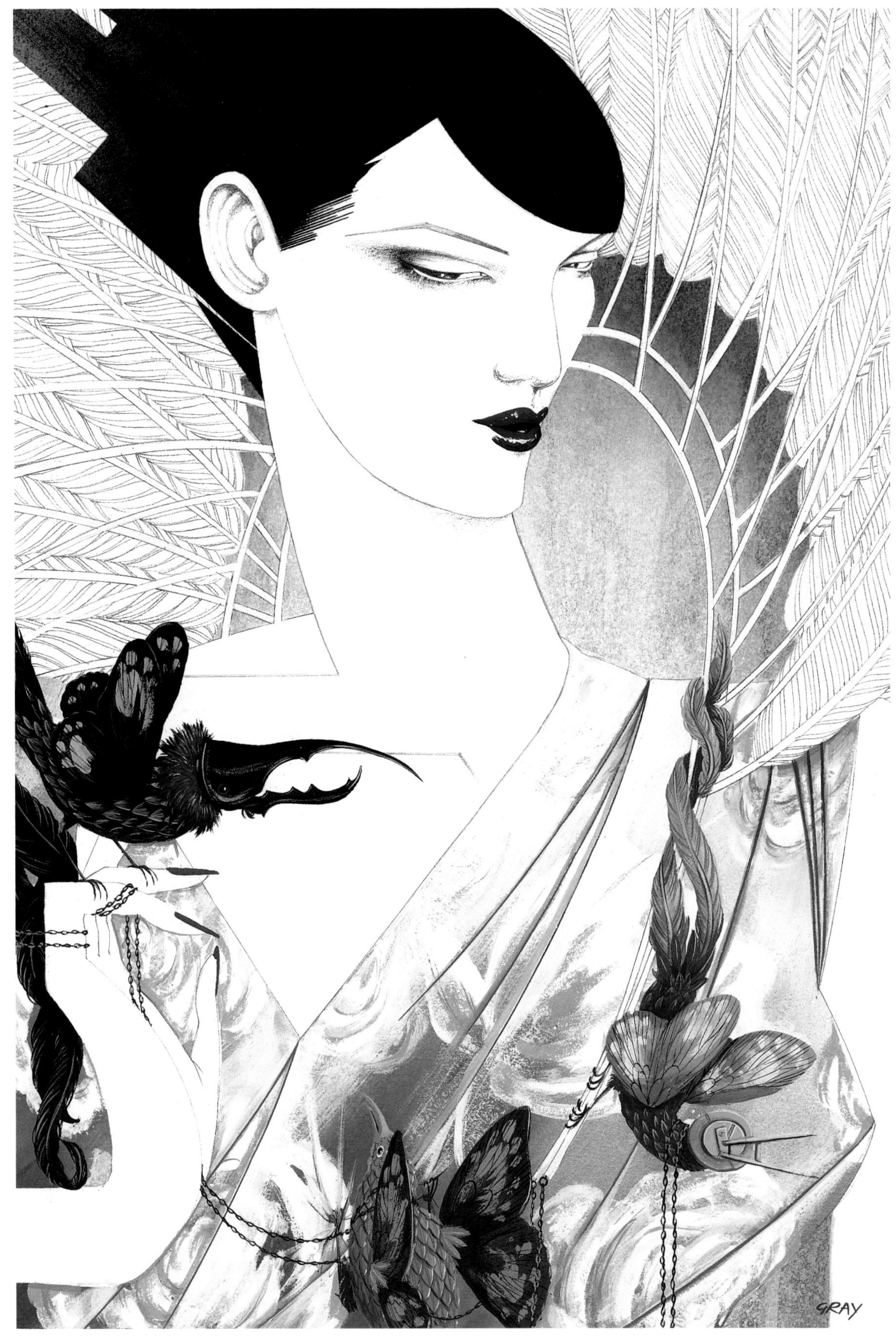
GRAY

PETER CLARK

What inspires you?

Looking everywhere and at everything! This can fire one's imagination. From a cloud to a piece of squashed chewing gum on a pavement; color next to color; or people-watching. Absolutely anything looked at with an open eye.

Are you interested in fashion?

Yes, the necessary constant changing is interesting in itself—the way clothes are worn or placed on a body can set one's imagination sprinting. How different garments affect people and their behavior is also fun.

Describe your work.

I use a comprehensive collection of found papers as my palette in my collages. These are colored, patterned, or textured by their printed, written, or worn surfaces. With these media, I "paint" my collages. I shade with density of print and create substance and movement with lines plucked from old maps or manuscripts. My pieces try to use mark-making in an innovative and humorous way to create a collection of clothing that exudes character and wit.

Which media and techniques do you use?

Paper collage is the source of my creativity. I prefer to use old paper because of the way that it can be manipulated, and I prefer the colors and texture. I also occasionally use fabric and metal, as nothing is actually ruled out.

What, for you, makes a successful fashion illustration?

One that gives a feel of the hero [garment] and hopefully adds movement and visual excitement in its execution.

What artistic training have you undertaken?

I was given great encouragement to look and draw at primary school. Secondary school then added belief in one's ability and also the first chance to deal with rejection. This was followed by a fabulous time of discovery and technique, learning at Manchester College of Art and Design (UK). I then worked in television and animation in the UK and the USA before developing my current working style in the UK and Europe.

If you could give one piece of advice to a student, what would it be?

Look, draw, and don't let anyone grind you down.

Describe yourself and your greatest achievement.

Be patient—I'm not there yet!

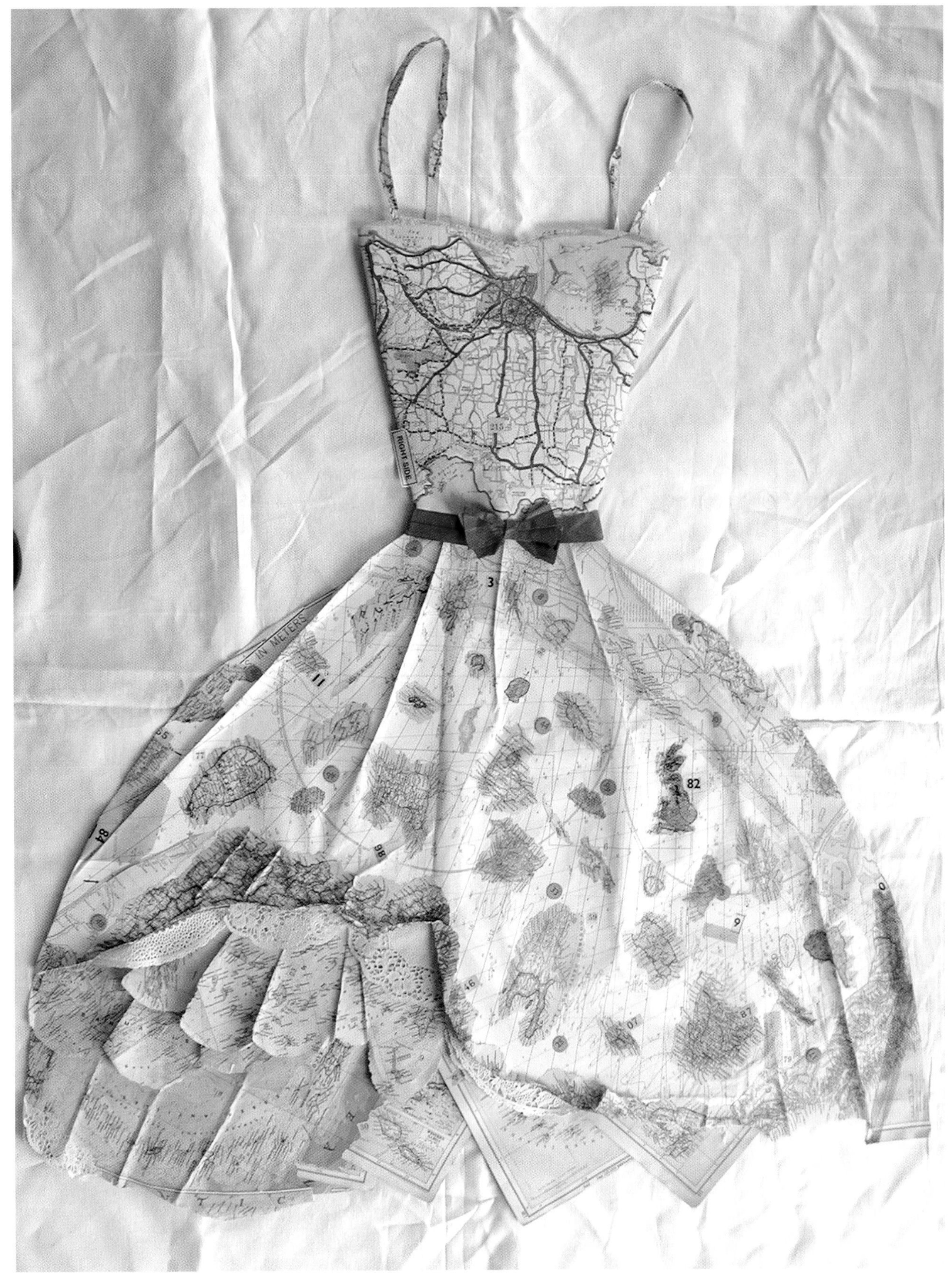
RIGHT SIDE
IN METERS
82

REBECCA ANTONIOU

What inspires you?
An eclectic mix of "good stuff." When my eyes are open, anything is up for grabs. It's a very colorful world we live in.

Are you interested in fashion?
My roots are in fashion. I studied fashion design for three years and worked as a designer for seven, so really I came into illustration from a fashion perspective. Fashion, by nature, is always about the future and looking ahead, so it's natural for me as an illustrator to think in the same way. I'm always looking for something new, something different. From a drawing standpoint, it's much easier to illustrate something when you understand it, say, how certain fabrics behave or how a garment would drape or fit. With fashion illustration, you definitely have to be a little bit of a stylist too. Without this experience, I don't think my work would be anything like it is today.

Describe your work.
It's an amalgamation of things. I've always loved the beauty and delicacy of Art Nouveau and, at the other end of the spectrum, the boldness of Constructivism. In my work, there's definitely an element of each of these, of intricate patterns and very graphic compositions. I like to throw a lot of elements into my work. Color, texture, nature, and ornamentation all play a part. In the end, my work is a melting pot, and it's always interesting to see the outcome of all these different influences, of how you can bring opposites together and create something new. The wonderful thing about illustration is that there really are no boundaries.

Which media and techniques do you use?
Predominantly Photoshop along with pencil, paper, photos, magazine tearsheets and fabric. Basically, anything I can scan in, sample, and scrap. The computer enables me to sample a lot of things visually. It's really like building a collage and then painting over it.

What, for you, makes a successful fashion illustration?
The same thing that makes any illustration successful—it should make you stop, make you want to tear it out of a magazine. It should evoke a mood, capture a period in time, or give you a sense of style, but overall it should just be an arresting image.

What artistic training have you undertaken?
One year in Fine Art at Nene College, Northamptonshire (UK).
Three years in Fashion Design at the Kent Institute of Art and Design (UK).

If you could give one piece of advice to a student, what would it be?
To not hold back, don't give yourself any boundaries. It's easy to get imprisoned by your own style, but artistically it's important to keep pushing forward and developing, otherwise your work just becomes stagnant.

Describe yourself and your greatest achievement.
I'm always restless and always searching for a new solution, I've got a lot more that I want to do, so hopefully I haven't yet reached my greatest achievement.

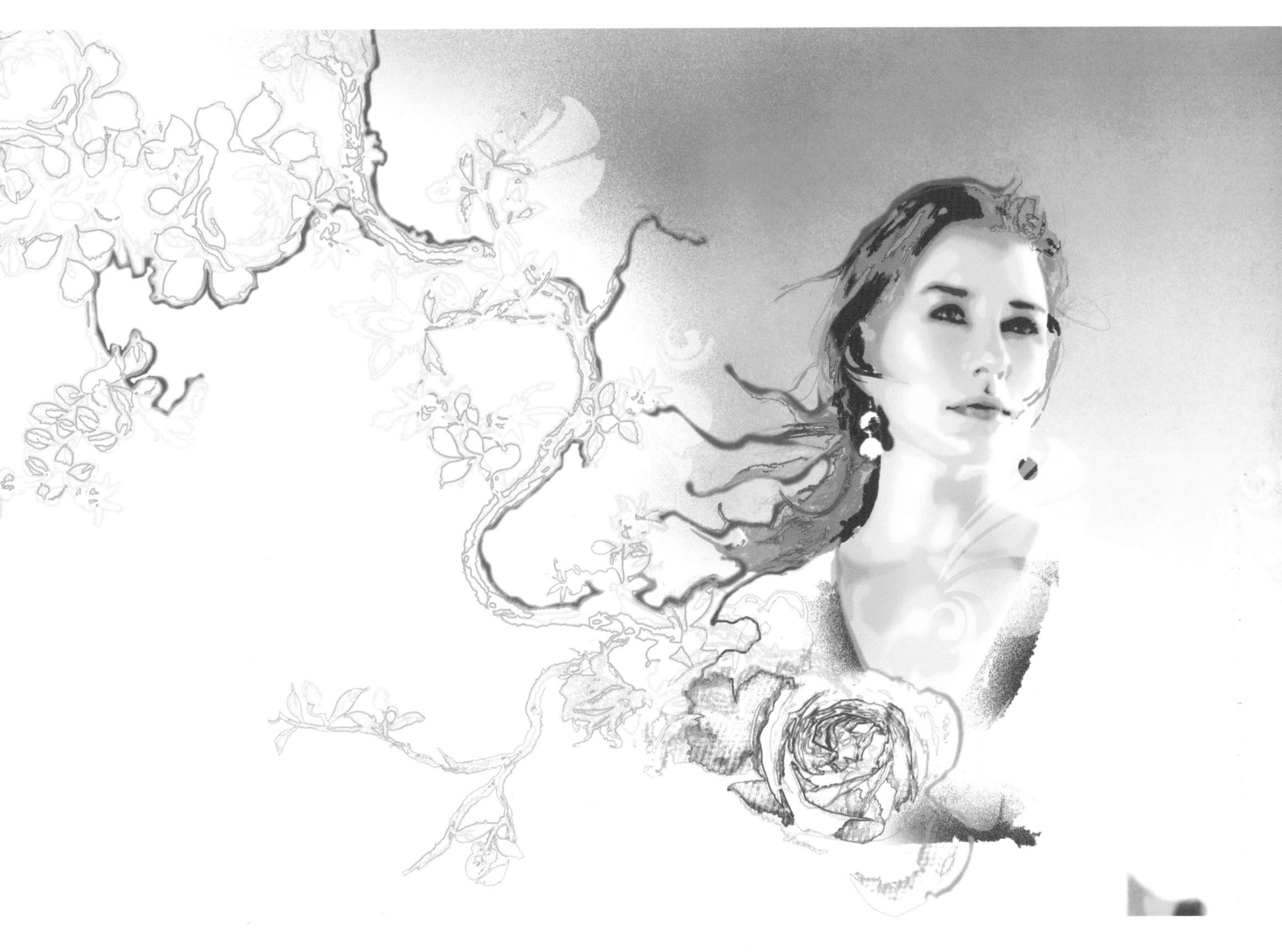

ROBERT WAGT

What inspires you?
Life.

Are you interested in fashion?
Not really.

Describe your work.
I think my illustration work has more to do with style and graphics than with fashion. I search for a solution in which composition, styling, wit, colors, and graphics and so on are in perfect balance with each other and create a sort of tension.

Which media and techniques do you use?
Collage, photography, drawing, and computer, not necessarily in that order.

What, for you, makes a successful fashion illustration?
The overall illustration has to add something to the clothes without getting in the way of the fashion. It should tell a story and add atmosphere.

What artistic training have you undertaken?
Art school (Minerva Academy of Fine Art and Design, The Netherlands), specializing in illustration and photography.

If you could give one piece of advice to a student, what would it be?
Never follow anything, and do what you believe in; it's in you, whatever you grasp for. You must have love, insight, and a strong point of view.

Describe yourself and your greatest achievement.
If I could describe myself, that would be my greatest achievement.

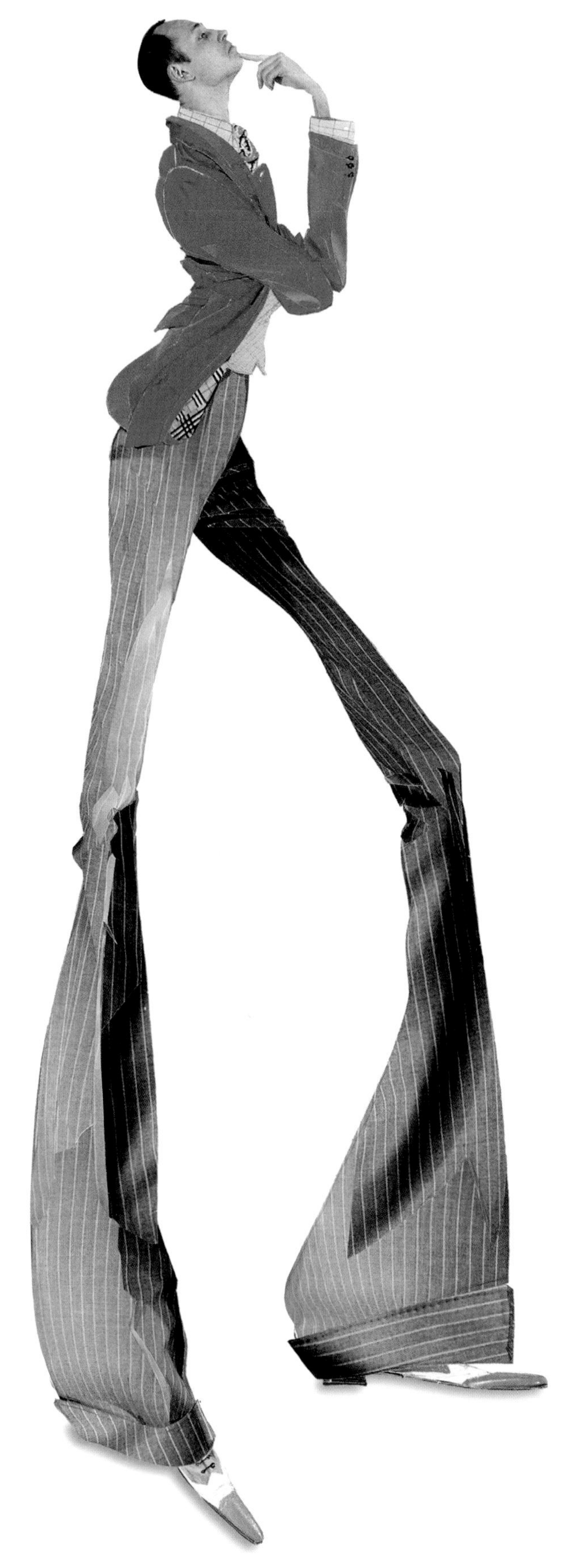

CHICO HAYASAKI

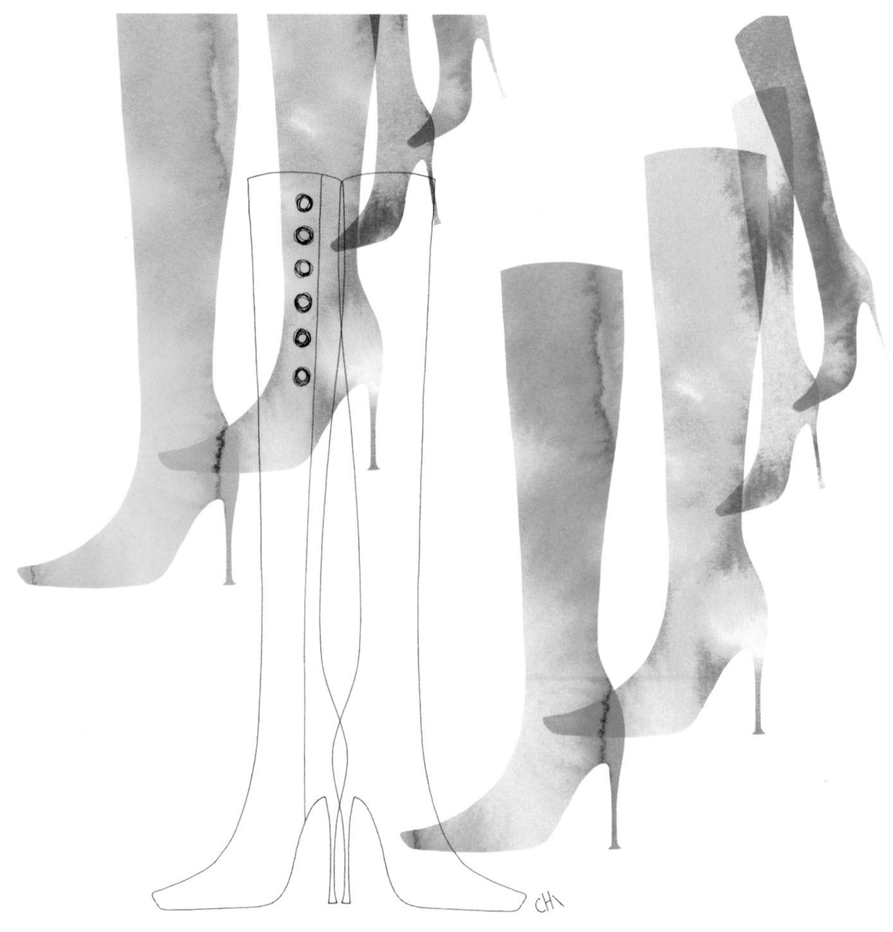

What inspires you?
Anything and everything that enters my daily field of vision. It is when I see beautiful and interesting forms that ideas start pouring out.

Are you interested in fashion?
Yes.

Describe your work.
The harmony of line, color, and space. When I illustrate, I want each work to have different elements—such as elegance, boldness, a playful spirit—that merge and coexist happily and comfortably with each other.

Which media and techniques do you use?
I use watercolor paper (HP) and brushes. For my line drawings, I use water-based pens (0.3 and 0.4) and colored ink. I occasionally use watercolor pencils and markers. I create the lines and colors separately by hand, then scan all the artwork into my Mac to create a composite image.

What, for you, makes a successful fashion illustration?
Work that possesses elegant beauty that can capture the viewer's eye.

What artistic training have you undertaken?
BA Hons in Graphic Design from Lewis and Clark College, in Portland, Oregon. I went on to work at an advertising production firm before launching my freelance career.

If you could give one piece of advice to a student, what would it be?
Just keep on drawing, whatever you like, without inhibition. That is how you will eventually come across your own artistic voice and style.

Describe yourself and your greatest achievement.
Low-key and generally at peace—I have the ability to be absorbed entirely by what I am doing. My greatest achievement would be all the wonderful friends I met during my college years.

VIRGINIA JOHNSON

What inspires you?
Color, texture, and rhythm in nature, circular shapes, decoration in everyday uses, women with confidence, and flowers.

Are you interested in fashion?
Very much—I am also a textile designer and clothing designer.

Describe your work.
Spontaneous, fun, spirited, elegant, slightly old-fashioned (I always add red lipstick and nail polish).

Which media and techniques do you use?
Watercolor. I don't plan out my drawings, but pick up a brush and start painting. I love texture and pattern and so try to incorporate these. Often the distinction between my illustrations and textiles blur; they come from the same place and inspire each other.

What, for you, makes a successful fashion illustration?
An illustration should be able to transport you and make you feel a bit of magic. There should be a sense of another time and place, another era or mood. It should make one dream.

I like my illustrations to read "fresh" and "spontaneous," so that I convey a feeling of energy, and a sense of excitement and anticipation. If I work too much at one image, I lose this.

What artistic training have you undertaken?
Majored in Art History at Queen's University, in Kingston, Ontario, Canada. Majored in Fashion Design at Parsons School of Design, in New York. Interned at Marc Jacobs and *Marie Claire* magazine, in New York. Designed shoes and bags for Helmut Lang, in New York. Took additional courses in silkscreen fabric printing at the Fashion Institute of Technology, in New York. Various stitching and quilting workshops at Sheridan College, in Oakville, Ontario, Canada.

If you could give one piece of advice to a student, what would it be?
To hold true to your own style and do what you really love to do. I didn't know illustration as a career existed, and my illustration teacher told me my drawings were not acceptable because they were far too loose and unfinished. In the end, I didn't—and couldn't—change the style, but it is now my greatest asset.

Also, in school you are taught to focus on one thing, and there are plenty of careers and opportunities that you don't learn about until you're out there in the real world. If you stick with what you love, doors will open for you in directions you never dreamed of. And you realize, as a creative person, that your life becomes integrated and whole when your creativity is allowed to express itself in many ways. I never knew you could do so many things simultaneously: illustrate, design clothes, design textiles. This way your happiness and success are guaranteed.

Describe yourself and your greatest achievement.
My biggest achievement was leaving my job as a design assistant and starting my own business. I had no clue what I was going to do, and thought that perhaps the best years of my fashion career were over. I could not have imagined that the best years lay just around the corner. I started illustrating for Kate Spade, eventually working on three books with them (*Occasions*, *Style*, and *Manners*); I found a great agent, Stephanie Pesakoff of Art Department; and I started designing a collection of resort clothing with my textiles, which is now sold across the USA and Canada. And all that has happened in less than three years.

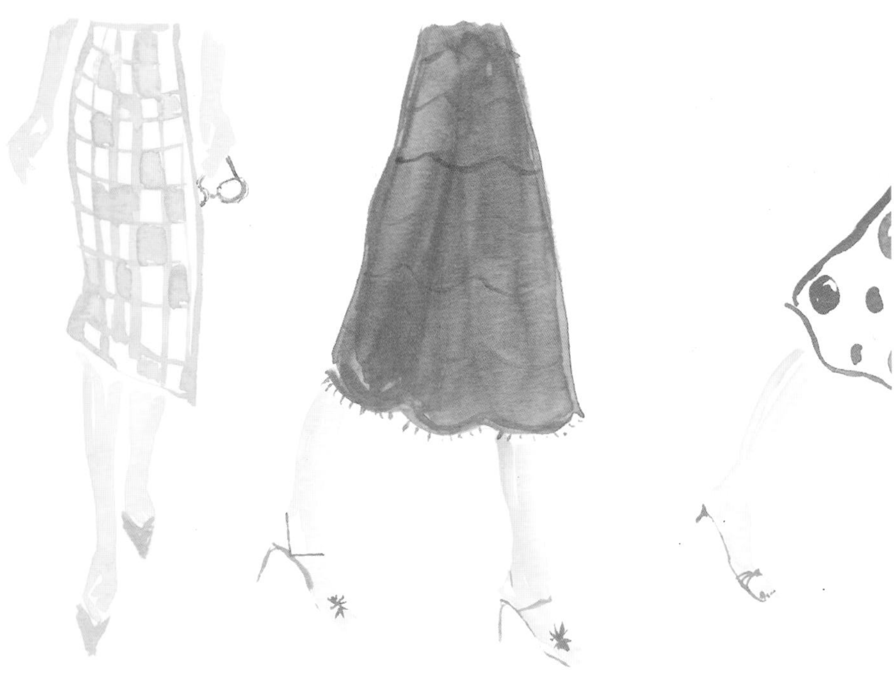

VINCENT BAKKUM

What inspires you?

I'm in love with the "object" woman, her graphic qualities. I fall for her outlines, her bone structure, the shadows under nose and lips, the knuckles of long slender fingers, the lightfall on her calves, pitch-black, cheek-brushing eyelashes. The person behind the "object" leaves me uninspired. In real life I love women for what they stand for, but in depicting them on canvas they are reduced to colorful graphic images only. The beauty of a woman to me is closely connected with the fruit, dead fish, and stuffed birds I also enjoy painting—death and decay is another undeniable source of inspiration. Beauty doomed to rot. Colors bound to fade away. Something that conforms to the Dutch tradition of still-life painting, I guess. A ripe and blossoming apple is already decaying. Although there's no thin line between flourishing and decaying, I still try to catch that moment. I'm desperately trying to save what there is left to save. Since death is also a source of inspiration for religion, and I'm stuck with Roman Catholic roots and a coquettish interest in the symbolic circus, I once in a while like to enrich my paintings with these symbols. Two more sources of inspiration are the hidden sensuality and thick outlines of the Art Nouveau artist Alphonse Mucha and the strong contrasts of the gentle black-and-white photography of the sixties. One could almost call my art a hybrid child of both art forms and periods.

Are you interested in fashion?

Fashion as an art form, as a way of enhancing female beauty, is followed by me. But I'm more interested in the end product than the mere garment or accessory itself. It is the collaboration of stylists, make-up artists, photographers, illustrators, models, etc., that can make fashion exciting and interesting.

Describe your work.

Colorful graphic images of the female, footwear, fish, fowl, fruit, and the feast of life. David Bailey's and Alphonse Mucha's delirious baby.

Which media and techniques do you use?

Acrylic on canvas or plywood. Nothing more, nothing less.

What, for you, makes a successful fashion illustration?

The lines have to feel good. There are many ways of drawing a shoulderline, the fitting of a skirt, or the necklace over a collarbone, but there are only a couple that feel, and therefore are, good. The brush, the stroke, the paint have to do the talking. A fashion illustration is the depiction of a mere split second that you must experience in the illustration.

What artistic training have you undertaken?

I haven't got any decent schooling. It has been a lonely search for beauty in my studio without any authorized guidance. I trust my instincts and my sense of beauty. People like Gruau, and Mucha, and Warhol have been my unpaid tutors. I did modeling for about fifteen years and gathered a lot of inspiration by being part of the scene and going through the magazines.

If you could give one piece of advice to a student, what would it be?

Stay true to yourself. Steal as much as you like from your artistic idols. In the long run you will build up your own style anyway. You have to start with what history has left you with. Just a starting point for a long and, hopefully, fulfilling journey.

Describe yourself and your greatest achievement.

Beauty is my goal, laziness my motor. Man, if I could be a bit harder on myself! I believe the invitation to be interviewed for this book is one of my greatest achievements. Still a student myself, I'm all of a sudden giving advice to other students. Eternal students we are ...

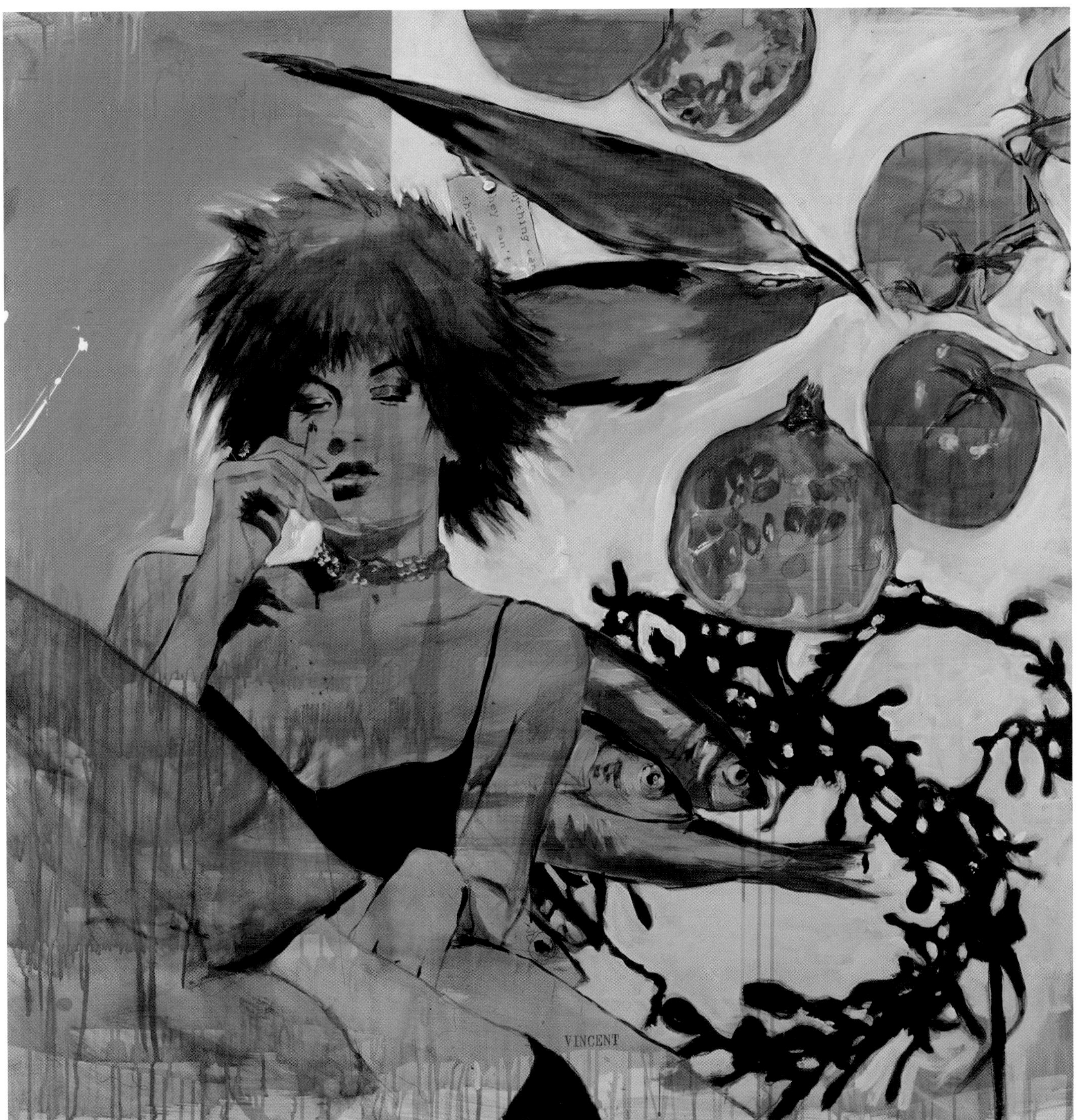
VINCENT

CARMEN GARCIA HUERTA

What inspires you?
Everything: people in the street, fashion magazines, art of all centuries and cultures, cinema, traveling, my friends.

Are you interested in fashion?
Sure. In fact, fashion photography is my biggest source of inspiration.

Describe your work.
I prefer other people to describe it, but I like to think that, though I work mostly with a computer, which normally makes figures look too correct and cold, I get some kind of warmth and human touch in the expressions. It's a personal mix between machine and handmade work that I like to achieve. Or at least I try to!

Which media and techniques do you use?
It's a whole process. First, I draw a sketch on paper with a pencil, then I scan it. I open the file in Illustrator and trace over the pencil drawing. At this point I choose the colors too (which is the best part of working with a computer: you can change and undo or redo as much as you want, like a game). When it's all traced, I export to Photoshop, where I do the final touch: volumes, lights, skin effects ...

What, for you, makes a successful fashion illustration?
Basically, newness. Something never done before but, at the same time, able to keep the essence of beauty and grace that for me defines fashion illustration through the ages.

What artistic training have you undertaken?
Advertising at Universidad Complutense de Madrid (Spain), but it was not much of an artistic training ... I took some lessons in classical drawing at a small academy for a few months. While studying at the university, I took a course in graphic design at an academy too. And that's all.

If you could give one piece of advice to a student, what would it be?
I'm not good at advice; I'm probably as lost as anybody else. But you must try to enjoy what you do, work from passion, pay attention to the trends but not too much, keep the feeling you had while playing alone when you were a child.

Describe yourself and your greatest achievement.
I'm a lonesome worker, very proud of making a living by doing what I love most.

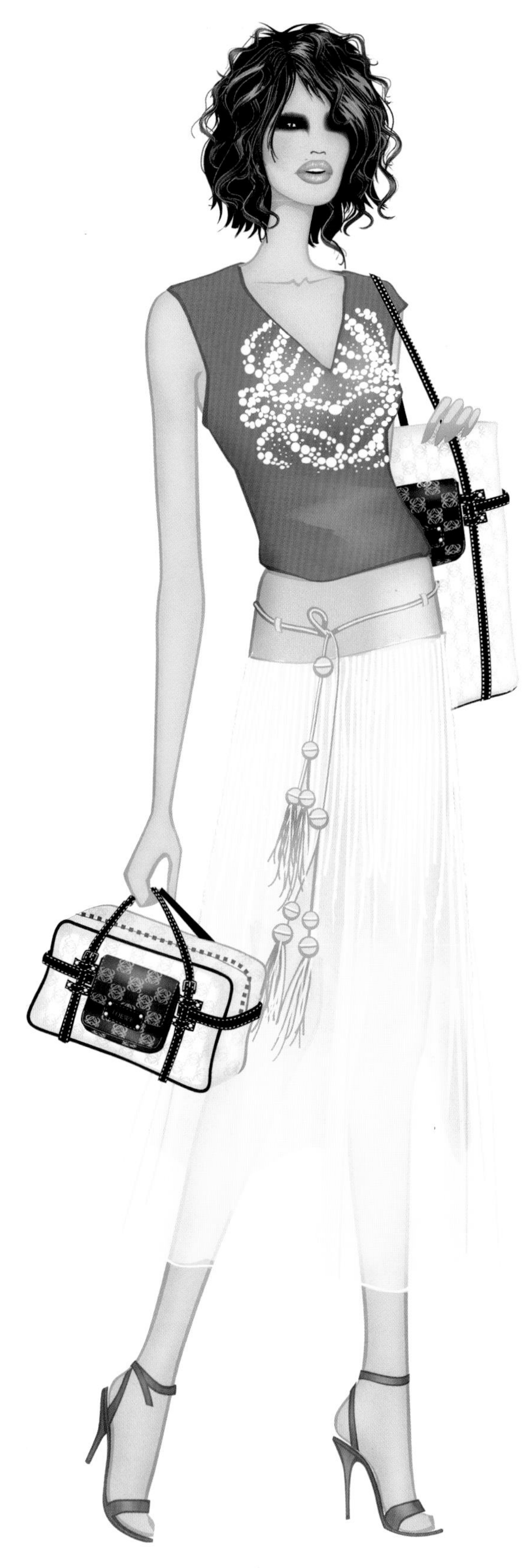

AYAKO MACHIDA

What inspires you?
Everything from my daily life—television, magazines, music, people on the streets, travels, etc. I often find hints and inspirations in conversations with friends, then proceed to expand on the situational imagery.

Are you interested in fashion?
Moderately. I do admire fashionable people, but don't quite have the sensibility to apply it to my own wardrobe—so I am mainly on the observing end.

Describe your work.
I don't feel that my artistic style is incredibly unique, but I do value the playful situations and subtle touch of humor in my works.

Which media and techniques do you use?
I draw sketches by hand, then scan them into my Mac to add color with Photoshop.

What, for you, makes a successful fashion illustration?
Something that has flavor, an edge, a "smell"—that's what I aspire to create, as it's too boring to be merely cute or stylish.

What artistic training have you undertaken?
Upon graduation from an art school in Saga, Japan, I worked at several design firms as design assistant. I started illustrating around 1996, and started receiving assignments around 1997. Now I continue to take commercial commissions while working on original projects and exhibitions.

If you could give one piece of advice to a student, what would it be?
As much as it is important to create what your heart desires, it is also important to create something original with the intention that it will be used and viewed by the public.

Describe yourself and your greatest achievement.
Mild and easygoing. I am most proud that I have fulfilled my wish of making illustration a profession, and that I have found something that I would like to do for a long time.

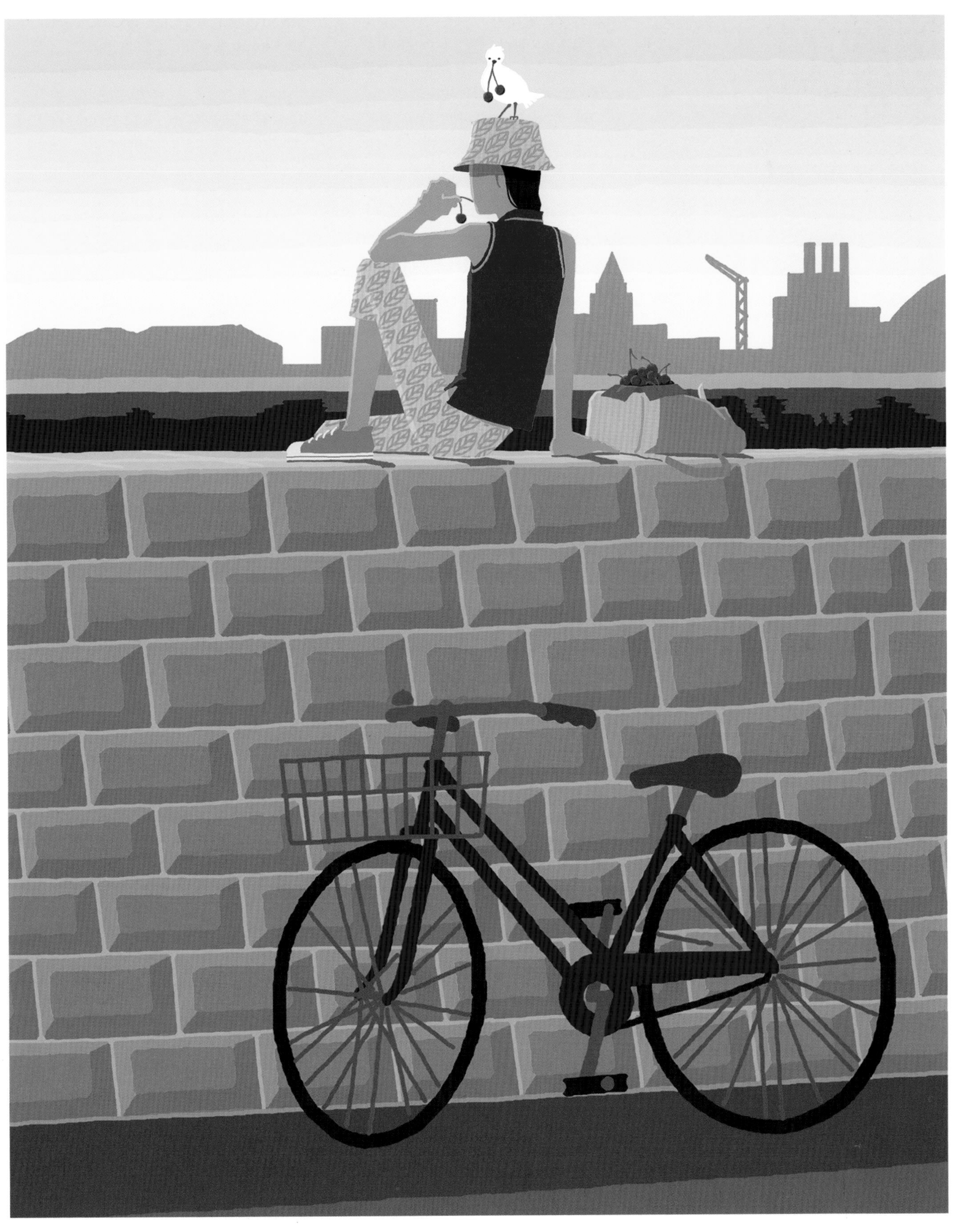

TINA BERNING

What inspires you?
The beauty of life, however it comes by.

Are you interested in fashion?
As a very tall person—always hopeless at finding long-enough clothes—I started sewing my own things very early, so I got interested in brands only very lately, actually not before my first fashion job, in 1999. I was always interested in wearing nice things but never really followed the trends that closely.

Describe your work.
I love to have a variety. That goes from fashion spreads, through to essays on social themes, to advertising jobs for car companies. Each theme deserves its own solution, and I love the challenge of finding the right solution every day.

Which media and techniques do you use?
I experiment with techniques, mix them up and see what's happening. Most times it is watercolor, ink, ballpoint pen, and a proper amount of Photoshop.

What, for you, makes a successful fashion illustration?
Style and information. With a drawing you can be very informative on textures, fittings, cuts, etc., but it would be nothing without a good style, and vice versa.

What artistic training have you undertaken?
After working for a German painter for two years, I started studying graphics, focusing on illustration, in Nuremberg. While studying, I worked for the music industry and spent one year at a magazine as a graphic designer before I decided to quit pushing letters around and do what I love most: illustration.

If you could give one piece of advice to a student, what would it be?
Be patient, explore, allow yourself to make mistakes, and do it all over again. It's the only time you can do that without getting into trouble. And go study in a different country. I never did, and I regret that.

Describe yourself and your greatest achievement.
I never ask what could please the client but do what pleases me. This often makes me do more than what is needed but also keeps the quality of my work high. I am thankful for the patience I have, no matter how late it is.

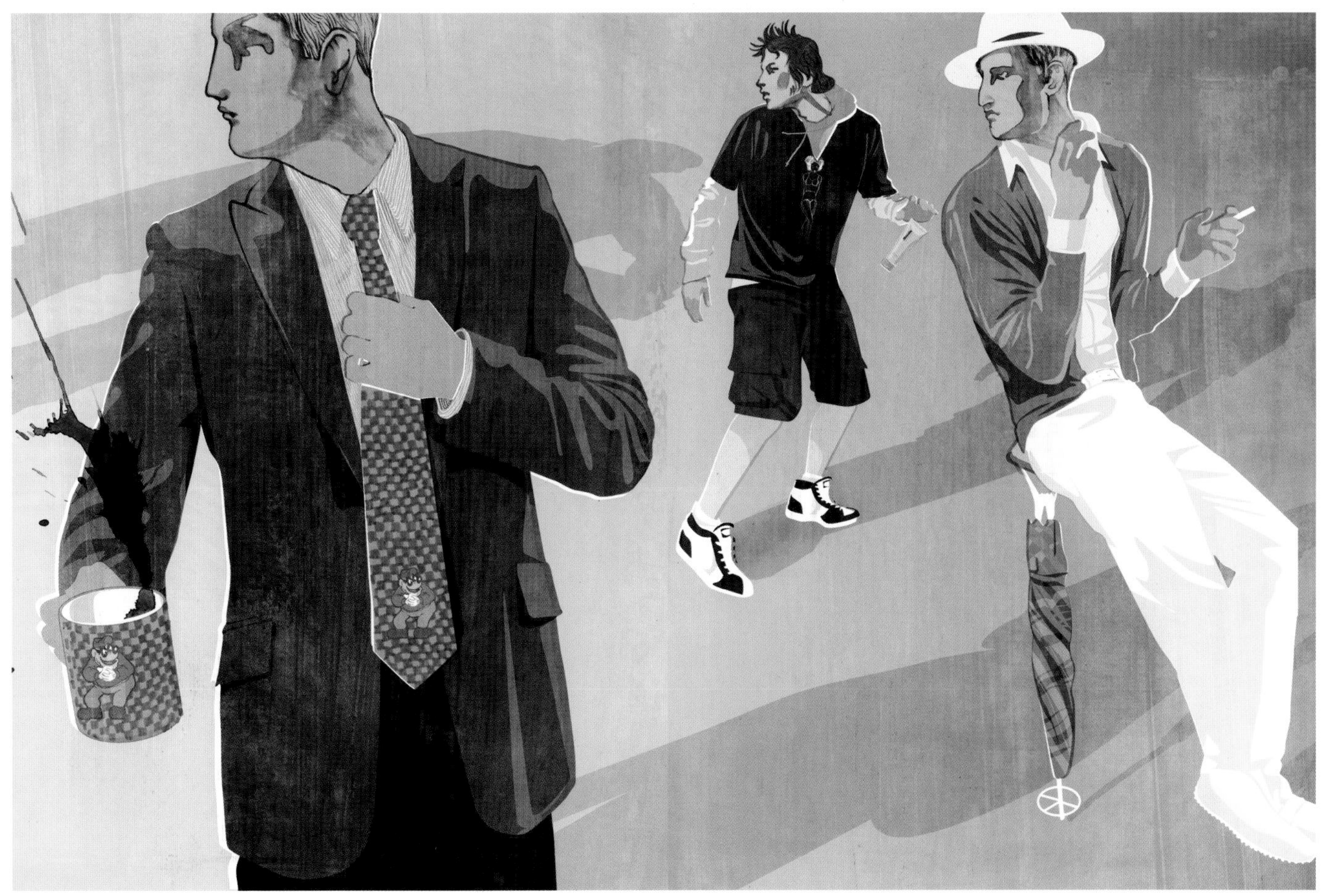

MARIE O'CONNOR

What inspires you?
That is a very tough question! It's always changing. I am inspired by the need to learn and think. I try to find out about new things (techniques, processes, or people) and this helps me to develop my work. My inspiration often comes from mistakes or from having to "make do," or things that are out of place or out of context: bad DIY, craft techniques, homemade and handmade items, chairs, mattresses on the street, Arte Povera, broken spectacles with tape, etc.

Are you interested in fashion?
Yes, but I think I am more interested in the idea of clothing than the fashion arena itself. In fact, I trained as a textile designer and, after graduating, moved to London to work as an assistant to a fashion label. I also work as a design consultant within the fashion industry. In my illustration and personal work, fashion is not the emphasis but could be the application.

Describe your work.
Another tough one! I say this because I feel there are a few strands to what I do and, although they can sometimes be very separate and seen in different contexts, they are inextricably linked for me. A lot of it is about cut-and-paste, as a technique but also as an aesthetic. This gives the tactility, which is probably the most interesting quality for me, along with exploring the relationship between things in two dimensions and three dimensions—flatness and fullness, the idea of construction, and the meeting of low-fi and hi-fi working methods. What tends to happen is a response to a process. Found materials, and odds and ends create a sensibility, and that determines my approach stylistically, which, in turn, can re-inform the concept of the piece, story, artwork, or print. It is very much about putting things together in a temporary way, moving things around and assembling in a way that, while being considered, is hopefully not contrived.

Which media and techniques do you use?
My illustration work is primarily collage-based, and I'm influenced by my training in textiles. I use a lot of thread and yarn, stitch by hand and machine, incorporate found ephemera, fabric, paper, buttons, and any bits and bobs that take my fancy really. I look out for interesting surface qualities and also use smaller objects, from electronic components to pieces from broken ceramic mugs. I keep things on my desk and in a series of boxes. I try to use it in the same way that I store it—in a non-precious yet still organized way.

What, for you, makes a successful fashion illustration?
Something that inspires and that can be odd or beautiful. It's not about the designer or their brand, but letting the clothes and the execution of the image evoke a mood or create a completely different environment.

What artistic training have you undertaken?
BA Hons in Embroidered and Woven Textiles from Glasgow School of Art (UK).

If you could give one piece of advice to a student, what would it be?
Find things out for yourself, but also ask questions. Don't view your discipline in a vacuum; experience other subjects, find out about their techniques and how you can adopt them for yourself. Be true to yourself, and try to enjoy being a student because you really can do anything you want to do at this point in your career.

Describe yourself and your greatest achievement.
I don't really think I have a greatest achievement. I guess it's all relevant to certain times and circumstances, and I think that still being excited by the prospect of creating artwork is quite an achievement. I feel that I'm only just scratching the surface, so hopefully I will have more to achieve in the future.

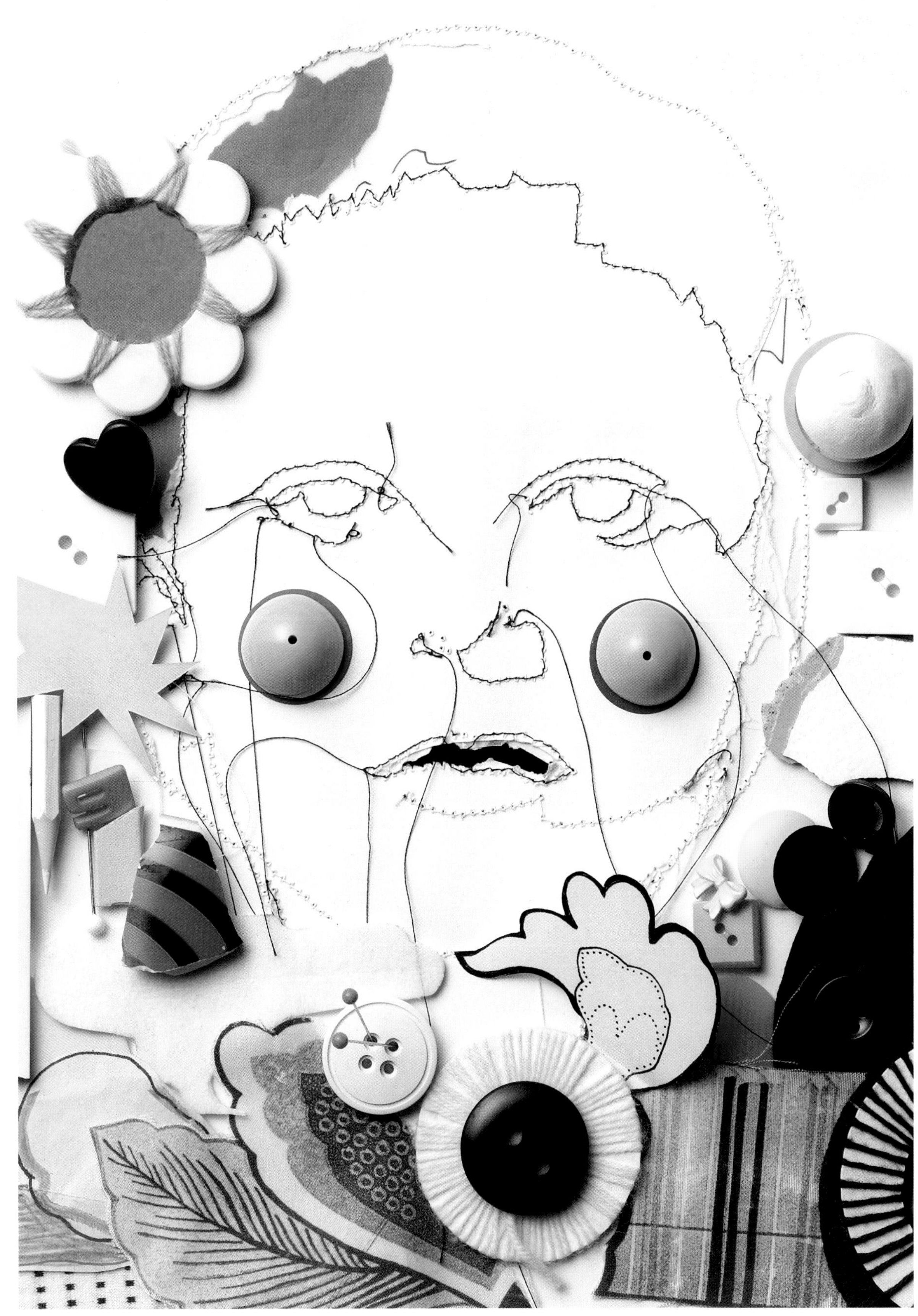

KAREEM ILIYA

What inspires you?
Everything, but in particular the space I live in and the nature that surrounds it.

Are you interested in fashion?
Yes, in fact, for many years while illustrating I was also working as a menswear designer for various companies including A/X Armani Exchange, Express Men, and Banana Republic.

Describe your work.
It often gets described as "ethereal." However, I think I usually aim for something graphic and yet soft and beautiful.

Which media and techniques do you use?
Watercolors, inks, pastels, charcoal, and various papers along with my Apple Mac and Adobe Photoshop—depending on the assignment, I may or may not involve any computer manipulation.

What, for you, makes a successful fashion illustration?
An image that grabs your attention and holds it, making you wish for more.

What artistic training have you undertaken?
When I was ten, my brother taught me to use watercolors, and my father showed me the best technique for coloring in maps for my school projects. I also took various art courses throughout my education, including high school and college. During my college years, my degree in fashion design focused my attention on selling my design ideas via my illustrations, and that is when I realized how much I loved to illustrate fashion.

If you could give one piece of advice to a student, what would it be?
Well, I was kicked out of my fashion illustration class in college because I refused to draw in the manner my professor requested. I was bored to death and let her know. I think developing your own style and not conforming to the masses is the best lesson one can have. Also, follow your passion rather than what is expected of you.

Describe yourself and your greatest achievement.
I've had several goals throughout my career. My earliest goal, in my early twenties, was to be published in *W* magazine) it was a publication I had followed since pre-college days and throughout my career as a designer). The day they gave me a call to work with them was one of the best, and I've since worked with them many times over the course of the past decade. The other publication I was longing to be a part of was *Visionaire*. From the moment the first issue was published, I became a collector. It was a great honor to be a part of what they were working on, and I was fortunate enough for my work to be in several of the early issues.

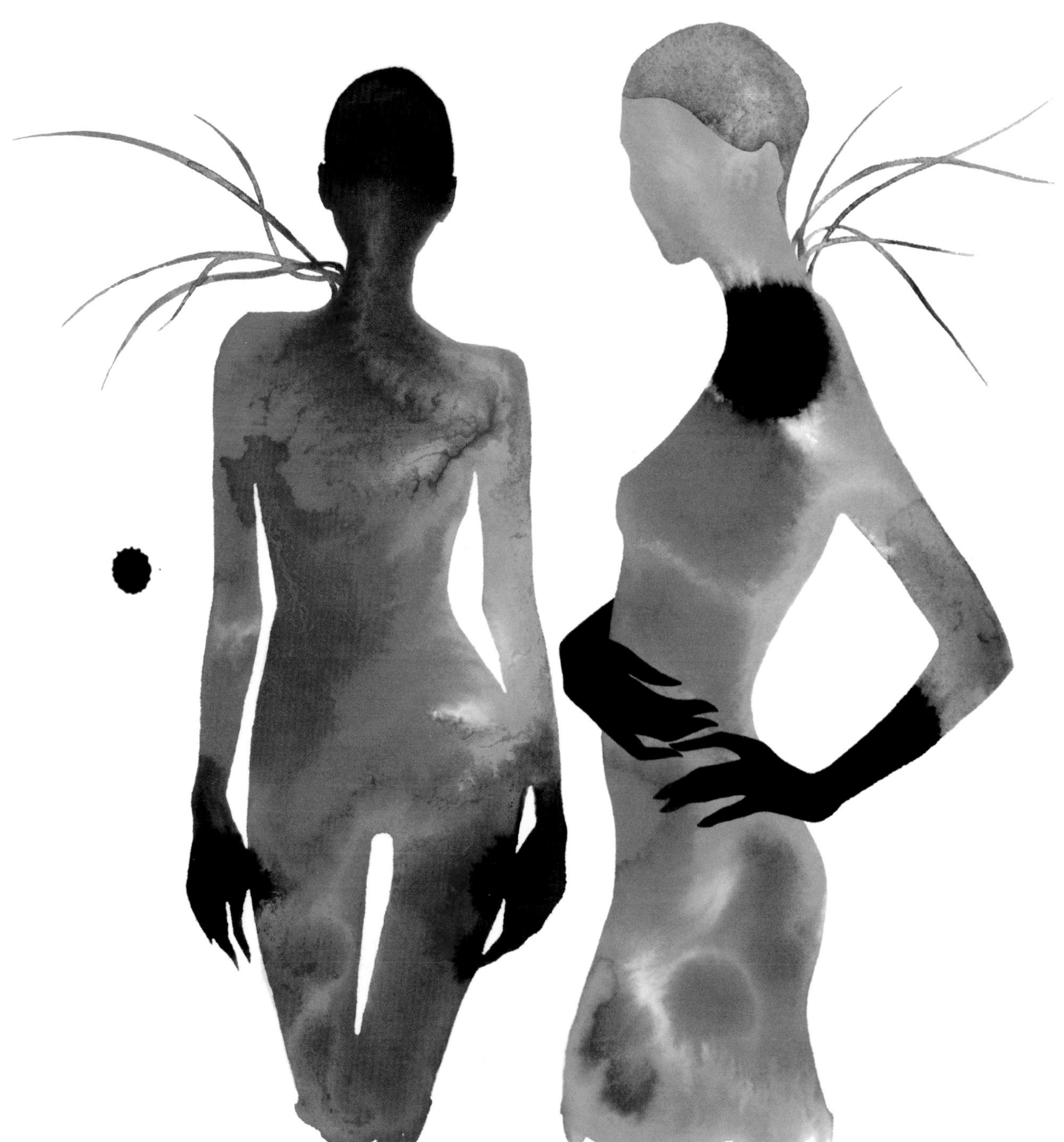

YUKO SHIMIZU

What inspires you?
Basically, everything I've experienced in my life, everyone whom I've encountered; my family, friends, people I like or don't like—these are all my inspirations. The whole experience makes me who I am, and that lets me do the work I do. Of course I have favorite artists, but they are only a small part of my inspiration.

Are you interested in fashion?
Of course. You should not work in a field you are not interested in.

Describe your work.
My work is somewhere in between Japanese woodblock prints and manga, with a Western influence. Basically, that was how I grew up. I started drawing and copying manga when I was little and got blown away by Hokusai and other woodblock artists when I got a little older. Although I am from Japan, I partially grew up in the USA and also came back later on to finish art school here, so I have a lot of American art and cultural influences.

Which media and techniques do you use?
I draw on paper with black India ink and Japanese or Chinese bamboo brushes. I then scan the drawing in and color it with Adobe Photoshop. I treat Photoshop as a computer-generated silk-screen processing machine.

What, for you, makes a successful fashion illustration?
I am not so much interested in the traditional terms of fashion illustration, meaning accurately drawing the texture and design of clothing. I was never trained in fashion anyway. My background is illustration and fine art, where concept is as important as or more important than the style of your drawing. So, for me, if I can make an image that reflects some kind of fashion or trend, as well as a concept or narrative with my personal voice in it, that is a successful illustration.

What artistic training have you undertaken?
My undergraduate degree was in advertising and marketing. After I had worked in corporate Japan for eleven years, I went back to art school—School of Visual Arts (SVA), New York. I did my first and second year in BFA Illustration, then switched over to MFA Illustration as Visual Essay at SVA. Now I teach BFA Illustration and Cartooning at SVA.

If you could give one piece of advice to a student, what would it be?
Being influenced is fine, but never copy other people's work. You should become an artist because no one has created what you want to create. What is most important is that your work reflects who you are. Your work has to have your personal voice. Have as much life experience as possible outside of art. That will ultimately make your work more interesting.

Describe yourself and your greatest achievement.
Creating drawings makes me alive. The greatest achievement is yet to come.

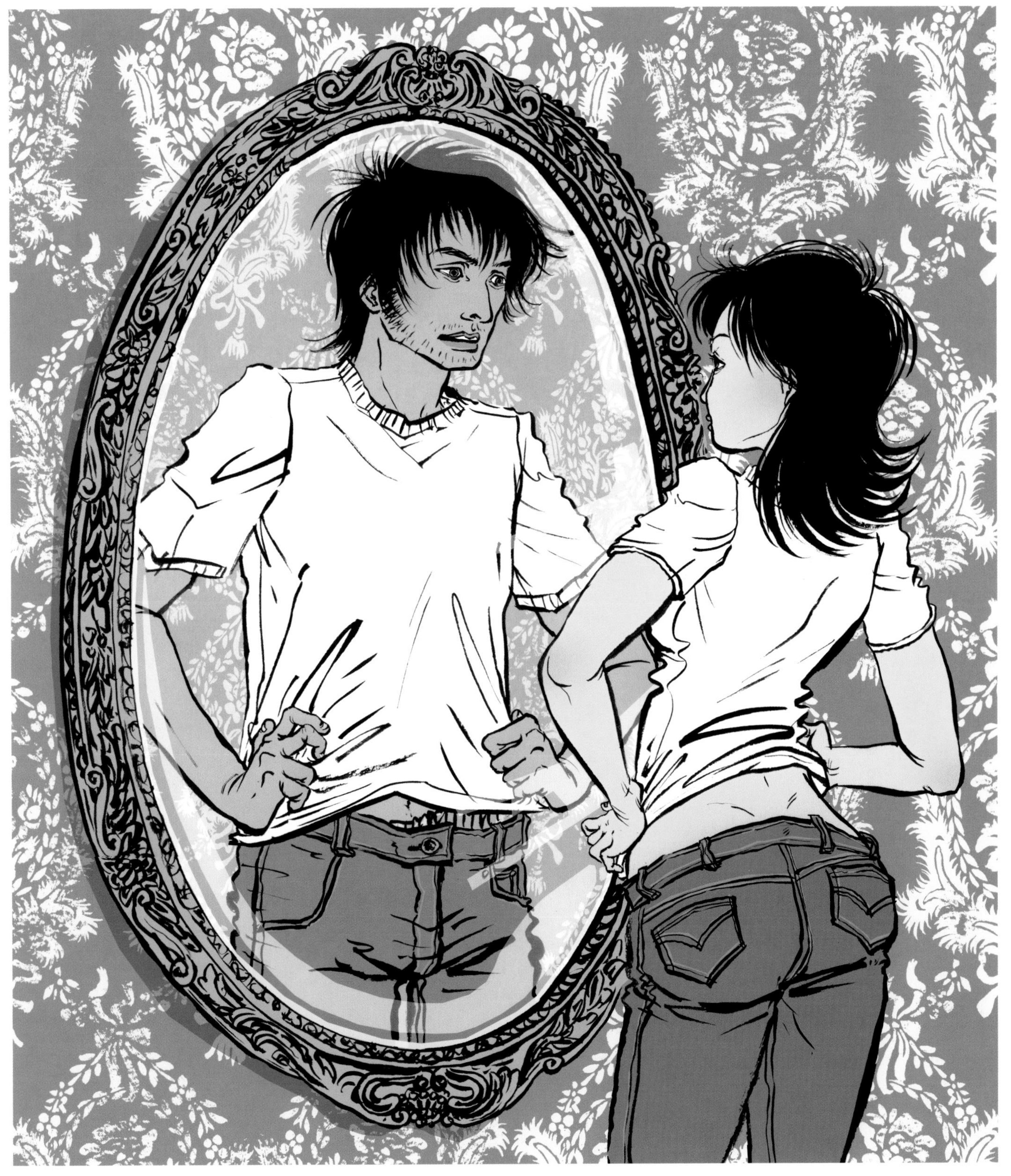

MILES DONOVAN

What inspires you?
New York, Saul Bass, Montana Gold Spray paints, Basquiat, Mike Mills, Michel Gondry, Peepshow Illustration Collective, Black Convoy, early mo wax sleeves, Spike Jonze, Shynola, Johnny Cash, Warhol, early Cuban posters.

Are you interested in fashion?
I think it's very important to see what is happening around you, not just in your particular field of expertise, but also within the arts in general. All sorts of things can inform your work, from obscure food packaging to film and gallery visits. It's important to keep your eye on fashion trends as a freelance individual, as many say: "Know your market and the market you don't know."

Describe your work.
Traditional painting mixed with the flexibility and approach of modern techniques and technology. It's portrait-based illustration, street-inspired.

Which media and techniques do you use?
Apple Powerbook, scanner, scalpel, paper, spray paint, fuse wire, A3 printer, tape, scissors, Photoshop, Illustrator.

Everything I do is based on photographs. These are scanned and manipulated in Photoshop, then the spray stencils are created in Illustrator, each individual stencil is printed out on thin card, cut, sprayed, scanned back into Photoshop, and the picture is reconstructed with layers and heavy color manipulation. It's a very long process, but enables me to have complete control over every element you see.

What, for you, makes a successful fashion illustration?
A successful illustration varies from job to job. If you achieve everything the client asked you to do, then, for me, I've completed everything I set out to achieve, but certain things must be considered and should be apparent in everything you do. These include a balanced composition, strong use of color, and considered media.

What artistic training have you undertaken?
BTEC National Diploma in Foundation Studies and BA Hons in Illustration, University of Brighton (UK). To be honest, though, the majority of my education within the field of illustration has been developed over a period of time since graduating. You can't beat actually going out there and learning from the mistakes you make, whilst trying to make it as a freelance illustrator, meeting clients, working on commissions, etc. I learnt very little about the business and client side of things while at university. The three years studying was essentially a time to develop a style I was happy with and that could be taken forward into something that would be commissioned.

If you could give one piece of advice to a student, what would it be?
Even if others doubt what you do, always go with what you believe in and work hard to prove them wrong.

Describe yourself and your greatest achievement.
110 illustrations for Maverick Records in two weeks.

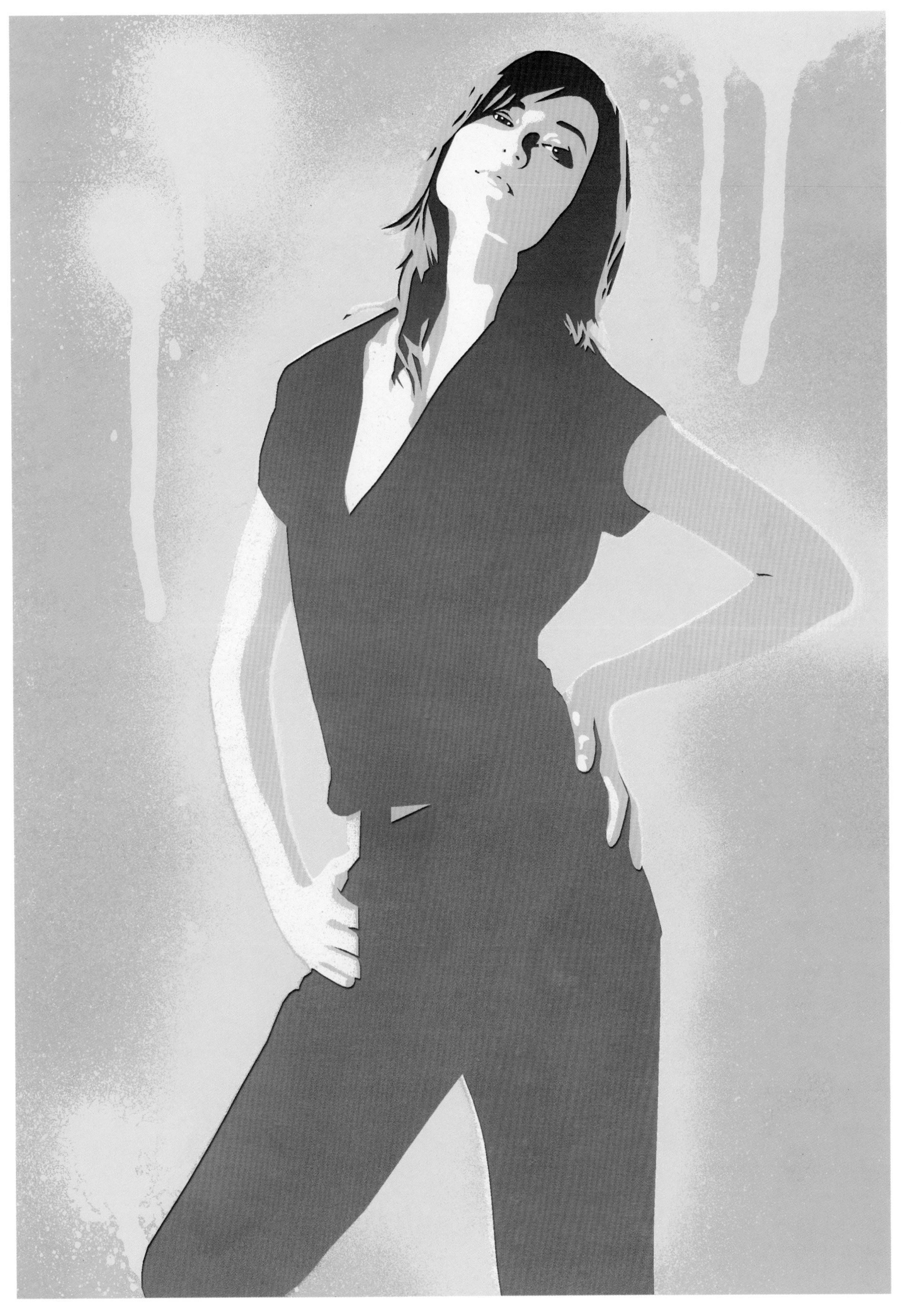

NINA CHAKRABARTI

What inspires you?
Junk inspires me. I have suitcases full of stuff other people throw away. Old milk cartons, sanitary towel bags, Indian sweet wrappers, torn pieces of wallpaper. One day all these things will make their way into my drawings. Also, I'm crazy about patterns, the more baroque and swirly, the better; and shoes. I love drawing them.

Are you interested in fashion?
I am interested in personal style rather than fashion. I don't read any current fashion magazines but prefer to look at old ones. Somehow I find them more interesting. Maybe I'll look at contemporary fashions in ten years' time. I'll be ready for them then! I also find what my friends wear very inspiring.

Describe your work.
My work is very detailed and decorative. I often use type, often as a decorative tool, but occasionally to express ideas. My work is primarily about the quality of line, although I have started to use found objects and create more layered work these days.

Which media and techniques do you use?
I'm addicted to Rotring pens. Even if illustrations end up being collaged with found objects and composed in Photoshop, I always start by drawing.

What, for you, makes a successful fashion illustration?
Something that makes me think, "Wow, wish I'd done that!"

What artistic training have you undertaken?
BA Hons in Graphic Design at Central Saint Martins, London (UK). MA in Communication, Art and Design at the Royal College of Art, London (UK).

If you could give one piece of advice to a student, what would it be?
Appreciate the library: a whole world, past and present, is waiting to inspire you there.

Describe yourself and your greatest achievement?
Small and brown, slightly hunchbacked! Generally of a happy disposition apart from winter, when I go a bit weird. My greatest achievement is learning how to ride a bike at age 28—and that's a pushbike I'm talking about, not a motorbike. It was hard, especially as I'd torn a ligament trying to learn the first time and had a fear of cycling. I remember the first time I cycled to work and feeling so exhilarated.

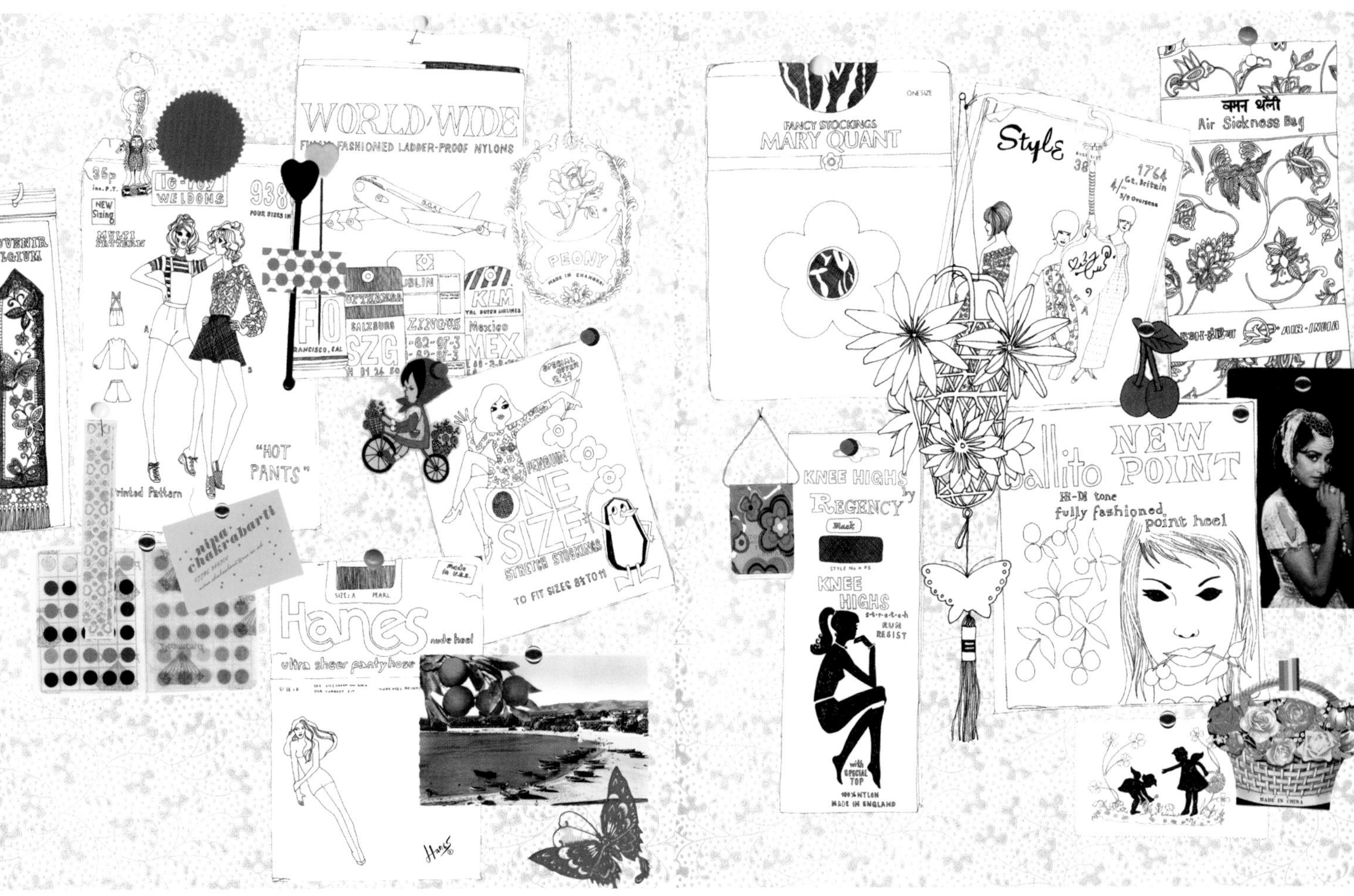
WORLD-WIDE
FULLY FASHIONED LADDER-PROOF NYLONS
WELDONS
MULTI PATTERN
"HOT PANTS"
PEONY
FANCY STOCKINGS
MARY QUANT
Style
Air Sickness Bag
AIR-INDIA
KNEE HIGHS
REGENCY
NEW POINT
fully fashioned point heel
ONE SIZE
STRETCH STOCKINGS
TO FIT SIZES 8½ TO 11
Hanes
ultra sheer panty hose
MADE IN ENGLAND
MADE IN CHINA

MATTHIAS FREY

What inspires you?
All kinds of music, design history (especially the seventies), people, everyday things. And Berlin—it's such a vibrant city with so many contradictions. You can be in ten different parts of the city and feel like you are in ten different cities. This contrast is inspiring. There are a lot of creative people in Berlin, which, although it means stiff competition, is also inspiring. There are just too many exhibitions to see—inspiration is interdisciplinary.

Are you interested in fashion?
Yes, I'm very much interested in fashion—but I'm not a fashion victim anymore. My urge to be fashionable was definitely stronger in my twenties than today. I still follow trends but not every single one. I am now comfortable and well dressed—rather than loud and outrageous.

Describe your work.
It is very "pop," very pretty. Its aim is always to please the viewer. My work is mostly very bright and colorful. It has improved over the years and still does. Every once in a while, I come up with a different way of doing something—for example, shading or colored outlines instead of solid black ones. Then I look at my older illustrations and think, "I should always have been using colored outlines."

Which media and techniques do you use?
I draw by hand, then scan my drawings and do everything else on computer. I work with Adobe Illustrator and Photoshop. I've been using this technique for a while now, but in between it's important to try out new techniques.

What, for you, makes a successful fashion illustration?
It should give you some information about the garments or a feeling of what they are like. I think a fashion illustration is more a piece of work than a piece of art—so it should be less about the self-expression of the illustrator.

What artistic training have you undertaken?
Diploma in Communication Design at the Fachhochschule, in Wiesbaden (Germany), with two semesters at the University of Technology (UTS), in Sydney, Australia. This had an immense impact on me, both personally and professionally.

If you could give one piece of advice to a student, what would it be?
Do go and study in a different country for a while. The Fachhochschule, in Wiesbaden, where I studied, is very industry-oriented. That's good, because at an early stage students get to know how the industry works: timings, meeting the client, presenting work, etc. The university in Sydney (UTS) was quite the opposite—the focus was on the idea, the creative process. Also, living in a foreign country broadens your horizon immensely. Dealing with a different mentality is fascinating. You start to adapt to parts of it, while at the same time you get in touch with your own country's mentality and become more aware of it. So, take my advice and take on the challenge—it will pay off.

Describe yourself and your greatest achievement.
I'm a graphic designer/illustrator. After I finished my studies, I worked in smaller design agencies for a while. Two years ago, I moved to Berlin, becoming self-employed. I love my work—I couldn't think of any work field that would suit me better and could make me happier. At the same time, I don't take it too seriously. I don't like designers who can only think and speak about design. There is a lot more to life, and I think it's healthy to acknowledge that fact. I love music. I think, along with flying, it's the best thing mankind has ever invented. My greatest achievement? Has yet to be achieved, I guess. I've had some of my work published in magazines and books, and I always find it very exciting. But I think my greatest achievement so far is staying a positive-thinking person!

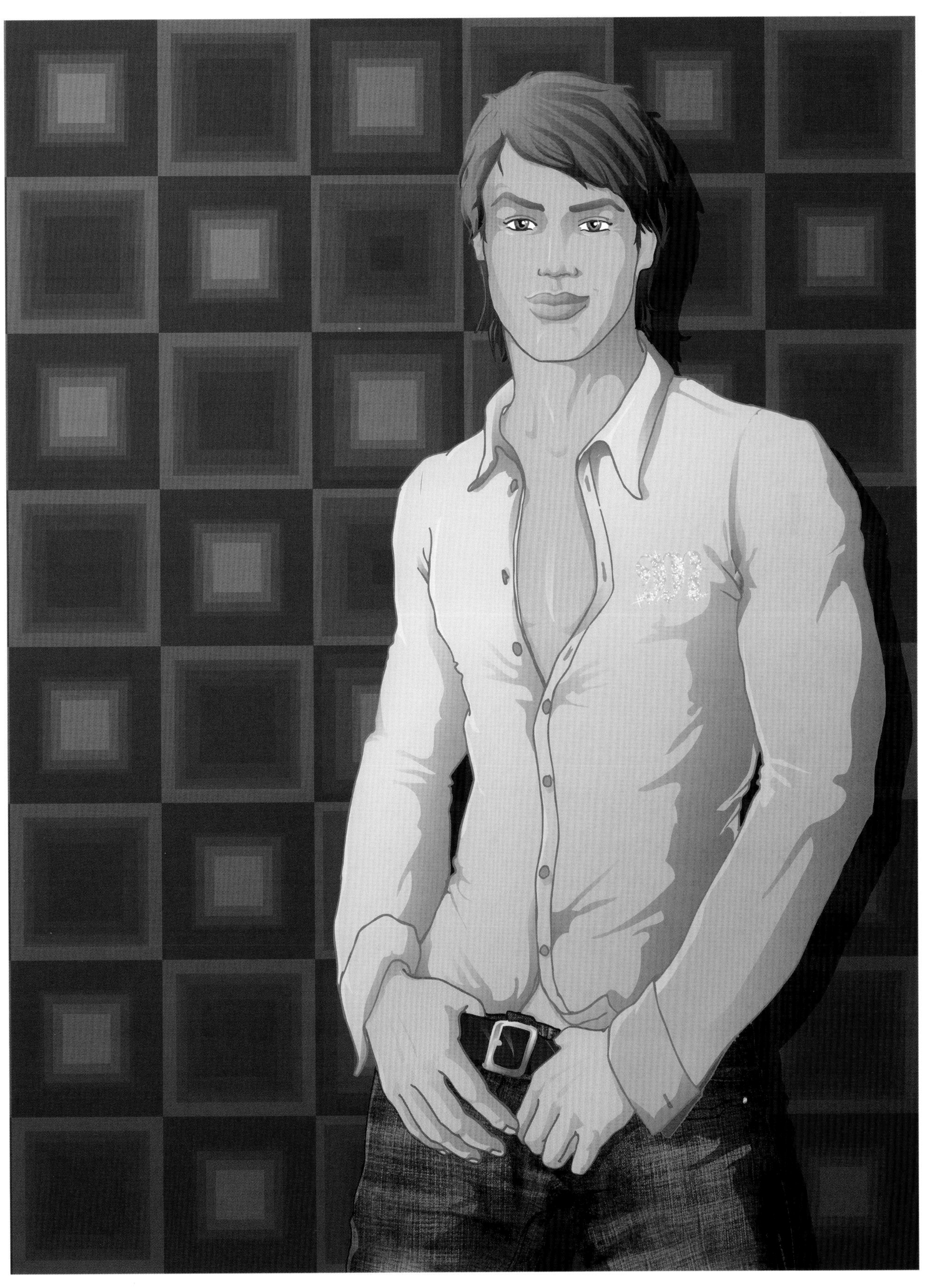

MICHOU AMELYNK

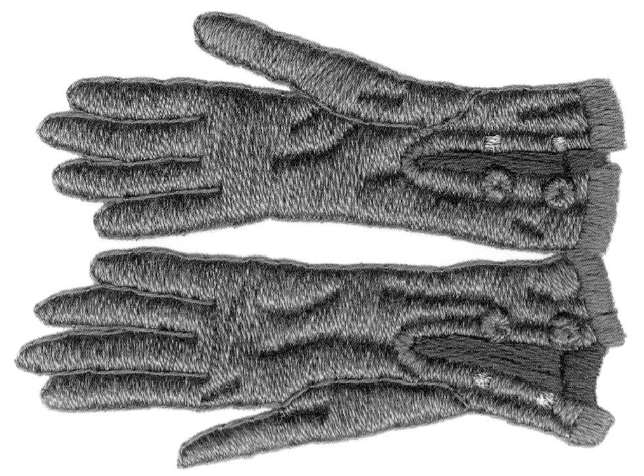

What inspires you?
My inspiration varies, ranging from a specific subject to images that come from reading a novel. It can be from scenes on stage, or in life, that touched me and that remain with me. For portraits, I choose relatives, famous people I like, or people with some distinctive feature.

Are you interested in fashion?
I'm not a fashion addict, but I appreciate the working part of fashion: the patterns, the fabrics, the details of the realizations, the accessories, etc.

Describe your work.
Contemporary hand embroidery.

Which media and techniques do you use?
The technique is traditional. Either I draw directly onto the fabric, or I transfer the main lines with carbon paper. After that, I fix the rough with an iron and place the piece of fabric on a little circular frame. I use cotton threads. The choice of stitches is wide, but I mainly use straight stitch.

What, for you, makes a successful fashion illustration?
A skillful blending of elegance and legibility.

What artistic training have you undertaken?
I have no real training in illustration, but am educated in dance (ballet, contemporary, and modern jazz dance). I have completed a preparatory year in interior design and short courses in professional makeup and video.

If you could give one piece of advice to a student, what would it be?
Explore your dreams.

Describe yourself and your greatest achievement.
I'm Belgian, of Korean origin, living in Brussels. I studied makeup and used to work for theaters, mainly at the opera. Coming to embroidery has been a slow journey, after being obstructed in adolescence. When I was a teenager, I started making clothes with the help of my mother, but then using the sewing machine alone was a stressful experience. Later on, there was a remnant of fear when I needed to do alterations or other needlework. I always chose to hand-sew. The idea of contemporary embroidery came when I saw some embroidery pieces. They were so modern, wonderful, and delicate that it motivated me to give embroidery a try. As I was used to hand-sewing, I started by teaching myself.

I guess my greatest achievement will be the next one.

YUKI HATORI

What inspires you?
People and cities. Late-night movies.

Are you interested in fashion?
Yes. It's hard not to observe unique and stylish people on the streets.

Describe your work.
I love to incorporate details and elements inspired by foreign cultures into my work, but the women I illustrate are the quintessential Japanese women—modest, shy, and ethereal.

Which media and techniques do you use?
I draw by hand, then work in Photoshop on my Mac.

What, for you, makes a successful fashion illustration?
Whether it grabs me or not. I've never really thought about what makes it successful per se.

What artistic training have you undertaken?
I graduated from Setsu Mode Seminar, an art school in Tokyo, Japan. Shortly after, in 1999, I entered and won the Chance Competition Award hosted by my current agent.

If you could give one piece of advice to a student, what would it be?
Cherish what you love.

Describe yourself and your greatest achievement.
I often come across as energetic and outgoing, but am actually shy. My greatest achievement would be giving birth to my son.

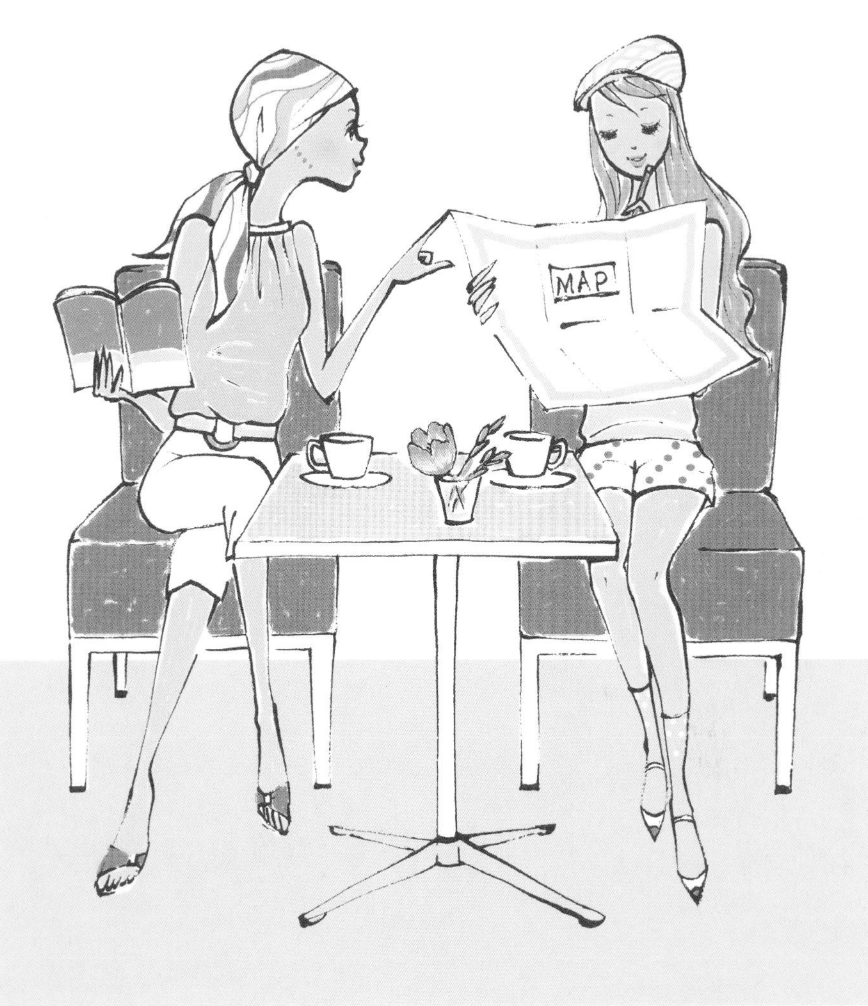

MARION LEFEBVRE

What inspires you?
God knows! That inspiration thing has a life of its own ... I'm inspired by architecture; soulful, abandoned places; abstract shapes; diagrams of all sorts; weird objects and creatures; and, at the moment, subtle colors.

Are you interested in fashion?
I like understated fashion, along with a nice detail that brings it all to life. Shoes are great too! In real life, I can appreciate a beautiful pair of shoes, the design of a piece of cloth or its texture, but what people wear is not what interests me most when I meet them. As an image-maker, I'm interested in the way fashion editorials or campaigns are art-directed and in what they reveal of the society we live in.

Describe your work.
Recently, my work has changed. I now use more drawing. I like subtle colors. Composition is a major aspect of my work, which mainly focuses on characters. I always start from the character, which then dictates the choice of the format, the background elements, and the style of the image. Each element participates in the elaboration of the image and has a reason for being there. I tend to create images with an atmosphere—they always contain the embryo of a story.

Which media and techniques do you use?
I use my own photography and drawings. I also cut out images from magazines and books, or scan objects. I then bring the whole image together in Photoshop.

What, for you, makes a successful fashion illustration?
It's an image that epitomizes the spirit of the clothes it portrays, or tells a story. It can also be that it just works by showing the clothes in the best light. It is either an image that works for a fashion element—a piece of cloth, shoes, or an accessory—that is brought out and made to look outstanding, or the opposite, an image that works with the element. In this last case, the image is a reflection of how these objects actually create the world around them.

What artistic training have you undertaken?
I studied Fine Art for five years at L'École Nationale Superieure des Beaux Arts, in France, as well as multimedia in a photography school in France. I also have a BA Hons in Illustration, which I took at the Kent Institute of Art and Design (UK).

If you could give one piece of advice to a student, what would it be?
It is crucial to be open and learn as much as you can. But it's just as important to forget it all at one point and to find your own way! Be curious of what others do and of what others have done before. Personally, I find history of art very important, as even the most cutting-edge style has sources that can be traced. Creation is mostly about reinvention. Be open, don't be afraid to experiment with new styles, always look further. Get real. Artists who make it are also very good at promoting themselves, so be prepared to develop your commercial skills!

Describe yourself and your greatest achievement.
My greatest achievement is always ahead! I guess that describes me as an optimist! Through my career as an illustrator, my style has changed a lot. It is said to be easier if you stick to a commercial style that you can be recognized for, but I find this very alienating. I want to keep exploring my skills and feel free to give up a style when I become bored of it, rather than become a prisoner of that same style from fear that clients won't follow if I change. In my eyes, a great achievement is not who you've worked for or how many people have seen your work. If you're managing to stay true to your creative self, that's a great achievement.

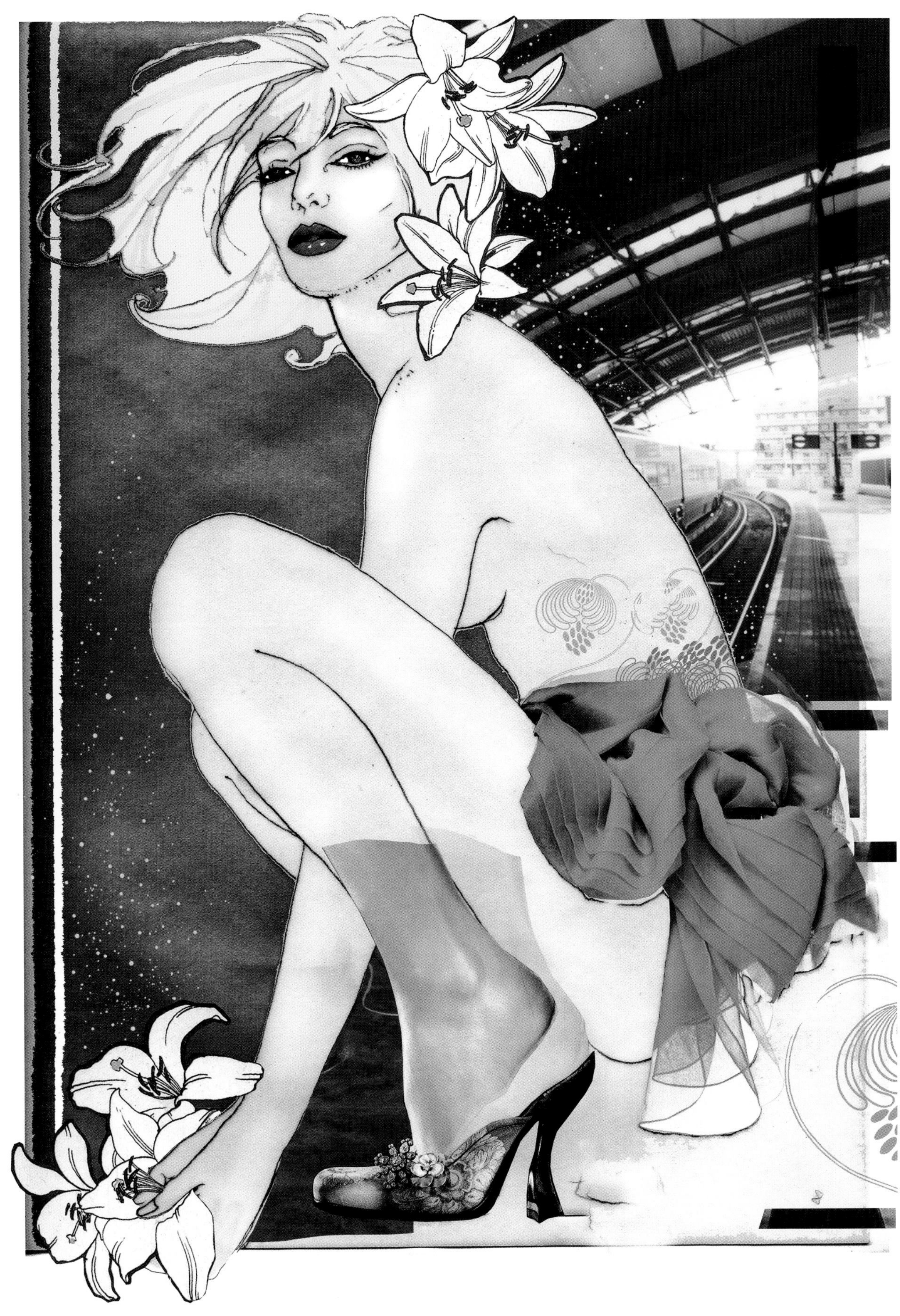

TOBIE GIDDIO

What inspires you?
People, places, and things uplifting to me ... music, nature, beautiful clothing, realized beings, true creators ... Agnes Martin, Tori Amos, "Yellow Submarine," meditation, London.

Are you interested in fashion?
Yes. Fashion photography has greatly influenced me over the years. I have learned what makes a solid and inspired story from the likes of Steven Meisel, Paolo Roversi, and Craig McDean. Fashion visionaries such as Alexander McQueen, Rei Kawakubo, and Yohji Yamamoto have influenced me a great deal as well. They remind me again and again of how far, inwardly and outwardly, I can take things. It's all about great beauty, liberation, and pure creativity with these guys.

Describe your work.
My work is ultimately about connecting to the universally innate beauty in all of us. I do my best to stay out of the way in order to allow these somewhat faraway beings to emerge onto the page. When I have an assignment for a fashion company, it's the same process, except I know what they will be wearing.

Which media and techniques do you use?
I almost always start off with a completely direct sumi-ink drawing. I never do a rough sketch or any type of underdrawing, and a lot of drawings get thrown away until I get to where I need to be. Then I apply Pantone transparency film in various colors and gradations with a straight-edge razor blade. This product was discontinued years ago, and so I am continually searching for what I need.

What, for you, makes a successful fashion illustration?
A successful fashion drawing illustrates a gorgeous woman in clothing, in a way that a photograph cannot. She is supremely elegant without a sense of comparison to a model per se.

A successful fashion illustration brings the viewer a pure sense of delight and pleasure. There is much left to the imagination, while what is necessary remains apparent. It bothers me to see drawings that are lacking in the knowledge of anatomy. I am very focused on the structure and balance of a drawing. Quality of line and composition is everything.

What artistic training have you undertaken?
Fashion Illustration at the Fashion Institute of Technology, New York. My primary mentor was Barbara Pearlman, a successful fashion illustrator from the sixties and seventies who went on to have a career in fine art. Other instructors included Jack Potter, Ana Ishikawa, Gertrude Stretton, and Dorothy Loverro.

If you could give one piece of advice to a student, what would it be?
Be yourself. Find your unique purpose. Do whatever it takes to find out what that is.

Describe yourself and your greatest achievement.
I think my greatest achievement has been that I have maintained my artistic integrity and independence throughout the years in a field that has evolved relatively slowly. I have learned humility, perseverance, and faith in the process.

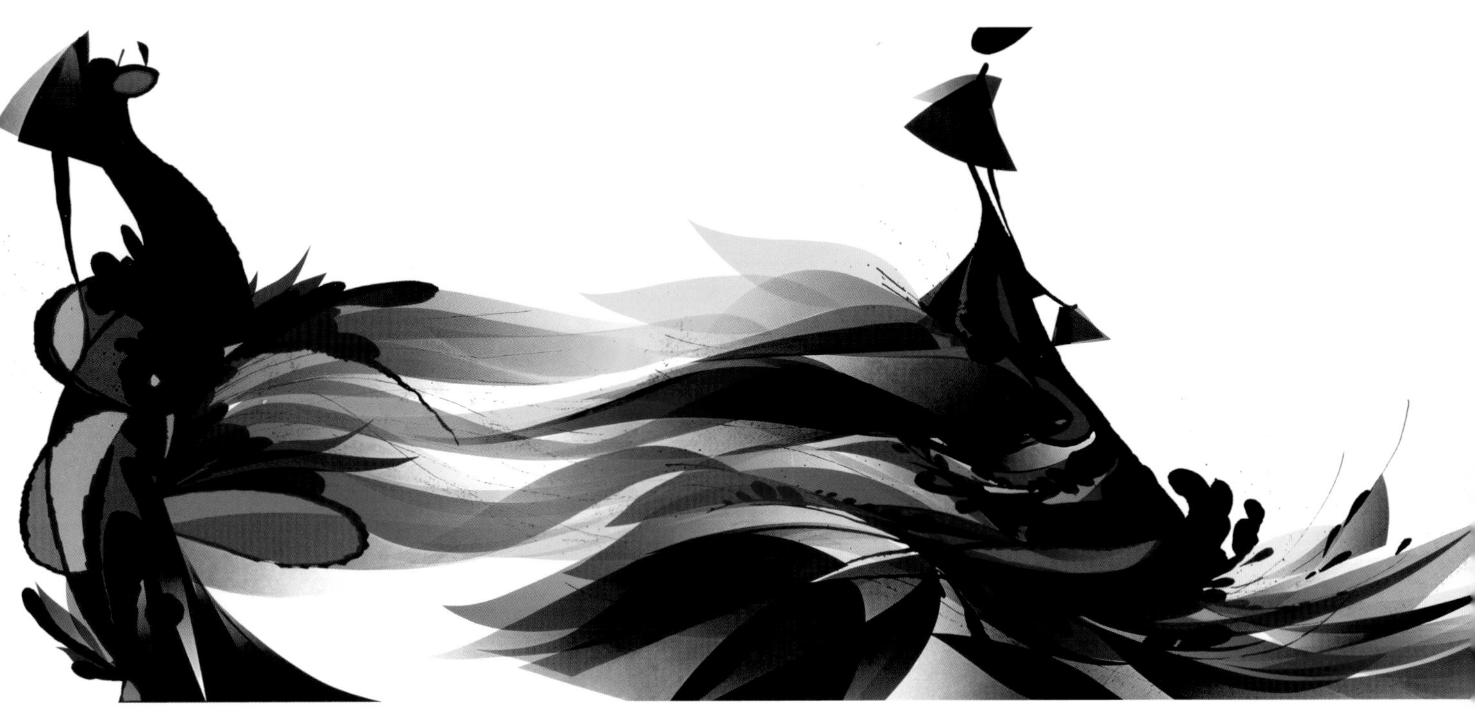

EDGARDO CAROSIA

What inspires you?
Really, I find inspiration in everything that surrounds me. Although that sounds like a cliché, it is true. Working for different types of magazines and periodicals, directed to different audiences, causes me to carry out a lot of investigation of specific themes. There is so much that corresponds to fashion and aesthetics, including the radio, music, newspapers, books, movies, television, urbanism, politics, etc. But many other things inspire me similarly—my friends, the friends of my friends, their inclinations and customs, my son, my wife, the sea that we see through the window, the parties, the festivals, the street, the people that pass along the street. Inspiration is constant for me, almost routine and always traps me into working.

Are you interested in fashion
Yes—from the types of clothes I buy for myself, to the textures and colors of the clothes (like stained-glass windows) of the models that parade on the runway. Fashion interests me as an area of perpetual investigation, although it seems that fashion always returns and is a constant recycling process. In every case a fashion always returns, but redefined, vague, and redrawn. It is infinite.

Describe your work.
Describing my work is a little difficult. I am very curious and investigate all the time, pushing my own limitations as I am attracted to different techniques. My work is based on the study of forms and technique, line and style. In general, mine are commercial works, by assignment for newspapers, magazines, publicity, and design. This work is what carries me forwards to discover in myself different styles every time.

Which media and techniques do you use?
The media that I utilize is everything that I find appropriate for each situation: ink, acrylic, pencils, cuts, clothes, and PC—a lot of PC. The scanner and the PC are the common denominators that help me to amalgamate everything.

What, for you, makes a successful fashion illustration?
The freedom of techniques that can be used in fashion illustration attracts me. One can experiment, mix, and propose, and it allows you to cross into artistic exaggeration. In my case, it is the line and colors that prevail, but I enjoy the illustrations of those that present different ideas and styles, mixing techniques at the same time. This is what inspires me in my less commercial works, which I enjoy a lot.

What artistic training have you undertaken?
I have done all kinds of workshops linked to illustration, but I am basically self-taught, since I did a university course not in illustration but in chemistry! From this comes my interest in collage—the mixture and investigation, I suppose. It is drawing as artistic expression that has always attracted me since I was very small. Therefore, I have tried to take classes in drawing, commercial illustration, drawing by PC, comic strip, animation, painting, humorous drawing, etc.

If you could give one piece of advice to a student, what would it be?
What I can tell students is what I apply to myself: value curiosity as an indispensable tool, since it links directly to investigation and, from there, to technique.

Describe yourself and your greatest achievement.
Being able to work doing what I enjoy is what I value most. The curiosity and investigation that go into my work are the things that define me as an author and illustrator.

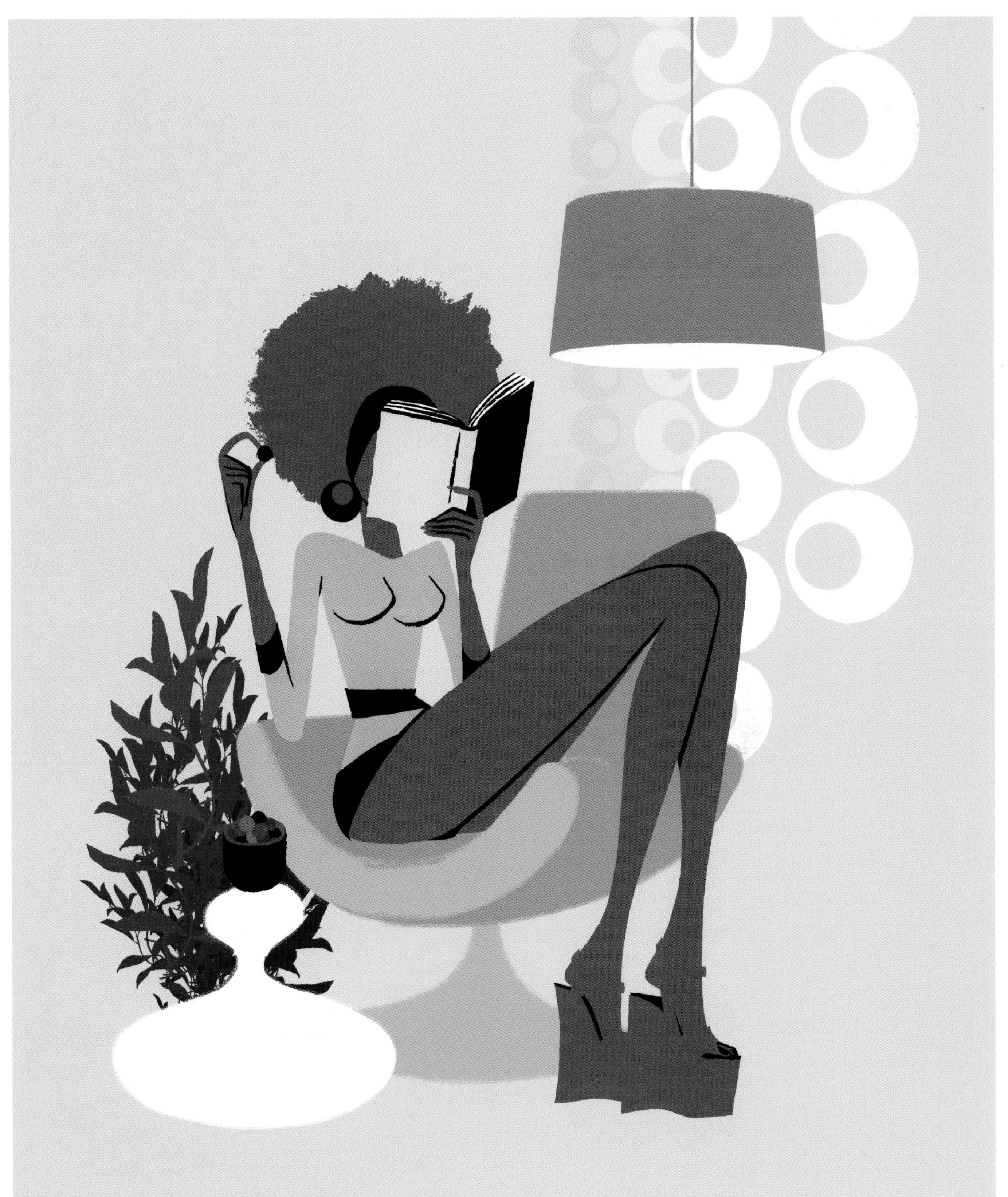

STEPHEN CAMPBELL

What inspires you?

The children and teenagers that I see at my day job as an art therapist at Bellevue Hospital, in New York City. Those New York City teens have amazing street style. Movies like Richardson's *Mademoiselle* or Godard's *Weekend*, Klein's *Polly Maggoo* or Tati's *Playtime*. My collections of *Snoopy* and *Tin Tin*. Travel. Photographers like Jean-Pierre Khazem and Sam Haskins. Icons like Polly Melon—they live and die with the fashion!

Are you interested in fashion?

Yes, but also many other things too. Growing up, I would always draw the fashions from the newspaper style page or fashion magazines.

Describe your work.

I think of my work as paper cutouts with many layers. My details, color, and humor are the most important. I like my figures to have just enough information to do their job. The rest is left up to the viewer to decide the figure's name, ethnicity, story, and qualities, etc.

Which media and techniques do you use?

My illustrations are created in Adobe Illustrator. I only draw with the mouse. The mouse gives a line quality like a marker for me. The computer allows me to paint and mix colors. I am able to see the color in my head. Then, with the computer color CMYK palette, I am able to mix the desired color. Instant gratification. In addition, I always carry a sketchbook and marker. When I travel, I am able to use my sketchbook to generate illustrations throughout the year. I am always sketching a bit of something. Later, I will incorporate these little sketch ideas when needed. Sometimes an illustration might come from the drawing of a bag or shoe seen on the street or subway.

What, for you, makes a successful fashion illustration?

The communication has to be clear. It needs to be reinforced by the details, color, and humor. There should be a reason to give the illustration a second look and study it.

What artistic training have you undertaken?

In college, my major was in Graphic Design/Packaging. I flunked out of the color-theory classes and program due to my inability to mix acrylic paints for color scales. I explored different media and types of art, while graduating with an art history major.

Growing up, I have to thank my mother and grandmother for providing me with creative art experiences. They made me aware that everything (and anything) can be made with your hands. This philosophy has helped me through all my development as an artist, whether I was sculpting, sewing, gardening, or embroidering a dog head on a sweater.

If you could give one piece of advice to a student, what would it be?

My advice is to pursue what you enjoy. Draw what you know. I draw or make something every day. If not, I am at least thinking about the next illustration in my mind. Even if I didn't have any success in my illustration career, I would still be drawing every day. Do your own thing. Trends come and go in illustration and fashion. Be aware of the world and history inside and outside of fashion, then illustrate your way. Develop your instincts, and know to listen to them. Those first instincts of choice are what make you different.

Describe yourself and your greatest achievement.

Observant, Lacoste-loving prep, hard worker, collector, art therapist, illustrator. The launch of my Ralph Pucci Mannequin lines—the thrill of seeing my work reinterpreted as a lifesize, three-dimensional object.

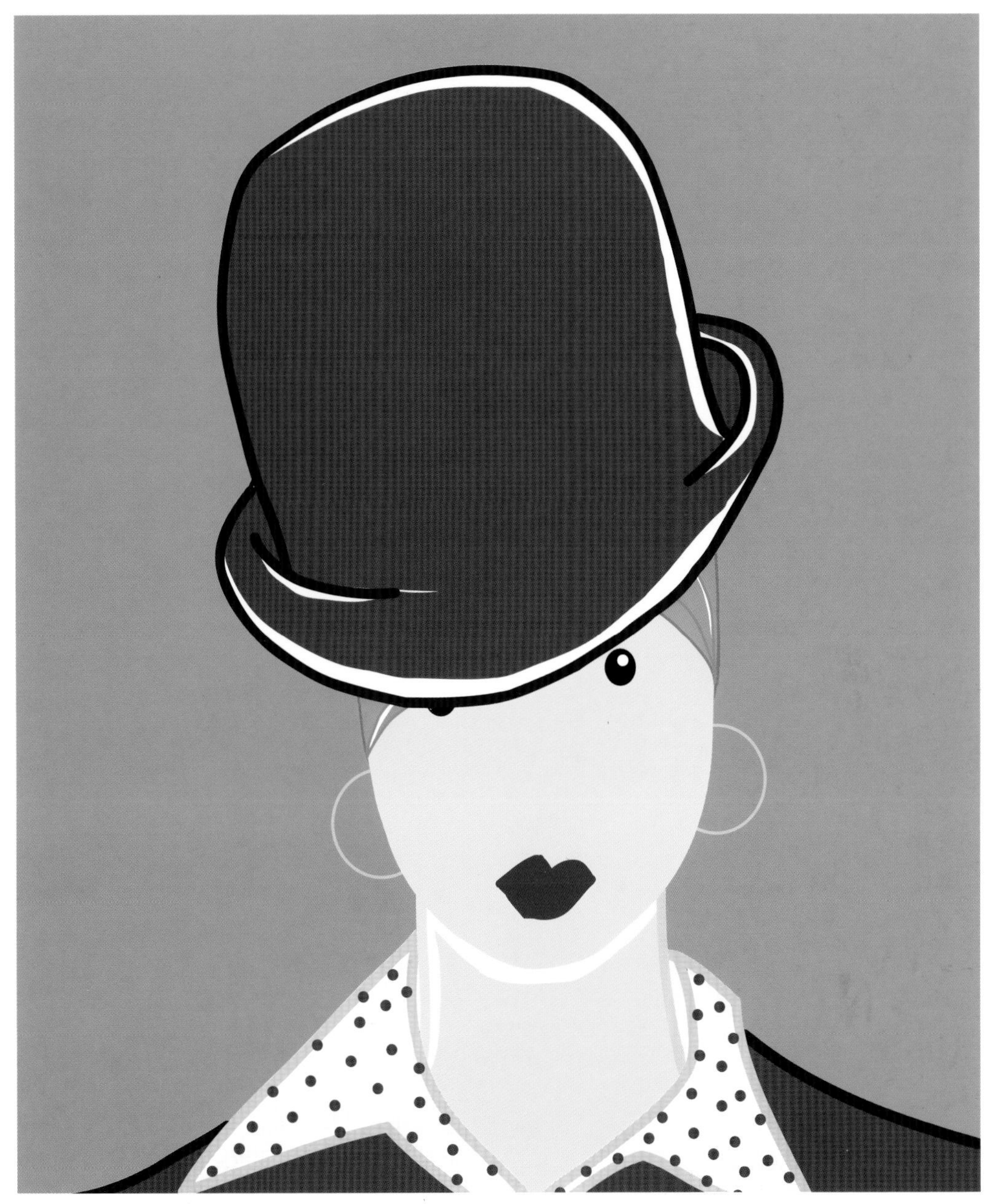

ALMA LARROCA

What inspires you?
Many things can serve as sources of inspiration, according to the moment and the work to be carried out, although I believe that inspiration does not always appear naturally when I seek or need it. It is something that comes to my mind for any reason and at any time. Ideas can arise from a movie, a newspaper, or from chatting with friends. Also, certain things can serve to make me begin a work: places or environments such as the sea, the clear horizon, the green of mountains, some music, the smile of my baby, are all inspirational starting points.

Are you interested in fashion?
Yes, it attracts me as an artistic area where several disciplines are mixed. I especially like the textures of the human body; the idea of dressing silhouettes in my illustrations entertains me.

Describe your work.
I work by assignment, creating illustrations for magazines, newspapers, book covers, etc. I have also carried out a project for a restaurant. The work was created with vectors so that printed giants covered the walls of the restaurant. I also designed the menu, cards, etc. Generally, when I receive an assignment, the first step is compiling information on the theme. I investigate through the Internet, books, and magazines. I write down my ideas, mixing information with fast sketches, which sometimes only I can understand. But sometimes I work directly on what will be the final work without a prior sketch, depending a little on the importance of each work and the time that I have to create it.

Which media and techniques do you use?
I utilize different techniques, doing as much manually as by computer, and I like to combine them for the final result. I am very interested in mixed media, especially collage in two and three dimensions (assemblage), where I combine objects and different materials. I also carry out a similar process with my computer, combining photographs or scanned objects with drawings carried out by hand or with vectors.

What, for you, makes a successful fashion illustration?
The use of original and attractive techniques, for representing the fashion world in many different and interesting plastic and graphic ways, where at times the role of the illustrator is mixed with the role of fashion designer.

What artistic training have you undertaken?
Graphic Design at the University of Buenos Aires, Argentina. I also studied traditional animation at the School of Cinema of Avellaneda, Buenos Aires, Argentina, and I have carried out some seminars and short courses: drawing, *cartapesta* (papier-mâché), etc. But I think that my vocation and special interest in collage and mixed media comes from practice and free experimentation.

If you could give one piece of advice to a student, what would it be?
You should be curious; you should experiment and investigate; you should be involved in what happens around you. Enjoy the boundaries of each project, considering it to be an attractive challenge, a play in which you will find the most appropriate way to transmit something with your personal seal.

Describe yourself and your greatest achievement.
Curious, obsessive, sleepless, worker. I think that my greatest achievement is to work doing what I enjoy, and recently my best work has been my little son!

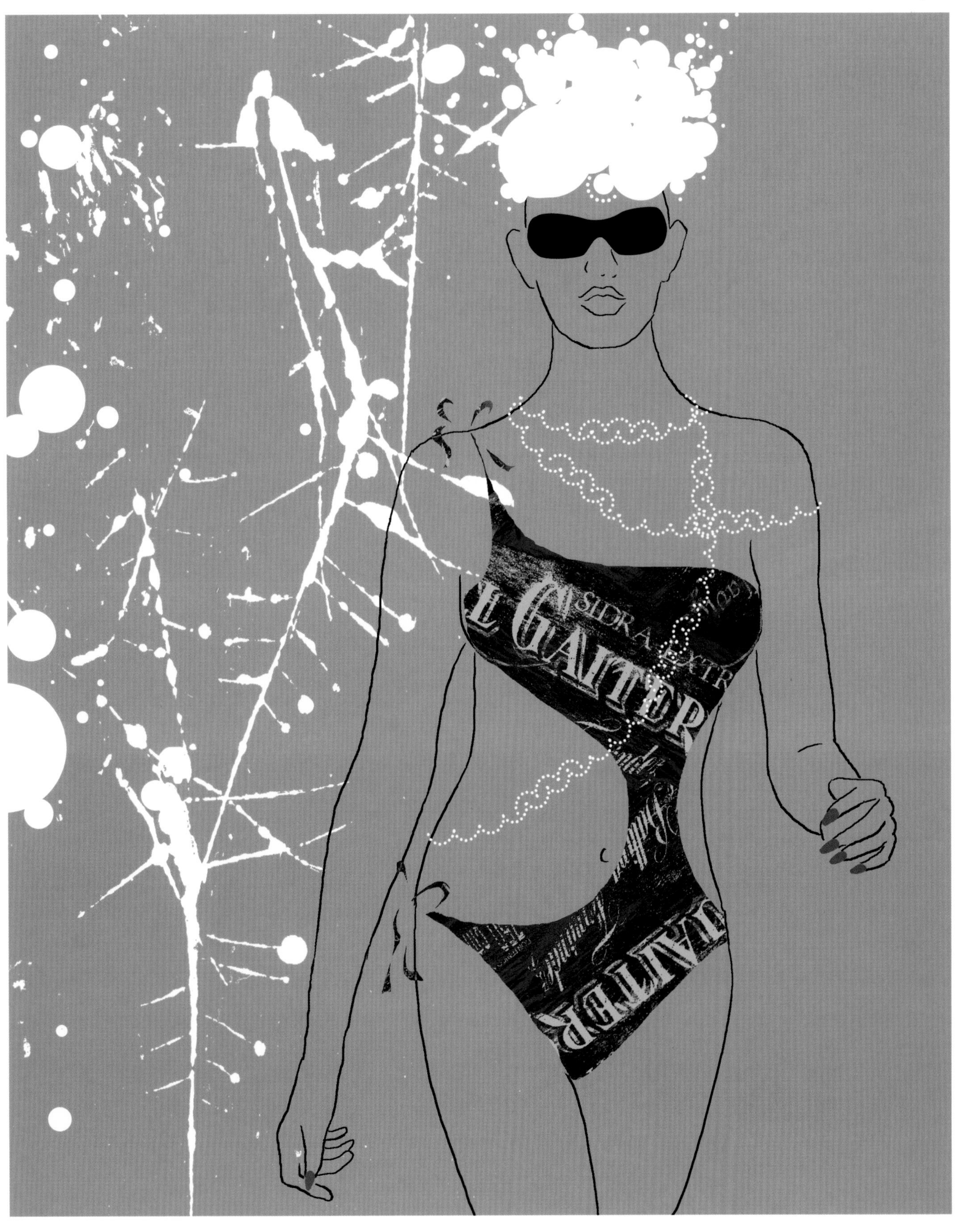

LOVISA BURFITT

What inspires you?
I collect my inspiration in the magic meetings and moments in life that are like little film-clips. Also, I have my heroes, who I return to all the time. They include Frida Kahlo, Coco Chanel, and Edith Piaf because of the heart and soul they bled into their work.

I think it is very important to flee from everyday life and dream away. I like a little touch of working-class hero mixed up with glamour and decadence.

Are you interested in fashion?
Yes, indeed. I also do my own line of clothing, and I love the combination of this and my illustration, gaining inspiration both ways.

Describe your work.
My work is very restless, sensual, and impulsive. Usually I work best when I feel I am doing the work on my "extra time," like bonus time. As if I have been stealing time from something else, that makes me really excited. Silly, I know. Really trying to work on that one.

Which media and techniques do you use?
I use everything from ink, felt pen, touch, crayons, and spray to Scotch [tape], which I cut out my drawings from.

What, for you, makes a successful fashion illustration?
A hit in the solar plexus, if it is full of emotions. It is, of course, a matter of taste. I am sure of that. But the best illustrations I ever made were done really quickly, sometimes I feel they were almost made by accident while I was supposed to do something else.

What artistic training have you undertaken?
Art school foundation diploma, stylist's assistant, designer's assistant at H&M, Beckman's School of Fashion Design and the Royal College of Art (UK).

If you could give one piece of advice to a student, what would it be?
Follow your heart and first intuition with an idea, but also be prepared to analyze it. Remember that creativity could be just that you are actually doing something more, rather than it having to be the best thing you've ever done.

Also for me, my work has saved me many times. My creativity is important. It is that, rather than my "career," that saves me.

Describe yourself and your greatest achievement.
First of all, I would like someone else to answer these questions. I am a very moody person, which I am sure you can also see in my work. All emotions have to be expressed in some way, and, in my case, it became through drawing and design. A person once said in a radio interview that looking at my illustrations made her feel self-confident and inspired, and I guess that it is a nice reflection of my work. Also, it is so wonderful when I see people in the street wearing my clothes. Then they are suddenly transformed by someone else who applies their own ideas and combinations.

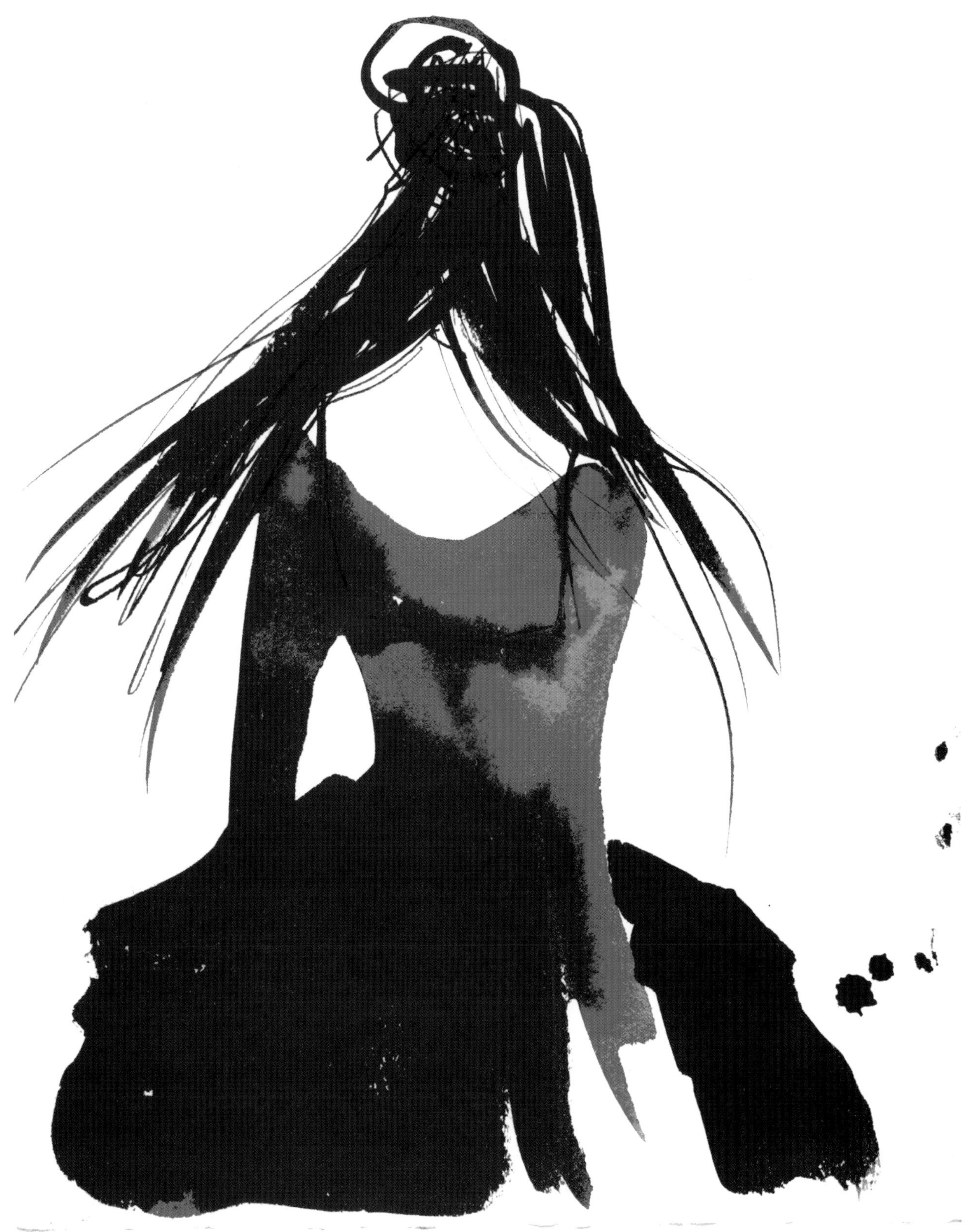

BILL BROWN

What inspires you?
Mostly I'm inspired by people-watching. Later, when I'm sketching, I might use a hairdo, or an overbite, or a stance that I have seen. When I can't watch people, I'll draw from magazines or my own photographs. I draw my friends a lot. I also enjoy redrawing existing artwork, such as early advertising cuts or clip art, but recreating the image in my own style.

Are you interested in fashion?
I've always enjoyed working on projects that ride on a rush of creativity and have too short a shelf-life to be over-managed. That would describe most of the fashion magazine work I do, but I have never been interested in designing clothing.

Describe your work.
I would describe my illustrations as sweet, yet smart-assed at the same time. I like having that duality in there. For example, if an illustration is sexy, it should also be silly. Nothing should be taken too seriously.

Which media and techniques do you use?
Nearly all the line art is drawn with ink on paper. In fact, I just use Sharpies and relatively inexpensive paper. Then the line art is scanned, and color is applied in Adobe Photoshop.

What, for you, makes a successful fashion illustration?
An illustration is a collaborative process, so the success of it depends on the work dynamic of the artist and the client. If the art director and the artist respect each other for their specific talents, the result should be a success. When I'm working, I want to feel free enough to do the sort of work that caught the client's eye in the first place. I'm proud of the work in my portfolio, and some of my most successful images were done without a lot of art direction. I'm one of those artists who works well unsupervised for a while, but I do like to have some boundaries to push against. Ultimately, it's important for me to at least do what's asked of me. They are paying for it, after all.

What artistic training have you undertaken?
BA Hons in Graphic Design from Montana State University.

If you could give one piece of advice to a student, what would it be?
Draw all the time. Draw every day if you can. I highly recommend a lot of nude, figure drawing. It's so much easier to draw a clothed figure when you know what it looks like underneath. If you can't get nude models, draw your clothed friends. It's always best to draw from life rather than a photograph, but photographs are good when you can't get someone to sit for you.

Describe yourself and your greatest achievement.
I'm a regular guy who happens to be very lucky. My greatest achievement has been making a living of my greatest passion. I love to draw, and I would do it anyway, whether people paid me or not. The fact that it's my job has kept me drawing steadily for years, and my style has evolved throughout that time. I can't wait to see how much I've improved in ten years.

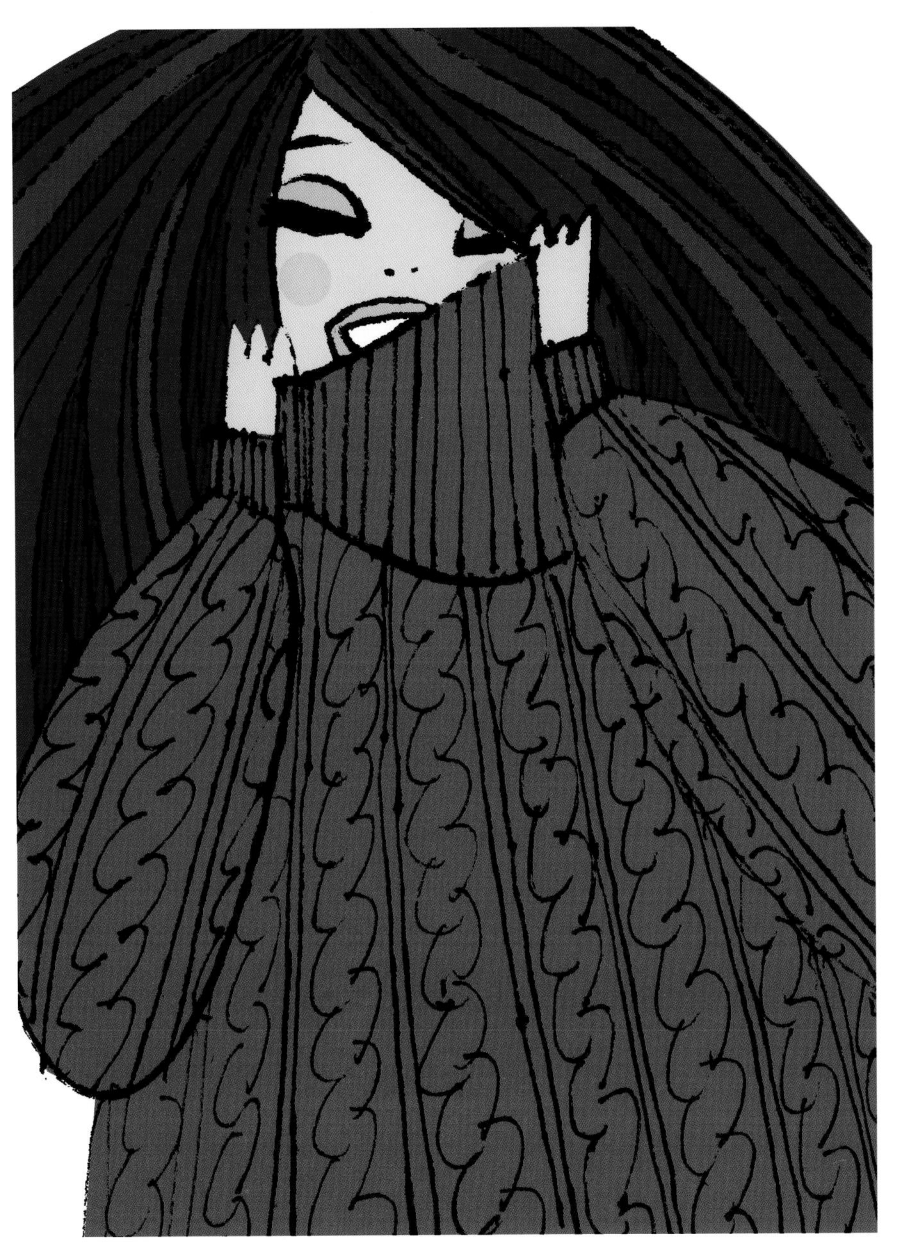

GIOVANNA CELLINI

What inspires you?
I can be inspired by many things—observing people and places around me, or discussing things with my friends and family can be really stimulating. I look at art, graphic design, fashion, and illustration, but also children's books and interior design. Sometimes, even a small detail can be the starting point for a piece of work; and trying a new technique, or some new paper, can give me the idea for a project. A frequent source of inspiration for me is nature, and especially the animal world. I am fascinated by the endless variety of their colors, skin, and eyes. I am interested in detail. I also like to go through objects, books, and photographs from my past, things that I loved as a child and I still hang onto. I like to incorporate personal reference in my illustrations, and I believe this helps me relate to the work, even if I am the only one to understand it.

Are you interested in fashion?
I studied fashion design, and I collaborate professionally with various clothing labels as a print designer. It's interesting how people relate to fashion, how everyone has a personal sense of style, a preference for certain colors, even if only in the minute details. I think that getting dressed is a form of art.

Describe your work.
My illustration work is heavily based on drawing. I also use the computer, but I like my images to have a handmade, sometimes sketchy quality to them. My drawings are often very intricate and detailed, and I tend to work adding and moving elements like in a collage. I think my illustration work has a fantastic side to it—I've always been fascinated by images with an unreal feel to them.

Which media and techniques do you use?
I always sketch first in pencil. As separate drawings, all the elements I intend to use in my illustration follow a general idea. Then I collage it together, either as an actual cut-and-paste object, or I compose the image on the computer and redraw it as a whole. I use various techniques, sometimes in combination—mainly black pencil and colored pencils. At the moment, I particularly like soft, colored pencils on colored paper. I also use black ink, adding color on the computer.

What, for you, makes a successful fashion illustration?
I think that a successful fashion illustration, or any illustration for that matter, is made by a combination of different elements. I think that respecting the brief and representing the garment are important, but the illustration should also possess an extra quality, an idea of style that is unique to the illustrator.

What artistic training have you undertaken?
Fashion Design at Istituto Europeo del Design in Rome, Italy. After that I moved to London, where I took a BA Hons in Graphic Design at Camberwell College (UK).

If you could give one piece of advice to a student, what would it be?
I think I would advise students to spend some time thinking about what made them want to study art and design—remember books, artists, and places that shaped their taste and inspired them—then center their work around what they really like and feel more passionately about, without worrying too much about what everyone else is doing. Also, I think that it is important to follow ideas through, remembering that what one has in mind and the finished product are often two completely different things, and sometimes unexpected results can be very exciting.

Describe yourself and your greatest achievement.
A fairly quiet Italian, living in London, who can't think of her greatest achievement. I hope it is yet to come.

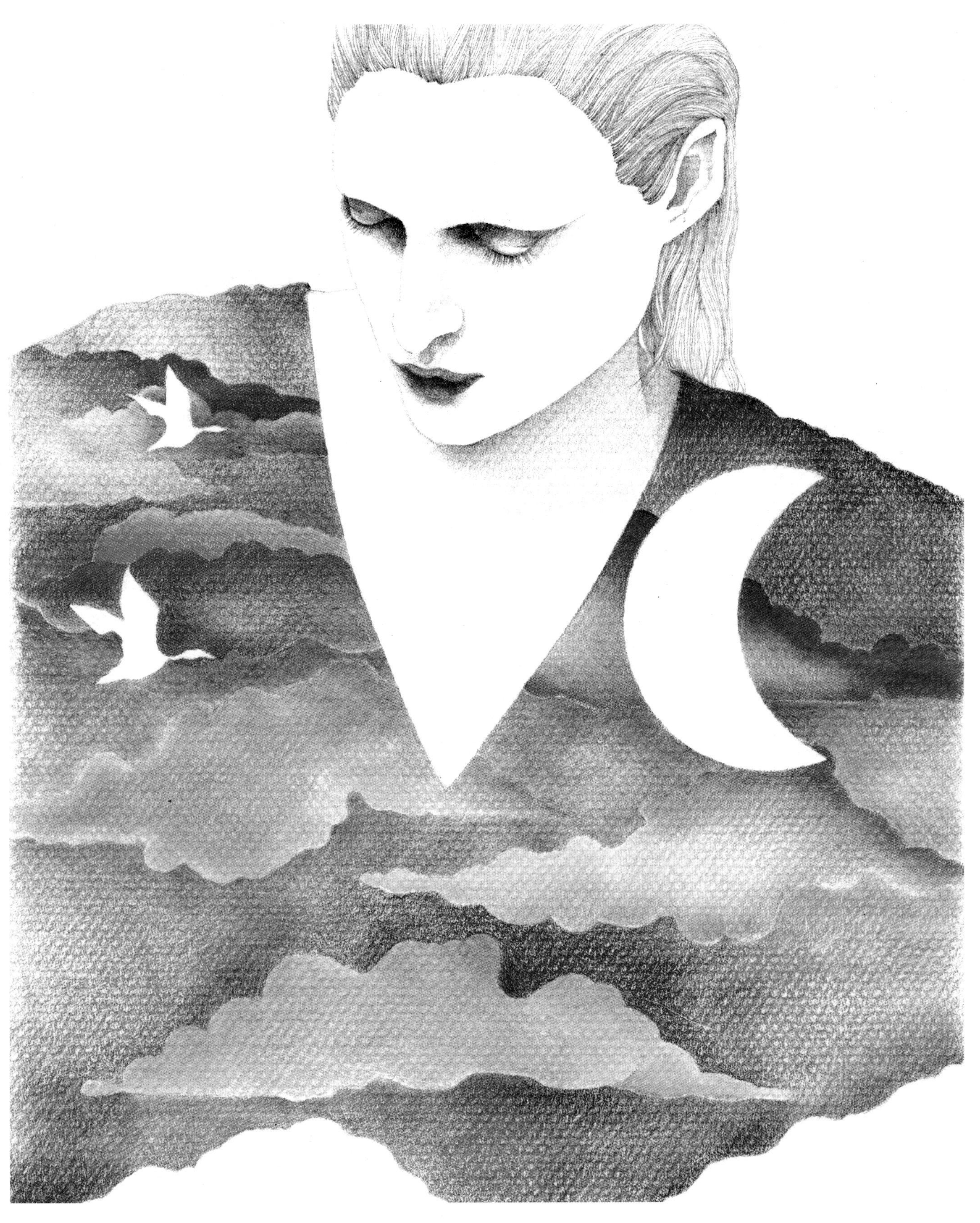

JASPER GOODALL

What inspires you?
Re-contextualizing elements in things like Japanese prints, natural-history illustration, and seventies' illustration and design. Erotic illustration, particularly at the moment Aubrey Beardsley's work. Also, female beauty, sexuality, and my love/hate for fashion photography.

Are you interested in fashion?
Yes, I have been for some years, not really specific clothes as such, more vibes conveyed by clothes—attitudes that come through certain looks.

Describe your work.
I guess I have a recurring theme of female sexuality; sometimes it's about the clothes, but more often it's about the attitudes of the women I present. Quite often it's about being powerful, confident, and playful. I think I'm really interested in desire, both my own and the audience's, and how one successfully pushes "desire buttons" through artwork.

Which media and techniques do you use?
I use a process of initial photomontage to create a photo-based image of my "character" from a vast library of photos. This method allows me to create a very good reference of someone doing virtually anything. By putting an arm here, then a leg there, and a head, etc., I can manufacture a photograph that I have neither the time nor money to actually take. I then redraw either on the computer or with traditional media—ink or felt-tip pens or pencils, so the illustration could end up either very clean or more organic and rough looking.

What, for you, makes a successful fashion illustration?
Fashion photography has become so sophisticated and has spawned so many celebrity photographers that an illustration is too often seen as a poor alternative. I think well-used fashion illustration is very rare. It's usually a small, single piece of fashion "news" or "suggestions." The serious work of the six-page-or-so story is left to the photographers and the models.

I think, personally speaking, fashion illustration can hold as much attitude as a photograph can. I want my work to be used positively and to be perceived as valid, valuable, and desirable, and to be taken as seriously as a photograph would be.

What artistic training have you undertaken?
Foundation at UCE Birmingham (UK). BA Hons in Illustration at University of Brighton (UK).

If you could give one piece of advice to a student, what would it be?
Don't get too hung up on your degree show or the mark you get. Your course is the very beginning of your artistic life, and you will change over and over. The illustrator/designer you are when you leave is not who you will continue to be. Your course isn't the only chance you'll get to do well and assemble your portfolio, so don't get too worried if you feel incomplete on leaving. When you leave, talk to as many art directors as you can—they are your new tutors, as well as yourself. Remember nobody will ever know who you are unless you go out and tell them you exist.

Describe yourself and your greatest achievement.
Perpetually unsure of my own ability, as I suspect (or hope) most artists really are! My greatest achievement has not yet come—I hope it will be to get my own book published within the next two years.

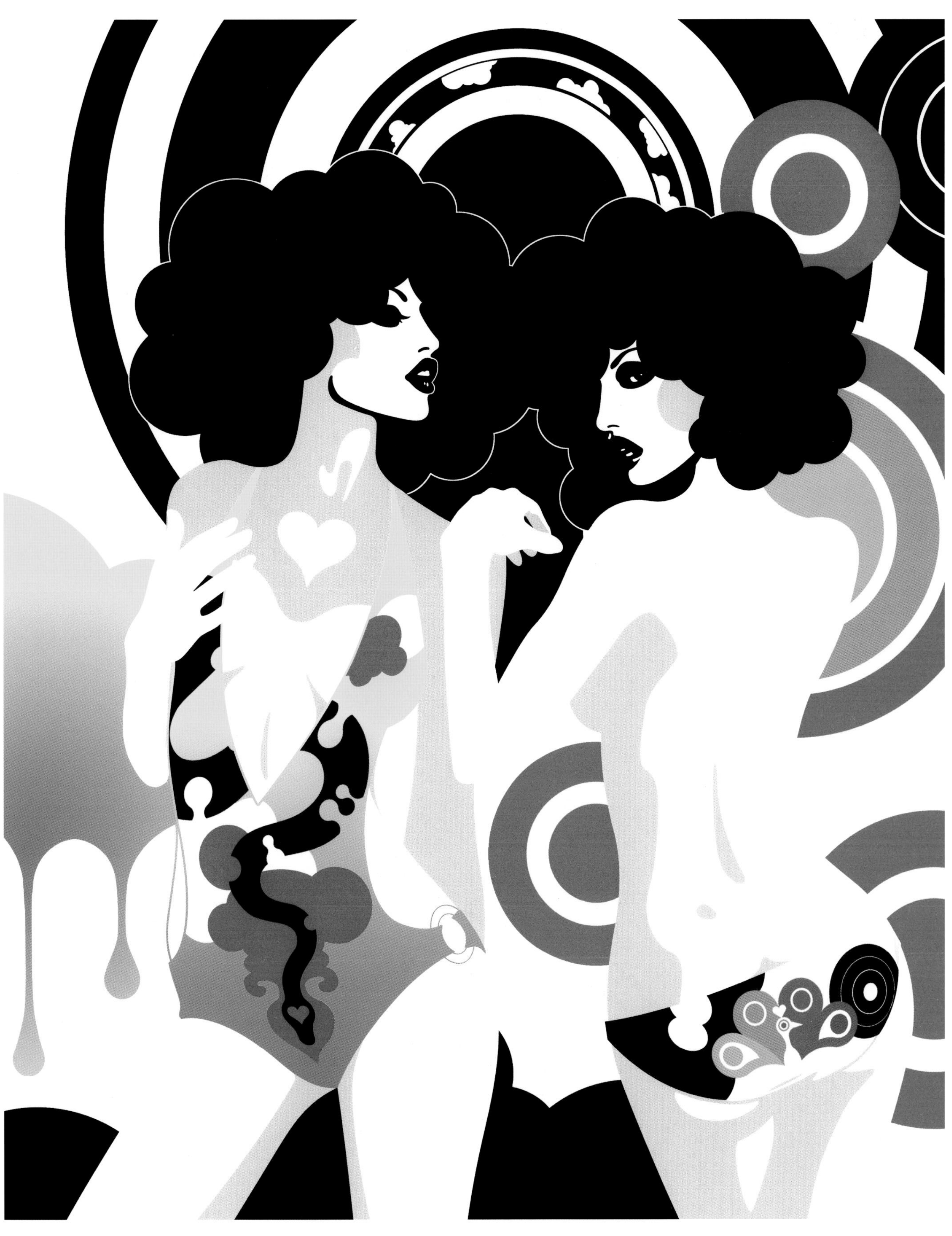

ANNABELLE VERHOYE

What inspires you?
She has that look. You know it. So pretty, she's ugly. So ugly, she's pretty. The ambivalence and double-sidedness of beauty has been the keynote to my art. The perfection of my models is clearly artificial. They seem flawless and arouse fascination through perfection, thus idealizing and elevating attractive female figures. Beauty becomes absolute.

Are you interested in fashion?
Yes. The combination of sex appeal with luxury, elegance, and romance are very attractive to me in fashion. The work of many of today's top designers is extremely captivating, and it influences my artwork. Fashion is one aspect of our culture that transcends the time in which it is made and also encapsulates it for us today.

Describe your work.
My approach and technique are closer to the realms of fine art than most typical illustrations. I try to produce the kind of images that stop you in your tracks, hold your attention, and prevent you turning the page. My goal is to deliver a piece that is beautiful and distinctive, and which is so congruent with the essence of the project that it manifestly advances its cause.

Which media and techniques do you use?
Chine-colléwhich combines delicate layers and precious webs of delightfully patterned Chinese and Japanese rice paper with a sophisticated line drawing. Each layer is scanned individually and further amalgamated in Photoshop.

I also work in a combination of spray paint and acrylics on Plexiglas. My paintings evoke seventeenth-century Japanese scrolls with their clean, smooth lines and often sensual figures. Inspired by Europe's stained-glass windows, I pour and layer the paint on the back of the Plexiglas, giving the work a clean elegance. Nothing is accidental or spontaneous in this process, as I am meticulous in the creation.

What, for you, makes a successful fashion illustration?
The drawing of the human figure is the most crucial aspect of a piece. The figure should be rendered in its aliveness and humanity, and dealt with more directly and on a higher level of thoughtfulness. Outstanding art is achieved through a defined personal vision.

What artistic training have you undertaken?
MFA at School of Visual Arts, New York. BFA diploma in Design at Professional College, Düsseldorf, Germany.

If you could give one piece of advice to a student, what would it be?
Develop your own body of work. Put together a portfolio that illustrates your own personality and the type of work that excites you. The keyword here is passion. When your work focuses on something deeply felt and earnestly expressed, it will naturally convey its importance and find a home. It will create a powerful connection and become true and compelling for others. Be true to yourself.

Describe yourself and your greatest achievements.
In lieu of fame and fortune, I have become aware of how hard-driving and disciplined today's successful artists are. In order to make it in the highly competitive and talented world of illustration, one needs to be passionate, hard-working, disciplined, and persistent. Shortly before graduating, I was honored to receive my first commission: an illustration for the *New Yorker*. My work has been honored with numerous awards and exhibitions at BMW (New York), Thomas Werner Gallery (New York), The Society of Illustrators, American Illustration, and La Samaritaine (Paris, France), just to name a few. I have also had the honor of working for the Walt Disney Company on a tote-bag design. My artwork has been chosen for the labels of Bonny Doon Vineyard, Santa Cruz.

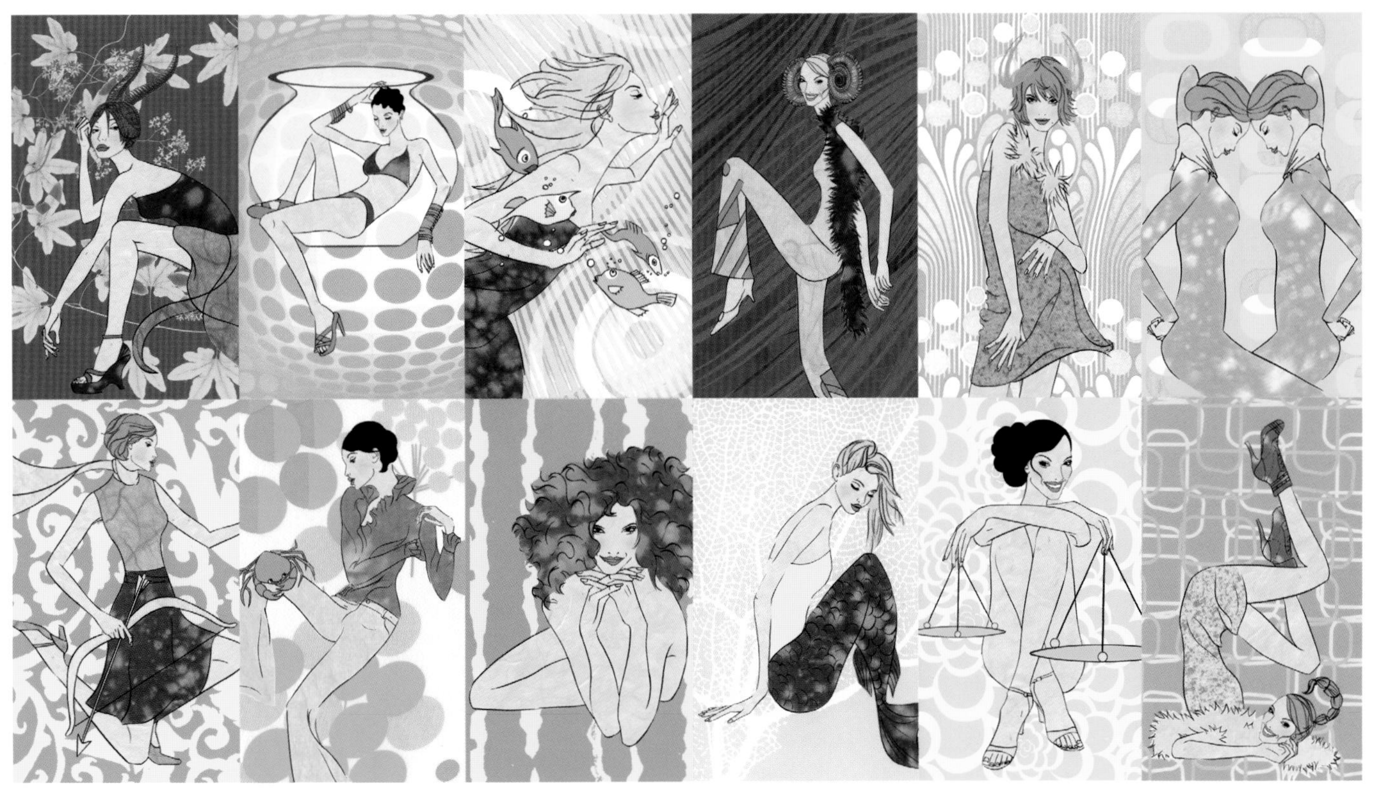

EDWINA CHRISTIANA WHITE

What inspires you?
Wordplay, stories, mishaps, a sharp pencil, colorfields, juxtapositions, a corner of fresh paper, exhausted material, rainy days, and music—it doesn't take much ...

Are you interested in fashion?
Yes. I think of fashion as in the same league as a visit to the zoo. I figure haute couture is the extraordinarily exotic: the fragile, wonderful, imagined creatures that are rarely, if ever, seen in real life. Those ones you can't take home. From feathered heads to dovetails—the best of the fashion game is alluring and watchable, well-adapted, spirited, and timeless. It can be quite difficult to leave a catsuit behind, pacing back and forth in its cage. My wardrobe is evolving.

Describe your work.
Imperfect with purposefully loose ends, it's narrative and figurative. It is quite lyrical and humorous—I figure beauty as melancholic. It is often quite layered with meaning, which is why I am attracted to editorial work. Oh, and I like to lengthen a neck or twist a pupil, to raise an eye socket or enlarge a hand, for the sake of expression.

Which media and techniques do you use?
I work pretty fast, so oils are rarely employed. I use tea, pencils, wire, inks, anything cheap and within reach—endpapers, wood, and fabric swatches. Recently I have been printing drawings on suede, and I have worked with chux (cleaning sponge) and shoe polish in my time ... I'll try anything hanging out in the cupboards or from a street collection.

What, for you, makes a successful fashion illustration?
Perhaps to adapt and redefine beauty—to make an impact and attract attention—just like in real life. I like to suggest and enhance the particular language of a designer and to create a particular feel. The best work is provocative.

What artistic training have you undertaken?
Visual Communications at the University of Technology, Sydney, Australia and an exchange term at Brighton University's Illustration course (UK). I taught different classes at university in Sydney for four years, so that allowed me to experiment further.

If you could give one piece of advice to a student, what would it be?
Work practice is redefined now—make every attempt to focus on how you want to live. My advice would be to continue to make time for what else you do—if you are acting, writing, surfing, playing in a band, whatever ... just play on and adapt those techniques and references to your work practice—whether it be improvised, structured, made solo, or in a group. The happiest designer/illustrator folk I know make room for their other stuff. And they relish their practice almost every day.

Describe yourself and your greatest achievement.
I am the colorful and friendly sort—footloose and searching for fascination ... consistently inconsistent ... I will change my outfit and pictures often. I tend to butterfly socially—and then sometimes I may disappear for a while and relish being mute and serious. My greatest achievement? I am most proud of a bountiful collection of idiosyncratic, warm, delightful, hilarious, and talented friends to keep me afloat. And the fact that I haven't lost any fingers.

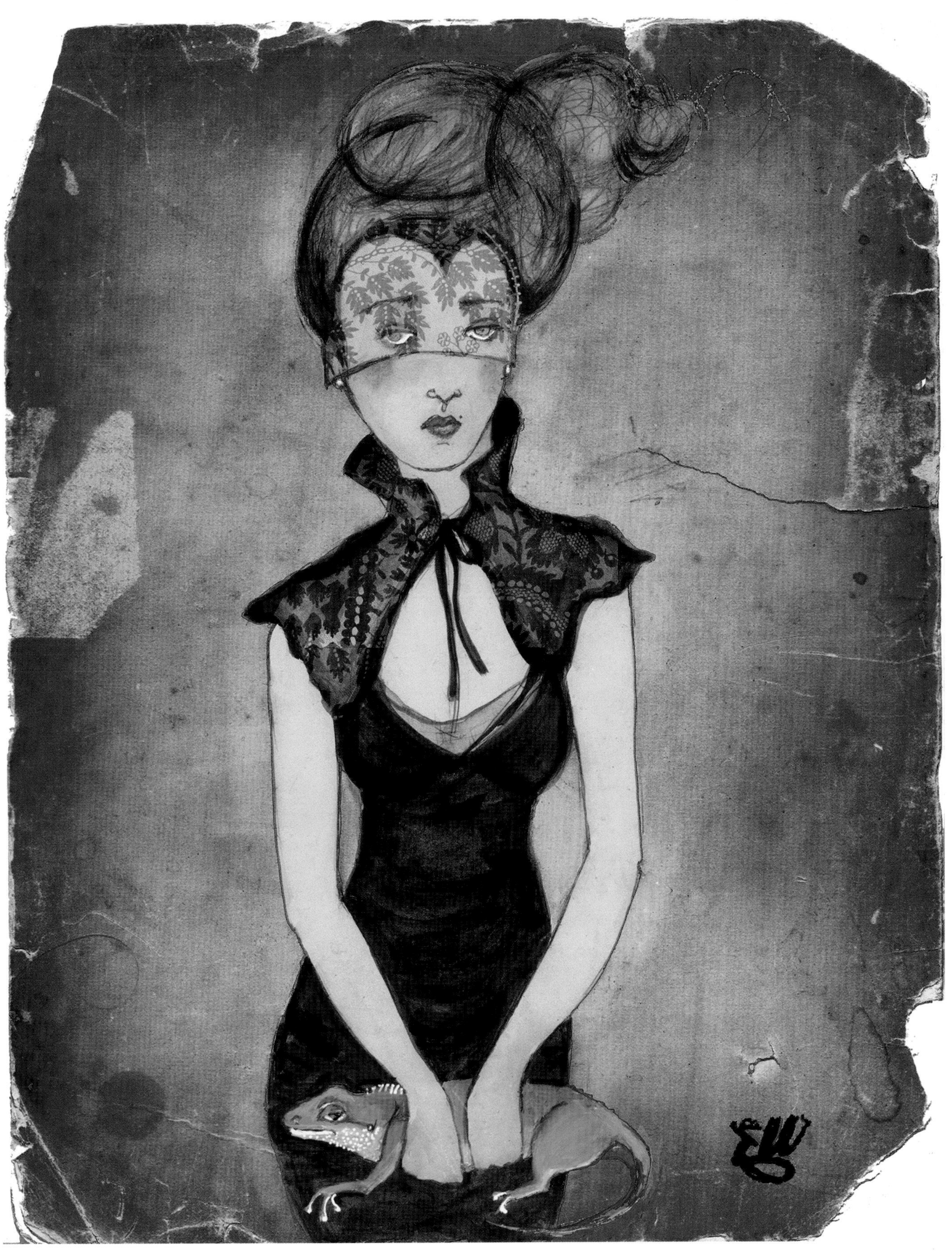

MARCOS CHIN

What inspires you?
Strangers, friends, books and stories, art, design, fashion, graffiti, music videos, cartoons, anime, manga, superheroes, traveling, patterns, wallpaper, doilies, and dolls.

Are you interested in fashion?
Yes, I have always been. I remember when I was very young, watching Fashion Television, and the designer Patrick Kelly's runway show was on. I sat there in awe of his colors and his ideas. I remember seeing garments turn into butterflies, with fabric draping and models swaying. I immediately went to my sketchbook and started drawing figures in my own Kelly-inspired outfits. I think I was twelve.

Describe your work.
I love drawing figures. If you look at my work, you'll see that often there is hardly any background, rather the drawing space is filled with people. I think, for the most part, my images are light and sometimes whimsical. I was heavily influenced by anime, and manga, and comic books as I was growing up, then I became interested in fashion. I think in some capacity, these two things have melded together.

Which media and techniques do you use?
I use Adobe Illustrator to create my work. I draw out the idea first in pencil but usually use that initial sketch only as a template, after which I redraw it using Illustrator.

What, for you, makes a successful fashion illustration?
I grew up seeing that fashion illustration was a good rendering of clothing on a figure—that the lines, colors, and shapes used were a good reflection of the garment it was supposed to illustrate. However, I think that way less so nowadays. I think fashion illustration has a much wider focus, and its appeal has broadened. Now, when you flip through magazines, illustrations that are themed "fashion" are funny, quirky, and abstract. They tell stories or are lone silhouettes, they're sexy and campy. Some are more surreal in their ideas, while others focus more on the elements of the image's aesthetics. I think a successful fashion illustration should be gauged no differently than any other work of art. Design and composition, I think, is key. Color, line quality, concept ... all these principles and elements come into play and, from them, a successful piece is derived, not just a successful fashion illustration.

What artistic training have you undertaken?
I studied at the Ontario College of Art and Design, in Toronto, Canada.

If you could give one piece of advice to a student, what would it be?
I think persistence and honesty is the key. If you love drawing, or painting, or creating, then it will show in your work. It will make you persistent at what you do, and will motivate you to continue to learn, and to be inspired, by people, and things, and experiences, which will help you become a better artist or, in this case, a better fashion illustrator.

Describe yourself and your greatest achievement.
Quirky, intense, hyper, melancholy, driven, neurotic, organized, excitable, honest, passionate. As for my greatest achievement, I would probably say being able to draw for a living.

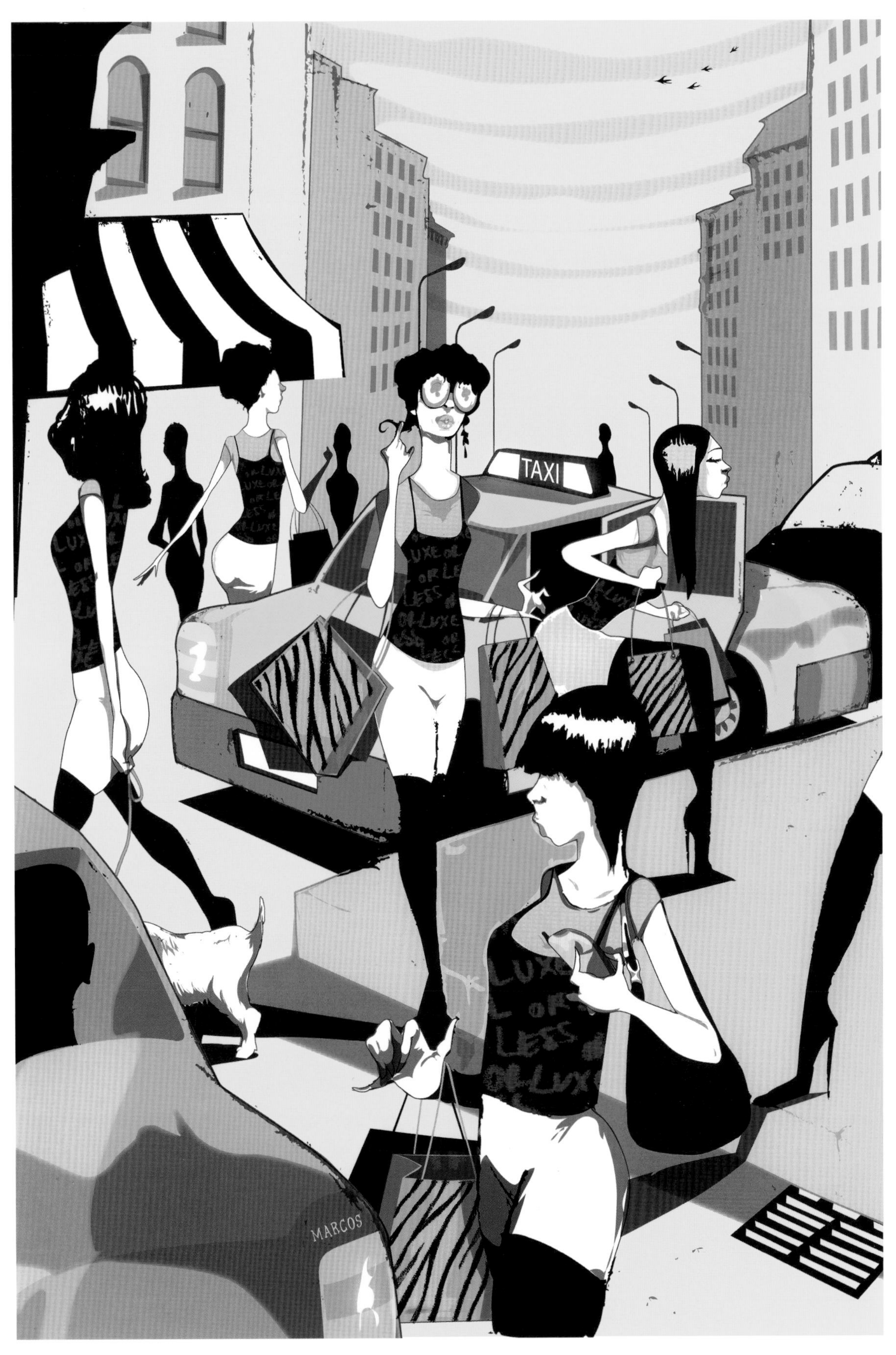
TAXI
MARCOS

OTA KOJI

What inspires you?
Various things that I touch in my daily life. All the stories that are around us; it's a question of looking and feeling. To create is to make alive these small things that we catch a glimpse of in our environment.

Are you interested in fashion?
Yes. Actually, when I was in Paris, I worked for a long time for Japanese boutiques. They asked me to discover new brands, to meet stylists, etc. I realized at this time that fashion is also an art, and I keep up to date by reading the latest fashion news.

Describe your work.
Usually I paint portraits, and about three times a year I have an exhibition. On the other hand, I do a lot of illustrations for Japanese newspapers, fashion magazines, or even for some authors. Also, I draw manga.

Which media and techniques do you use?
Acrylic on canvas, markers, crayons, and PC—it depends what I'm working on. I prefer acrylic because it is easy to manipulate, quick to dry, and many deep nuances are possible.

What, for you, makes a successful fashion illustration?
Something that speaks to you, even if you don't know exactly why. A good illustration is a silent and mysterious story of a brief meeting between someone who draws and someone who looks and adopts in a personal way what he is looking at.

What artistic training have you undertaken?
In my case, I didn't learn through academic training. This wasn't so much a question of choice but lack of opportunity. I think it is important to be curious about everything and never to stop drawing. Sometimes I draw all day.

If you could give one piece of advice to a student, what would it be?
There are many ways to become professional, and I have no idea which is the best one. The most important thing, to me, is to practice a lot and leave the thinking until afterwards.

Describe yourself and your greatest achievement.
My painting should describe me better than my words. My greatest achievement? I don't know exactly, but I do enjoy meeting people who can feel my work, even if we don't speak the same language, and even if we have a very different personal history.

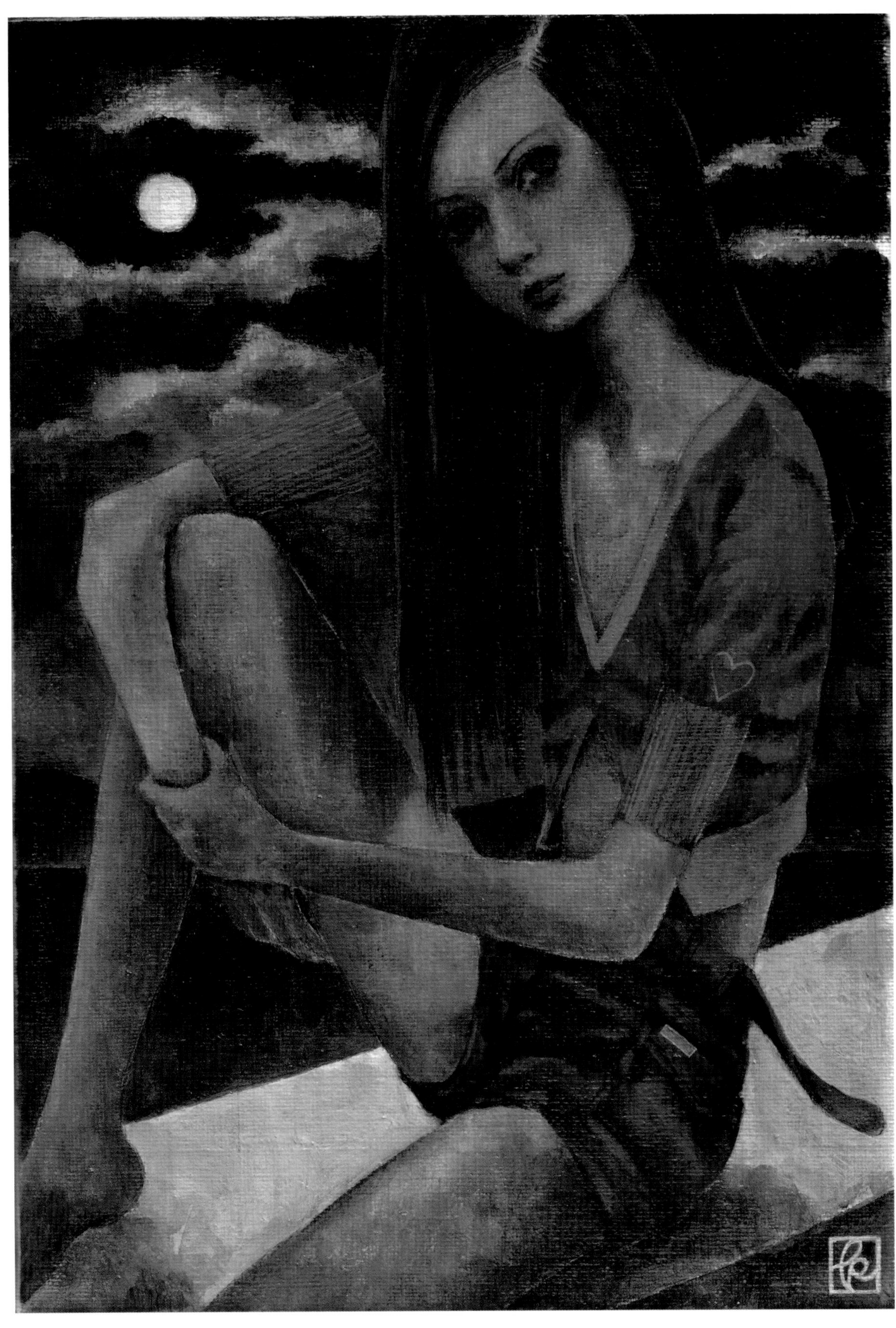

ANNE BOURBEAU

What inspires you?
Simple everyday things. Objects that can be found around the house that may often be overlooked: an old knitted cap, a pair of muddy wellies, an empty tea box. I am often drawn to the graphics of the banal, like the pictures you might find in old children's books, and packaging from that of gum wrappers to soda cans—all things that have snuck into what we might call the "visual vernacular."

Are you interested in fashion?
I love fashion, and love seeing it in action. I find it very energizing! Clothes are a great reflection of the culture and interests of the time to which they belong. How they are worn and combined is pure expression.

Describe your work.
I try to represent objects and images from the everyday or banal in a new way. I enjoy the fun that can be had through shifting the expectations of the viewer. There are endless possibilities for this by simply playing with color, texture, materials, etc.

Which media and techniques do you use?
I love materials that evoke memory. In terms of technique, I prefer the good old-fashioned ones: a simple running stitch, blanket stitch, appliqué. To me, simplicity is best: a hand-tied pom-pom, a crisp pleat, or grandmotherly smocking.

What, for you, makes a successful fashion illustration?
I can only talk about what I enjoy seeing in fashion illustration, and that is the ability of the artist to capture the mood or essence of a piece. Technical accuracy is, of course, an admirable quality and has its place, but if the personality of the piece is not present, then what good is it?

What artistic training have you undertaken?
I have always loved art and design. My formal education is as follows: BFA degree in Graphic Design and Packaging at the Art Center College of Design, in Pasadena, California; Post-Baccalaureate Degree in Fiber Arts at the School of the Art Institute of Chicago; MA in Visual Arts: Textiles at Goldsmiths College, University of London (UK).

If you could give one piece of advice to a student, what would it be?
Take chances.

Describe yourself and your greatest achievement.
I am interested in so many things. Sometimes this works to my advantage and sometimes to my disadvantage. But I think I am at my best when I am learning something new, which makes me always believe that my greatest achievements are still to come.

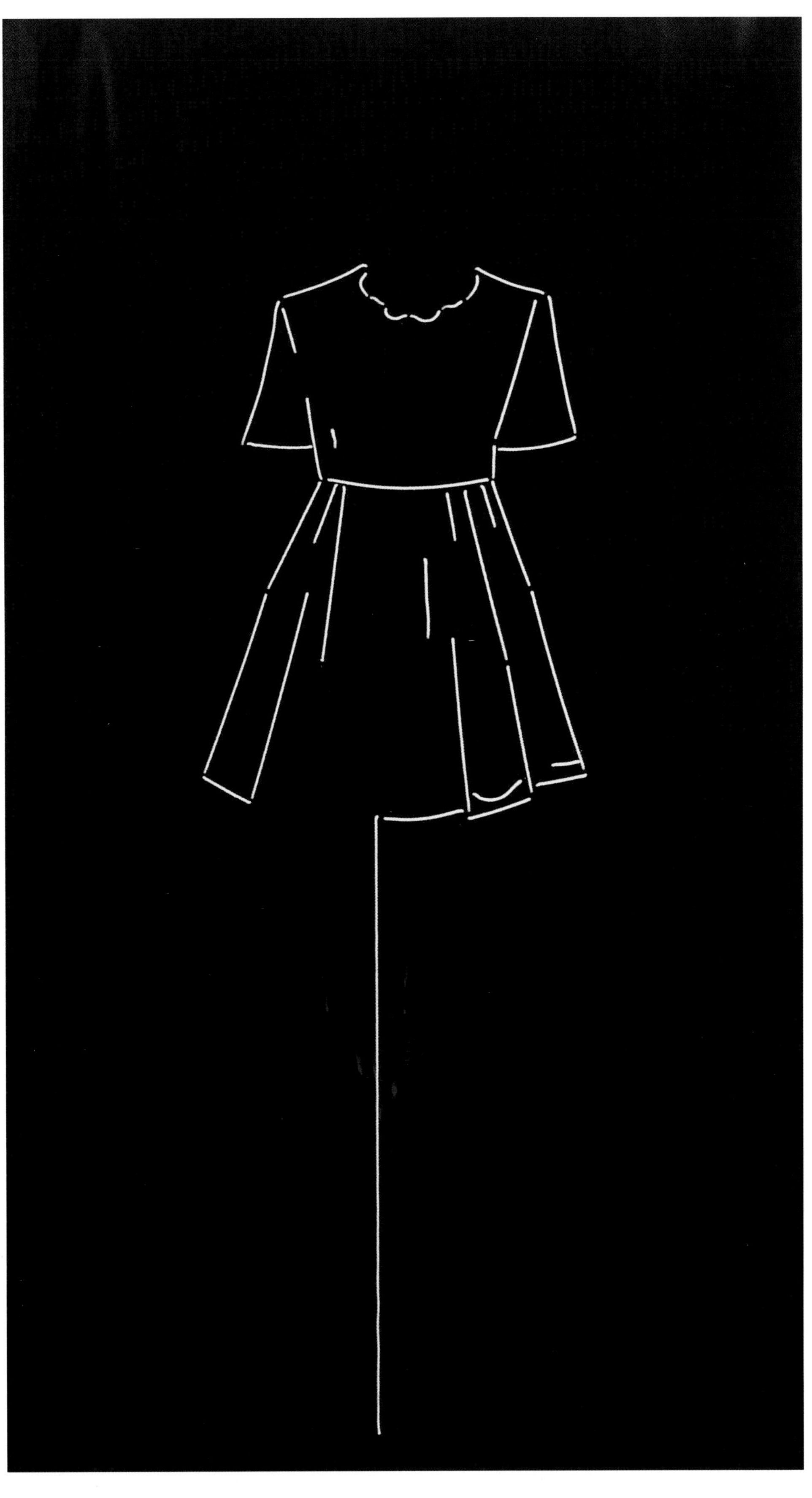

LOUISE GARDINER

What inspires you?
People-watching mainly. I am a very observant person, and I absorb what goes on around me like a sponge. I remember funny things that other people may not notice and log them in my head. They all get mixed together and appear in work quite randomly.

Other than that, my inspiration is eclectic, like a large bowl of minestrone. Almost anything can inspire me, sometimes quite unexpectedly. Music is particularly important; I listen to music to suit the work I am doing. As far as other artists are concerned, I love all sorts of work, such as Ralph Steadman, Tilleke Schwarz, Erté, Piet Paris, Aubrey Beardsley, Mats Gustafson, Modigliani, Klimt, Schiele. However, a lot of the time, people say I am a fusion of Beryl Cook and Lowry when they see my work!

Are you interested in fashion?
I am interested in the way people express themselves with their clothes and accessories. I love rich and interesting fabrics, and I am mad about color and pattern. My characters dress in very decorative and colorful clothes. If I had the time, I would learn to make clothes like these. I would wear heels and elaborate, beautifully cut, feminine outfits every day if I could be wheeled around and did not have to walk. As it is, I wear jeans and trainers most days, with spots of paint here and there.

Describe your work.
My work is an elaborate depiction of everyday people, glimpses of characters, conversations, and actions that go on around me. I dress life up and try to celebrate the diversity of human beings.

Which media and techniques do you use?
I collect ideas in sketchbooks and do figurative drawing as often as possible. Then, with a Bernina sewing machine, I either draw freely onto canvas (see *Crowd Sketch in Stitch*, facing page), or I plan commissioned illustrations carefully on tracing paper, then, once I am happy with the design, stitch through it onto canvas. I paint with acrylic onto the stitched drawings and then embroider again, mixing intricate, colored-thread patterns into the shapes and spaces within the drawing.

What, for you, makes a successful fashion illustration?
Fluidity of line, glimpses of movement and confident yet simple mark-making. I love old fashion plates in Art Deco style, especially Erté, and the simplicity of modern work by Tanya Ling.

What artistic training have you undertaken?
BA Hons in Textiles at Goldsmiths College, London University (UK). MA in Communication Design at Manchester Metropolitan University (UK).

If you could give one piece of advice to a student, what would it be?
Be positive, proactive, patient yet persistent, and a perfectionist.

Describe yourself and your greatest achievement.
My greatest achievement is that I am still doing what I trained to do! My work has improved year by year. And, most of all, I have managed to make a lot of people smile with my creative work, which is wonderful.

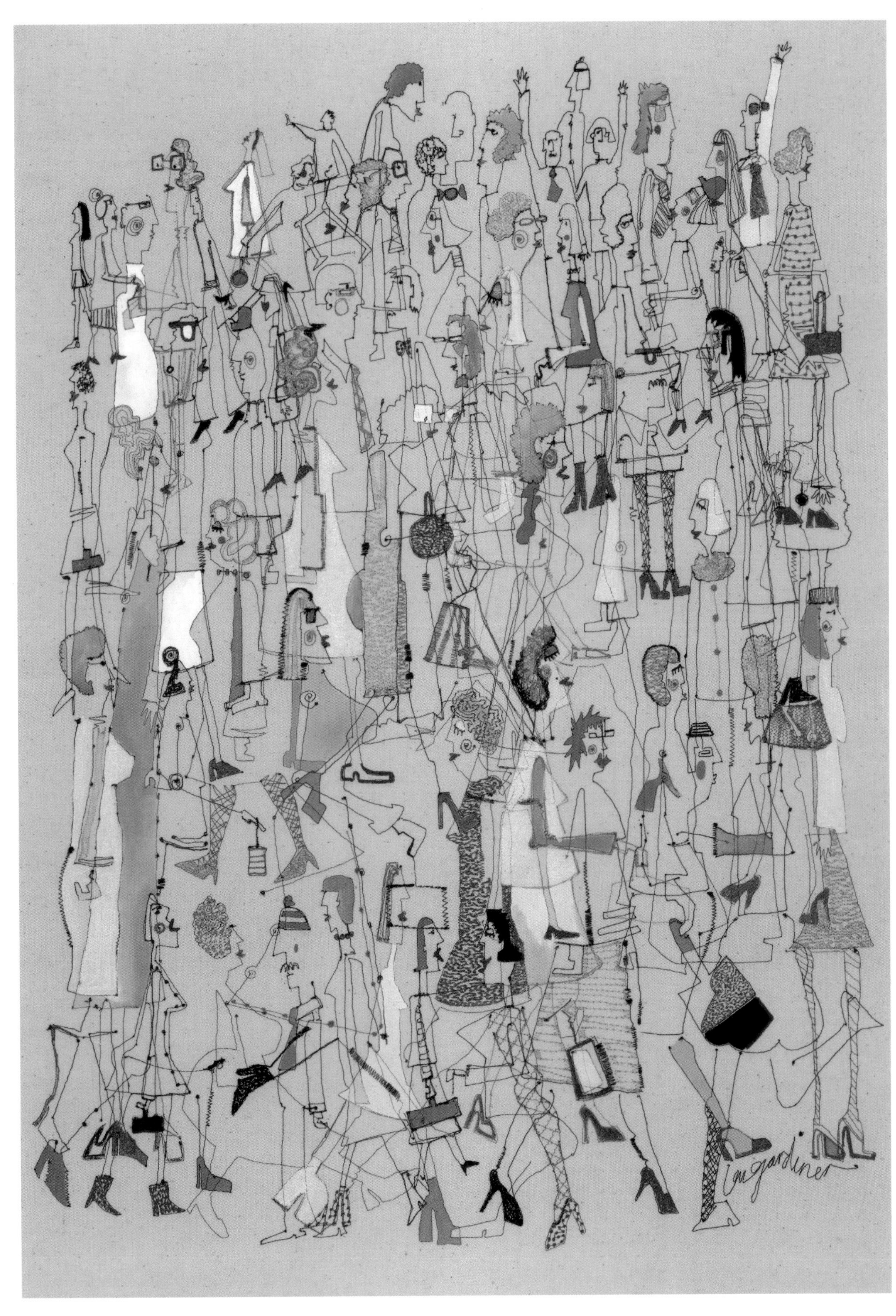

JULIA GRIFFITHS JONES

What inspires you?
Folk art is my greatest inspiration, particularly Eastern European. But poetry and literature also inspire me, particularly Margaret Atwood, Carol Shields, and Michelle Roberts.

Are you interested in fashion?
Yes, I am interested, but don't slavishly follow it. I am interested in wearing clothes that are highly decorated and embroidered, and in clothes that are an unusual cut or shape.

Describe your work.
I make metal pieces, which at the moment are taking the form of dresses, shirts, coats, and aprons. They are wall pieces, but I am also exploring moving sculpture pieces for my next exhibition.

Which media and techniques do you use?
I use mild steel wire in different gauges, which I weld and spray, and very often intricately paint. I am also using aluminum sheet, which I drill and stitch.

What, for you, makes a successful fashion illustration?
Quite minimal mark, with a lot of movement contained within it. Understated—I suppose you have got to know what it feels like to wear the clothes to draw them.

What artistic training have you undertaken?
BA Hons in Printed Textiles, at Winchester School of Art (UK). Master of Arts, also in Printed Textiles, at the Royal College of Art, London (UK).

If you could give one piece of advice to a student, what would it be?
Work hard, and be prepared to knock on doors: it won't necessarily land in your lap!

Describe yourself and your greatest achievement.
I am fifty, married with two children, and live and work in Llanybri, west Wales. Besides producing my children, my greatest achievement was seeing my work exhibited in a museum in Slovakia, where I had studied as a student twenty-five years earlier.

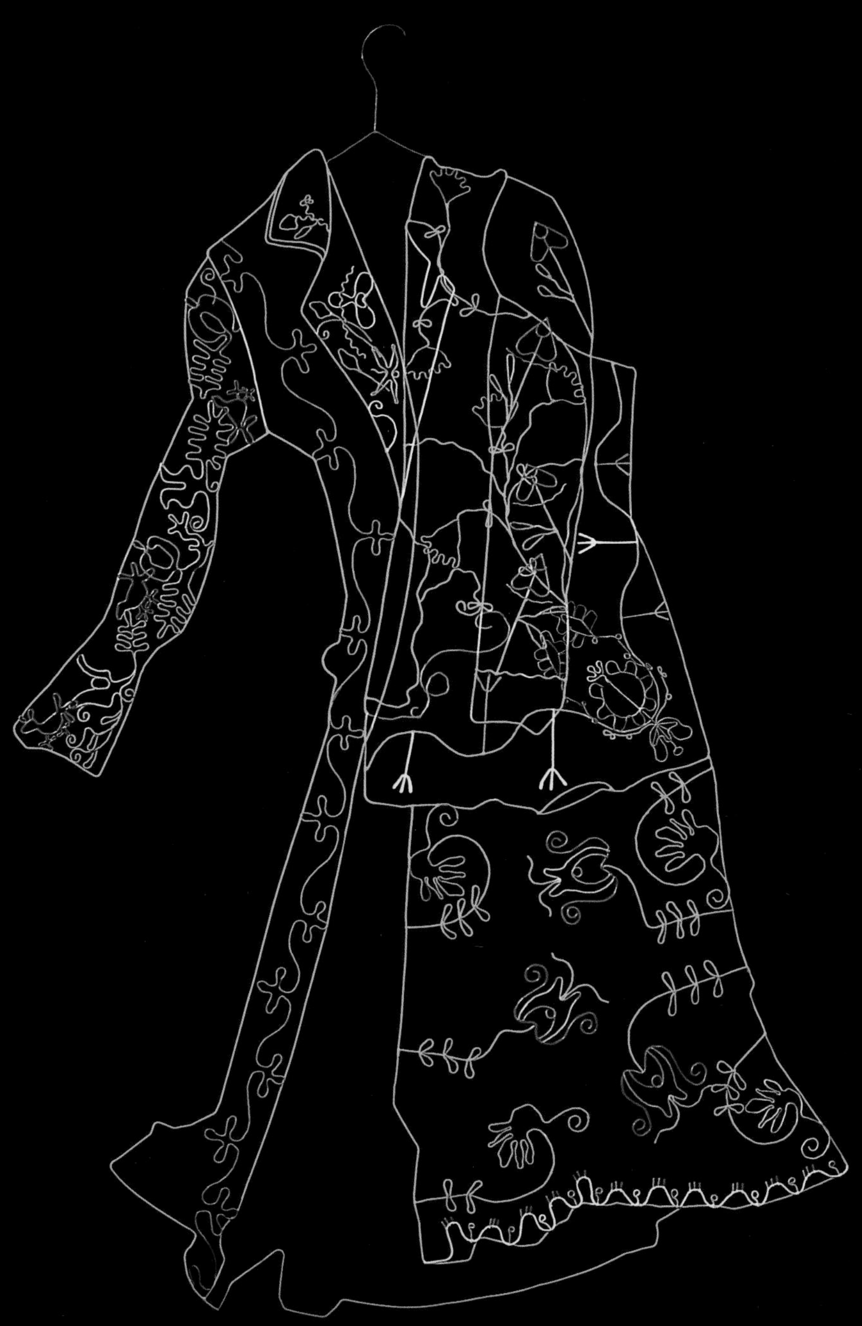

DEANNE CHEUK

What inspires you?
Originality. That moment when you see something so original, and striking, and memorable. It's something to strive for.

Are you interested in fashion?
Yes, of course! I have a clothing brand, and I contribute to many others. Fashion is a large part of my life. You can often see trends in fashion spreading to design, and vice versa, particularly in fabric patterns, advertising, photography, etc.

Describe your work.
My illustration work is laborious and many layered, sometimes psychedelic, always involving movement and other worlds, and mostly girls and mushrooms. I start on paper and never know what the end product will look like. I usually keep adding to it, and I hope that the time that passes in real time gets conveyed in the illustrations. I like each piece to feel heavy with experience. I always try to convey that feeling you have when you wake up from a dream, and you feel like you have just experienced everything and nothing.

Which media and techniques do you use?
Watercolor, pencil, ink, heavy watercolor paper, and, on the computer, Photoshop, and Illustrator. I also work in oil on canvas for exhibition pieces.

What, for you, makes a successful fashion illustration?
Something striking that you'll linger over. It can be simple or complicated.

What artistic training have you undertaken?
BA Hons in Graphic Design at Curtin University, Perth (Australia).

If you could give one piece of advice to a student, what would it be?
Create, don't imitate.

Describe yourself and your greatest achievement.
My first book, *Mushroom Girls Virus.*

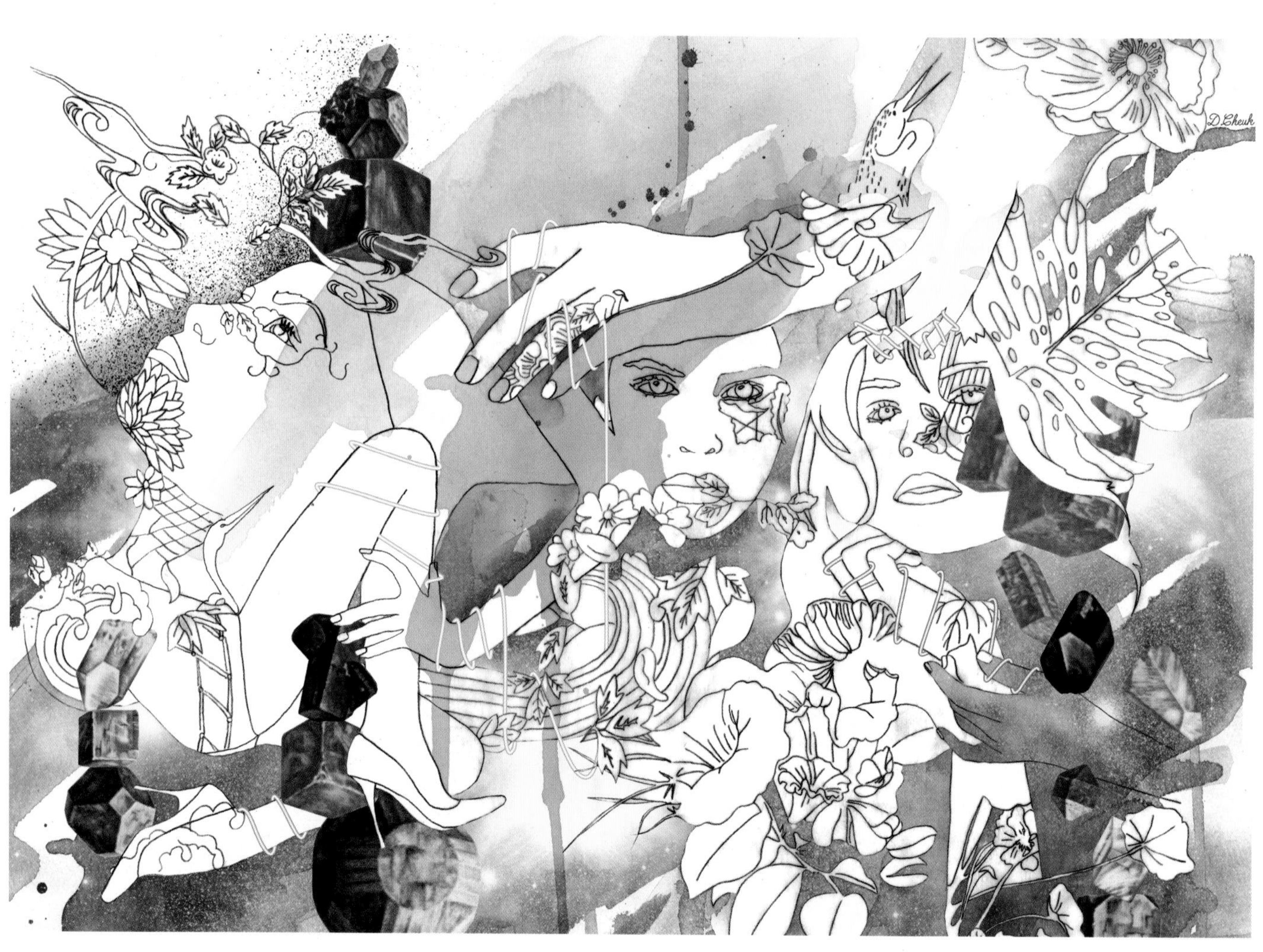

TUTORIALS

6

The previous chapter identified the many techniques used by artists and illustrators to represent clothing and the fashion figure. We have seen traditional methods such as drawing, painting, and print, alongside collage, stitch, sculpture, and digital manipulation to illustrate fashion.

So, how do you produce such inspired creations? Where should you start—with a sewing needle or a mouse? This chapter explores some of the many methods recognized by contemporary illustrators and artists of the moment.

HAND EMBROIDERY

Bethan Morris

For well over a thousand years, embroidery has been a means of adding decoration to clothing, personal accessories, and household or church furnishings. Embroidery is the art of applying decoration by needle and thread to the surface of a piece of cloth or canvas, often being a picture or pattern.

Hand embroidery does not rely on complicated equipment and techniques. It is a process in which the simplest of materials can suffice to enable you to create beautiful artwork. In recent years, there has been a return to the popularity of hand-created craft styles, such as sewing, knitting, and crochet. In a world that is now dominated by computers and digital technology, many people find these straightforward old-fashioned activities enjoyable.

Many variations of stitches and techniques have evolved over the centuries. All you need to begin is a needle, some fabric, and a selection of embroidery threads. If you are new to embroidery, it would be a good idea to refer to the stitch book listed in the Further Reading section (p. 196) for extra guidance.

ILLUSTRATING A HANDBAG WITH HAND STITCH

You will need:

Original drawing
Light box
Background fabric (calico)
Marker pens
Embroidery threads
Embroidery frame or hoop
Sewing needle

Stitches used:

Running stitch
Whipped running stitch
Satin stitch
French knot

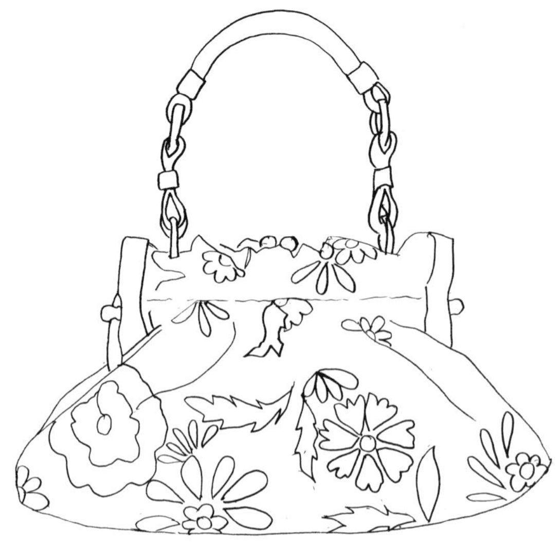

1

No matter which creative technique you are aiming to experiment with, it is essential to plan and organize your thought process. For hand-embroidered pieces you should always illustrate on paper first. By producing a plain line drawing of a handbag, you can clearly see the shapes to be filled with stitch and therefore plan the stitches to use.

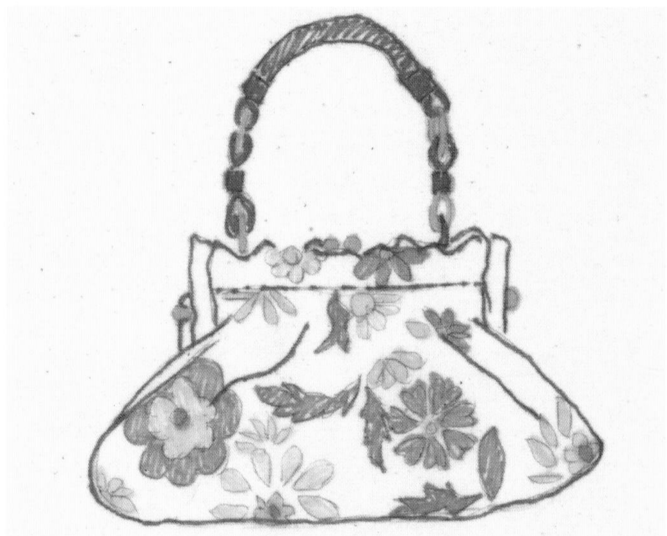

2

Transfer the handbag illustration onto fabric, using a light box or window to trace the image. In this case, a lightweight calico has been used. If you are a beginner, calico is firm and easy to control for stitch—a good starting fabric. It is a good idea to plan the colors of your artwork at this stage, too. This way you can choose the appropriate colored embroidery threads. This example has been shaded in complementary tones, using marker pens.

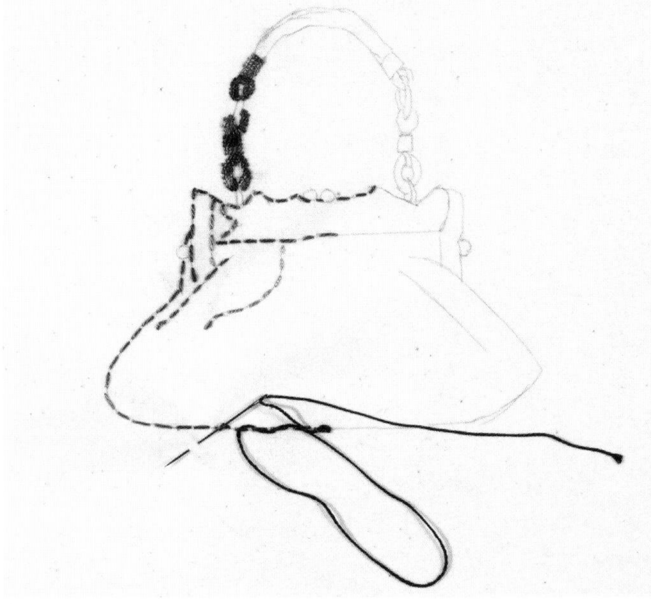

3
Mount the fabric image in an embroidery hoop to create a taut surface for stitching. This outline is stitched in a dark blue variegated thread. This type of thread is made up of various tones of the same color, adding a sense of light and shade. A running stitch is the most basic and versatile of all stitches and should be used for the outline. Pass the needle through the fabric at regular intervals with an in-and-out movement. To lend the outline more definition, a whipped running stitch gives a heavier line: following your running stitches, take a darker thread and weave (whip) the needle in and out of them alternately to form an almost corded effect.

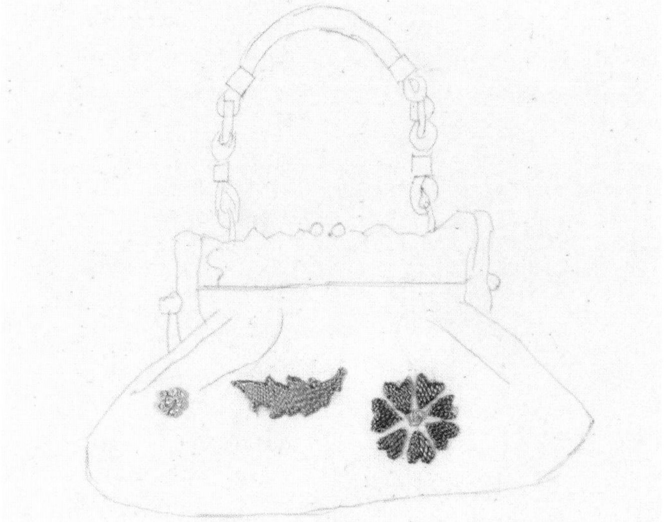

4
The flower petals and leaves need to be treated differently from the outline of the bag: these areas should be filled with a solid embroidery stitch. Satin stitch looks deceptively simple, but it takes practice to sew it neatly. Satin stitch can be worked in any direction. First, carry the thread right across the shape to be filled, and then return the needle under the fabric close to the point where it emerged. Build the stitches up close together so they lie flat and create an edge to the shape.

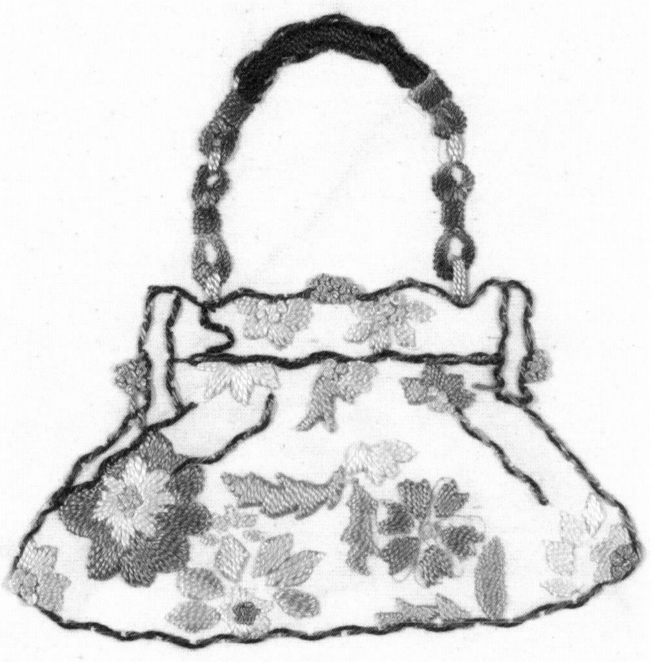

5
The center of each flower has been created with a singular stitch known as a French knot. This is a fairly difficult stitch to master initially, but will become easier with practice. Take the thread through the fabric and hold it taut with your free hand. Next, wind the thread around the needle; then, still holding the thread tightly, turn the needle and insert it back into the fabric where it originally emerged. A circular knotted stitch will form on the fabric surface. You can alter the size of the knots by increasing the number of times you wind the thread around the needle.

This exercise has shown how to create an embroidered fashion illustration in just a couple of hours. Once you have mastered hand embroidery, similar decorative techniques could also be applied to your own clothes and accessories.

PAINTING

Louise Gardiner

Painting is a traditional technique that is sometimes overlooked by students. It is often easier to fill an illustration with color using technology rather than mixing the colors yourself in a palette. However, acrylics produce strong colors and can be applied straight from the tube or watered down, making them an incredibly versatile medium for fashion illustration. Watercolor paints are also a fairly flexible medium, especially when mixed with water to create exciting patterns.

CREATING A FASHION FIGURE USING PAINT

You will need:

Magazine or original drawing
Light box
Pencil
Watercolor paper
Brushes (a variety of sizes)
Masking fluid
Masking tape
Watercolor paint
Acrylic paint

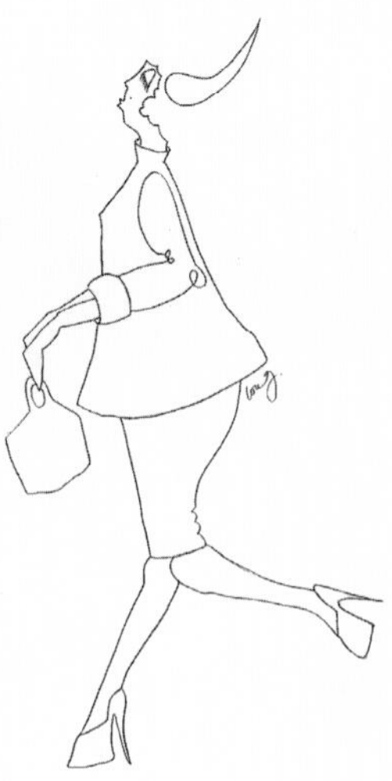

1

Select an image from a magazine that you want to re-create in your own illustrative style. Using a light box or window, trace the figure onto your page. You could also draw your own figure from a photograph or a previous piece of artwork. Ensure you draw your image straight onto watercolor or stretched paper, as you will later be working in a wet medium that will buckle ordinary paper. Always think about the characteristics of each material before choosing which ones will suit your final piece.

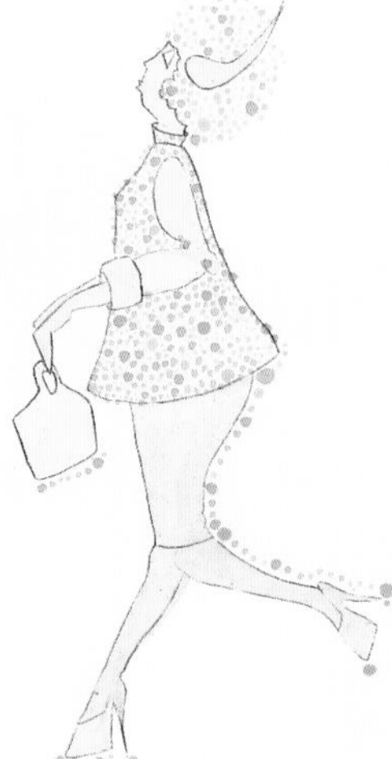

2

Carefully paint masking fluid with a thin brush over the areas you want to remain as white paper. Remember, you can either block in whole shapes or develop patterns, as shown here with dots. Let the masking fluid dry completely before the next stage. While you wait, decide on the colors you want to use in your illustration, bearing in mind that the watercolors will be blended to create interesting effects. In this illustration, navy blue mixed with a burnt umber will be used to create a washy blue/gray/brown effect.

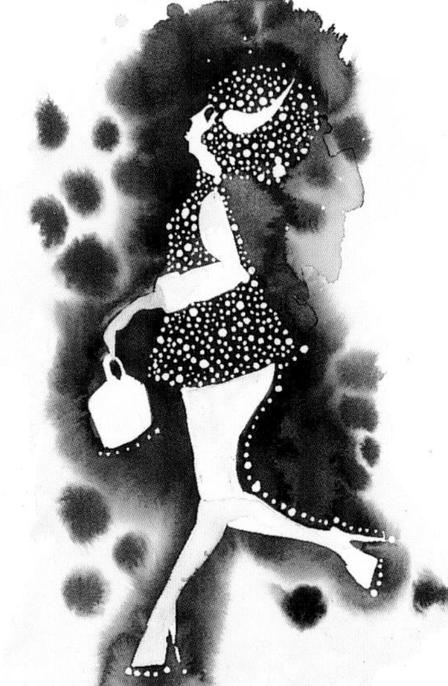

3
Once the fluid is completely dry, secure the paper with masking tape to prevent the paper from buckling. Then add a wash of water, being careful not to miss any areas. While the paper is still wet, add the color wash you have chosen. Here, the paint has been allowed to bleed and run around the paper in the water to create a washy dappled effect. Droplets of color have been added around the edges to create a pattern in the background. Watercolor naturally bleeds and reacts with water, so take advantage of this when using this medium.

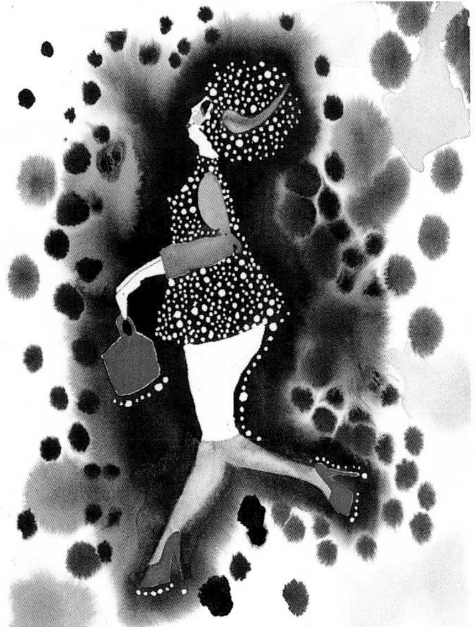

4
Once the wash is completely dry, the masking fluid can be fairly easily peeled off or removed with an eraser. Next, you can add blocks of color and subtle washes to represent the clothes. More water has been added to the figure's legs to create a subtle shadow to suggest nylon tights, and also to differentiate between the skirt and the skin tones. Acrylic has been used for the bag and the shoes to vary the intensity of the paint. Also, eyelashes have been added in acrylic with a very fine brush, along with a beauty spot to give the figure character.

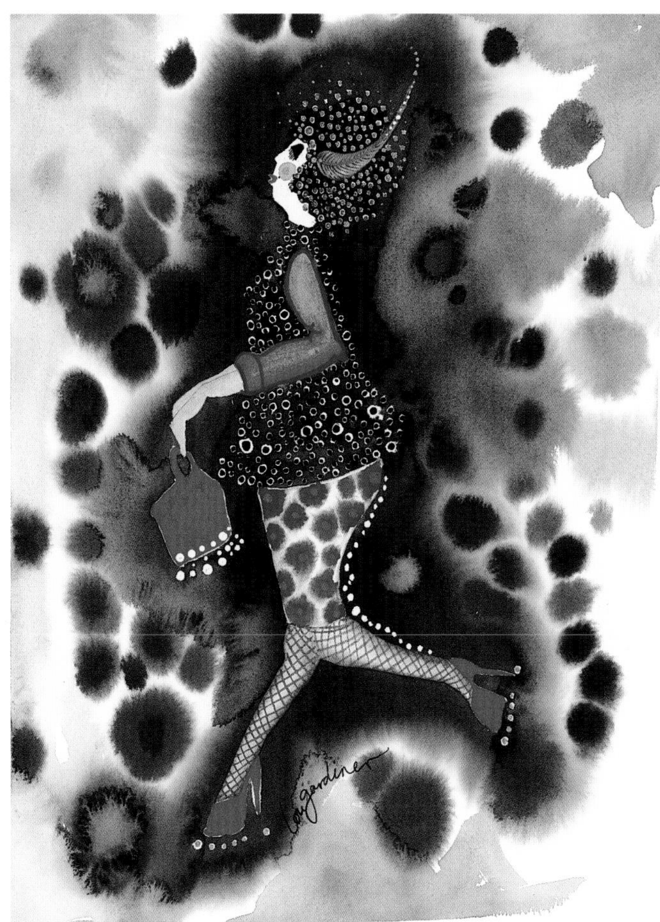

5
Now it is time to add the final details. Here, small drops of gold are added to the hair, and droplets of black in the coat create an interesting decorative counterpart to the white paper spots. These were added using the the end of the paintbrush, as well as the bristles, to achieve more texture. The delicate lines of the feather and the fishnet tights were added with a fine paintbrush as a finishing touch. This delightfully humorous image has been created using a fairly limited color palette, thus proving the "less-is-sometimes-more" theory.

DRAWING WITH INK

Will Knight

Ink is an alternative medium to paint that, if used properly, can create an interesting fashion illustration. Depending on the type of ink you use, you can make a variety of marks. Waterproof ink will produce solid, bold line drawings to which washes can be added, while non-waterproof ink will disperse in water, creating marvelous patterns. India ink has been used for centuries and, because of its versatility, is the first choice of medium for many illustrators. You can use ink directly from the jar or choose from a large selection of pens.

CREATING A FASHION FIGURE USING PENS AND INK

You will need:

Magazine or original drawing
Tracing paper
Ballpoint pen
Paper for final artwork
Light box
Waterproof India ink
Brushes
Rotring art pen
0.2 Pilot drawing pen
White pencil crayon

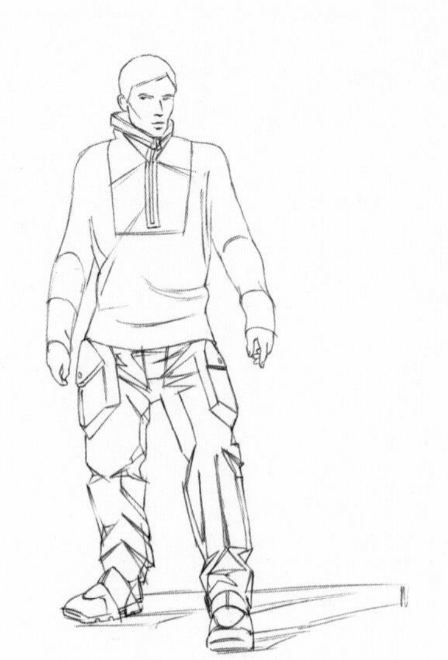

1

Having decided on the mood or theme for your illustration, source a couple of appropriate lifestyle magazines for inspiration and visual reference. Choose some clothing and details that you think will work, and find a character with the right sort of pose. You can trace from this figure directly, or use it as a guide to construct your own figure, taking the opportunity to make the pose more dramatic. Using a ballpoint pen prevents you becoming too precious and allows you to capture some dynamic line work as you block out the main shadows and apply the chosen designs. Keep detail simple here and make notes to yourself about what you wish to communicate.

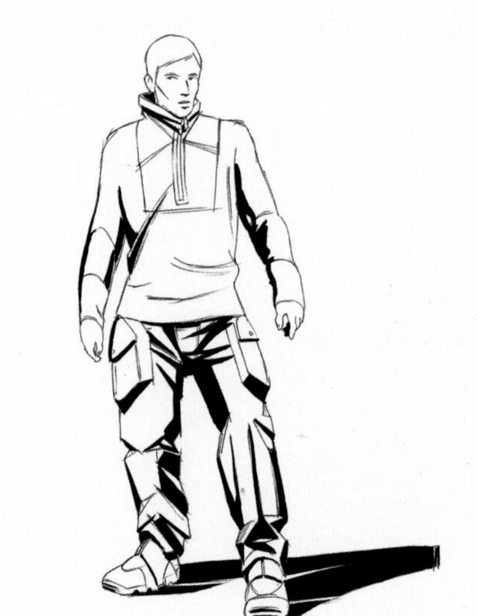

2

Using the first sketch as an underlay, start on a fresh piece of paper. Using a light box, trace the figure and main lines, again with a ballpoint pen. Try to use as few lines as possible, picking out the stronger lines from the underlay. Note the softer, more flowing lines used for the sweater, in contrast to the hard, angular lines of the trousers. Use your magazine references for drawing hands, eyes, mouth, and nose, again using as few lines as possible.

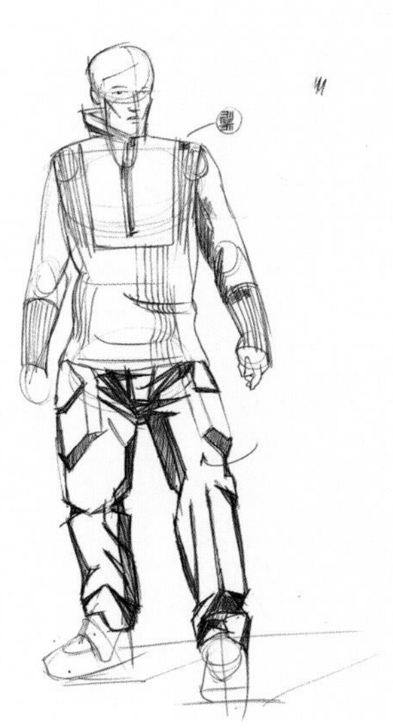

3

Next, block in the shadows using black drawing ink and a sable (or synthetic) brush. Make sure your brush is large enough to fill the area swiftly, but fine enough for smaller areas. If at any stage you are unsure as to where to apply your ink, use a separate piece of paper for testing out your ideas. Top tip: accidents will happen, so before you bring the ink to the drawing area, make sure you have a good supply of tissue at hand! The tissue can also be employed to manage the amount of ink on your brush.

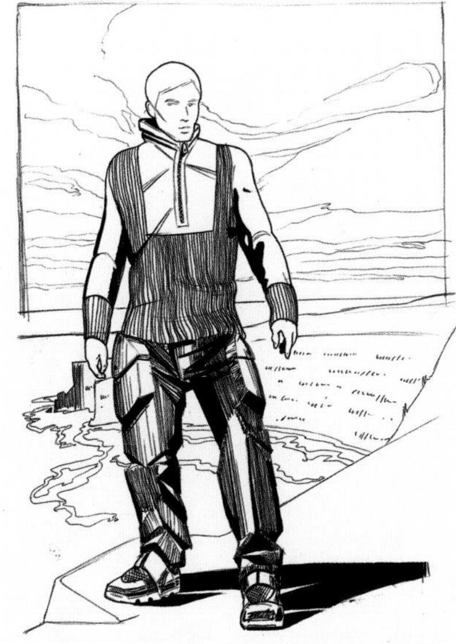

4

When the ink has dried, it is time to add the line work. You can use a felt nib, such as a technical drawing pen, for this stage, but a Rotring art pen with a stainless-steel nib will provide a looser and more interesting illustration. Note the flowing lines of the sweater in contrast to the straighter hatching on the trousers. Use the white space and denser line work to show form and shadow. At this point, you may wish to think about adding a suitable background scene for the illustration. In this instance, a rocky cliff top with dark storm clouds above and swirling seas below was decided as fitting the tone of our character and his apparel.

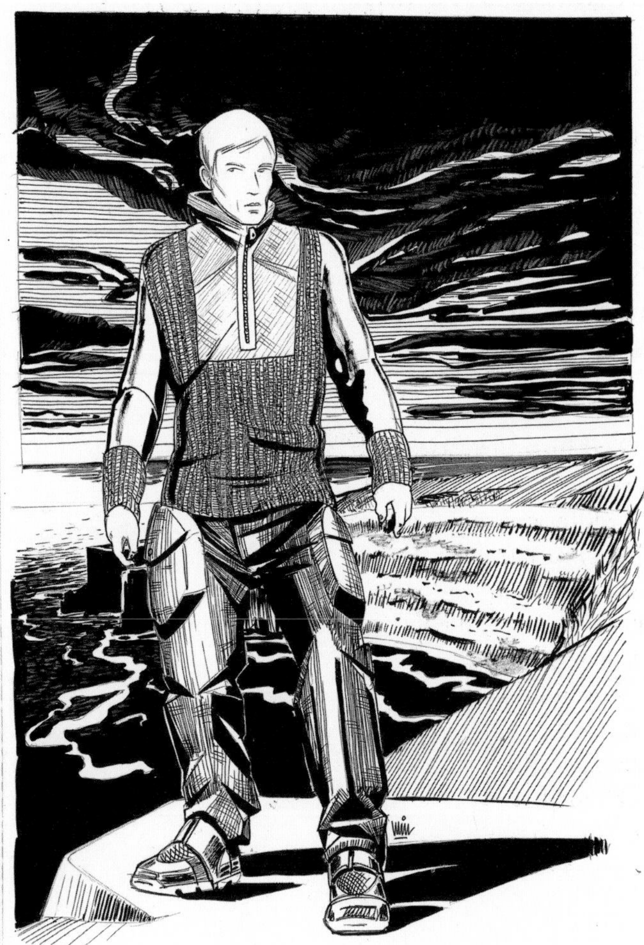

5

The art pen is used here again to add touches of texture to the trousers and chest panel. It is too thick, however, for the sweater texture, so an 0.2 Pilot drawing pen is used to add the detail that suggests the knitwear. A combination of art pen and brush are now used to paint in the scenery, to provide a strong and moody backdrop. Again, make sure you have some reference imagery from your magazine or the Internet to guide your decisions. Note that the clouds and sea were blocked in solid black, with the sea blending into white through a combination of lighter, smaller brush strokes and a final touch of white pencil crayon to pick out the ripples. White crayon is also used to suggest the sunlight catching the undersides of the storm clouds, thus adding dramatic atmosphere to the completed illustration.

COLLAGE

Adriano Gazza

Collage has always been an extremely effective way of using flat color, either by creating crisp cut lines or exploring abstract torn edges. Collage is an excellent technique for creating impact. In its simplest form, papers can be collaged by cutting, tearing, and gluing. However, new technology has allowed for more complicated experimentation by collaging scanned original images on the computer. With the advent of the digital camera, the possibilities for collage as an expressive medium have widened greatly, and photomontage is increasingly popular.

CREATING A SILHOUETTE

You will need:
Photograph
Magazine or original drawing
Tracing paper
Light box
Pencil
Black, colored, and white paper or card
Scissors or utility knife and cutting mat
Spray glue

For further embellishments:
Scanner
Computer
Adobe Photoshop program

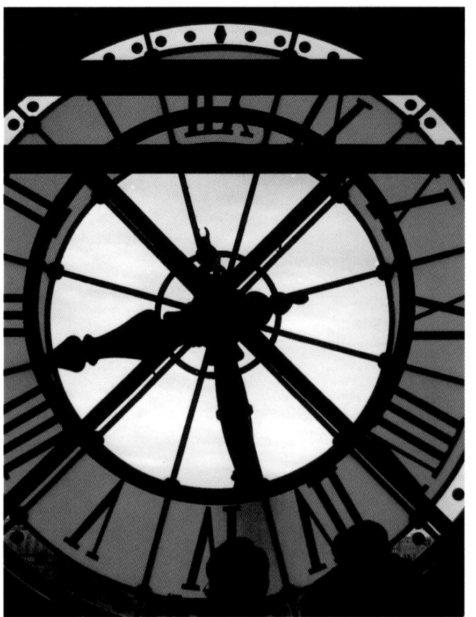

1
As a starting point for a fashion illustration, rather than taking an existing pattern or plain paper background, why not use a photograph that inspires you instead? The one used throughout this example was taken at the Musée d'Orsay, in Paris. The building was formerly a train station, and this photograph shows the original station clock. If you look closely, the strong black-and-white coloring of the clock emphasizes the figures outlined in silhouette beneath.

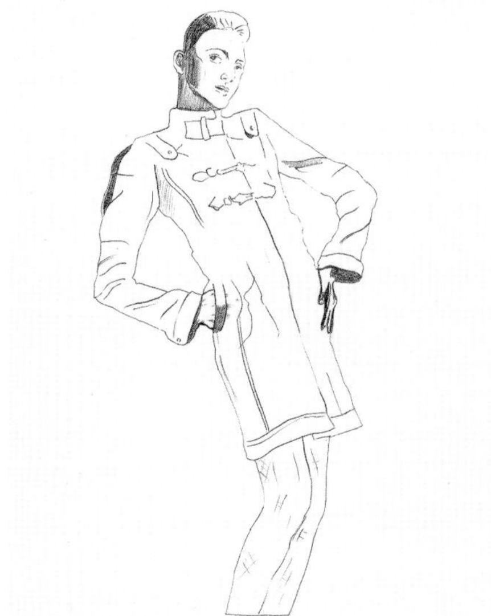

2
The next stage is to think about the figure that will be the focus of your illustration. The figure in this example will be collaged in card stock so that it is silhouetted like the figures in the original background photograph. Find a figure in a magazine with a strong, bold silhouette, and trace in pencil around the outline, using a light box, or create your own original outline.

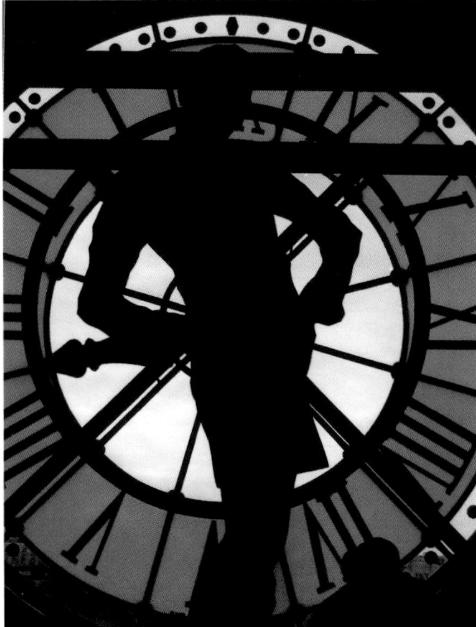

3

Next, using scissors, or a utility knife and cutting mat, cut the figure out to create a template. Draw around the edges of this template onto black card stock. Cut this out, and stick it onto the background photograph, using spray glue, laying the basis for your collaged silhouette figure.

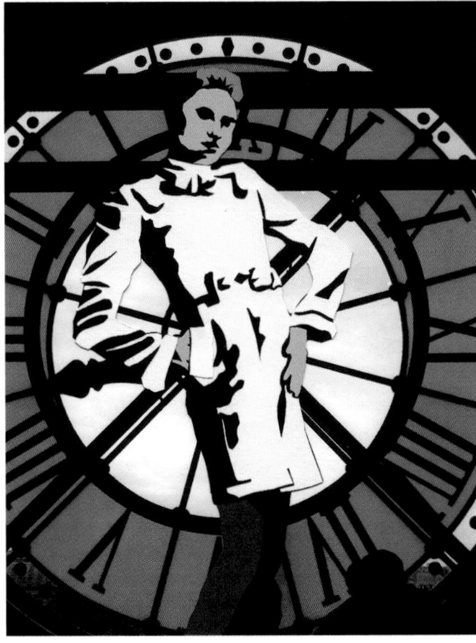

4

Using white and colored card stock, add quirky highlights and areas of shade to your silhouetted figure. This is where you can really start to see the illustration coming together. You can add hairstyles or facial features to give your figure character.

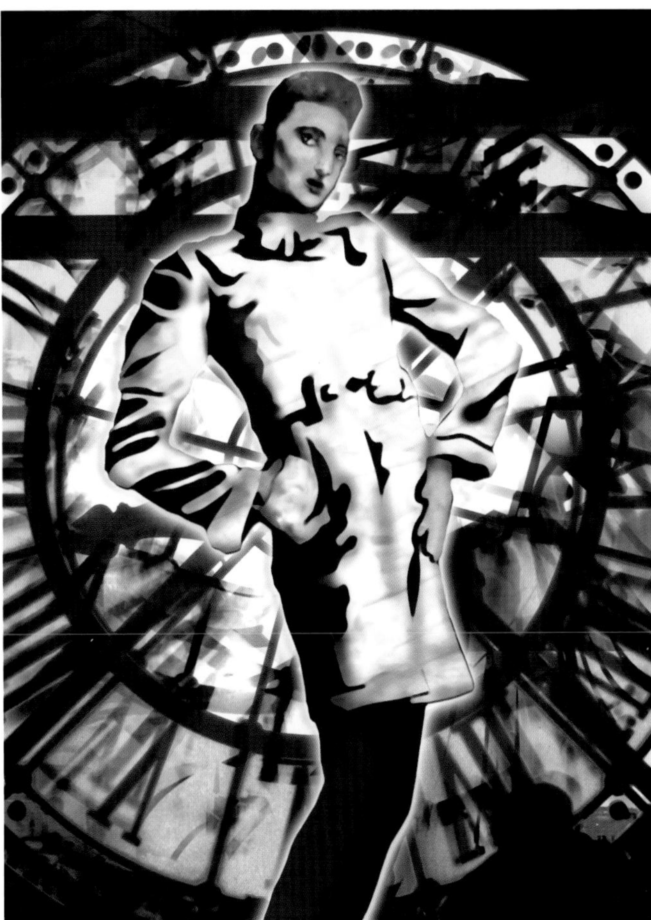

5

You could embellish your final fashion illustration by scanning it into your computer and working further detail into it on a specially designed computer program. Adobe Photoshop is ideal for this type of project and is used by many professional fashion illustrators worldwide. Here, the effects have been created using the magic wand and clone stamp tools. Filters were also used and the opacity levels adjusted to give varying balances and contrasts to the collage. The collage is finally complete when a drop shadow and an outer glow are added to the fashion figure.

COMPUTERIZED MACHINE EMBROIDERY

Patricia Joyner

Computerized machine embroidery is almost like drawing with a digital needle instead of a pencil. The fabric is your canvas, and the needle and threads are your brush and paint. You can plot your fashion illustration on a computer, transfer it to a digital embroidery program, and send the information digitally to your sewing machine. As the machine begins to sew, stitched lines appear on the fabric beneath, and an instant piece of art is formed.

As with any new activity, practice makes perfect. You will need to spend time familiarizing yourself with your sewing machine and computer programs. Do not be scared of the mistakes you make. You may even find that these mishaps turn out to be "happy accidents," quite by chance.

BUILDING UP A PICTURE: ILLUSTRATING A FIGURE FROM A MAGAZINE

You will need:

Magazine
Scanner
Computer
Computerized embroidery program (this tutorial uses Pfaff 3D Creative)
A sewing machine (this tutorial uses a Pfaff 2144)
Background fabric
Sewing threads

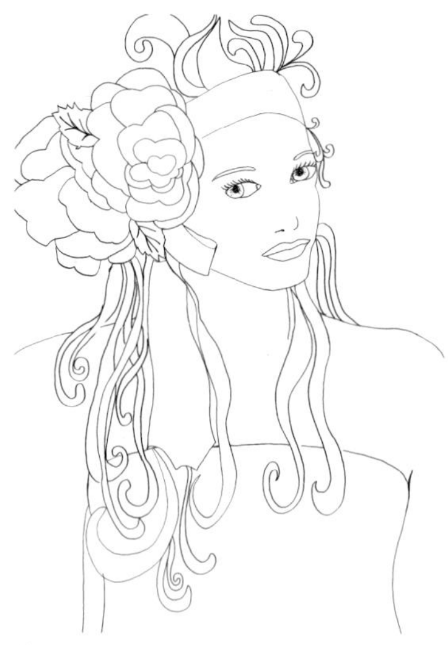

1

As with most of these tutorials, the obvious starting point, even for embroidery, is a drawing. This simple image has been copied from a fashion magazine. It has been drawn in pencil, and the lines have been kept sharp. When choosing an image for computerized embroidery, you need to be aware that all lines must be joined. This is because when sections are filled with stitches, if there are any gaps the stitches will leak out.

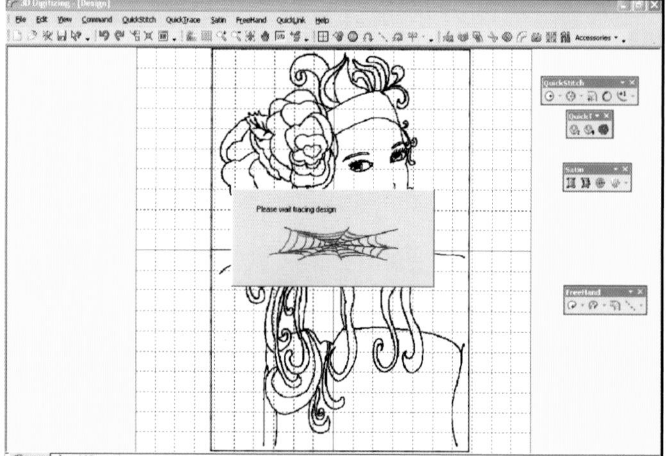

2

The next stage is to scan the image into the computer software. Most programs will accept familiar formats such as bmp, tiff, jpeg, etc. Open the digitizing module from the menu by selecting the icon, and click on Acquire Picture to obtain the original image. You can then select a trace option to do the digitizing automatically.

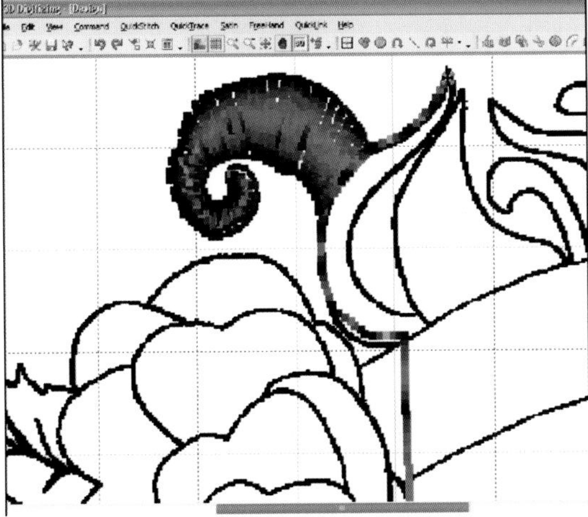

3

Once you have the image on screen, you can use the program to help plot the stitches. In this tutorial, satin stitches are used for the hair. The eyelashes will be double stitch, while the iris is created using a satin ring. A running stitch is plotted along the top of the headband to move from curl to curl. The curls are then filled on screen with a bronze satin stitch.

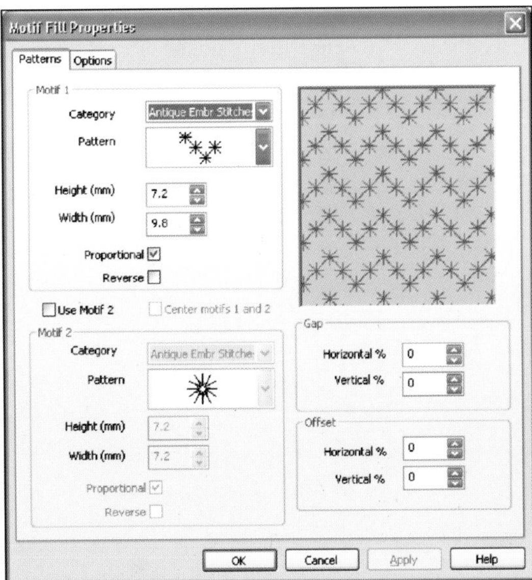

4

At this stage you can also think about the garments. How will you fill the dress and headband with embroidery stitches? This can all be plotted on screen too. Go to the Motif Fill menu, and select your patterns. These can be adjusted in size, color, depth, etc.

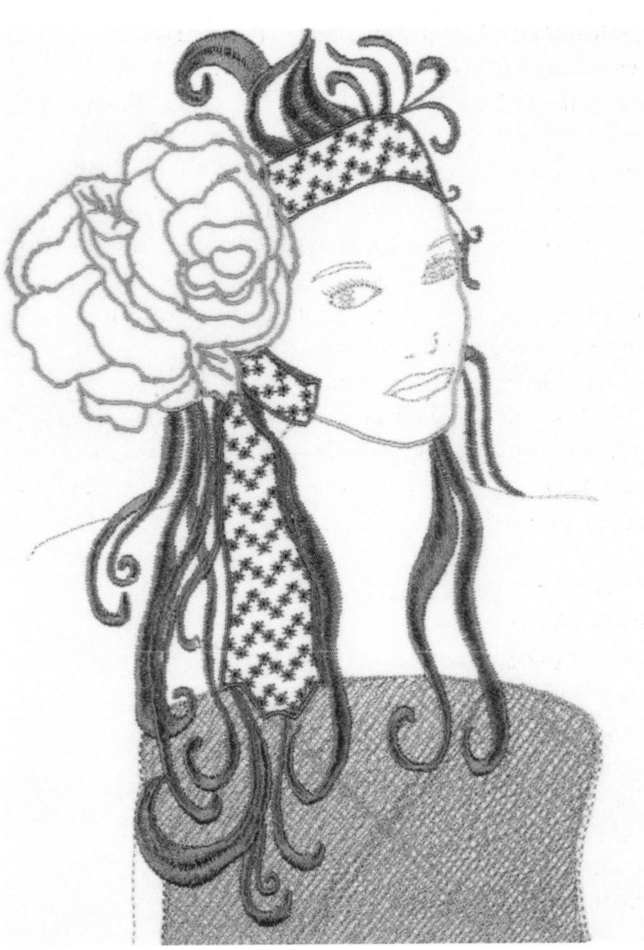

5

When you have completed the plotting, you can save your selections and send the design to your sewing machine to stitch it out. Place a suitable fabric in the machine's embroidery hoop (stabilizer), and the machine is ready to go. Watch in amazement as your original plain drawing becomes a beautiful color-embroidered fashion illustration.

ADOBE ILLUSTRATOR

Simone Legno

Adobe Illustrator offers incredible control to those who want to use the package to draw almost from scratch. When working digitally, there are two main types of picture-making applications: bitmap (or raster) and object-oriented (or vector). Adobe Illustrator is object-oriented, and drawings are composed of separate, distinct, mathematically defined objects or groups of objects (vectors).

BUILDING A FASHION FIGURE ON THE COMPUTER

You will need:

Original drawing
Scanner
Computer
Adobe Illustrator program

Website help:
www.adobe.com/support/products/illustrator.html

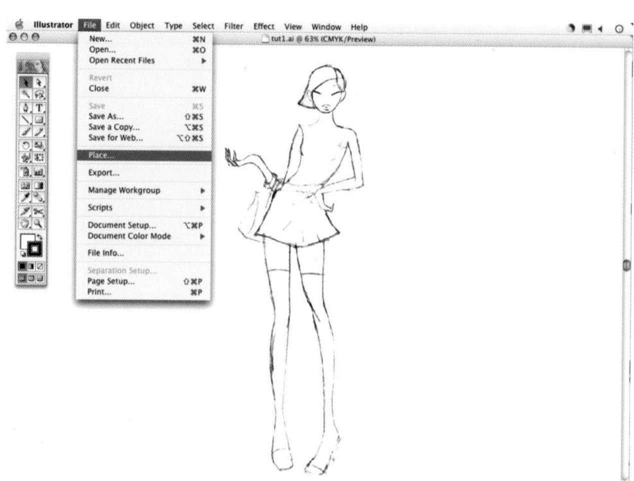

1

First, you need to create a base image on which your digital fashion figure can grow. You can do this by drawing a simple sketch in pencil, then scan and save it onto your hard drive. Next, open Adobe Illustrator, go to File > Place, and select the saved scan. The handmade sketch will appear on your blank page in a standard layer. So that you can work freely adding vectors without moving the guide sketch below, you will need to secure the image. You can do this by selecting Object > Lock. Remember to save your file, and keep doing so as you add new work.

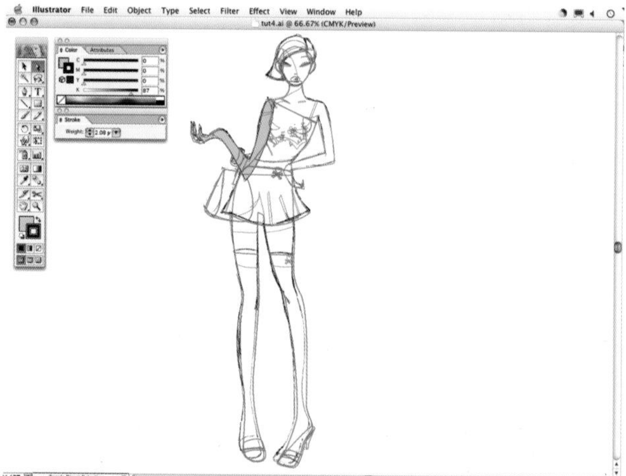

2

The next stage is to build image vectors. Using the Pen Tool menu, choose a bright color from the palette, so you can see the lines you draw on screen. In this example, red has been used. As you draw in red over the original sketch lines, you need to close the paths. Paths are the basis of all objects in Adobe Illustrator and can be open or closed. To close a path and divide your image into zones, you should select the path, using the direction selection tool, and then choose Object > Join. This takes a little practice. When you have completed your drawing, you can unlock the original guidance sketch and delete it from the screen.

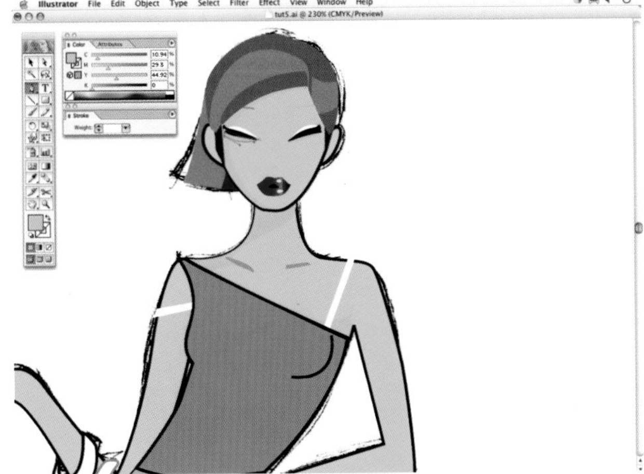

3
The next step is to start filling in the required colors for the fashion illustration. Adobe Illustrator has thirty-one movable palettes, all of which can be opened from the Window menu. Use the color palette to mix, choose, and switch between colors. You can view the color you have selected in color squares on the toolbox. The Stroke palette displays the weight and style of the stroke, and can be used to change those attributes. You can also use the Eyedropper tool to select and drop repetitive colors (such as skin tone) into your illustration.

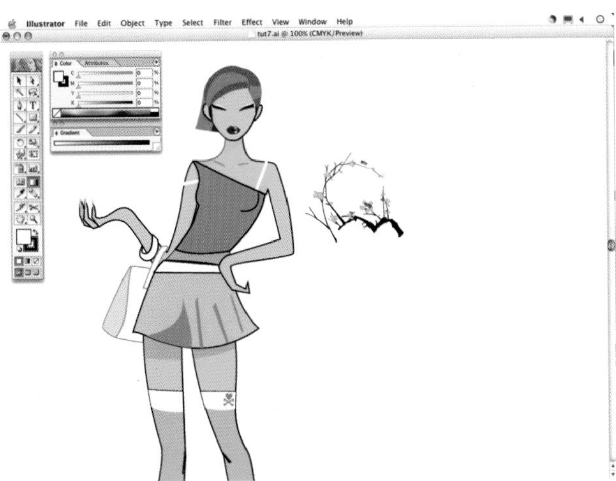

4
To add some decoration to the clothes your figure is wearing, you will need to create a pattern. This one has been created in Adobe Illustrator and imported into the art space. Using Adobe Illustrator's transparency controls, you can also add a touch of realism to your fashion illustrations. The tools will help you add light, shade, and density. The opacity slider on the transparency palette controls the transparency of each object; the blending modes control how an object's color is affected by the colors in underlying objects.

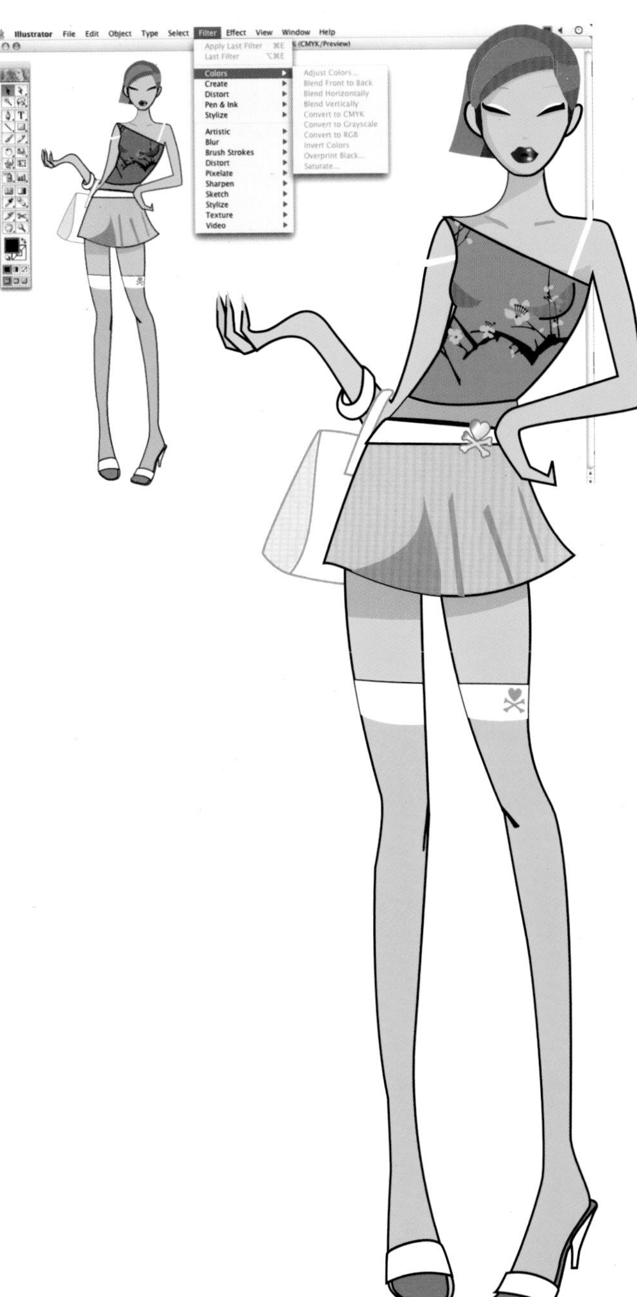

5
When you are happy with the embellishments you have made to the clothing, you can group all the elements by recoloring the garment. This can be achieved by selecting Filters > Colors > Adjust Colors. You have now built a fashion figure on the computer. As you become accustomed to the endless possibilities this program offers, you can create backgrounds on which to place your figures.

ADOBE PHOTOSHOP

Anna Bailey

Adobe Photoshop is a bitmap (or raster) picture-making application. It is ideal for creating soft, painterly effects and allows you the freedom to create fashion illustrations from many starting points. Imagery can be gathered and imported from various sources, such as scanners, drawing applications, digital cameras, photo CDs, and video capture. A Photoshop file is a digital picture made up of a monolayer of picture elements, or pixels for short (tiny square dots of color). A typical file is built up in layers, so you can work on specific areas independently.

BUILDING A FASHION FIGURE ON THE COMPUTER

You will need:

Original drawing
Scanner
Computer
Adobe Photoshop program

Website help:
www.adobe.com/support/products/photoshop.html

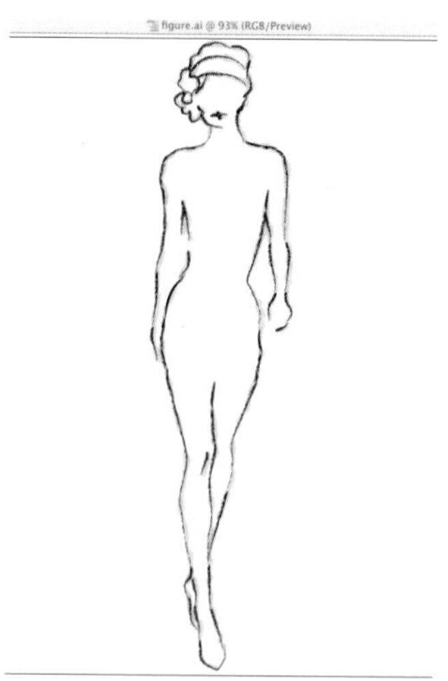

1

To begin, you need to create a figure upon which you can place your clothing designs, rather like playing "dress the doll!" You can do this by drawing your figure freehand and then scanning it directly into Adobe Photoshop. Once you have opened your figure in the program, save it as a Photoshop file (.psd). You will know when the image is saved correctly, as its new title (figure.psd) will appear on the file's title bar.

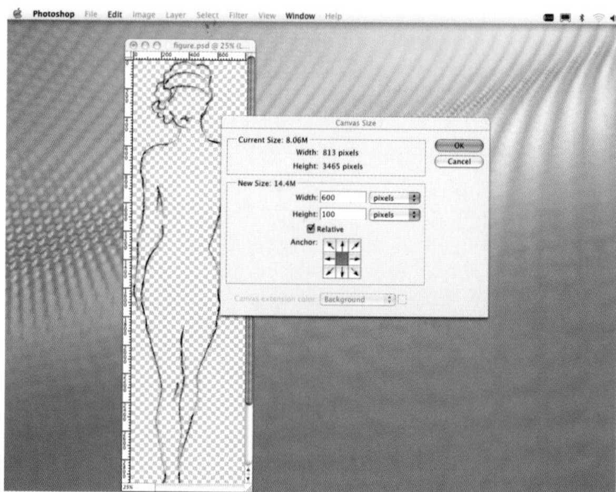

2

Next, you will probably need to increase the canvas space around the figure. This will give you plenty of space to work. Go to the Image menu and select Canvas Size, and a dialogue box will appear. Here the canvas has been increased relatively, by adding 600 pixels to the width and 100 pixels to the height. The figure is currently displayed on the default Photoshop checkerboard background (this indicates that you're working on an image file with a transparent background).

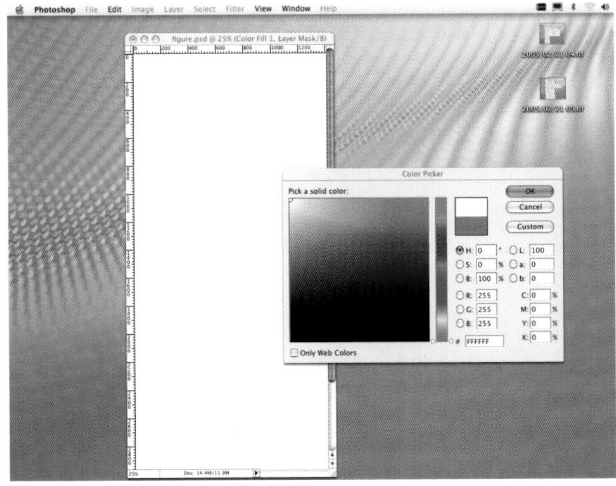

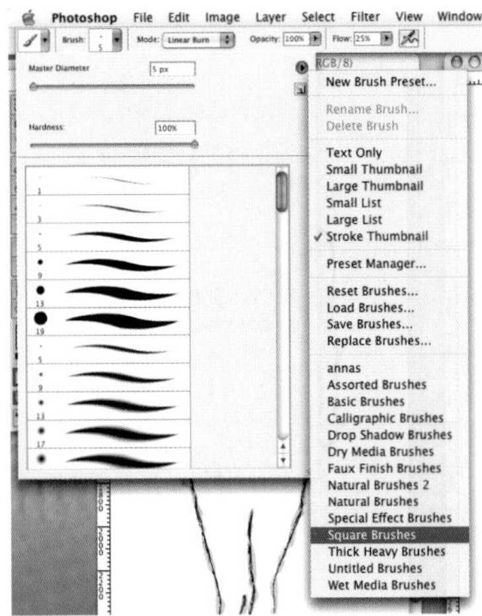

3

To create a solid, colored background layer, select New Fill Layer > Solid Color, from the Layer menu. A dialogue box will appear, enabling you to name this layer, if you wish. You will notice that the new color layer you have created is placed over the original figure layer: new layers are always placed above the currently selected layer; however, their stacking order can easily be rearranged. Once you've selected the color you wish to work on, simply drag the color-fill layer below the layer that contains your figure. For the purpose of this tutorial, a white background layer has been created.

5

There are many different brush presets available in addition to the default selection. To access new presets, select the brush tool, then on the options bar (at the top of the screen), click on the brush dropdown. This dropdown enables you to change the style of the currently selected brush, change the brush, or open a new set of brushes. Click on the arrow at the top right of the brushes dropdown, and select the brush set you wish to open from the list.

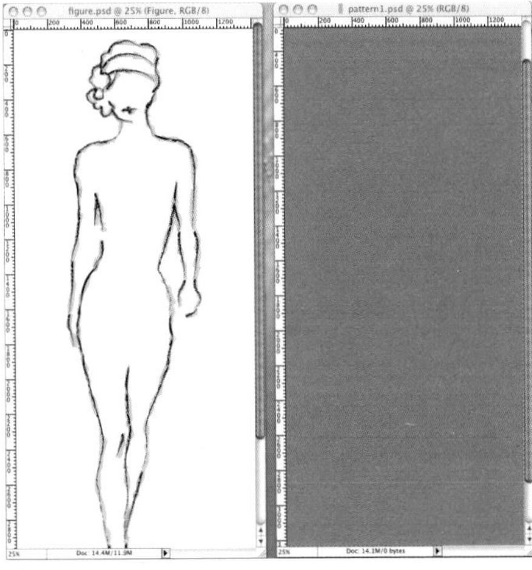

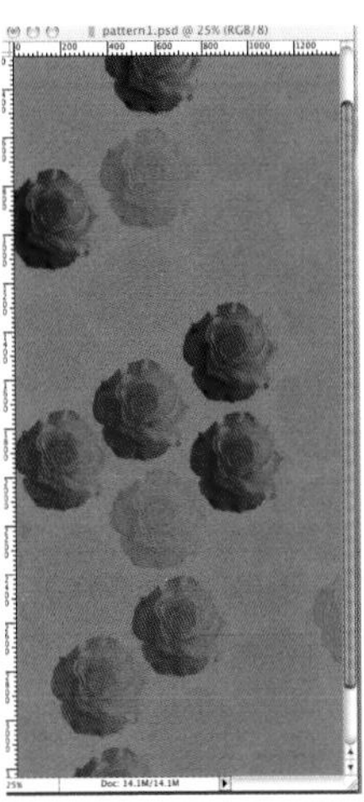

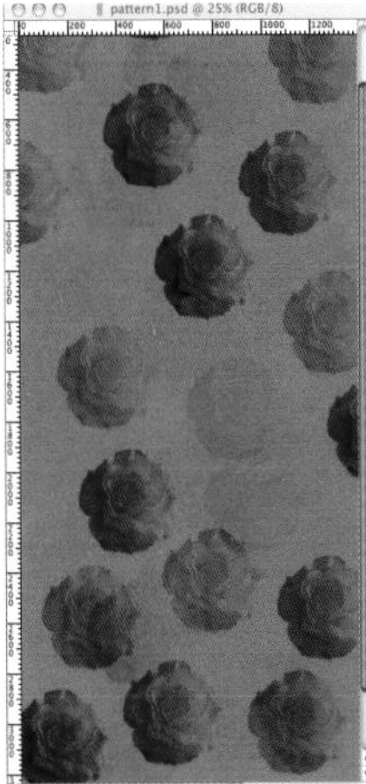

4

Now create a new Photoshop file, in which you can work on your fabric pattern. Make sure your pattern file is the same resolution and roughly the same size as the file containing your figure. This will ensure that the pattern retains its appearance when transferred to the figure file. It also helps to be consistent with units of measurement here! This pattern file has been given a strong pink background color. Now you can create your pattern. There are many ways of creating patterns in Photoshop: you could scan an existing fabric or pattern, or create a pattern from scratch, using paintbrush or shape tools and/or the define pattern command, under the Edit menu.

6

Once you've selected the brush you wish to use, you can edit its behavior via the dock, to the right of the options bar, under the brushes tab. The rose brush was selected here, and from the brushes tab, you can highlight Scatter and drag the slider toward 100 percent, then highlight Brush Tip Shape and do the same, in order to increase the spacing. If you are creating a geometric pattern, or a pattern from scratch, you may find the guides and grid helpful. These can be shown or hidden via the View menu. This tutorial takes a more random approach, using the scatter settings to paint roses all over the pattern canvas.

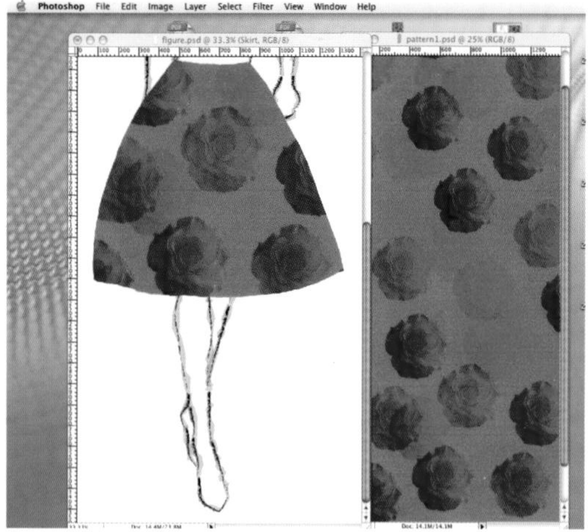

7
Once you have created and saved your pattern file, return to the file containing your figure. Now you can start to create areas onto which your pattern can be transferred. Draw a selection area around the skirt. Go to the Select menu and choose Load Selection. Select the Clone Stamp tool from the tool box. Holding down the "alt" key, click the brush to define a source point. Next, click on the file containing your figure, and paint the pattern onto the new layer. The brush's movements will be traced onto the pattern file. Notice that the selection area constrains the paint strokes, ensuring a tidy finish. Now repeat these steps to complete your outfit.

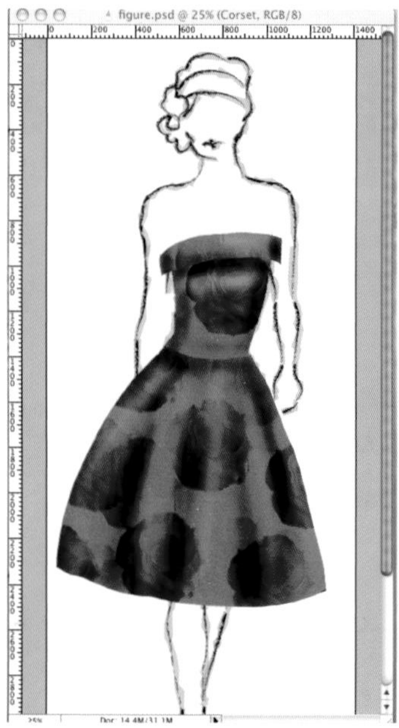

8
Finally, to add a hint of dimension to the clothing, use the burn and dodge tools to add shadows and highlights. You can either paint these on freehand, or draw a selection area to constrain your shading, for more predictable results. Remember, you can change the strength of the shadows and highlights you apply by adjusting the exposure level on the options bar.

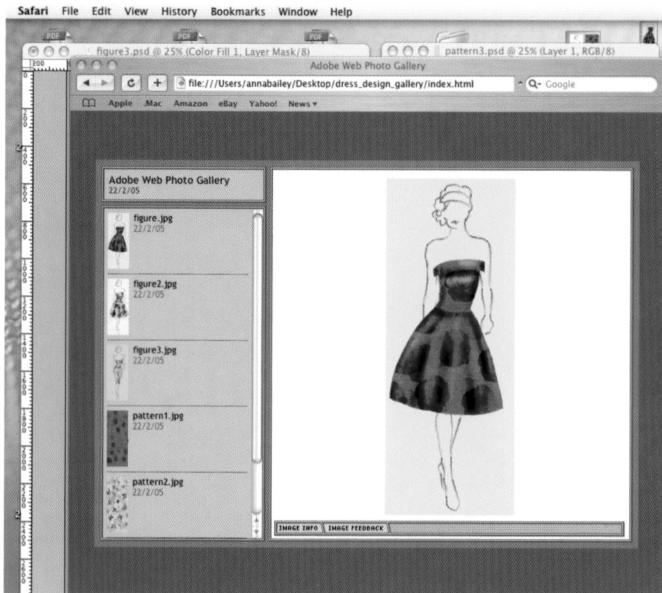

9
As a finishing touch, you may wish to change the background color to suit your illustration—simply double click on the color swatch to the left of your color-fill layer, and select a suitable color, using the color picker. A great way to present your design ideas is with a Web Photo Gallery. Photoshop enables you to very easily collate and present images professionally. Most of this process is automated, making it fairly straightforward to display your finished fashion artworks.

THE FUTURE: GUIDANCE

7

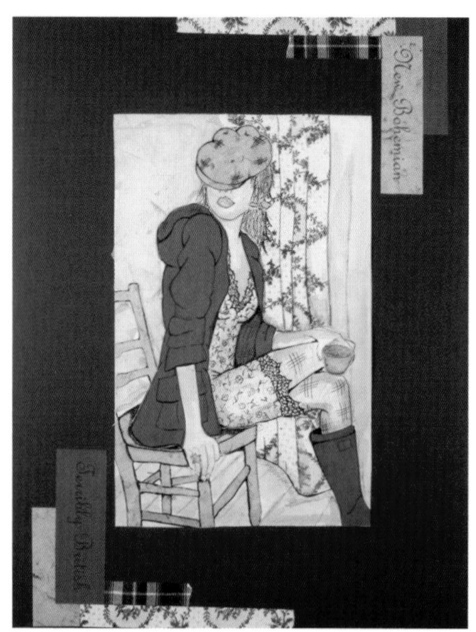

Above
New Bohemian fashion illustration presentation board. Mounting fashion illustrations is a time-consuming business, but it is worth taking time to display your work to its best advantage. This image has been planned meticulously, and the student has evidently thought carefully about colors and materials before securing anything onto the board. The most striking feature of the board is its simplicity, with the color palette kept to a minimum, and the same patterned papers used for the mounting as for the artwork. The illustration has been created by painting the figure in ink over a paper collage. The borders and text are in keeping with the image.

Sticking to the following rules has ensured the success of the above simple illustration as a portfolio piece:

- Keep lines that should be straight, straight.
- Unless your handwriting is beautiful, type all text.
- Use a quality adhesive, and ensure all corners are stuck down neatly.
- Use the same-colored mount board, in a color that complements your illustrations, throughout a project, to guarantee continuity.
- Foam board can be used to raise areas of importance.

The purpose of this book is to help you move through the artistic journey of fashion illustration by learning imaginative techniques and thinking creatively about fashion presentation. Alone, this is not enough to succeed in your chosen career—there are practical steps to take to secure a foothold in the fashion industry. Whether you are applying to study fashion design, with illustration only a small element within the course, or you are choosing fashion illustration as a career, this final chapter aims to guide you through the issues that may be causing you concern. It also features advice and practical recommendations from industry specialists to help you face the future confidently in this competitive world.

PORTFOLIO PRESENTATION

Whether you are applying to study at college or university, or seeking employment as an illustrator, you need a portfolio—a flat, portable case for presenting your artwork. Your portfolio is like a résumé showing the viewer what you are capable of achieving. Effective visual communication is vital in the fashion world, and first impressions count, so your portfolio should be a powerful self-marketing tool.

Portfolios range from A4 to A1 in size, but A3 (16½ x 11½ inches) or A2 (23½ x 16½ inches) types are most suitable for fashion artwork. These sizes ensure that the work is large enough to view but still portable. Unless you can afford more than one portfolio, it is probably best to decide at an early stage which size suits your personal working style. This allows you to plan your artwork to fit your portfolio. However, don't let portfolio size restrict your creativity—add fold-out sections for larger pieces, or reduce them to fit, on a color photocopier.

A strong portfolio case enables you to keep work neat and flat. Take pride in your artwork by looking after it properly. In the highly visual world of fashion, curled edges or tatty, smudged sheets do not create a good impression. Protect your work by presenting it in transparent plastic sleeves that clip into the spine of the portfolio case.

The running order of the artwork in your portfolio needs to flow smoothly. The aim is to encourage the viewer to keep turning the pages in anticipation of impressive work. It is often a good idea to put your best pieces at the start and end of the portfolio, as they will become the most memorable. These are often known as "conversation pieces"—artwork that the viewer may want to discuss further. It is important to note that you should only choose to show work that you feel comfortable talking about. If you are not particularly confident about a piece, leave it out of the portfolio entirely.

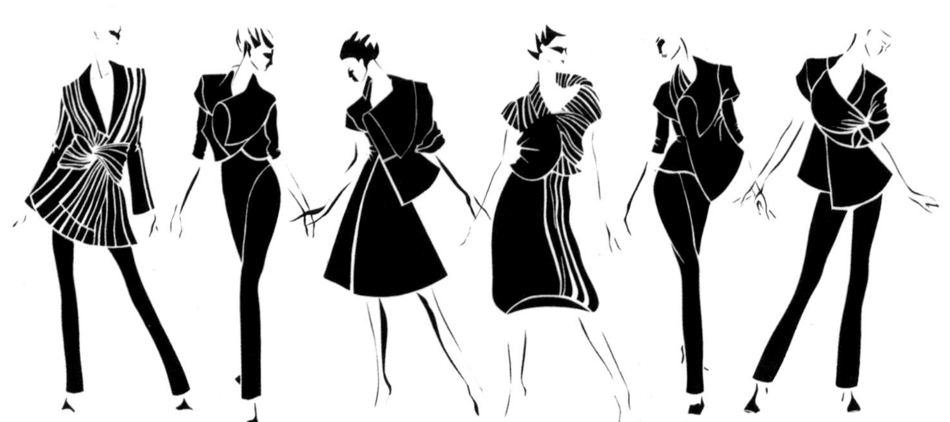

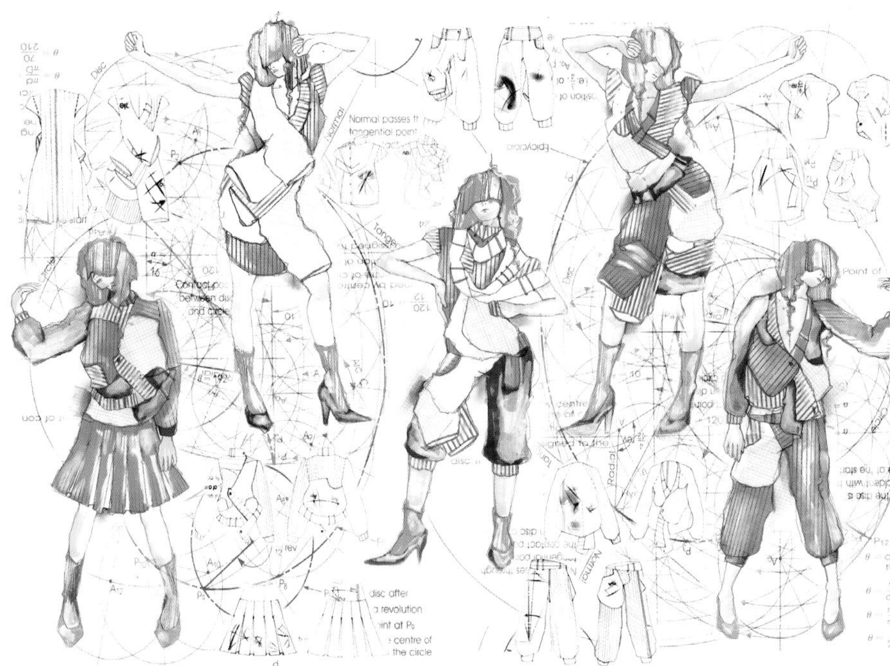

Left and opposite, below
This portfolio collection lineup (*Left*) shows figures illustrated using colored marker pens, mounted on a black-and-white sketchy background, which also contains specification drawings of the garments. The figures are arranged in a haphazard manner compared to the straight lineup of six black outfits (*Opposite, below*). This arrangement is equally striking, even though only one color has been used.

You can group your work in assorted ways. Chronological order will show development, while varying project themes and styles will add diversity to the running order. Remember that the viewer will be looking at the work for the first time, so your portfolio should clearly tell the story of how you researched and resolved a brief. It should not be necessary to question you. Likewise, the viewer should not have to turn your portfolio at all angles to see the work—keep the orientation of your pages the same. For continuity, organize your work logically, grouping projects together for clarity.

FURTHER-EDUCATION PORTFOLIO

If you are applying to further your education in a fashion-based course or entering a fashion degree program, assemble a portfolio that shows your strengths and abilities. Much of the advice above is applicable, but focus on showing the interviewer the development of your creative work, so that your future potential is evident. Display a range of visual studies, including life drawing, still-life studies, textile sampling, and imaginative observational work. Although the portfolio should have a slight fashion focus, you will be learning fashion skills during the course or degree program. The interviewer will want to see wide-ranging artistic abilities in your portfolio that can be developed in a fashion environment. At this stage, it is not your technical expertise or fine-tuned fashion illustrations that are important, but your ideas. With this in mind, keep a few sketchbooks in the back of your portfolio, and possibly some examples of written work, so the interviewer discovers as much as possible about your creative talents.

GRADUATE PORTFOLIO

When selecting artwork for your portfolio, remember that professionalism is key. You will not be able to carry garments to interviews, so you are reliant on your portfolio to impress clients. If you are seeking employment as a graduate, include any live projects that you have completed. These are often projects linked to

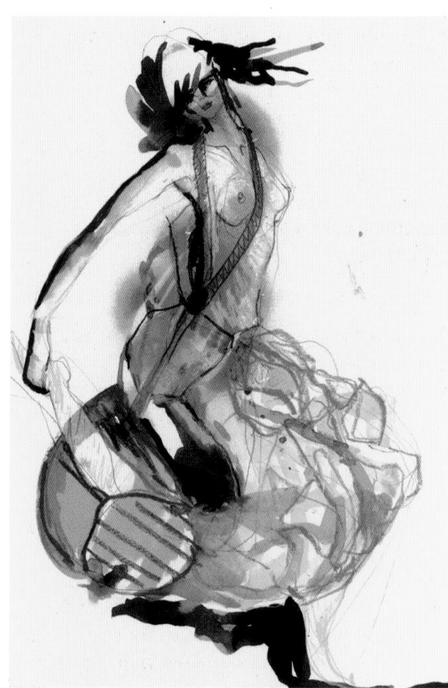

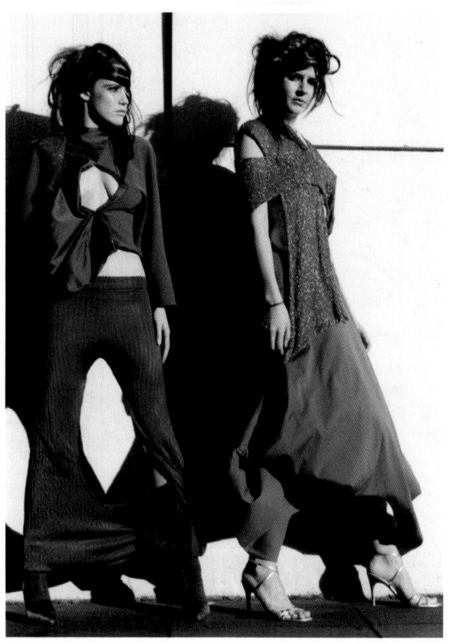

Designers use many ilustration techniques to enhance their garments. This one (*Top*) was created by a student using watercolor and pastels on tinted paper. The student has a particularly good eye for cropping the image for maximum impact. Once the garments had been constructed, the same student set up a photo shoot to record the creations further (*Below*). You can see the original skirt from the illustration has been teamed with other designs to complete the look. Remember, photographs of your garments are an essential part of your portfolio. Prospective employers will want to see "the real thing" as well as the artwork.

reputable businesses, companies, or industry specialists that have sponsored a university or college fashion course, usually donating fabrics or offering appropriate payment and prizes. Many fashion companies also reward students with work placements or internships. By including live work in your portfolio, you demonstrate that you are aware of the industry you are entering. An interviewer will be interested to know how you coped with meeting deadlines, working to a brief, and presenting your final ideas. This creates a valuable snapshot of you as a potential employee. Display in your portfolio national and international competition entries, too, because they provide evidence that you are ambitious, enthusiastic, and keen to be the finest in your chosen field. A fashion-design graduate should also include promotional photographs of garments, setting up photo shoots on location or in a studio.

PROFESSIONAL PORTFOLIO

Your portfolio will have gone through many changes by the time you reach professional status. Now you should have a clear direction and focus, reflected in your portfolio. You can be more selective about the pieces you include, and you will be able to organize your portfolio to appeal to a specific employer. Your portfolio will be either predominantly fashion design or promotional illustration. Like many professionals, you might show a portfolio of work on your own website.

DIGITAL PORTFOLIO

In today's technical society, you should always save your work digitally, too. Scan the contents of your portfolio at high resolution, and save it onto a disk. This version of your portfolio can be sent to potential employers. You can also email work-sample files instantly if requested, making your work even more accessible. Creating a convenient digital portfolio can save you from carrying the real thing to interviews. However, always check what clients prefer, as some would rather look through the original portfolio than digital copies.

There are many ways of presenting fashion artwork. The images in this section are all portfolio pieces produced by students enrolled in various fashion courses and degree programs. In your portfolio, aim for continuity, diversity, stunning imagery, and a professional approach to organization and presentation. Then be proud of what your portfolio holds, and your confidence will communicate itself.

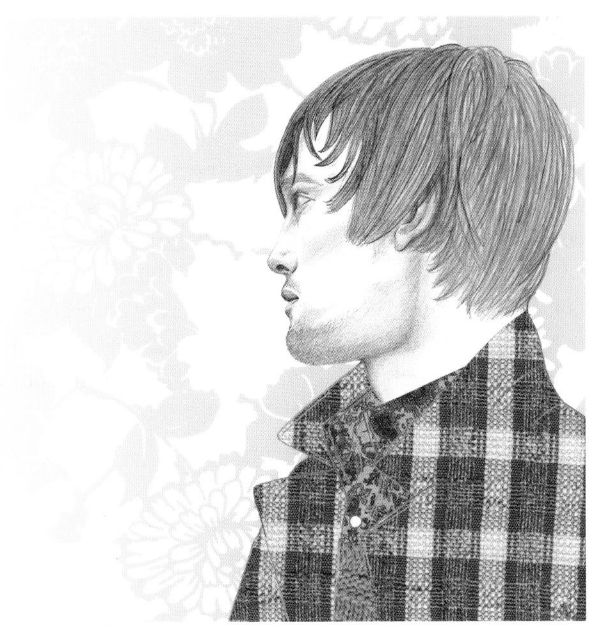

Left
When preparing your portfolio pages, don't cram in so much that they become cluttered. The "less-is-more" theory has been successfully applied to this illustration by a student who enhances her drawings on the computer using Photoshop. The sense of serenity conveyed by her uncluttered approach is emphasized by a soothing color palette and minimalist style of illustration.

Below left
In contrast to the previous image, a full figure is required to promote the outfit in this digitally enhanced illustration. Again, the artist ensures that the fashion item is the main subject of interest; this time by not over-complicating the image with a fussy background.

Below right
The energy of this figure is emphasized by allowing her to explode across the edges of the page. This effect can also be created by carefully cropping your artwork using a paper cutter. The original drawing has been adapted on the computer.

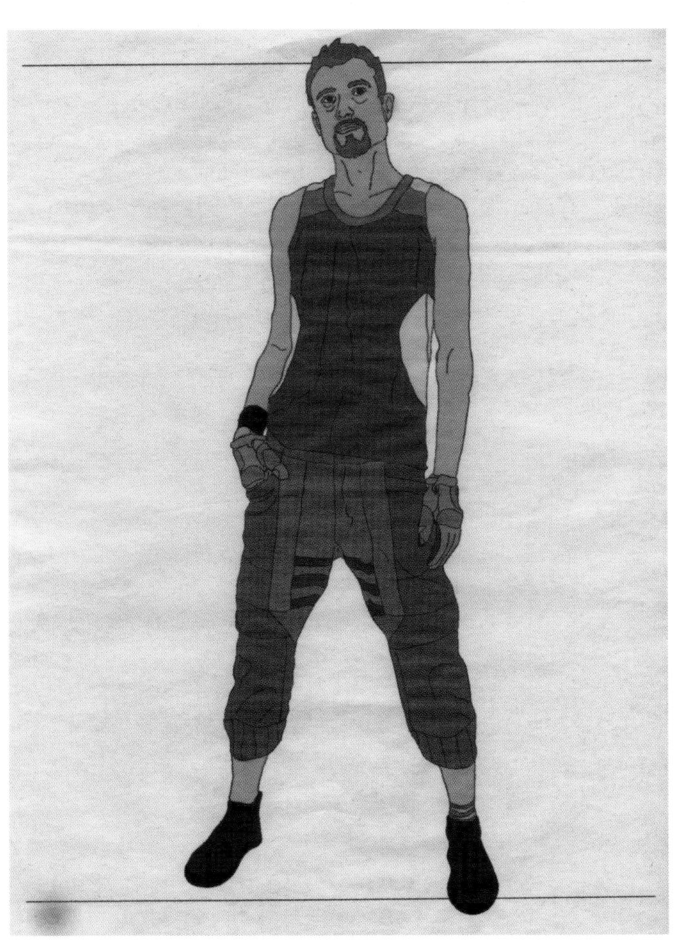

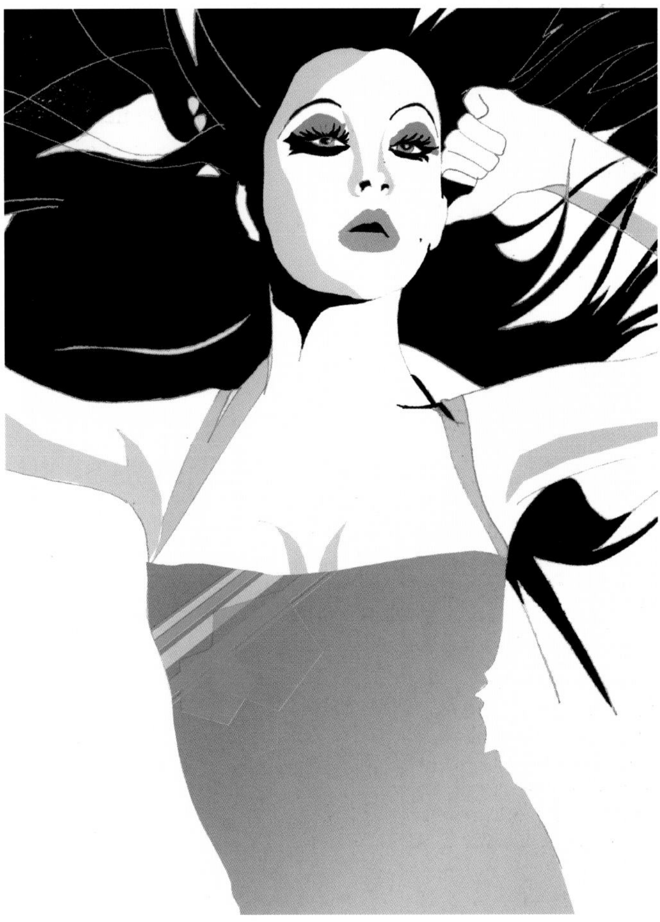

THE FUTURE: MAKING CHOICES

FURTHER EDUCATION

Fashion is a "glamorous" industry that many find attractive, resulting in much competition for places in fashion degree programs. Before applying, research the type of course that will suit you best. The aim of a college or university program is to make your training as relevant as possible to a job in the fashion industry, so the correct program choice at this stage is vital. It is no longer as simple as choosing to study "fashion"; programs with similar-sounding titles vary considerably. Fashion design and garment construction dominate many degree programs, but fashion illustration and promotion are also often key areas. The following list demonstrates the variety of fashion degree programs offered:

- Costume Design
- Fashion Accessories
- Fashion Art
- Fashion Brand Promotion and Journalism
- Fashion Design
- Fashion Design with Business Studies
- Fashion Design with Retail Management
- Fashion Enterprise
- Fashion Promotion and Illustration
- Fashion Photography
- Fashion Knitwear
- Product Development for the Fashion Industry

When you have narrowed your field, a good starting point is to search the Internet for possible study locations. Most institutions offer a catalog that you can order online or by telephone. Catalogs and brochures are the marketing tools that colleges and universities use to sell their courses to you. They provide a wealth of information about degree program outlines, educational procedures, the school's location, and success rates. Many catalogs also include student opinions about what it is like to study at the school and information about social activities and nightlife. Some cities hold annual career fairs in large exhibition centers, packed with stands from major institutions offering art and design courses. Visiting such an event is an ideal opportunity to talk to members of staff and collect catalogs.

The next step, and probably the most important in the decision-making process, is to visit the institutions that you are interested in. Attend their open house days, taking the following checklist with you on the visit, and noting the answers to help you decide on your future.

- What is it like to be a student at the institution?
- What is the structure of the program?
- What proportion of the program is dedicated to written work and contextual studies?
- Is there up-to-date machinery, technology, and facilities?
- Will I have my own work space?
- What are the studio and workshop hours?
- Are the staff team skilled and inspiring?
- What is the student-to-staff ratio?
- Are there links with other departments?

- Are there links with industry?
- Are study visits organized to major cities at home and abroad?
- Where are the student shows held?
- What have previous graduates from the institution achieved?
- Which key elements will the interviewer be looking for in a portfolio?
- How many candidates applied last year?
- Do I like the location and atmosphere of the institution? Is its surrounding area somewhere I would enjoy living? Are there student accommodations? What are the opportunities for socializing?

With all your queries answered and the decision made, it is time for your college or university selection interview. Try not think of this as a terrifying ordeal, but as an opportunity to impress. Practice your interview technique beforehand. Ask a teacher to set up mock interviews, or get your family to test you with suitable questions. Interviewing differs greatly from one institution to another. Some review portfolios before deciding whether to interview a student, while others ask you to bring your portfolio to the interview and dedicate time to the questioning and answering process. Questions vary, too, so prepare answers on a wide range of subjects. Remember that questions are not meant to trick you but are asked to discover more about you. The interview is not an examination, so there are no right or wrong answers. Before making a selection, the interviewer wants to learn about your personality and your commitment. The following list shows a small range of questions that you may be asked at an interview:

- Why have you chosen this degree program?
- Why do you want to study in … (name of town or city)?
- Did you come to the open house?
- Where do you see yourself in five years' time?
- Have you completed any work experience?
- Which is your strongest piece of work and why?
- Which fashion designers do you admire?
- Which fashion illustrators inspire you?
- What do you like/dislike about the fashion industry?
- Which is your favorite fashion retailer?
- Which television programs do you enjoy watching?
- What are you reading at the moment?
- What is your favorite piece of clothing and why?
- Which magazines do you read?
- Where do you wish to travel?
- What was the last exhibition you saw?
- What do you like best about your personality?
- Do you have any weaknesses?
- What is your greatest achievement to date?

Another issue for students attending a fashion-based interview is what to wear. Selecting the right outfit is difficult if you are worried about the scrutiny of the interviewer. It is fair to say that the interviewer's main objective is to scrutinize your work rather than your dress, but a little effort in this area will not go unnoticed. Choose something you feel comfortable wearing—your clothes should reflect your personality. Don't try to be someone you are not just to impress. It can be a good idea to wear a garment or accessory that you have made yourself to display your creativity.

Most importantly when attending interviews at this level, remain calm and confident. Think about the questions carefully and answer with considered sentences. Your main aim is to make the interviewer think they would be making a mistake if they were to reject you. Believe in yourself, and others will believe in you.

THE BIG WIDE WORLD

Many students embark on their education as a clear route to a career, while for others it is more of a personal challenge—they enjoy a subject, such as fashion, and want to develop their work as far as possible. After many years of study, and probably a great deal of expense, you are no longer a student but a graduate ready to enter the big wide world. At this stage, you will probably ask yourself: "How do I decide what to do next?"

There will be many others in a similar position when you leave the safety of the study environment. Most courses showcase graduate work in annual, specialized graduate exhibitions attended by members of the fashion industry and the press. This is a wonderful opportunity for graduates to network and establish contacts for possible future employment. It is also a chance to receive feedback about your work and observe the work of others. Fashion scouts visit these events to hunt for emerging talent, so label your work clearly with your name and contact details. Printing memorable postcards or business cards for possible employers to take away is worthwhile to try to ensure you make a lasting impression.

A degree program is not the only route to a career in fashion illustration. Many people become self-taught illustrators or attend night classes to gain extra artistic skills to build a suitable portfolio. To succeed in this way, you need to be committed and passionate about your future. You should network actively and promote yourself, as you will not have the support of an educational establishment. This is probably a slightly tougher journey, but not an impossible one if you are dedicated.

Many jobs in the creative field are not advertised but found through personal contacts, networking, or by approaching an employer directly with a résumé. If you are seeking employment you need to "sell" yourself. Just like in the college or university selection interview, encourage employers to think they will be making a mistake if they do not hire you. Conduct a thorough and organized search for an appropriate job vacancy, attending career fairs and consulting websites, national, regional, and local newspapers, industry-specific journals and publications, and most importantly, specialist fashion-recruitment agencies. Listed on page 199 are some useful addresses giving information on finding employment.

Self-employment, or freelancing, is another avenue to explore. Many fashion illustrators work on a freelance basis, being employed for a specific job, then moving on to the next when that is complete. For an illustrator, this is an excellent way to build a diverse portfolio with a varied range of clients. You need to be highly motivated to work in this way, and may require an agent to help promote your skills.

Postgraduate study is an opportunity to further your education. Many graduates return to college or university to continue studying the subject they enjoy, or to gain higher-level training and qualifications to increase their employment opportunities. This is a costly process, so, before applying, find out about any available funding such as scholarships. Postgraduate study can be undertaken at any time. Some employers may fund your study on a part-time basis if your new qualifications and skills will also be advantageous to them.

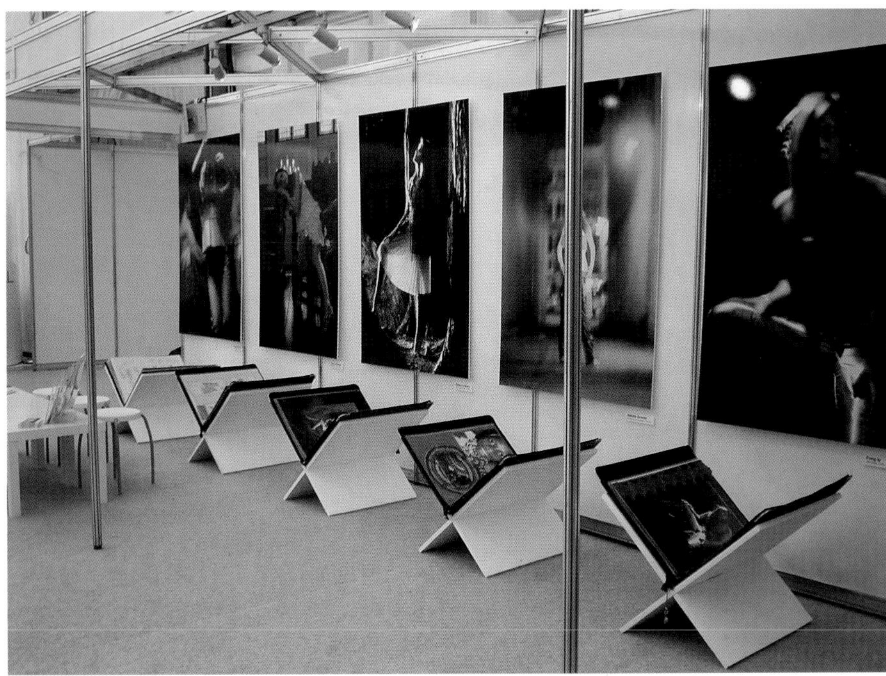

A stand at London Graduate Fashion week—an annual event showcasing the work of fashion graduates.

Residencies offer an income and work space in return for producing a work of art that meets a particular brief. Clients can range from schools, hospitals, galleries, and community spaces to industrial and commercial settings. Becoming a resident at an appropriate location is an excellent way to gain experience and enhance your development as an artist.

Taking time out to travel in between graduating and joining the workforce can also be a valuable learning experience, giving you inspiration and confidence. Travel with a camera, sketchbook, and diary to record different cultures and lifestyles. When you return to the job market, you will be competing against a new set of graduates, so use your traveling observations to demonstrate the connection between this experience and your work.

SELLING YOURSELF

Your résumé is a personal marketing tool presenting qualifications, skills, and attributes that demonstrate your suitability for a job. It must be accurate, interesting, and up-to-date to make the best impression possible and get you noticed. Advice about the best style and layout for a résumé differs widely. Frequently asked questions include: How many pages should it be? Which font size should I use? Should I list my interests? The final decisions rest with you. Make your curriculum vitae a personal record of your life that promotes you to your best advantage.

If you are unsure about what to list on your résumé, start by analyzing the skills and interests you have to offer in relation to your career choice. Your experience in higher education is not just about what you learned from studying, but about your life. Consider your academic achievements, social life, work experience, hobbies, and responsibilities. All can provide evidence of the qualities sought by employers. The following checklist will help you to compile the relevant information for your résumé:

• Name
• Contact details
• Personal profile/statement
• Education
• Qualifications
• Employment/work experience
• Responsibilities
• Skills/abilities/specialist areas
• Achievements/competitions/awards
• Interests/hobbies
• References

As an artist, consider the visual aspect of your résumé. Including images of your work will make you memorable to an employer. Think of ways to promote yourself further, perhaps creating a marketing pack that includes a résumé, business card with contact details, and postcards or photographs of your artwork. Some people send digital visual résumés online in the form of a PDF file. Most importantly, always follow up with a phone call to a potential employer. There are many ways of selling yourself effectively and making sure that you stand out from the crowd.

When it is time to enter the world of employment, it may take you a little while to know exactly what you want to do. The following interviews with industry professionals may help you to decide the path you wish to take. Stephanie Pesakoff, from Art Department, describes the role of an illustration agent. David Downton tells of his fascinating life as a fashion illustrator. Lysiane de Royère, from Promostyl, discusses how to illustrate future fashion trends, and Jeffrey Fulvimari tells of his growing empire as a commercially led fashion illustrator.

STEPHANIE PESAKOFF

ILLUSTRATION AGENT FOR ART DEPARTMENT

Fashion illustrators often work on a self-employed, freelance basis whereby they are hired to illustrate specific assignments. Working as a freelancer involves learning to juggle several commissions at once, invoicing clients, and managing all administration. Many freelancers gain the representation of a reputable agent, who promotes them. The services of an agent vary depending on the individual illustrator, but in general, they handle all inquiries, portfolio requests, negotiations, scheduling, and invoicing. In addition, a good agent maintains portfolios and an agency website with samples of illustrators' work, and perhaps orchestrates agency promotions.

Stephanie Pesakoff is an illustration agent at Art Department, based in New York. Art Department also represents photographers, fashion stylists, hair and makeup artists, and prop and set designers. Stephanie suggests: "An illustrator should have some professional experience under their belt before approaching an agent, as they then have a better idea of the agent's job and more realistic expectations and appreciation of the agent."

It is not easy to get onto the books of Art Department. They receive enquiries from an average of five illustrators a week, yet take on only approximately four new illustrators a year. However, Stephanie says she is "always happy to see new work" and suggests "email contact with jpeg samples is the best way to approach an agency." When looking for the right agent, Stephanie advises: "It's a really personal thing. First and foremost, the illustrator should do their homework and learn about various agencies. The illustrator should like the work that an agency represents and also the branding or positioning of the agency. I also think it is really important to meet the owner, or agent, and get a sense of whether you like and trust them as a person. This is someone you might well be speaking with on a daily basis, so I think it's necessary to like each other. I think it is appropriate to check around and inquire about the reputation of the agency; you can ask industry people, or even ask the agent if you can speak directly with some artists already on their roster."

When Stephanie is selecting an illustrator to be represented by Art Department, she says: "They must first be nice, communicative, and professional people; I then have to love their work. And finally, I think it's important that their style fits in with the look and client base of our agency."

So, how important is fashion illustration in the commercial world? Stephanie states adamantly: "Not important enough! Historically, there is a very rich and varied legacy of fashion illustration, so it seems ironic that today illustration is often considered a 'risky' or 'edgy' option. Look at any issue of *Vogue* from the 1940s, and you will find it's *all* illustration. I still consider a big part of my job to be education. It is surprising how many art directors have never worked with illustration. It's great to be able to enlighten them to all its benefits and possibilities."

Art Department aims to secure freelance projects for illustrators in many areas, including advertising, editorial, design projects, CD covers, book jackets, and so on. When discussing payment, Stephanie says: "It really depends on the project and can vary greatly. We have illustrators earning anywhere from $20,000 to $300,000 a year." If becoming a freelance fashion illustrator appeals to you, Stephanie advises: "Do what you really love, and focus on having an individual and recognizable style. Good luck."

DAVID DOWNTON

FASHION ILLUSTRATOR

Although David Downton describes his role in the fashion industry modestly as "peripheral," it could be argued that it is set firmly in the center. Born in London, he trained at Canterbury and Wolverhampton Art Colleges (UK) in graphics and illustration. On graduating, David's first commission was to illustrate a cover for *Which Computer?* magazine, but it didn't take long for his distinctive style of portraying figures to be recognized, transporting him into a very different environment. "I didn't set out to become a fashion illustrator, and came at it via a circuitous route," says David. "The job that changed everything for me was in 1996, when I was sent to Paris by a magazine to cover the couture shows. I'd dabbled in fashion illustration prior to this, but then I'd also done all the usual jobs that an illustrator tackles, from educational books to packaging design." David became a familiar face, backstage and front of house, in the lavish and illustrious Paris haute couture shows. His reports from the collections have appeared in *The Times, The Daily Telegraph, The Independent,* and *Harper's Bazaar* (Australia).

David has spent time in Paris drawing the world's greatest models wearing couture clothes from Dior, Chanel, and Valentino. Following a seven-hour sitting with Linda Evangelista at the George V Hotel for *Visionnaire* magazine, he said: "I could retire now—it doesn't get any better than this."

Like René Gruau, René Bouché, and Antonio Lopez before him, drawing beautiful women has become second nature to David, who has captured the likenesses of some of the world's most striking women. He has created portraits of Jerry Hall, Carmen, Elizabeth Hurley, Iman, Paloma Picasso, Joely Richardson, and Anna Piaggi. His friendship and many collaborations with the model Erin O'Connor has brought him further recognition. In an article for the Association of Illustrators, David says of Erin: "I can never decide whether she looks like a drawing, or whether she is how a drawing ought to look." David also advises: "Drawing from a model (famous or not) is vital; in many ways the model is the drawing."

Asked how he achieves the perfect fashion illustration, David answers simply: "I don't think it is possible to achieve a perfect illustration. But hope springs eternal. I think it involves a lot of work and a lot of drawing, and my mantra is always 'keep working until it looks effortless.'" It is fair to say that David Downton's working process is far from effortless. For the Association of Illustrators, he describes how he captures the moment with a model such as Erin O'Connor: "Between us we come up with a pose that will look good on the page and will show whatever is interesting or important about the clothes. I then take maybe half a dozen photographs. Then I make between ten and twenty drawings of each pose during the sitting, using pen or graphite on cheap cartridge or layout paper." When the preparatory stage is complete David begins again, this time working on watercolor paper, "refining the image while trying to maintain the spontaneity of the first drawing."

The importance of practice cannot be emphasized enough for David: "To get one good fashion illustration, I have often completed twenty sketches beforehand. Forests have perished in the name of this! As an illustrator, you should be constantly learning and striving to get better." The art materials and techniques he uses vary: "It depends on the situation, the job, or my mood. I use watercolor, gouache, Doctor Martin's inks, cut paper, pencil, and lots of Rotring black ink—I am keen to develop my skills and would like to try oils, and I am going to take a screen-printing course."

When talking about different styles and techniques for fashion illustration, David says: "There are no rules." Although computer-generated work is not for him, David explains: "It's great if used with skill and imagination. Jason Brooks showed us all how it could be done." Aspiring illustrators are often concerned about capturing their

Opposite, top left
This watercolor illustration of a Christian Lacroix ensemble was shown at David Downton's first solo exhibition, in London, in 1998, and is described by him as a "happy accident." During this exhibition, Downton was surprised that practically every piece sold—this was one he refused to sell.

Opposite, top right
Another illustration from David Downton's first solo exhibition shows a Thierry Mugler couture dress portayed in flat colors, cut paper, and acetate overlay. This image became iconic, selling instantly. It is still well-remembered and is pictured on cards for The Art Group and Ikea.

Opposite, below
In 2003, David Downton drew Carmen at the Hardy Amies Couture House, in Savile Row, London. This watercolor image was also featured as a cover for the *Telegraph* magazine. Carmen has modeled for more than sixty years. Downton says: "She understands how to edit herself for the page. She is so wonderful to draw, because she understands what it is that you see and knows how to make pictures."

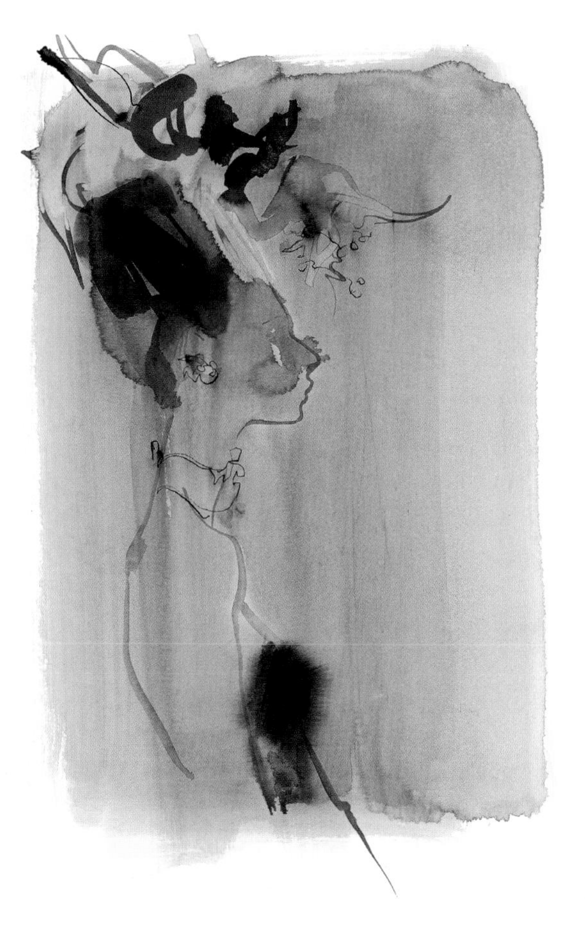

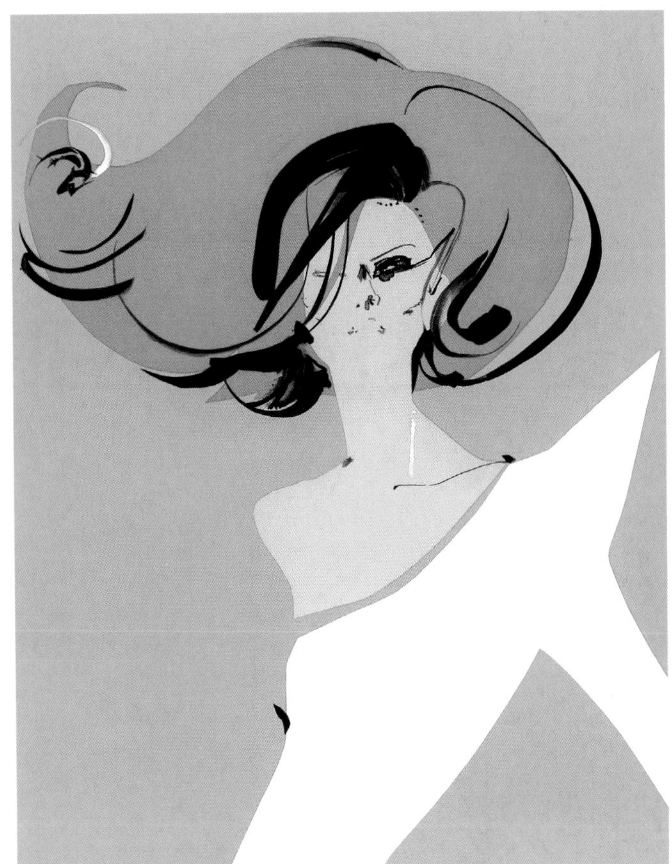

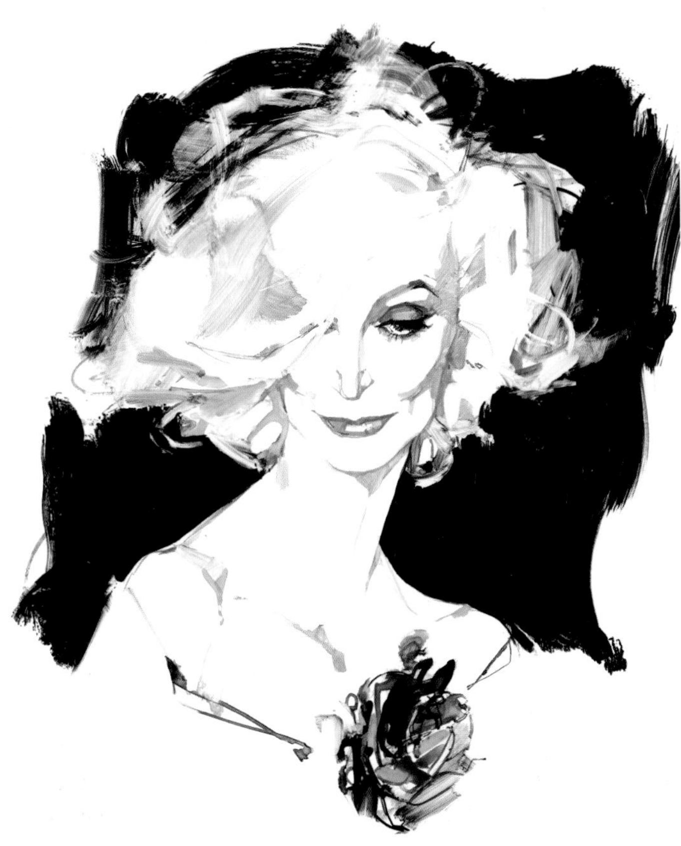

Right
Illustration of Erin O'Connor backstage at a Galliano/Christian Dior Haute Couture summer show.

Below
For this image for a Topshop advertisement, David Downton spent days drawing Lily Cole and Erin O'Connor. He describes it as: "A perfect job—when you draw from models like these, so much of your work is done. They wear the clothes so well, creating a fashion illustration came easily."

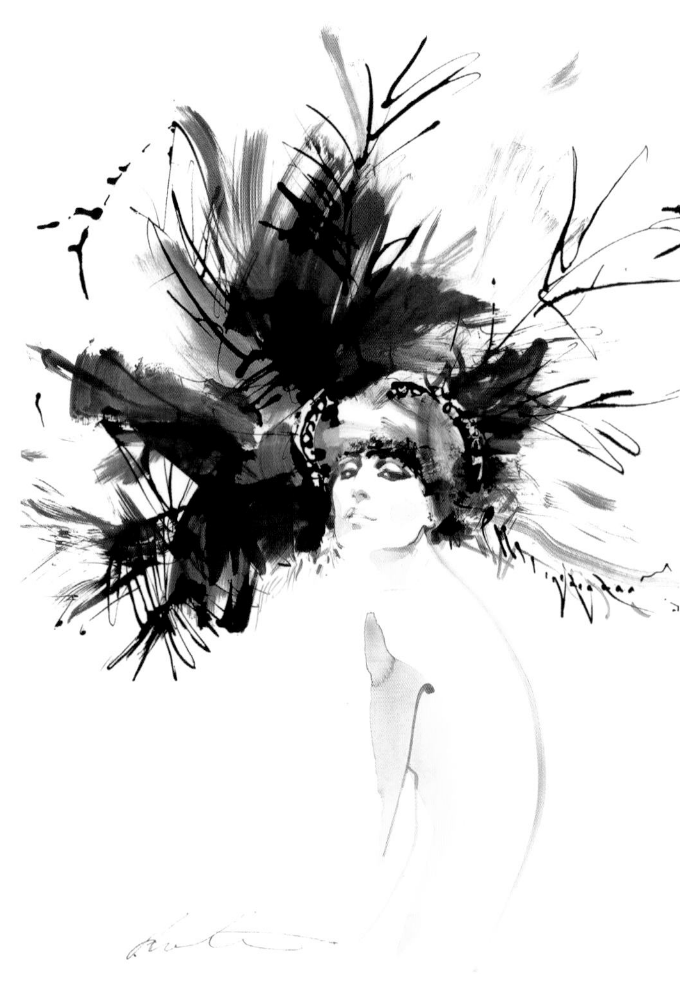

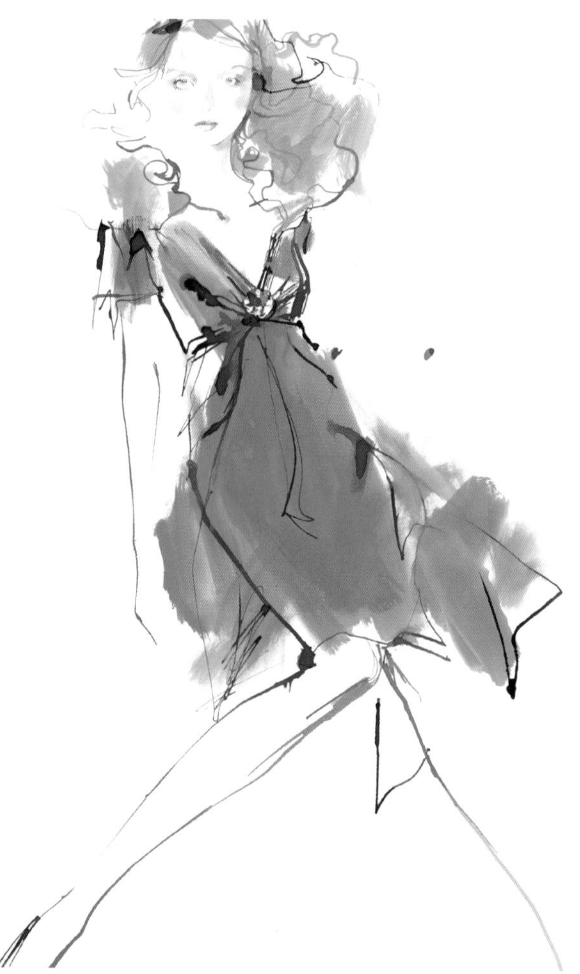

own style, but David advises: "Don't worry about it. Very few people start out with a 'style' as such. It will evolve the more you work—in fact, most illustrators work in several styles. Above all, I think drawing is at the center of it, whether you finally end up producing work digitally or not. So, my advice would be to keep drawing, and be very persistent."

As well as looking to the future, David has an eye on the past. He admires the work of René Gruau for his peerless graphic sense and glamour; Eric for his draftsmanship and consistency; and René Bouché for his way with a likeness. Today, David thinks Mats Gustafson is the illustrator's illustrator. When speaking of his own fashion illustration career, David believes: "It is important to never really be in fashion. I was never really the illustrator of the moment, and never having been exactly 'in,' I've also never really gone 'out.'" This theory has made for a successful career spanning over two decades. David recognizes his many achievements and says: "I have been lucky enough to work with some extraordinary people—designers, models, some of the most iconic faces of our time—but I think probably my greatest achievement is to have had solo exhibitions in London, Paris, and New York."

David is keen to point out that, following a brief interlude when fashion illustration fell out of favor, the industry is growing again. He acknowledges: "There are a lot of illustrators out there—but thankfully, there is also a lot of work today. You can work editorially in newspapers, magazines, and publishing; for card companies; in advertising—in conjunction with designers or fashion houses; or alternatively, pursue fashion as 'art' rather than illustration, and work with galleries and on limited-edition prints."

Finally, what for David Downton is the best thing about his job as a fashion illustrator? "I don't have to shave! Independence! Drawing every day! But most of all, having a window onto the world of couture and all its craziness, and then going home to a real family situation. As I said before, 'It's peripheral!'"

LYSIANE DE ROYÈRE

PROMOSTYL

In the constantly changing world of fashion, trend-forecasting companies offer a prediction service to members of the industry. Promostyl is an independent company specializing in style, design, and trend research. Created in 1967, Promostyl now has a large international client base, including companies such as Adidas, Chanel, Coca Cola, L'Oréal, Orange, Swarovski, Waterman, and Zara on their books. Promostyl employs fashion illustrators on a regular basis to help sell its trends.

Launched in the early seventies by Danielle de Diesbach, of Promostyl, the *Trend Book* has become an indispensable tool for fashion and textile professionals. Today the *Trend Book* is a full-color publication created using computer graphics with many color fashion illustrations, in volume and in flats. These show clearly the accessories, color ranges and garment shapes, prints, badges, and logos of the future. Each fashion trend is divided into various stories, as outlined in the images (facing page). The pages are filled with themed fashion illustrations, fabrics, and color details destined for the future.

Promostyl creates fifteen different illustrated *Trend Books* per season, including *Colors, Fabrics, Influences, Home, Baby-Layette, Sport and Street, Lingerie, Women, Ultimates* (for young women), *Men, Children, Junior, Shoes, Swimwear, Knit,* and *Men's Body and Beach Wear.* Promostyl's *Trend Books* are published eighteen months in advance of the season they are predicting and are compiled for spinners and weavers, garment-makers, fashion designers, accessory brands, cosmetic and sports companies, industrial designers, marketing people, and all those whose products must be in step with changing trends and lifestyles.

The Head of Communications at Promostyl, Lysiane de Royère, says: "Curiosity and intuition are very important qualities in this business. It is very important to know as early as possible everything that is new on our planet. At Promostyl, we have a network of agents, and information is continually gathered through travel, the international press, and by consulting the Internet."

To make these books as original as possible, Promostyl employs just over ten fashion illustrators. "They are employed on a freelance basis, with some illustrators working three to four months every year for us," states Lysiane. "We select an illustrator because of the allure or the modernity of their sketches, as well as the legibility of the items," she explains. "A Promostyl fashion illustration needs to be nice to look at but easy to understand and translate into a garment." The illustrators are given as much information as possible to complete their work: a brief, rough sketches, colors, and the names of the trends. "They use a range of materials, including pens, pencils, markers, and the computer. Very often, we ask them to scan their sketches and add fabric and colors onto them using Photoshop," says Lysiane.

When asked which qualities Promostyl look for when employing a fashion illustrator, Lysiane replies: "They need to have a good sense of themselves, be fashion-oriented, and passionate about their work!" Lysiane also explains: "Our illustrators come from all over Europe. It is important to speak languages in order to be able to work with various countries around the world." With its offices in Paris, New York, and Tokyo—and its widespread network of exclusive agents spanning Europe, Brazil, Asia, and Australia—Promostyl's influence is truly felt around the world.

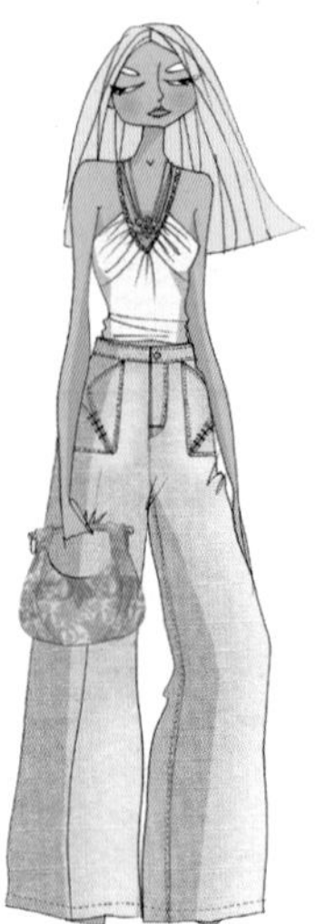
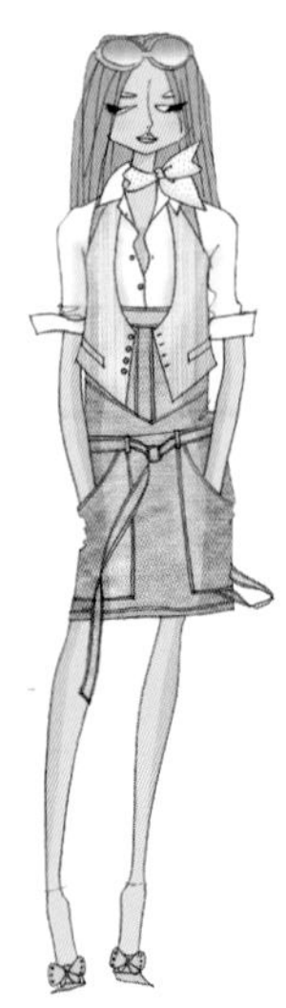
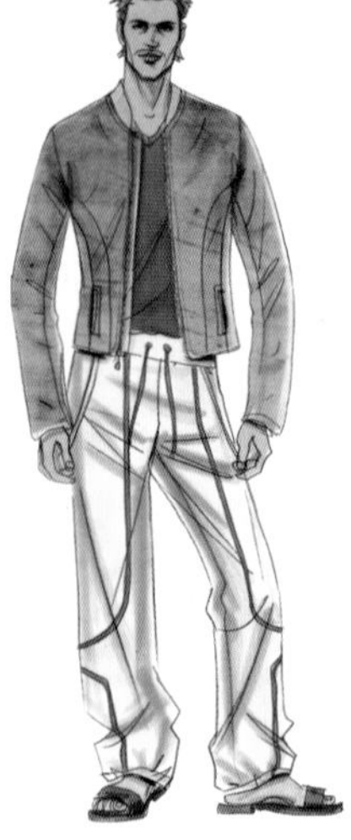
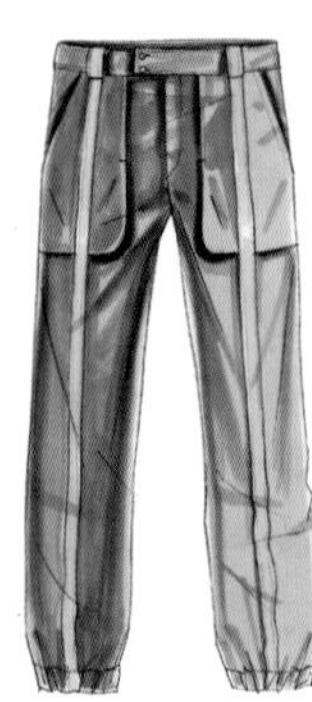

A selection of womenswear and menswear fashion illustrations and flats that feature in Promostyl's *Trend Book* pages. The illustration styles usually vary according to the story of the season.

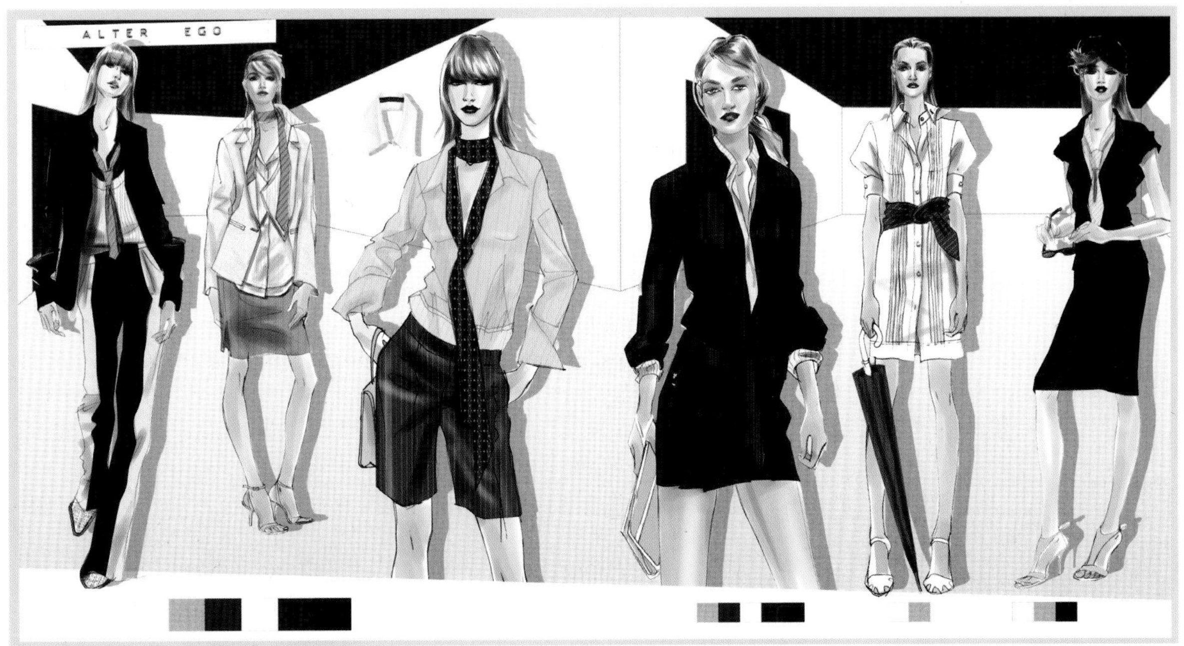

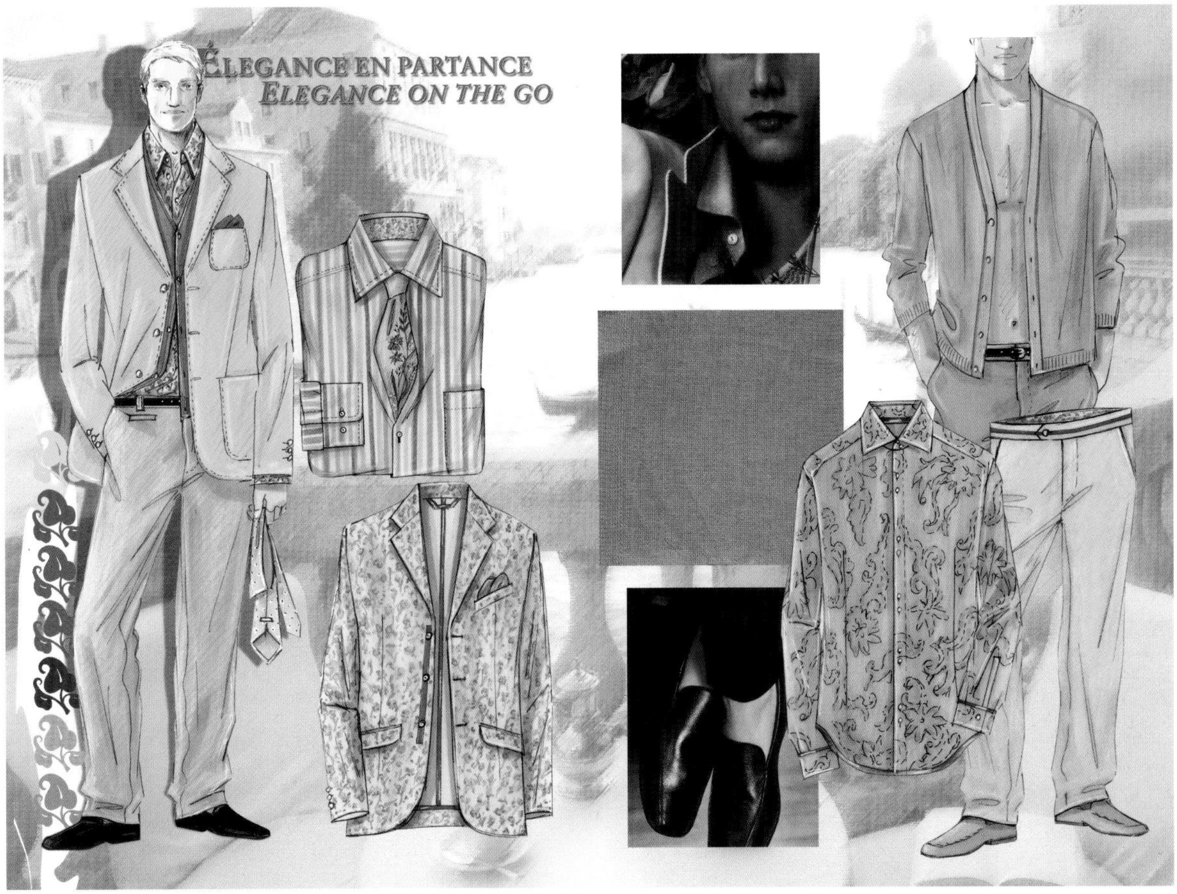

ÉLEGANCE EN PARTANCE
ELEGANCE ON THE GO

Promostyl's *Trend Book* pages display future trends for fashion, fabrics, and accessories. Colorways for future seasons are also outlined.

JEFFREY FULVIMARI

COMMERCIAL FASHION ILLUSTRATOR

"I overstep gallery structures and head straight for the shopping mall," says Jeffrey Fulvimari, creator of the doe-eyed fashionable girls that grace numerous products worldwide. Jeffrey's highly successful fashion illustrations have appeared on everything from Stila cosmetics and Louis Vuitton scarves to a Grammy award-winning CD cover for *The Complete Ella Fitzgerald Songbooks*.

Even as a child Jeffrey was always enthusiastic about art. He says: "I was encouraged by my teachers to express opinions, and they often held up my work as an example for other pupils. I won a big art award when I was very young, so I guess you could say I had a following since first grade!" Jeffrey continued his education at The Cooper Union, New York, and the Cleveland Institute of Art. He originally trained as a fine artist, producing conceptual art. However, to generate an income, he decided on illustration as a career. "Fashion illustration drew me in because it was not museum art. I wanted to do something that was as far removed from my education as possible. I am very proud of my fashion illustration career. In the art world, everybody should be different, we do not all have to be on the same page."

Fulvimari has made his name by embracing the commercial world with open arms. He has launched his own range of illustrated clothing, bags, and wallets across the USA and UK. His fashion brand has been steadily building in Japan since 1998, and his "Bobbypin" girls feature on teenage cosmetics, nightwear, and greeting cards in large department stores worldwide. "My work is both my career and my hobby. I like to make statements with the jobs I take," says Jeffrey. "I was at my happiest when a magazine wrote about my merchandise from both ends of the spectrum in the same article. I don't ever want to be labeled as 'prejudiced' in the fashion world. I want my audience to be from all walks of life. So, to have both top-end and cheaper fashion ranges featuring alongside one another really told my story."

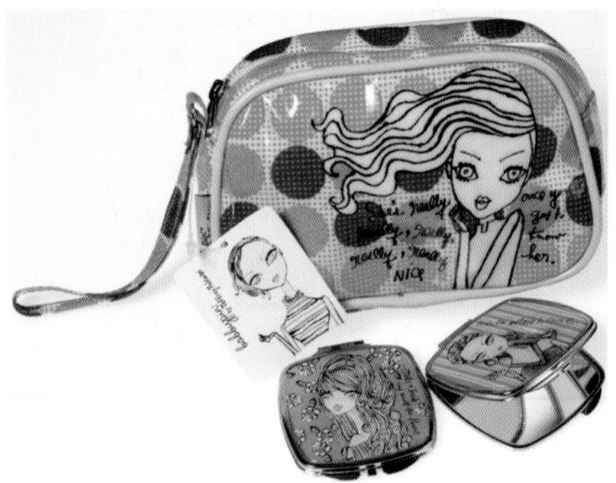

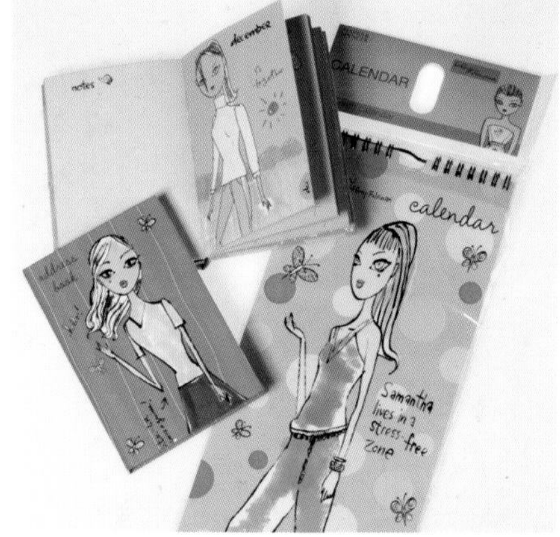

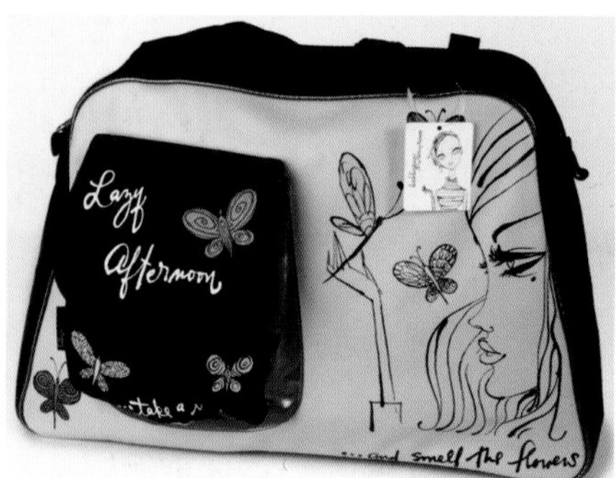

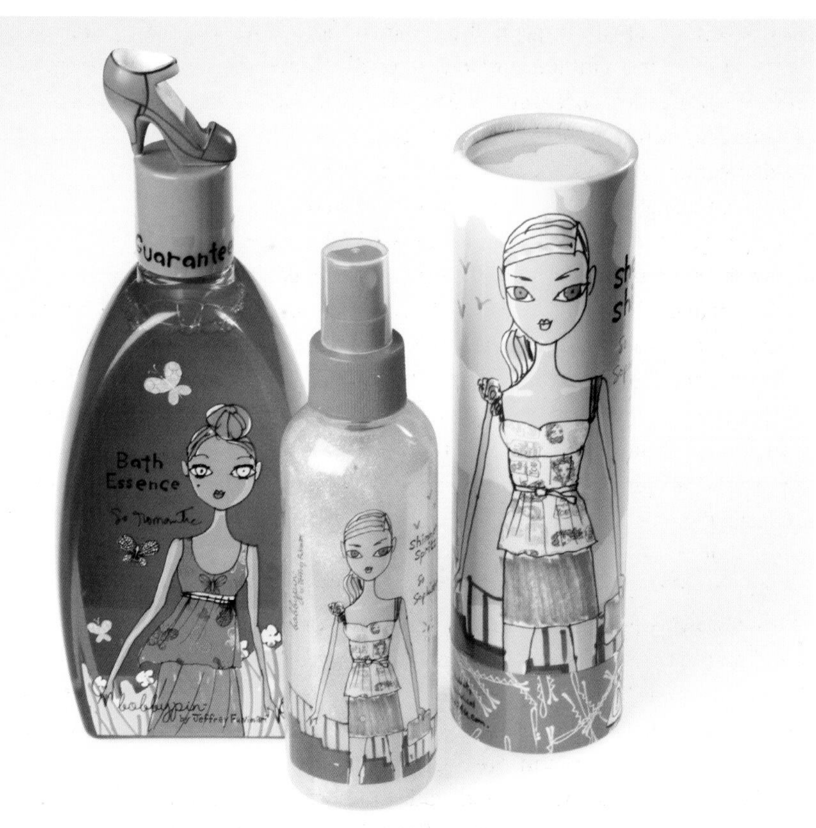

A selection of Jeffrey Fulvimari's illustrated products. His trademark doe-eyed girls feature on, among other things, bags, compacts, stationery, and toiletries.

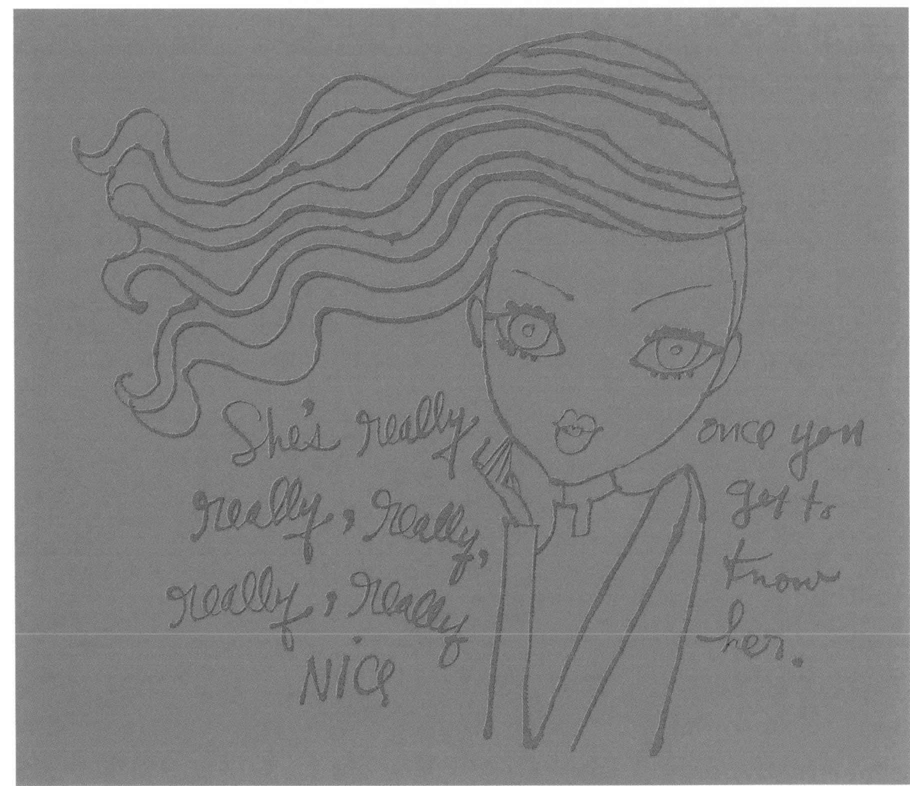

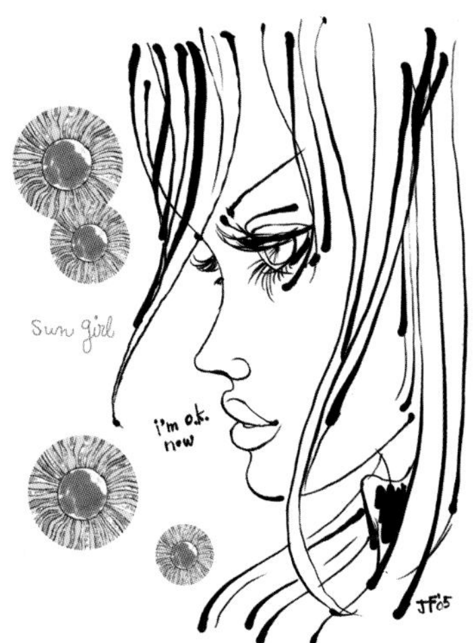

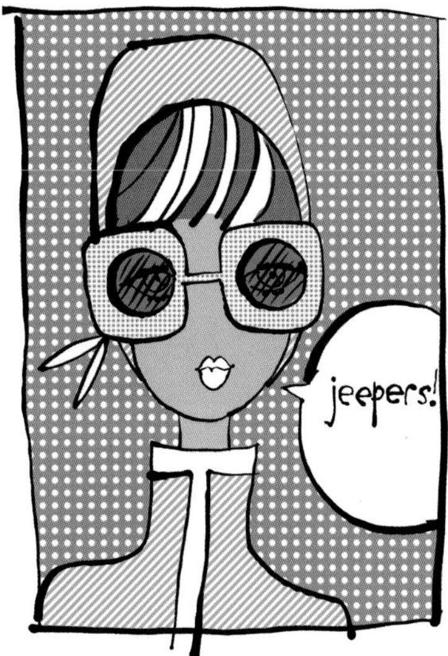

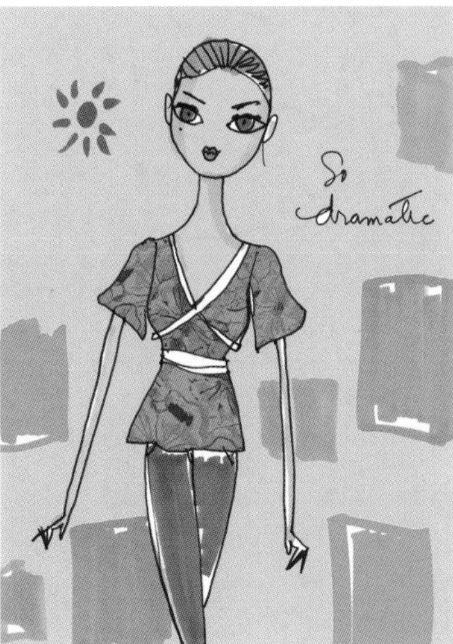

Fashion illustrations by Jeffrey Fulvimari, featuring his distinctively featured girls and his hallmark quirky captions.

Long before he became a successful fashion illustrator, Jeffrey was given a piece of advice that has guided his life since: "Aim high—and you'll go straight to the top." His first job was illustrating a nightclub invitation for a weekly event called "Smashing." It was a folded card with each illustrated panel telling a story. The intriguing invitations became a talking point, and people in the fashion world, such as Anna Sui, started to collect them. Soon he was working for American *Vogue* and the department store Barneys without the aid of an agent. Unafraid to voice his own talents, he had guts and a determination to succeed. He advises: "Launch your career in a big city. Go to the top, and don't be afraid. I had confidence and self-belief and just willed everything to happen. I've never stopped working since."

Jeffrey describes fashion illustration as "a notion of blank pages being filled with notes. It is a starting point that some people take and turn into a career." He also warns: "I chose illustration because fifteen years ago it seemed to be a dead medium. It was easier to get to the top and make some money. Now, you have to be individual, as there are so many illustrators out there." When discussing his inspiration, he replies: "I don't really look at other fashion illustrators much, as I don't want to be influenced by their styles. I limit the amount of art I look at because I want to make new art for myself."

Admiring the simple lines of Charles M. Schulz—the creator of Snoopy and Charlie Brown—Jeffrey explains, "Schulz's artwork is perfection—there is not a leaf out of place in Snoopy's world." Another creative influence was the work of Maxfield Parrish, who was one of the best-known illustrators in America. Parrish's first work, created specifically for reproduction as an art print in 1922, became his signature piece. The atmospheric, sun-drenched *Daybreak*, which depicted a reclining classical female figure in a toga, with a nude child standing over her on a columned portico, looking out onto a rich landscape of flowering trees and purple mountains, became

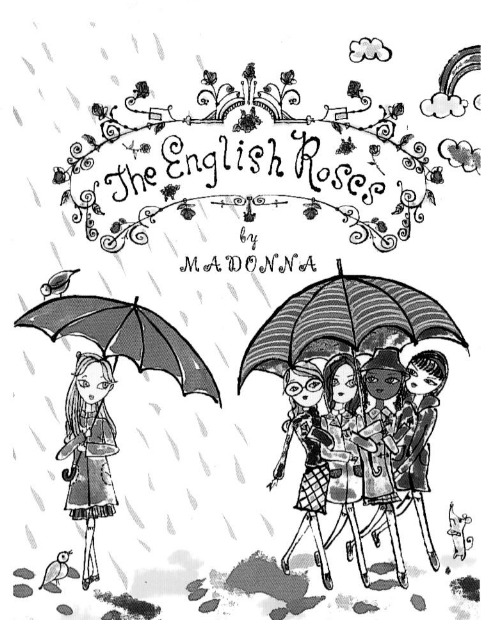

The English Roses book, written by Madonna and illustrated by Jeffrey Fulvimari.

an almost instant icon, found on many American families' walls. "I love his work so much that I sign my illustrations with just simple initials, as Maxfield Parrish once did. I admire how many people Parrish's art has touched."

Jeffrey caught the world's attention in 2003, when Madonna asked him to illustrate her children's book, *The English Roses.* Madonna's team conducted a Cinderella-style search for the person who could bring her *English Roses* to life. In a top-secret mission, they sent people all over the globe to see if the "illustrator slipper" fitted. When Jeffrey was first approached, he remembers that he was initially unsure: "I had held off illustrating children's books for so long because one day I would like to produce my own. But, how could I refuse? This was Madonna asking! I thoroughly enjoyed working with Madonna. I was involved in the creation of the book at all levels, and the art director for the project was excellent. The best thing for me was my grandmother was named Rose, so I hope my involvement with the book would have made her very happy."

When asked about the greatest element of his job, he answers: "I get all the credit, because I did it myself—it is an intensely satisfying role." He also points out: "I am very lucky that I need do very little self-promotion or marketing. I do not have a portfolio, as I am approached personally through my agent for new projects. I have worked very hard to be in this position, though it has not been an easy ride." So, is there anything Jeffrey Fulvimari doesn't like about being a fashion illustrator? "Oh, yes," he states, "the isolation is so hard. Sometimes I work for days on a project without seeing a single soul. The frustration when things are out of your control is also difficult. My advice is to try and turn any negativity around. Collect rejections and disappointments, because with every ten rejections comes one acceptance. Having a positive attitude is vital in this game!"

With so many commercial fashion illustration projects under his belt, you wouldn't be alone in thinking Jeffrey lives a glamorous lifestyle, but when questioned about his role in the industry, he argues: "I rarely go to fashion shows. I'm a total outsider really—a fly on the wall. I just enjoy watching people and then using the characters in my illustrations. The truth is, I often find my characters very close to home. I live in an imaginative Woodstock house that can only be described as the Hobbit meets Heidi's grandfather! There is even a friendly bear living in my yard!"

IN SUMMARY

Fashion Illustrator is intended as a rewarding reference book of practical advice and inspirational ideas to form a basis from which individual creativity can develop, and not as a bible to be followed word for word. As Coco Chanel is reputed to have said, "To be irreplaceable in life, one must be different"—excellent advice for your sketchbooks and portfolio, and for life in general! The following pages offer useful information to help you on your journey. You will find recommended further reading, addresses and websites of institutions and other worthwhile contacts, and a glossary of important words.

FURTHER READING

1 INSPIRATION

Gerald Celente, *Trend Tracking*, New York, Warner Books, 1991
Gwen Diehn, *The Decorated Page: Journals, Scrapbooks & Albums Made Simply Beautiful*, New York, Lark Books, 2002
Alan Fletcher, *The Art of Looking Sideways*, London, Phaidon Press, 2001
Carolyn Genders, *Sources of Inspiration*, London, A&C Black, 2002
Kay Greenlees, *Creating Sketchbooks for Embroiderers and Textile Artists: Exploring the Embroiderers' Sketchbook*, London, Batsford, 2005
Holly Harrison, *Altered Books, Collaborative Journals and Other Adventures in Bookmaking*, Rockport, Mass., Rockport Publishers Inc., 2003
Leonardo Da Vinci *The Notebooks of Leonardo Da Vinci: Selections*, Oxford, Oxford World's Classics, 1998
Dorte Nielsen and Kiki Hartmann, *Inspired: How Creative People Think, Work and Find Inspiration*, Book Industry Services, 2005
Lynne Perrella, *Artists' Journal and Sketchbooks: Exploring and Creating Personal Pages*, Rockport, Mass., Rockport Publishers Inc., 2004
Jan Bode Smiley, *Altered Board Book Basics and Beyond: For Creative Scrapbooks, Altered Books and Artful Journals*, Concord, CF, C & T Publishing, Inc., 2005
Paul Smith, *You Can Find Inspiration in Everything*, London, Violette Editions, 2001
Petrula Vrontikis, *Inspiration Ideas: Creativity Sourcebook*, Rockport, Mass., Rockport, 2002

2 THE FIGURE

100 Ways to Paint People and Figures (How Did You Paint That?), Central Islip, NY, North Light Books, 2004
Bina Abling, *The Advanced Fashion Sketchbook*, New York, Fairchild Group, 1991
Anne Allen and Julian Seaman, *Fashion Drawing: The Basic Principles*, London, Batsford, 1996
Sandra Burke, *Fashion Artist: Drawing Techniques to Portfolio Presentation*, London, Burke Publishing, 2003
Diana Constance, *An Introduction to Drawing the Nude: Anatomy, Proportion, Balance, Movement, Light, Composition*, Newton Abbot, David & Charles, 2002
Elisabetta Drudi and Tiziana Paci, *Figure Drawing For Fashion Design*, Amsterdam, The Pepin Press, 2001
Gustavo Fernandez, *Illustration for Fashion Design: Twelve Steps to the Fashion Figure*, New Jersey, Prentice Hall, 2005
Robert Beverly Hale, *Master Class in Figure Drawing*, New York, Watson-Guptill Publications Inc., 1991
Patrick John Ireland, *Figure Templates for Fashion Illustration*, London, Batsford, 2002
Andrew Loomis, *Figure Drawing For All It's Worth*, New York, The Viking Press, 1949
Kathryn McKelvey and Janine Munslow, *Illustrating Fashion*, Oxford, Blackwell Science (UK), 1997
Jennifer New, *Drawing from Life: The Journal as Art*, Princeton, Princeton Architectural Press, 2005
John Raynes, *Figure Drawing and Anatomy for the Artist*, London, Octopus Books, 1979
John Raynes and Jody Raynes, *How to Draw The Human Figure: A Complete Guide*, Bath, Parragon Books, 2001
Nancy Riegelman, *9 Heads*, New Jersey, Prentice Hall, 2002
Julian Seaman, *Professional Fashion Illustration*, London, Batsford, 1995

Mark Simon, *Facial Expressions: A Visual Reference for Artists*, New York, Watson-Guptill Publications Inc., 2005
Ray Smith, *Drawing Figures*, London, Dorling Kindersley, 1994
Bridget Woods, *Life Drawing*, Marlborough, The Crowood Press, 2003

3 ARTISTIC TECHNIQUES

Bina Abling, *Fashion Rendering with Color*, New Jersey, Prentice Hall, 2001
Jennifer Atkinson, Holly Harrison and Paula Grasdal, *Collage Sourcebook: Exploring the Art and Techniques of Collage*, Hove, Apple Press, 2004
EL Brannon, *Fashion Forecasting*, New York, Fairchild, 2002
Steve Caplin, *How to Cheat in Photoshop: The Art of Creating Photorealistic Montages—Updated for CS2*, Focal Press, 2005
Tom Cassidy and Tracey Diange, *Colour Forecasting*, Oxford, Blackwell Publishing 2005
David Dabner, *Graphic Design School: The Principles and Practices of Graphic Design*, London, Thames and Hudson, 2004
Brian Gorst, *The Complete Oil Painter*, London, Batsford, 2003
Hazel Harrison, *The Encyclopedia of Drawing Techniques*, Tunbridge Wells, Search Press Ltd, 2004
Hazel Harrison, *The Encyclopedia of Watercolour Techniques: A Step-by-step Visual Directory, with an Inspirational Gallery of Finished Works*, Tunbridge Wells, Search Press Ltd, 2004
David Hornung, *Colour: A Workshop for Artists and Designers*, London, Laurence King Publishing, 2004
Wendy Jelbert, *Collins Pen and Wash* (Collins Learn to Paint Series), London, Collins, 2004
Bonny Lhotka, et al, *Digital Art Studio: Techniques for Combining Inkjet Printing with Traditional Art Materials*, New York, Watson-Guptill Publications Inc., 2004
Vicky Perry with Barry Schwabsky (Introduction), *Abstract Painting Techniques and Strategies*, New York, Watson-Guptill Publications Inc., 2005
Melvyn Petterson, *The Instant Printmaker*, London, Collins & Brown, 2003
Sarah Simblet, *The Drawing Book*, London, Dorling Kindersley, 2005
Lawrence Zeegen, *The Fundamentals of Illustration*, Lausannne, Ava Publishing, 2005

4 PRESENTATION FOR FASHION DESIGN

Anvil Graphic Design Inc. (compiler), *Pattern and Palette Sourcebook: A Complete Guide to Using Color in Design*, Rockport, Mass., Rockport Publishers Inc., 2005
Terry Bond and Alison Beazley, *Computer-Aided Pattern Design and Product Development*, Oxford, Blackwell Science (UK), 2003
Janet Boyes, *Essential Fashion Design: Illustration Theme Boards, Body Coverings, Projects, Portfolios*, London, Batsford, 1997
Sandra Burke, *Fashion Computing: Design Techniques and CAD*, London, Burke Publishing, 2005
Akiko Fukai et al, *Fashion in Colors*, New York, Editions Assouline, 2005
Richard M. Jones, *The Apparel Industry*, Oxford, Blackwell Science (UK), 2003
Oei Loan and Cecile de Kegel, *The Elements of Design*, London, Thames and Hudson, 2002
Kathryn McKelvey and Janine Munslow, *Fashion Design: Process, Innovation and Practice*, Oxford, Blackwell Science (UK), 2003
Kathryn McKelvey and Janine Munslow, *Fashion Source Book*, Oxford, Blackwell Publishing, 2006
Steven Stipelman, *Illustrating Fashion: Concept to Creation*, New York, Fairchild, 1996
Sharon Lee Tate, *The Complete Book of Fashion Illustration*, New Jersey, Prentice Hall, 1996
Caroline Tatham and Julian Seaman, *Fashion Design Drawing Course*, London, Thames and Hudson, 2004

5 HISTORICAL AND CONTEMPORARY FASHION ILLUSTRATION

Francoise Baudot, *Gruau*, Paris, Editions Assouline, 2003
Laird Borrelli, *Fashion Illustration Now*, London, Thames and Hudson, 2000
Laird Borrelli, *Fashion Illustration Next*, London, Thames and Hudson, 2004
Laird Borelli, *Stylishly Drawn*, New York, Harry N. Abrams, 2000
CameraWork, *Unified Message In Fashion: Photography Meets Drawing*, London, Steidl Publishers, 2002
Paul Caranicas and Laird Borrelli, *Antonio's People*, London, Thames and Hudson, 2004
Bethan Cole, *Julie Verhoeven: FatBottomedGirls 003*, Paris, Tdm Editions, 2002
Martin Dawber, *Imagemakers: Cutting Edge Fashion Illustration*, London, Mitchell Beazley, 2004
Martin Dawber, *New Fashion Illustration*, London, Batsford, 2005
Delicatessen, *Fashionize: The Art of Fashion Illustration*, Corte Madera, CF, Gingko Press, 2004
Delicatessen, *Mondofragile: Modern Fashion Illustrators From Japan*, Italy, Happy Books, 2002
Simon Doonan, *Andy Warhol Fashion*, San Francisco, Chronicle Books, 2004
Hendrick Hellige, *Romantik*, Berlin, Die Gestalten Verlag, 2004
Angus Hyland, *Pen and Mouse*, London, Laurence King Publishing, 2001
Angus Hyland and Roanne Bell, *Hand to Eye: Contemporary Illustration*, London, Laurence King Publishing, 2003
Yajima Isao, *Fashion Illustration in Europe*, Tokyo, Graphic-Sha Publishing, 1988
Robert Klanten, *Illusive: Contemporary Illustration and Its Context*, Berlin, Die Gestalten Verlag, 2005

Robert Klanten, *Wonderland*, Berlin, Die Gestalten Verlag, 2004
Alice Mackrell, *An Illustrated History of Fashion: 500 Years of Fashion Illustration*, New York, Costume and Fashion Press, 1997
Francis Marshall, *Fashion Drawing*, London and New York, The Studio Publications, 1942
William Packer, *The Art of Vogue Covers: 1909–1940*, London, Octopus Books, 1983
William Packer, *Fashion Drawing in Vogue*, New York, Coward-McCann Inc., 1983
Pao & Paws, *Clin d'oeil: A New Look at Modern Illustration*, Book Industry Services, 2004
Pater Sato, *Fashion Illustration in New York*, Japan, Graphic-sha Publishing, 1985
M. Spoljaric, S. Johnston, R. Klanten, *Demanifest*, Berlin, Die Gestalten Verlag, 2003
Anna Wintour, Michael Roberts, Anna Piaggi, Andre Leon Talley and Manolo Blahnik Manolo, *Blahnik Drawings*, London, Thames and Hudson, 2003

6 TUTORIALS

Jemi Armstrong, et al, *From Pencil to Pen Tool: Understanding and Creating the Digital Fashion Image*, New York, Fairchild Books, 2006
M. Kathleen Colussy, Steve Greenberg, *Rendering Fashion, Fabric and Prints with Adobe Photoshop 7*, New Jersey, Prentice Hall, 2003
Val Holmes, *Encyclopedia of Machine Embroidery*, London, Batsford, 2003
Susan Lazear, *Adobe Illustrator for Fashion Design*, New Jersey, Prentice Hall, to be published 2007
Susan Lazear, *Adobe Photoshop for Fashion Design*, New Jersey, Prentice Hall, to be published 2007
Janice Saunders Maresh, *Sewing for Dummies*, New York, Hungry Minds Inc., 2004
Kevin Tallon, *Creative Computer Fashion Design: With Abobe Illustrator*, Batsford, 2006
Mary Thomas's Dictionary of Embroidery Stitches, new edition by Jan Eaton, London, Brockhampton Press, 1998
Elaine Weinmann and Peter Lourekas, *Visual QuickStart Guide: Illustrator CS For Windows and Macintosh*, Canada, Peachpit Press, 2004
Elaine Weinmann and Peter Lourekas, *Visual QuickStart Guide: Photoshop CS For Windows and Macintosh*, Canada, Peachpit Press, 2004

7 THE FUTURE: GUIDANCE

Noel Chapman and Carole Chester, *Careers in Fashion*, London, Kogan Page, 1999
David Ellwand, *Fairie-ality: The Fashion Collection*, Massachusetts, Candlewick Press, 2002
Mary Gehlhar, *The Fashion Designer Survival Guide: An Insider's Look at Starting and Running Your Own Fashion Business*, New York, Dearborn Trade, Kaplan Publishing, 2005
Sue Jenkyn Jones, *Fashion Design*, second edition, London, Laurence King Publishing, 2005
Astrid Katcharyan, *Getting Jobs in Fashion Design*, London, Cassell, 1988
Anne Matthews, *Vogue Guide to a Career in Fashion*, London, Chatto and Windus, 1989
Margaret McAlpine, *So You Want to Work in Fashion?*, London, Hodder Wayland, 2005
Steve Shipside and Joyce Lain Kennedy, *CVs for Dummies: UK Edition*, London, John Wiley and Sons, Ltd, 2003
M. Sones, *Getting into Fashion: A Career Guide*, New York, Ballatine, 1984
Linda Tain, *Portfolio Presentation for Fashion Designers*, New York, Fairchild, 1998
Robert A. Williams, *Illustration: Basics for Careers*, New Jersey, Prentice Hall, 2003
Theo Stephen Williams, *Streetwise Guide to Freelance Design and Illustration*, Central Islip, NY, North Light Books, 1998
Peter Vogt, *Career Opportunities in the Fashion Industry*, New York, Checkmark, 2002

TRADE PUBLICATIONS AND MAGAZINES

Another Magazine
Arena Homme
Bloom
Bridal Buyer
California Apparel News
Computer Arts
Daily News Record (DNR)
Dazed and Confused
Drapers: Drapers Record and Menswear
Elle
Elle Decoration
Embroidery
Fashion Line
Fashion Reporter
Girls Like Us
Graphic magazine
ID
In Style
International Textiles
Juxtapoz
Living etc
Marie Claire
Marmalade
Numero
Oyster
Pop
Purple Fashion
Retail Week
Self Service
Sneaker Freaker
Tank
10
Textile View
Tobe Report
V
View on Colour
Victor and Rolf
Visionaire
Vogue
W
Womens Wear Daily (WWD)
World of Interiors

USEFUL ADDRESSES

UK

The Association Of Illustrators
2nd Floor, Back Building
150 Curtain Road,
London EC2A 3AR
Tel +44 (0)20 7613 4328
www.theaoi.com
The Association of Illustrators was established to promote illustration, advance and protect illustrators' rights, and encourage professional standards. The website contains professional resources for illustrators and for commissioners of illustration. It carries a growing catalog consisting of nearly 8,000 images, including self-managed illustrators' portfolios.

The British Fashion Council (BFC)
5 Portland Place
London W1N 3AA
Tel +44 (0)20 7636 7788
www.londonfashionweek.co.uk
The BFC supports British fashion designers and manufacturers, especially with export enterprises. It encourages new talent through annual awards to students, such as the "Innovative Pattern Cutting Award" as well as awards for Graduate Fashion Week presentations.

The Crafts Council
44a Pentonville Road
London N1 9BY
Tel +44 (0)20 7278 7700
www.craftscouncil.org.uk
In addition to having an excellent contemporary gallery and crafts bookshop at this address, the Crafts Council offers many services, such as advice, a reference library and development grants. It also publishes a magazine that promotes crafts.

Design Wales
PO Box 383
Cardiff CF5 2W2
Tel 0845 3031400
Email enquiries@designwales.org.uk
www.designwales.org.uk
Design Wales provides comprehensive advice and support services on all issues related to design. Their services are provided free to all businesses in Wales.

The Department of Trade and Industry (DTI)
(Clothing, Textiles and Footwear Unit)
1 Victoria Street
London SW1H 0ET
Tel +44 (0)20 7215 5000
www.dti.gov.uk
A government department that advises UK businesses on legal issues, the DTI also provides information concerning export regulations.

Embroiderers' Guild
Apt 41, Hampton Court Palace,
Surrey KT8 9AU
Tel +44 (0)20 8943 1229
Email administrator@embroiderersguild.com
www.embroiderersguild.com
The Guild was set up in 1906 by sixteen graduates of the Royal School of Needlework and is now the largest crafts association in the UK. The Embroiderers' Guild is a leading educational charity and registered museum, with a lively program of exhibitions, events, and workshops.

Fashion Awareness Direct (FAD)
10a Wellesley Terrace
London N1 7NA
Tel 0870 751 4449
Email info@fad.org.uk
www.fad.org.uk
An organization committed to helping young designers succeed in their careers by bringing students and professionals together at introductory events.

The Prince's Youth Business Trust (PYBT)
18 Park Square East
London NW1 4LH
Tel +44 (0)20 7543 1234
www.princes-trust.org.uk
The Prince's Trust gives business advice, professional support, and awards funding for young and unemployed people planning to set up a potentially successful new idea in business.

USA

The Color Association of the US (CAUS)
315 West 39th Street, Studio 507
New York, NY 10018
Tel +1 212 947 7774
Email caus@colorassociation.com
www.colorassociation.com

Fashion Information
The Fashion Center Kiosk
249 West 39th St
New York, NY 10018
Tel +1 212 398 7943
Email info@fashioncenter.com
www.fashioncenter.com

National Art Education Association
1916 Association Drive
Reston
VA 20191-1590
Tel +1 703 860 8000
www.naea-reston.org
Fabric and resources

National Network for Artist Placement
935 West Ave #37
Los Angeles, CA 90065
Tel +1 213 222 4035
www.artistplacement.com

New York Fashion Council
153 East 87th Street
New York, NY 10008
Tel +1 212 2890420

Pantone Color Institute
590 Commerce Boulevard
Carlstadt, NJ 07072-3098
Tel +1 201 935 5500
www.pantone.com

The Society of Illustrators
128 East 63rd Street
New York, NY 10021-7303
Tel: +1 212 838 2560
www.societyillustrators.org
The Society of Illustrators can be joined via a membership application. It is home to a wonderful illustration museum and library. The website contains useful information for students, and there are annual competitions and scholarships.

United States Small Business Administration
26 Federal Plaza, Suite 3100
New York, NY 10278
Tel +1 212 264 4354

MUSEUMS, ILLUSTRATION AND COSTUME GALLERIES

A number of museums offer reduced rates to students or free admission on certain days.

UK & EUROPE

Centro Internazionale Arti e del Costume
Palazzo Grassi
Campo San Samuele
San Marco 3231
20124 Venice
Italy
Tel +39 41 523 1680
www.palazzograssi.it

Galeria del Costume
Piazza Pitti
50125 Firenze
Italy
Tel +39 55 238 8615
Located in a wing of the Palazzo Pitti

Kobe Fashion Museum
Rokko Island
Kobe
Japan
www.fashionmuseum.or.jp

Kostümforschungs Institut
Kemnatenstrasse 50
8 Munich 19
Germany

Lipperheidesche Kostümbibliothek
Kunstbibliothek
Staatliche Museen zu Berlin
Matthaikirchplatz 6
10785 Berlin
Germany

MoMu
Antwerp Fashion ModeMuseum
Nationalestraat 28
B - 2000 Antwerpen
Belgium
Tel + 32 (0)3 470 2770
Email info@momu.be

Musée des Arts de la Mode et du Textile
Palais du Louvre
107 rue de Rivoli
75001 Paris
France
Tel +33 1 44 5557 5750
www.ucad.fr

Musée de la Mode et du Costume
10 Avenue Pierre 1er de Serbie
75016 Paris
France
Tel +33 1 5652 8600

Le Musée des Tissus et des Arts Décoratifs
34 rue de la Charité
F-69002 Lyon
France
Tel +33 (4)78 3842 00
www.musee-des-tissus.com

Museum of Costume
Assembly Rooms
Bennett Street
Bath BA1 2QH
UK
Tel +44 (0)1225 477 173
www.museumofcostume.co.uk

Museum Salvatore Ferragamo
Palazzo Spini Feroni
Via Tornabuoni 2
Florence 50123
Italy
Tel + 39 055 336 0456

Victoria and Albert Museum (V&A)
Cromwell Road
South Kensington
London SW7 2RL
UK
Tel +44 (0)20 7942 2000
www.vam.ac.uk

USA

Costume Gallery
Los Angeles County Museum of Art
5905 Wilshire Boulevard
Los Angeles , CA 90036
Tel +1 323 857 6000
www.lacma.org

Costume Institute
Metropolitan Museum of Art
1000 Fifth Avenue at 82nd Street
New York, NY 10028-0198
Tel +1 212 535 7710
www.metmuseum.org

The Museum of American Illustration
Society of Illustrators and Norman Price Library
128 East 63rd Street
New York, NY 10021
Tel +1 212 838 2560
www.societyillustrators.org

Museum at the Fashion Institute of Technology
Seventh Avenue at 27th Street
New York, NY 10001-5992
Tel +1 212 217 5970
Email museuminfo@fitnyc.edu

The National Museum of American Illustration (NMAI)
Vernon Court
492 Bellevue Avenue
Newport
Rhode Island 02840
Tel +1 401 851 8949
Fax +1 401 851 8974
Email art@americanillustration.org

ILLUSTRATION AGENTS

Agent 002
Contact: Michel Lagarde
70 rue de laFolie
Mericourt
75011 Paris
France
Tel +33 (0)1 40 21 03 48
Fax +33 (0)1 40 21 03 49
Email michel@agent002.com
www.agent002.com

Art Department
Contact: Stephanie Pesakoff (see p. 185)
420 West 24th Street, #1F
New York, NY 10011
USA
Tel +1 212 243 2103
Fax +1 212 243 2104
Email stephaniep@art-dept.com
www.art-dept.com

Big Active
Warehouse D4, Metropolitan Whaf,
Wapping Wall
London E1W 3SS
UK
Tel +44 (0)20 7702 9365
Fax +44 (0)20 7702 9366
Email contact@bigactive.com
www.bigactive.com

CWC International, INC
Contact: Koko Nakano
296 Elizabeth St 1F
New York City, NY 10012
USA
Tel +1 646 486 6586
Fax +1 646 486 7633
Email agent@cwc-i.com
www.cwc-i-com

WEBSITES

www.adobe.com
The home page for all Adobe software packages.

www.collezionionline.com
View shows, videos, and magazines on line.

www.computerarts.co.uk
Offers creative suggestions, tutorials, and the latest news from the world of computer illustration.

www.costumes.org
Links to many other sites covering all aspects of costume.

www.daviddownton.com
Website of fashion illustrator David Downton (see pp. 186–189).

www.fashion-enterprise.com
Website of the Centre of Fashion Enterprise, London College of Fashion.

www.fashionoffice.org
Online magazine covering fashion, beauty, and lifestyle.

www.ideasfactory.com
Online "Art and Design" zone.

www.jeffreyfulvimari.com
Website of commercial fashion illustrator Jeffrey Fulvimari (see pp. 192–194).

www.marquise.de
A site all about period costume, from the Middle Ages to the early twentieth century.

www.promostyl.com
Website of the trendforecasting agency (see pp. 190–191).

www.vogue.co.uk
With links to the websites of all other Vogue International editions.

GLOSSARY

Adobe Illustrator An object-oriented (or vector) digital computer package.

Adobe Photoshop A bitmap (or raster) digital computer package.

Advertising The promotion through public announcements in newspapers or on the radio, television, or Internet of something such as a product, service, event, or vacancy, in order to attract or increase interest in it.

Avant-garde A fashion or concept that is ahead of its time.

Bespoke Individual made-to-measure tailoring for men's suits.

Boutique French word for an independent, usually small, shop with unique stock and atmosphere.

Brainstorming Open discussion among colleagues or peers to introduce new ideas and concepts.

Brand A name or trademark used to identify a product and denote quality, value, or a particular ethos.

Buyer The person responsible for planning and and managing the buying and selling of merchandise.

CAD/CAM Computer-aided design and computer-aided manufacturing.

Canvas A strong, heavy, closely woven fabric that is stretched around wood to create a surface for painting.

Capsule collection A small range of related styles with a special purpose or impact.

Classic A term for a style that remains constantly popular and changes very little in detail, e.g., men's shirts, the cardigan, jeans.

Clothed life-drawing or fashion-life The act of drawing the clothed human figure from life.

CMYK palette A shortened term for cyan, magenta, yellow, and black (the last "k" abbreviation used to avoid confusion with blue), the ink colors used for printing.

Collage The art of making pictures by sticking cloth, pieces of paper, photographs, and other objects onto a surface.

Collection The term used for fashion clothes that have related features or are designated for a specific season. "The Collections" is a colloquial description used for the Paris fashion shows.

Color forecasting The prediction of future color trends by analyzing data from trade shows, etc.

Color palette/gamme A limited selection of linked colors used in fashion design and illustration.

Colorway The limited range of colors that a style of garment, or a collection, may be offered in; also the term for the choice of colors in which a printed textile is available.

Composition The way in which the parts of something are arranged, especially the elements in a visual image.

Contemporary Distinctly modern and in existence now.

Coordinates Fabrics or items of clothing that relate in coloring or style, and which can be worn together.

Costing The base price of the garment, determined by the materials, trimmings, labor, and transportation. An illustration might accompany a costing.

Couturier French word for fashion designer.

Critique/Crit Discussion and evaluation of work, often held as a group session at the end of a project or assignment.

Degree show The exhibition of work which is assessed to ascertain a student's degree classification.

Design board A visual presentation board in a portfolio that represents a final design.

Design developments Drawings that progress through desirable or successful elements within a design theme.

Design roughs First-stage drawings for designs, usually made quickly in pencil and without extraneous detail.

Diffusion line A secondary, usually lower-priced garment line that allows consumers on a budget to buy into the designer look.

Digital imagery The process of transforming or altering a digital image by manipulating it on the computer.

Digital portfolio Examples of artwork saved digitally to be emailed or put on compact disks to mail to prospective employers.

Draping A method of making a fashion style or pattern by manipulating fabric on a body or dress form.

Editorial An article in a newspaper or magazine that expresses the opinion of its editor or publisher. If the article is on fashion, it will often feature fashion illustrations.

Embellishment The adding of ornaments or decorations to something, such as a garment, or accessory such as a bag or item of footwear, to make it more interesting.

Embroidery Decorative stitching that may be produced by hand or machine, in a range of different types of thread.

Exhibition A public display, usually for a limited period, of a collection of works of art, illustrations or objects of special interest.

Fabric rendering The artistic, and perhaps accurate, representation of fabric using various media.

Fad A very short-lived fashion.

Fashion cycle The calendar by which a company will plan, design, make, and market its ranges.

Fashion designer A person who devises and executes designs for clothes.

Fashion illustration An artistic image produced to promote a particular fashion.

Freelancer Self-employed person working, or available to work, for a number of employers, rather than being committed to one, and usually hired for a limited period.

Final collection The last college collection before graduation.

Flapper A young woman of the 1920s who disdained prior conventions of decorum and fashion.

Flats Diagrammatic drawings (see Specification drawings).

Glossies The high-quality magazines.

Graduation The completion of a course of academic study.

Graduate exhibition A display of graduates' work visited by potential employers.

Grain The direction of a fabric's threads. Fabric may be cut along a straight grain or "on the bias," which gives it a draping, figure-hugging quality that may be emphasized in a drawing.

Handwriting, signature A personal design style, design features, or way of drawing.

Haute couture French term for the highest quality of dressmaking. A designer or company cannot call themselves *haute couture* unless they have passed the stringent criteria of the Chambre Syndical of the Fédération Française de la Couture.

Illustration agent A company or an individual that can represent and promote the work of an illustrator.

Internship A period of study, usually between two weeks and nine months, spent within a business to gain work experience. Also known as a placement.

Label This term is sometimes used synonymously with logo, but is also used to describe the tag that identifies the designer or manufacturer and the origin, fiber contents, and wash care of the product.

Layout pad A sketchbook with sheets of thin paper that can be traced through.

Light box A device with an illuminated surface that can be used for tracing an image.

Life-drawing The act of drawing the nude human figure.

Lineup A preview of toiles (see below) or finished garments on models to determine the balance, range, and order of a collection. A lineup can also be illustrated and presented in a portfolio.

Logo A brand name or symbol used to identify a product or designer.

Mac A shortened term for an Apple Macintosh computer.

Manga A Japanese style of comic books or animated cartoons.

Mannequin A model, usually life-size, of the human body used to display or fit clothes. Smaller wooden mannequins are used to draw body proportions and poses.

Masking fluid A liquid that acts as a resist to paint.

Memorabilia Objects collected as souvenirs of important personal events or experiences. Sometimes such objects are generally considered to be collectors' items.

Mood board A presentation board that shows the overall concept and direction of a design collection. It captures the style and theme for a set of designs by displaying defining images, fabrics, and colors that are influential in the design process.

Objective or observational drawing The act of creating an image to represent what is seen during direct observation.

Outline The edge or outer shape of something.

Palette In illustration, this refers to the range of colors used in an artwork.

Pantone A worldwide color referencing system.

PC A shortened term for a personal computer.

Photomontage The technique of combining a number of photographs, or parts of photographs, to form a composite picture. Photomontage is popularly used in art and advertising.

Pixel An individual tiny dot of light that is the basic unit from which the images on a computer or television screen are made.

Pochoir Line drawings that are highlighted with watercolor applied through finely cut stencils. The technique originated in Japan and was a popular form of fashion illustration in the early 1900s.

Portfolio A large, portable holder for flat artwork and press cuttings that should give a potential client a comprehensive view of the illustrator's or designer's capabilities.

Pose A particular physical posture or stance. The pose of the figure is a vital component of a fashion illustration, giving it impact and mood.

Postgraduate study The opportunity for a student to continue to learn, or carry out research, in an academic environment following graduation.

Première vision*, also known as *PV French for "first look" and the name of the major fabric trade fair held twice a year in Paris.

Prêt-à-porter French for ready-to-wear, a term used for better quality and designer separates; it is also the name of a major fashion exhibition.

Price point Different ranges of price indicate quality and market level, e.g. budget, designer, and luxury. An illustrator's specification drawings (see below) assist in establishing a price point.

Primary colors These are the colors that cannot be made by mixing other colors, but from which other colors are mixed.

Promotion Any means by which something is marketed to become better known and more popular. Promotional fashion illustration is mainly used in advertising to encourage the clothing to sell.

Proportion The relationship and balance between one aspect of a design and another. A principle of fashion design, proportion also relates in fashion illustration to the comparative size and shape of different elements of the human body.

Psychedelic A term often used to describe distorted or wildy colorful artwork that resembles images that may be experienced by someone under the influence of a halluconogenic drug.

Range building The process of building a series of connected ideas that are realized in a clothing range.

Ready-to-wear Also known as off-the-peg, prêt-à-porter, and clothing separates.

Research A methodical investigation into a subject or theme in order to discover facts and visual data.

Résumé A chronological personal summary detailing educational and employment achievements and attributes. (Also known as a CV, or curriculum vitae.)

Retail The selling of goods from a business to an individual consumer.

Scanner A device used to convert an image into digital form for storage, retrieval, and transmission.

Secondary colors These are colors produced by mixing two primary colors.

Shade The result of mixing a color with black.

Silhouette The overall shape of a garment or person, without detail.

Sketchbook A visual notebook or diary used to create a personal response to the world and inspire ideas for finished works.

Snapshot A record or view of a particular moment in a sequence of events, or in a continuing process.

Specification drawings (also known as specs) A design drawing annotated with measurements and manufacturing details, such as the stitching and trimmings that are to be used in manufacturing a garment.

Stories Design themes comprising fabric, color, or style associations that are used within a particular collection.

Storyboard Also known as a theme board, this is a presentation of the concept for a collection with a detailed breakdown of styles and coordinates.

Stylist A fashion expert who prepares fashion items for photographs or presentations.

Tear sheets Also known as swipes, these are pictures lifted from magazines, etc., which are used as initial inspiration or corroboration for a concept, not to copy.

Template A master, or pattern, that serves as a guide from which other, similar shapes can be made. A figure template is used as a guide for fashion design and can also be used for illustration.

Tertiary colors These are colors made by mixing a primary color with its adjacent secondary color.

Theme A unifying image or concept that, in fashion design or illustration, appears repeatedly in a collection or throughout a series of sketches or illustrations.

Tint The result of mixing color with white.

Toile Literally the French for a lightweight muslin but used to describe a sample or test garment.

Tone The result of mixing gray with a color.

Tracing A copy of an image made by tracing it onto a sheet of translucent paper laid on top of it.

Trend A current fashion or mode.

Trend book A color publication that outlines the predicted future trends up to two years ahead.

Trimming A term used in fashion illustration to describe the decorative detail on a garment, but which is also used for the finishing and cutting of loose threads.

Tutor In British universities, an academic who is responsible for teaching and advising an allocated group of students.

Tutorial A meeting with a tutor to discuss a student's progress.

Vector A mathematically defined object or group of objects that in computing can be a range of lengths, but which appear only in one dimension.

Viewfinder A simple device that helps to select how much of a figure's surroundings to include within the confines of a picture. This allows the selection of the view that works best.

INDEX

Page numbers in **bold** refer to illustration captions.

A

accent color 59
acetate 48-49
acrylics 53, **53**, 162
adhesive, spray 54
Adobe Illustrator 55, 170, **170**, **171**
Adobe Photoshop 55, **167**, 172, **172**, **173**, **174**
agents 8, 185
Amelynk, Michou 124, **124**
anatomy 25
Andri, Ferdinand 60, **60**
angora 63
Antoniou, Rebecca 7, 98, **98**
Argyle pattern 63
Armani, Giorgio **13**
Art Department 185
art materials 48-55
artistic techniques 8

B

bad weather theme **20**, **21**
Bailey, Anna 172, **172**, **173**
Bakkum, Vincent 104, **104**
Bakst, Leon 83
ballpoint pens 54, **55**, 164
Barbier, Georges 84
beads 62
Beaton, Cecil 86
Bellows, George 10
Benito, Eduardo Garcia 85
Bérard, Christian 86
Berning, Tina 110, **110**
Berthold, François 92
body proportions 25, 27, 36-46
Bolin, Guillermo 85
books 12
Botero, Fernando 91
Bouché, René 87, **87**
bouclé 63
Bouët-Willaumez, René 86, 87, **87**
Bourbeau, Anne 152, **152**
brainstorming 14
briefs 6
Brissaud, Pierre 84, **84**
brocade 62
Brooks, Jason 88, 88, 92, 92
Brown, Bill 138, **138**
Burfitt, Lovisa 136, **136**
butterfly theme 14, **14**, **15**
buyers 80, 80

C

CAD/CAM systems 76
cameras 10, 86
Campbell, Stephen 85, **85**, 132, **132**
card stock 49
Carosia, Edgardo 130, **130**
cartridge paper 48
cashmere 63
Cellini, Giovanna 140, **140**
Chakrabarti, Nina 120, **120**
Chanel, Gabrielle "Coco" 85
charcoal 51, **51**
charcoal pencils 51
checks 61
chenille 63
Cheuk, Deanne 158, **158**
chiffon 62
Chin, Marcus 84, **84**, 148, **148**
cities, trends 10
Clark, Ossie **31**
Clark, Peter 12, 96, **96**
clients 6, 78
clothing, construction **26**, 27
collage **17**, 166, **166**, **167**
collecting inspirational items 11-13
collections 70, 73
  displaying 75, **75**, **78**, **177**
  planning **22**
color **16**, 56-59
  design roughs 73
  fashion illustration 58-59, **58**, **59**
  forecasting 58
color palettes, fashion 58, 69
color-prediction agencies 58
color wheel **56**, 57
colored backing paper 49
colored pencils 50
complementary colors 57
computers 55
  embroidery 168, **168**, **169**
  flats **76**
  production costs 76
  templates 33
concept boards 68
continuous-line exercise, drawing 31, **31**
"conversation pieces" 176
cool colors 57
costing 76
customer profile 70
cutting mats 54

D

Dagmar 88
Dalí, Salvador 82
dance cards **16**
Degas 82
degree courses 180
Delhomme, Jean-Philippe 92
denim 63, 66
design roughs 70-73, **70**, **72**, **73**, **74**
Diesbach, Danielle de 190
digital portfolios 178
Dior 87
dip pens **52**
Donovan, Miles 118, **118**
"don't-look-back" exercise, drawing 30, **30**
Downton, David 8, **86**, 92, 186, **186**, **188**, 189
drawing 8
  exercises 30-31
  human figure 6, 8, 24-31, 36-46
  ink 164, **164**, **165**
  shoes **46**
dressing for interviews 181
Dryden, Helen 85

E

ears 43
embellished fabrics 63, **63**
embroidered fabrics 63, **63**
embroidery
  computerized machine 168, 168, 169
  hand 16, 160, **160**, 161
  threads 54, **55**
employment 182
English Roses, The (Madonna) 194, **194**
equipment 54-55
Eric (Erikson, Carl) 86, **86**
Erté 84
exaggeration, body proportions 8, 36, 38, 39, **39**, **40**, **85**
exhibitions **13**
eyelashes **43**
eyes **43**

F

fabrics
  design roughs 72
  embellished 63, **63**
  embroidered 63, **63**
  knitted 63, **63**
  patterns 63, **63**
  prints 63, **63**
  rendering 60-66, **65**
  samples 69
  sheer 62, **62**
  shiny 62, **62**
  striped and checked 61, **61**
  woollen 61, **61**
faces *see* heads
Fair Isle pattern 63
fashion designers 6
fashion designs **70**
fashion illustration 6
fashion range 70
fashionable ideal, human figure 36
feathers 63, **63**
feet 41, 46
figure *see* human figure
figure drawing 6, 8, 24-31
fineliner pens 54
flannel 61

flats 76, **76**
fleece 61
found objects 16
freelancing 182
Frey, Matthias 122, 122
Fulvimari, Jeffrey 8, 192-194, **192**, **193**, **194**
fur 63, **63**
further education 180-182
portfolios 177

G

gabardine 61
galleries 10
Garcia Huerta, Carmen 106, **106**
Gardiner, Louise 154, **154**, 162, **162**
garments, photographs 178, **178**
Gazza, Adriano 166, **166**
georgette 62
Gibson, Charles Dana 82, **82**, 83
"Gibson Girl" **82**, 83
Giddio, Tobie 128, **128**
Goodall, Jasper 142, **142**
gouache 53
graduate exhibitions 182
graduate portfolios 177-178
Grafstrom, Ruth 86
graphite sticks 49-50
Gray, Richard 94, **94**
Griffiths Jones, Julia 156, **156**
Gruau, René 87
Gustafson, Mats 84, 90, 92

H

hair **44**
hand embroidery **16**, 160, **160**, **161**
threads 54
hands 41, **45**
hard pastels 51
Harper's Bazaar 84, 86
Hatori, Yuki 125, **125**
Hayasaki, Chico 102, **102**
heads 41, **42, 43**
Held, John, Jr 85, **85**
herringbone 61
history 82-92
Hollar, Wenceslaus 82
"Hot Metal" sketchbook research 18, **18**
hue 57
human figure 24-26
clothed 27
differences between sexes 38
drawing 6, 8, 24-31, 36-46
fashionable ideal 36
feet 41, **46**
hair **44**
hands 41, **45**
heads 41, **42**, **43**
height 38, **38**
nude 24, 25
parts **36**
poses 41, **41**
proportions 25, 27, 36-46, **39**
scale 27
templates 33, **33**

I

idea bank 7, 11
Iliya, Kareem 114, **114**
illustration agents **8**
Illustrator (Adobe) 55, 170, **170**, **171**
illustrators 8
image inspiration 17
imagination 14
India ink 52, **52**
ink 52
drawing with 164, **164**, **165**
India 52, **52**
inspiration 6, 7-8, 10-22
image 17
inventive 16
inspirational items, collecting 11-13
interviews 181
intuitive exercises, drawing 30-31
inventive inspiration 16
Iribe, Paul 83

J

jobs 182
Johnson, Virginia 103, **103**
Joyner, Patricia 168, **168**

K

Keogh, Tom 86
Kiraz 88, **88**
Klimt, Gustav 60, **60**
Knight, Will 164, **164**, **165**
knitted fabrics 63, **63**
knives 54
knowledge base 14
Koji, Ota 150, **150**

L

laces 62
Lady's Magazine 82
lamé 62
Larroca, Alma 134, **134**
layout pads 73
layout paper 48
leather 62
Lefebvre, Marion 126, **126**
leg elongation 38, 39, **40**
Legno, Simone 170, **170**
Leonardo da Vinci **24**, 25
Lepape, Georges 83, **83**
life drawing 28, **28**, **29**
light boxes 54, **55**
lips **43**
location, sketching on 27
London Graduate Fashion **183**
Lopez, Antonio 88, **88**, 90, 91

M

Machida, Ayako 108, **108**
machine embroidery
computerized 168, **168**, **169**
threads 54
Madonna 194
magazines 13
mannequins, wooden 37, **37**
markers 54
Marshall, Francis **29**, 86
Martin, Charles 84
masking tape 54
Matisse **31**, 82
Mattatotti, Lorenzo 84, 90
measuring methods, human figure 38
medium, finding 48
metallic yarn 63
Michelangelo **24**, 25
mind mapping 14, **15**
mixed media **17**, **25**, **48**, **55**, **59**
mohair 61, 63
mood boards 68-69, **68**, **69**, **78**
Mucha, Alphonse 82
museums 10, 11

N

net 62
non-waterproof ink 52
noses **43**
nude figure 24, **24**, 25, **25**

O

objective drawing 30
objects, found 16
observational drawing 30
O'Connor, Marie 112, **112**
oil pastels 51
oils 53
organdie 62
organza 62
outline exercise, drawing 31, **31**

P

packaging 49
painting 162, **162**, **163**
paints 52-53, **53**
Palmer, Gladys Perint 91
paper **49**
cartridge 48
colored backing 49
layout 48
pastel 48
tissue 49
tracing 48
wallpaper 49
watercolor 49

wrapping 49
Parrish, Maxfield 193
past, nostalgia for 11
pastel paper 48
pastel pencils 51
pastels 51, **51**
patterns, fabrics 63, **63**
pencils 49-50, **50**
pens 54, **55**
Pesakoff, Stephanie 185
photocopiers 55
photographers 86
photographs
garments 178, **178**
tracing from 32-33, **32**
photomontage 166
Photoshop (Adobe) 55, **167**, 172, **172**, **173**, **174**
Picasso, Pablo 10, 18, 25, **25**
pinstripes 61
Plank, George 85
planning, collections **22**, 70
pochoir 83, 83
Poiret, Paul 83
Pollard, Douglas 85
portfolios 8, 176, **176**, **177**, **178**, **179**
digital 178
fashion design presentation 78
further education 177
graduate 177-178
presentation 8, 176-179
professional 178
poses 41, **4**1
postcards 13
postgraduate study 182
presentation 8
fashion design 78-80
presentation boards **176**
primary colors **56**
prints, fabrics 63, **63**
professional approach 80
professional portfolios 178
Promostyl 58, 190, **190**, **191**
proportions, human figure 25, 27, 36-46

R

range building 73-75
rendering fabrics 60-66, **65**
repeat patterns 63
reptile skins 62
researching themes 14-17
residencies 183
résumé 183-184
Rounthwaite, Graham 92, **92**
Royère, Lysiane de 8, 190

S

satin 62
saturation 57
scale, human figure 27
scalpels 54
schematics 76
Schulz, Charles M. 193
secondary colors **56**
self-employment 182
selling yourself 183-184
sequins 62
sewing machines 54
shade 57
sheer fabrics 62
Shimizu, Yuko 116, **116**
shiny fabrics 62, **62**
shoes, drawing **46**
sketchbooks 8, 10, 18-22, **26**
bad weather theme **20**, **21**
collection planning 22
"Hot Metal" research 18, **18**
Marshall, Francis 29
sketching **26**, 27
see also drawing
Smith, Sir Paul 10
soft pastels 51
software 55
specification drawings 76, **76**
spray adhesive 54
spray paint 53
steel rulers 54
stenciling 83
stitching 63
storyboards 68
stripes 61
sweet wrappers 49

T

taffeta 62
target market 70
technical drawings 76
templates 32-33, **33**, 70, **70**, 73
tertiary colors **56**
themes
bad weather **20**, **21**
butterfly 14, **14**, **15**
researching 14-17
tint 57
tissue paper 49
tone 57
Toulouse-Lautrec, Henri 82
tracing 32-33
tracing paper 48
transparent fabrics 62
travel 10, 183
Trend Book 190, **190**, **191**
trend-forecasting companies 190
trends, cities 10
trims 72
tulle 62
tutorials 8, 160-174
tweeds 61

U

university 180
interviews 181

V

value (color) 57
Vanity Fair 86
velour 62
velvet 62
Verhoye, Annabelle 144, **144**
Vertes, Marcel 86
viewfinders 27, **27**
Vionnet, Madame Madeleine 85
Viramontes, Tony 90, **90**
Vogue 84, 85, 86, 87, 88
voile 62

W

Wagt, Robert 100, **100**
wallpaper 49
warm colors 57
watercolor paints 52-53, **53**, 162
watercolor papers 49
waterproof ink 52
water-soluble crayons 50
water-soluble pencils 50, **51**
wax crayons 51, 51
White, Edwina Christiana 146, **146**
wooden mannequins 37, **37**
wools 63
working drawings 76
wrapping paper 49

Y

yarns 63

Z

Zoltan 91, **91**

PICTURE SOURCES AND CREDITS

Every effort has been made to contact the copyright holders, but should there be any errors or omissions, Laurence King Publishing Ltd would be pleased to insert the appropriate acknowledgment in any subsequent printing of this publication.

Illustrators, artists, and photographers are listed alphabetically; numbers listed refer to the pages on which the work appears.

Michou Amelynck 125 c/o www.agent002.com; michel@agent002.com
Ferdinand Andri 60 (left) Leopold Museum, Vienna
Rebecca Antoniou 7, 99 c/o Art Department – Illustration Division, stephaniep@art-dept.com
Anna Bailey 172, 173, 174 www.annabailey.co.uk
Vincent Bakkum 53 (top), 105 vincent.b@koumbus.fi
Tina Berning 54 (top), 111 c/o CWC International, Inc., agent@cwc-i.com
Emily Blunt 77 (top left), 179 (top) eablunt@yahoo.co.uk
René Bouché 87 (right) ©Condé Nast Archive
René Bouët Willaumez 87 (left) ©Condé Nast Archive
Anne Bourbeau 152 annebourbeau@earthlink.net
Louise Brandreth 30 (bottom left) looeb@yahoo.co.uk
Pierre Brissau 84 (left) Mary Evans Picture Library
Jason Brooks 88 (below), 92 (right) Courtesy the artist
Bill Brown 139 c/o Art Department – Illustration Division, stephaniep@art-dept.com
Lovisa Burfitt 137 lovisa@burfitt.com
Stephen Campbell 85 (right), 133 c/o Art Department - Illustration Division, stephaniep@art-dept.com
Edgardo Carosia 58 (left), 131 info@carosia.com, www.carosia.com
Giovanna Cellini 141 gio.cellini@virgin.net
Nina Chakrabarti 121 nina.chakrabarti@alumni.rca.ac.uk
Deanne Cheuk 159 neomuworld@aol.com
Marcos Chin 84 (right), 149 www.marcoschin.com, mchin@sympatico.ca
Ossie Clark 31 (right) Courtesy of Celia Birtwell
Peter Clark 97 peterclark2000@hotmail.com
Lindsey Collison 33
Ann Dahle 72, 74 ankada9@hotmail.com
Miles Donovan 119 c/o Art Department – Illustration Division, stephaniep@art-dept.com
David Downton 86 (right), 187, 188 www.daviddownton.com
Eric Carl Erikson 86 (left) ©Condé Nast Archive
Matthias Frey 123 www.matthiasfrey.de
Jeffrey Fulvimari 192 (alicia@drilicensing.com), 193 (susanchungnyc@earthlink.net), 194 (*The English Roses*, pubished by Callaway Editions, Inc. ©2003 Madonna. All rights reserved.) www.jeffreyfulvimari.com
Louise Gardiner 155, 162, 163 loulougardiner@hotmail.com, www.houlaloula.com
Adriano Gazza 166, 167 adrianogazza@hotmail.com
Ludnuila Gelbutoyskaya 59 (right), 178 lgelbutovskaya@yandex.ru
Charles Dana Gibson 82 Private Collection, London
Tobie Giddio 129 tobie@tobiegiddio.com, www.tobiegiddio.com
Chris Glynn 26 (top left and top right) glynngraphics@hotmail.com
Jasper Goodall 143 jasper.goodall@sukie.co.uk
Cat Gray (176 (bottom) catgray10@hotmail.com
Richard Gray 95 All clothing by Boudicca; c/o Art Department - Illustration Division, stephaniep@art-dept.com
Julia Hall 48 joolshall@yahoo.co.uk
Yuki Hatori 125 c/o CWC International, Inc., agent@cwc-i.com
Chico Hayasaki 102 c/o CWC International, Inc., agent@cwc-i.com
John Held Jr 85 (left) Private Collection, London
Carmen Heurta 107 c/o CWC International, Inc., agent@cwc-i.com; cghuerta2@yahoo.es
Bryan Hollingsworth 59 (left) bryan_hollingsworth@hotmail.com
Megan Huish 10 meganhuish@mac.com; model: Hannah Warren
Kareen Iliya 114 kareemiliya@earthlink.net
Marcus James 29 (right column) marcus@marcusjames.co.uk
Rebecca Jenkins 41, 179 (bottom right) bexj@aol.com
Virginia Johnson 103 virginia@virginiajohnson.com
Julia Griffiths Jones 157 julia@dyffrynolcwm.plus.com
Patricia Joyner 54 (with Bethan Morris), 168, 169 patricia.j@tiscali.co.uk
Anna Kelso 52 (bottom) kelsac@hotmail.com
Kiraz 88 (top) Private Collection, London
Claire Kemp 177 clairekemp@lycos.com
Gustav Klimt 60 (right) Osterreichische Galerie Belvedere, Vienna/Bridgeman Art Library
Will Knight 164, 165 will@willknight.com, www.willknight.com
Ota Koji 151 Iwashi347@yahoo.co.jp c/o www.agent002.com; michel@agent002.com
Alma Larroca 135 info@carosia.com, www.almalarroca.com
Marion Lefebvre 127 sugargrafiks@hotmail.com
Simone Legno 170, 171 simone@tokidoki.it
Georges Le Pape 83 Art Archive/©ADAGP, Paris and DACS, London 2006
Peter Lindbergh (photographer) 13 (right)
Fredrika Lökholm and Martin Slivka (photographers) 16 (top), 49 (left), 50 (left), 51, 52 (right), 53 (bottom), 54 (photographs centre and bottom), 55 (top), 61, 62, 63, 192 © Laurence King Publishing Ltd
Antonio Lopez 89 © The Estate of Antonio Lopez
Gilly Lovegrove 12 (right), 13 (left), 26 (bottom), 27, 32 (top right and bottom), 34, 35, 36, 37, 38, 39 (top), 40, 42, 43, 44, 45, 46, 64, 65 © Laurence King Publishing; gilly@love-grove.fsnet.co.uk
Avako Machida 109 c/o CWC International, Inc., agent@cwc-i.com
Sam Strauss Malcolm 55 (bottom), 80 (right), 179 (bottom left) simontuesday@mac.com
Francis Marshall 29 (left) Francis Marshall Archive/Victoria & Albert Museum/The Archive of Art & Design/©ADAGP, Paris and DACS London, 2006
Henri Matisse 31 (left) ©Succession H Matisse/DACS 2006
Michelangelo 24 (right) British Museum, London/Bridgeman Art Library
Mary McCarthy 49 (right) mazmccarthy1@hotmail.com
Lizzie Mcquade 58 (right) lizzie_mcquade@hotmail.com
Dawn Mooney 80 (left) dawnm21@hotmail.com
Charlotte Morice 19 charlotte_morice@hotmail.com
Bethan Morris 10, 11 (right and bottom), 12 (left), 14, 16 (bottom), 17, 20, 21, 28 (centre), 30 (top), 32 (top left), 52 (top left), 54 (with Patricia Joyner), 68, 69, 77 (top right), 160, 161, 183 Bethanmorris1@yahoo.co.uk
Jacqueline Nsirim 15 (below), 39 (bottom), 50 (right) jnsirim@hotmail.com
Marie O'Connor 113 info@marieoconnor.co.uk
Rosie O'Reilly 30 (bottom right) rosieoreilly@hotmail.com
Marega Palser 28 (left and right) marega@ntlworld.com
Sima Patel 22, 70, 74 sima_patel27@hotmail.com
Pablo Picasso 25 (left) [Museu Picasso, Barcelona/"AHCB-ARXIU Fotogràfic - J.Calafell/©Succession Picasso/DACS 2006]; 25 (right) [Musée Picasso, Paris/Photo RMN "Gérard Blot/©Succession Picasso/DACS 2006]
Marina Polo 71 minapolo@hotmail.com
Promostyl 190, 191 www.promostyl.com
Liisa Riski 2, 11 (top), 75 liisa_riski@hotmail.com
Graham Rownthwaite 92 (left)

The Royal Collection 2005, Her Majesty Queen Elizabeth II 24 (left)
Yuko Shimizu 117 First appeared in *Z* magazine, Canada; yuko@yukoart.com
Laura Smart 73 flipflop@hotmail.com
Lewis Smith 78 lewis205@hotmail.co.uk
Liesel Taylor 77 (bottom) Liesel.Taylor@colegsirgar.ac.uk
Victoria Thomas 176 (top) vicksthomas@hotmail.co.uk
Annabelle Verhoye 145 anna@annabelleverhoye.com
Tony Viramontes 90 © The Estate of Tony Viramontes
Robert Wagt 101 rwagt@free.fr
Edwina Christiana White 147 www.larkworthy.com
Hannah Wood 79 wood_hannah@hotmail.com
Zoltan 91 Courtesy the artist

p. 49
Papers supplied by Faulkner Fine Papers, 74 Southampton Row, London WC1

pp. 50–55
Art materials supplied by the London Graphic Centre, 16-18 Shelton St, London WC2 wwww.londongraphics.co.uk

pp. 61–63
Fabrics supplied by Cloth House, 98 Berwick St, London W1 www.clothhouse.com

ACKNOWLEDGMENTS

I wish to thank the professional and graduate illustrators who have contributed so generously—you are the heart and soul of this book and an inspiration to us all.

This is my first book, so the learning curve gets steeper every day ... my sincere thanks go to Jo Lightfoot, Anne Townley, and Jessica Spencer of Laurence King, who have helped me grow. Your advice, guidance, and support have been exceptional, and it has been an honor and a pleasure to work with you all.

To the art and design academics who have greatly influenced my education. For your support and constant motivational guidance, I thank Elizabeth Ashton, Gillian St. John Griffiths, Dave Gould, Julie Pinches, John Miles, Jane Davison, and Steve Thompson.

To all those who gave their time and experience so freely, especially David Downton, Jeffrey Fulvimari, Lysiane de Royère, Stephanie Pesakoff, KoKo Nakano, Michel Lagarde, Matthew Jeatt, Alicia Davenport, Carlos Taylor, Susan Chung, Katherine Bradwell, Sue Jenkyn Jones, Gilly Staples, Don Parker, Lucy Richardson, Virginia Hole, Adriano Gazza, Will Knight, Anna Bailey, Simone Legno, Patricia Joyner, and Louise Gardiner.

To Frances Wellington of London Graduate Fashion Week who helped to track down the best graduate illustrators, and to Peter Kent for your tireless picture research. Thanks also to Samantha Gray for her excellent copy-editing and to David Tanguy for the wonderful design and layout. A special mention to Kareem Iliya, Annabelle Verhoye, Stephen Campbell, Edgardo Carosia, Matthias Frey, and Marion Lefebvre for your fantastic cover images, and Gilly Lovegrove for your valuable diagrams and illustrations throughout the entire book.

Thank you to the London Graphic Centre, The Cloth House, Faulkner Fine Papers, Madeira Threads, and Husqvarna-Viking for your generous sponsorship.

I'm happy to say that, when times were tough, I was saved by Karen posting me endless supplies of chocolate brownies, and by Rosie, my cat, whose unconditional love and companionship made me smile.

Finally a very special thank you must also go to my remarkable family and friends who have showered me with patience, understanding, and kindness over the last few years. I do not need to make a list because you all know who you are, and how much you will always mean to me.

DEDICATION

To my mum who taught me to believe I can do anything in life, and to my wonderful husband who helps turn those beliefs into reality every day. I thank you both from the bottom of my heart.